MOON

VERMONT

JEN ROSE SMITH

Contents

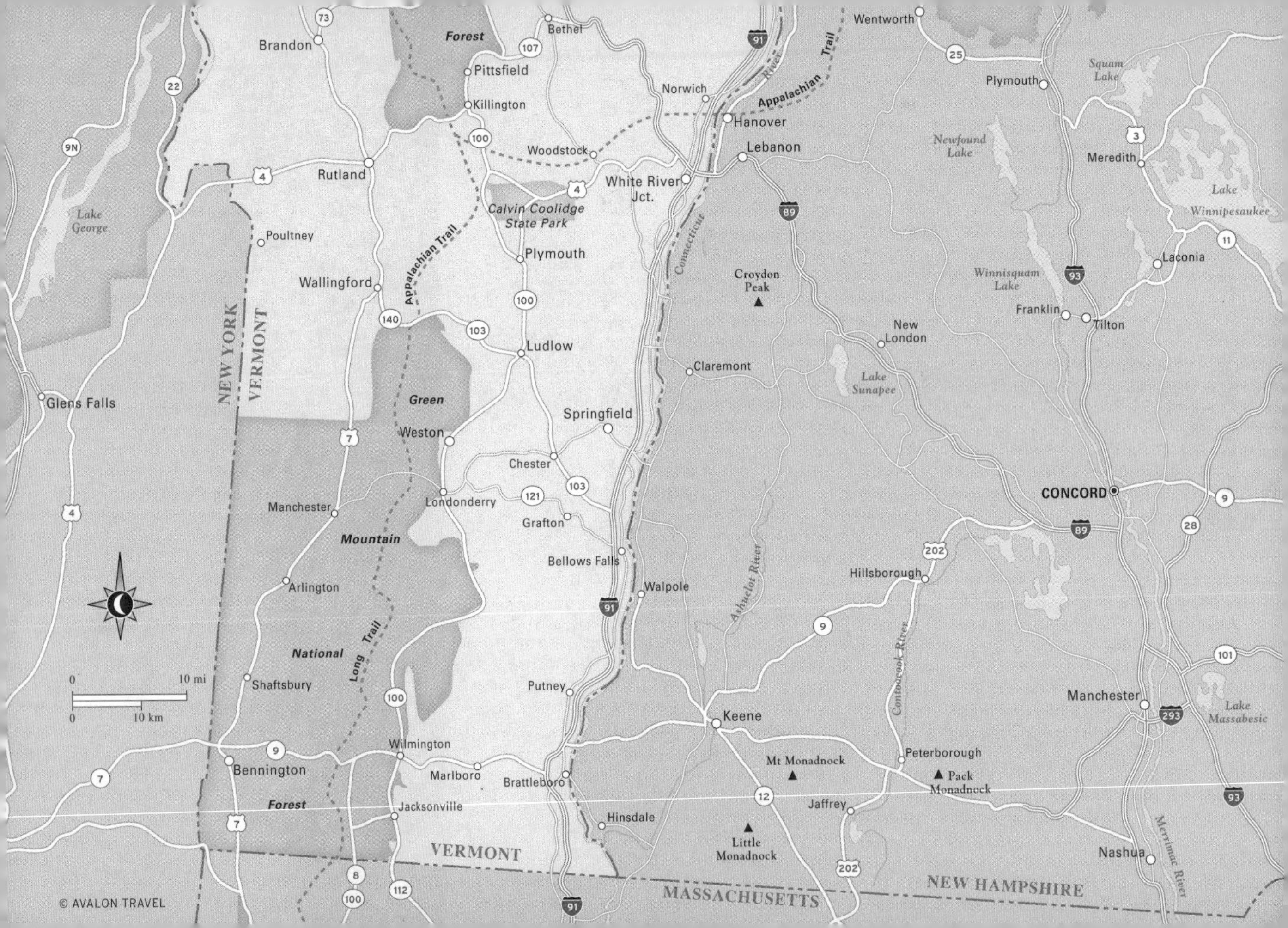

NEW YORK
VERMONT
MASSACHUSETTS
NEW HAMPSHIRE
Green Mountain National Forest
Long Trail
Appalachian Trail
Glens Falls
Lake George
Brandon
Pittsfield
Killington
Bethel
Rutland
Poultney
Wallingford
Woodstock
Calvin Coolidge State Park
Plymouth
Ludlow
Weston
Londonderry
Chester
Springfield
Grafton
Bellows Falls
Manchester
Arlington
Shaftsbury
Bennington
Wilmington
Marlboro
Brattleboro
Jacksonville
Putney
Hinsdale
Norwich
Hanover
Lebanon
White River Jct.
Connecticut River
Croydon Peak
Claremont
New London
Lake Sunapee
Walpole
Ashuelot River
Keene
Mt Monadnock
Little Monadnock
Jaffrey
Peterborough
Pack Monadnock
Contoocook River
Hillsborough
Wentworth
Plymouth
Newfound Lake
Squam Lake
Meredith
Lake Winnipesaukee
Laconia
Winnisquam Lake
Franklin
Tilton
CONCORD
Manchester
Lake Massabesic
Nashua
Merrimac River
0
10 mi
0
10 km
© AVALON TRAVEL

VERMONT
QUÉBEC
VERMONT
CANADA
U.S.A.
Swanton
Enosburg Falls
St. Albans
Jay
Newport
Lowell
Island Pond
Colebrook
Lake Francis
Lake
Champlain
Plattsburgh
Adirondak
State
Park
Milton
Jeffersonville
Craftsbury
Long Trail
Mt Mansfield
Burlington
Stowe
East Burke
Lyndonville
North Stratford
Lancaster
White Mountain National Forest
St. Johnsbury
Cabot
West Danville
Shelburne
Waterbury
MONTPELIER
Barre
Littleton
Mt Washington
Vergennes
Waitsfield
Orange
Woodsville
Franconia Notch
Crawford Notch
Pemigewasset River
Bristol
Green
Mountain
Middlebury
Randolph
Corinth
Haverhill
Orford
White
Mountain
Lincoln
White Mountains
National
Forest

DISCOVER

Vermont

In a blissfully rural state at the edge of densely populated New England, Vermont's rolling Green Mountains are dotted with sugar shacks and ski slopes. Life here is wrapped around the seasons and can recall another era: locals spend summer days in swimming holes, turn out for autumn's colorful display, then keep wintertime bright with sledding and pond skating.

But while the tiny town greens and whitewashed steeples may seem lost in time, the Green Mountain State is very much alive, with fascinating cultural vibrancy. Vermont has more cheese makers and brewers per capita than any other state, and its farms, festivals, and innovative restaurants have proved an appealing refuge for many visitors looking to unwind, unplug, and get a taste of the simple life—even if it's just for the afternoon.

There's a founding tension here that's summed up in the state's official motto, "Freedom and Unity," which presages Vermont's intriguing blend of innovation and tradition. In the Northeast Kingdom, generations-old dairy families partner with young cheese makers. Maple syrup producers collect sap on horse-drawn sleds, gathering it into state-of-the-art sugarhouses powered by the sun. And in a territory that played a key role in the American Revolution, Vermonters

Clockwise from top left: Vermont dairy cow; hitting the slopes at Mad River Glen; entries at an autumn apple pie contest; winding country lane in winter; farmers market supporting local agriculture; fall foliage at Elmore State Park.

have explored what freedom means today by electing a legislature that was the first to legalize gay marriage, lift restrictions on marijuana, and require labeling of genetically modified foods.

Community life thrives at church suppers and yearly town meetings. But even the taciturn American president—and local—Calvin Coolidge waxed eloquent while praising the independent spirit he found in the "brave little state of Vermont."

All that means visitors to Vermont have a unique opportunity to pick and choose, weaving between old and new as they explore. Opt for historical sites along old farm roads glowing with fall foliage, then head for Vermont's artsy cutting edge in cities like Burlington, craft cocktail in hand. For adventurers, the Green Mountains hold a lifetime of afternoons spent summiting rocky peaks and skiing perfect lines. Or as "Silent Cal" might have done, travelers to Vermont can simply find a quiet place to sit still, take it in, and watch the seasons transform the landscape.

Clockwise from top left: skiing at Stowe Mountain Resort; deeply colored evergreen trees contrasting with bright fall foliage; local spirits, infusing Vermont's cocktail culture with regional flavor; Old First Church in Bennington.

9 TOP EXPERIENCES

1 **Watch fall foliage light up the hills:** Autumn is Vermont's star season, when nights turn cool and the hillsides explode into a riot of color (page 24).

2 **Ski and ride the Green Mountains:** Snowy Vermont shines in winter, with all that powder turning the state into the perfect playground (page 26).

3 **Hike the Long Trail's iconic peaks:** The country's oldest long-distance hiking trail, the 272-mile Long Trail follows the spine of the Green Mountains, rising over some of Vermont's most beloved summits along the way (page 181).

4 Make a craft beer pilgrimage: The Green Mountain State is experiencing a golden age of brewing, with craft beers that have garnered national acclaim (page 23).

<<<

5 Bike scenic paths and trails: With a vast network of dirt roads and plenty of off-road bike paths, there's destination-worthy pedaling across the state (page 118).

>>>

6 Watch revolutionary art at Bread & Puppet: A former dairy barn houses rabble-rousing political theater and thought-provoking "cheap art" (page 236).

<<<

7 **Cool off in a swimming hole:** When summer brings hot, sticky days, skip the air-conditioning and head for one of the state's many rivers (page 201).

8 **Go back to the land on a working farm:** Experience the bounty in the Champlain Valley, where the farms range from elegant historic properties to down-home orchards (page 140).

9 **Taste Vermont's artisanal cheese:** It's only fitting that a place speckled with dairy cows should have cheese makers to match, and Vermont's got more of them per capita than any other state (page 38).

Planning Your Trip

Where to Go

Southern Green Mountains

The southernmost part of Vermont is a jumble of forested slopes and valleys that shelter postcard-ready villages. Country stores are stocked with maple syrup from family-run **sugar shacks,** and back roads are dotted with farm stands overflowing with summertime produce. With easy access from Boston and New York, the southern Green Mountains have been **New England's getaway** since the Civil War. Vacation like a Lincoln in upscale **Manchester,** wander orchards and art galleries in funky **Brattleboro,** and drive the Revolutionary-era **Molly Stark Trail,** a scenic byway that spans the Green Mountains and shines in foliage season.

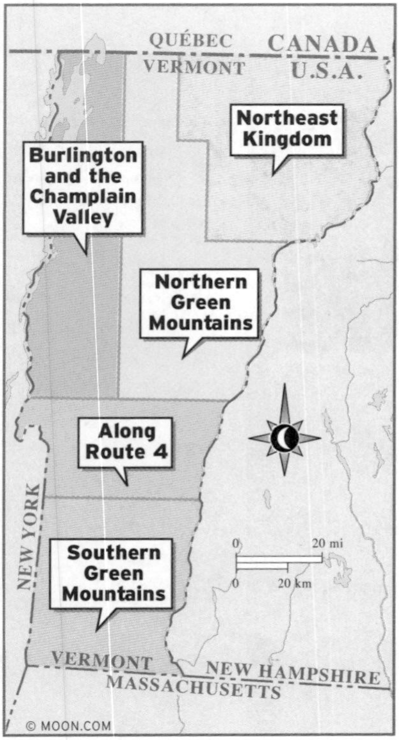

Along Route 4

U.S. 4 slices across the middle of the state, separating the two halves of the Green Mountain National Forest. This corridor offers a cross section of Vermont's colonial and industrial eras, with a detour into 21st-century mountain life. Visit **Rutland,** once a national center for marble production, or **Woodstock,** a quintessential New England village. In between them lies the ski resort of **Killington,** otherwise known as the "Beast of the East."

Burlington and the Champlain Valley

This rich swath of agricultural land is dotted with **farms and dairies** rimmed by the Green Mountains to the east and the sinuous coastline of **Lake Champlain** to the west. Its "Queen City" is **Burlington,** a dynamic college town and **culinary hot spot** that's home to many academics and artisans.

Northern Green Mountains

As you travel northward, the mountains get bigger and woollier, culminating with **Mount Mansfield,** an imposing peak that towers above the alpine village of Stowe. In this part of the state, you'll find easy access to outdoor adventures—especially in the compact **Mad River Valley,** whose romantic inns gaze out at mountains and **ski slopes** on all sides. This region is also the home of Vermont's diminutive state capital, **Montpelier,** and the ice cream factory that

Woodstock's adorable downtown is ideal for leisurely gallery browsing.

made **Ben & Jerry's** a household name; after you get your fill of ice cream, explore craft brews in downtown **Waterbury** and **Stowe.**

Northeast Kingdom

This **wild and rural country** is a glimpse of old Vermont and home to attractions that are as eclectic and memorable as the fiercely independent locals. The extraordinary **Kingdom Trails Network** offers the best **mountain biking** in the state—perhaps in New England—with views that rival the swooping single-track. Explore the flavors of the Kingdom at the **Northeast Kingdom Tasting Center** in Newport, or catch a revolutionary puppet show at Barton's **Bread & Puppet Theater.**

When to Go

In Vermont, there's something to love about every season, but it's important to come prepared.

If you don't mind the cold, Vermont is paradise in **winter,** when mountain resorts come alive under piles of snow. This is the time to explore the Green Mountains on everything from skis to sleds and horse-drawn sleighs. Temperatures are consistently in the mid-20s, but can be much colder with windchill, so pack plenty of warm layers. If there's any downside to visiting during winter, it's that major ski resorts attract crowds—but on big holiday weekends, you can always avoid the "Boston effect" by seeking out a quieter local hill.

When all that snow begins to melt, **spring**—otherwise known as "mud season"—is on the way. April and early May bring sleety drizzle, which makes outdoor adventures and back road driving a challenge. There's one sweet reason to come to Vermont this time of year: maple syrup. This is when the forests come out of their deep freeze, and sugarhouses boil sap day and night until the trees dry up.

Hike to the top of a Green Mountain peak to find views and unique alpine environments.

Summer is many locals' favorite season. Sunny weather turns mountainsides lush and green, and the hills are traced with endless hiking and biking trails. Temperatures tend to hover in the mid-70s, with a few hot weeks in July or August that offer perfect conditions for lolling around in a shady river. The countryside yields an abundance of farm-fresh produce and artisanal cheeses. Visitors tend to be dispersed across the state, so it rarely seems crowded.

Autumn is spectacular. The **fall foliage** is most dramatic in late September through October and leaf peepers arrive in droves. Prices rise along with the crowds, but it's easy to avoid the tourist rush by finding your own back road to explore. Temperatures can be unpredictable this time of year—some days might reach the low 60s, while others may creep toward freezing—so pack accordingly.

The Best of Vermont

Vermont's mountains and valleys are webbed with endless back roads—many of them dirt—and the best way to explore the state is to hop in the car and hit the road. This weeklong road trip is an easygoing circle around the state that includes some of Vermont's most beloved attractions. The pace leaves some time for exploring the places between the destinations, where you may just find your most memorable experiences.

Day 1

Start in **Brattleboro.** Spend the day exploring Brattleboro's **galleries** and **shops** on quirky Main Street, or pick some heirloom fruit at **Scott Farm,** orchards on a gorgeous property that includes Rudyard Kipling's former home. To soak in the creative spirit of the city, try to plan your visit to correspond to the first Friday night of the month to experience Brattleboro's **Gallery Walk.**

Day 2

From Brattleboro head north along winding Route 30, stopping in **Townshend** (25 min.) for a stroll around its adorable **village green** before taking the turn north onto Route 35 to Grafton (20 min.). Here, head to **Grafton Ponds Outdoor Center** for a hike or a round of croquet before a meal and stay at the historical **Grafton Inn.**

Day 3

Head west on Routes 121 and 11, then north on Route 100 to **Weston** (30 min.) to take in the kitschy charm of the **Vermont Country Store.** After lunch, continue north along scenic Route 100 to **Plymouth** (35 min.), where the **President Calvin Coolidge State Historic Site** is nestled in a splendid valley (with excellent cheese that's worth a trip all its own). Push on north along 100A and east on Route 4 to spend the night at

Colorful autumn leaves are one of Vermont's most unforgettable sights.

Best Romantic Getaways

If you're escaping to the country for a couple of days, these spots are dreamy places to unwind.

Woodstock *(page 90)*

Galleries, inns, and romantic restaurants line the quiet streets of this charming village, which is just 2.5 hours from Boston. The historical downtown is rimmed with rolling fields and imposing peaks, and the surrounding countryside is full of generations-old family farms. The iconic **Woodstock Inn & Resort** is a luxurious haven, with rolling trails, well-appointed rooms, and a daily pause for teatime in the Conservatory.

Manchester *(page 56)*

This town has drawn posh escapees since the Civil War, and present-day Manchester is a jumble of vacation culture, old and new. Wander the golf courses and gardens that Robert Todd Lincoln loved, or hit the outlet stores for a frenzy of shopping. The broad Battenkill River is a dream for fly-fishing, paddling, or simply floating. Only four hours from New York City, it may be the perfect weekend getaway. Lay your head at the quirky **Wilburton Inn** or the grand **Equinox Resort & Spa,** built in the 18th century.

Mad River Valley *(page 195)*

Self-contained and secretive, the Mad River Valley would be easy to miss, but it's a perfect distillation of Vermont beauty. Discover romantic inns, towering peaks, and a wide river that passes covered bridges and cows. The tiny valley claims two of the state's most beloved ski resorts, Sugarbush and Mad River Glen; after a day on the slopes warm up by the fireplace at the idyllic **Inn at the Round Barn Farm**.

Hot summer days in the Mad River Valley are perfect for swimming.

Stowe *(page 174)*

Spas and skiing are just the beginning in this village, which cast the mold for New England's mountain retreats. In wintertime this is an outdoor wonderland: If the world-class skiing doesn't appeal, simply bundle up in a horse-drawn sleigh and explore the countryside to the sound of silver bells. This is also a favorite foodie destination, and nearby Waterbury is the heart of Vermont's craft beer revival. This alpine town has sumptuous spas and refined inns. Try the isolated **Edson Hill,** which stuns with views across the valley.

the super-romantic **Woodstock Inn & Resort** in **Woodstock** (25 min.).

Day 4

Commune with the cows at Woodstock's **Billings Farm & Museum,** or eyeball the raptors at the nearby **Vermont Institute of Natural Science** in Quechee. From Woodstock, take in the scenic drive north along Route 12, east on Route 107, and then north along Route 100, ending up in the Mad River Valley town of **Warren** (90 min.). **Ski slopes** or **swimming holes** await, depending on the season. Spend the afternoon exploring **The Warren Store** and the picturesque village center, or take advantage of the nearby mountains with a hike up **Camel's Hump,** a bike ride through town, or a slow inner tube drift down the Mad River. Spend the night in **Waitsfield,** the cultural heart of the valley.

Day 5

Head north along Route 100 to **Waterbury** (30 min.), the original home of the beloved Heady Topper beer, and the **Ben & Jerry's factory.** After tasting some beer, ice cream, and fresh apple cider, drive west along I-89 to the lakeside college town of **Burlington** (45 min.), Vermont's "Queen City." Spend the morning strolling among the shops on **Church Street** before heading to the **Waterfront Park,** where you can take a spin on the bike path, go paddling on the lake, or visit the **ECHO Leahy Center for Lake Champlain.** After catching sunset on the lakefront, take in some music at one of downtown's many venues.

Day 6

Meander south down Route 7 to **Middlebury** (1 hr.), where you can get a morning tour of **Middlebury College**'s pristine gray granite campus, or just visit some of the small town's big-name brewers and distillers.

Continue south to the covered bridge capital of **Proctor** (35 min.), near the incongruous and ornate **Wilson Castle.** Stop for lunch in nearby **Rutland** (15 min.) and then drive to sophisticated **Manchester** (50 min.) to wander streets lined with vacation homes built in the 19th century by New England's elite families. Lincoln lovers can spot his stovepipe hat at **Hildene,** whose formal gardens are a dramatic contrast to the mountain scenery. Spend the night in Manchester at the **Equinox Resort & Spa** or the **Wilburton Inn,** full of historical charm and grandeur.

Day 7

Spend the morning driving up the **Mount Equinox Skyline Drive** for a beautiful view of the Green Mountains. Then head south down Route 7 to **Bennington** (40 min.), where you can check out the **Bennington Battle Monument** and the distinctive folk art of Grandma Moses at the **Bennington Museum** before spending the night in this quiet historical town.

Vermont Tasting Tour

Vermont's cuisine has gone local, from forest-foraged ingredients to small-batch cheese and beer. Eat and drink your way through the Green Mountain State on this weeklong tour, with a few favorite stops along the way.

Day 1: Burlington

Kick off your trip in the Queen City.

- **EAT:** Head to **Church Street** for a meal—alfresco or fireside, depending on the season. **American Flatbread** is a cozy brewpub and pizza joint, and it's hard to beat a burger and pint in the outdoor beer garden at **The Farmhouse Tap & Grill.**
- **DRINK:** Pay a visit to one (or more) of Burlington's **breweries,** which are among the best in the state.
- **EXPERIENCE:** Go straight to the source with a **farm visit** in the lower Champlain Valley. If it's a Saturday, visit the **Burlington Farmers' Market,** the biggest in the state. Afterward, work up an appetite with a stroll through the waterfront park.

Day 2: South to Middlebury

It's a leisurely drive south on **Route 7** to Middlebury (1 hr.), so you've got plenty of time to make stops along the way. Spend the night at one of Middlebury's quiet inns.

- **EAT:** If you're exploring **Shelburne Farms,** pause for a casual, outdoor lunch at their **Farm Cart**—on the weekend, though, it's worth splashing out for the delightful brunch at the farm's **Inn.** For dinner in Middlebury, try to snag an outdoor, riverside table for dinner at **The Lobby.**

- **DRINK:** Pick a few stops to visit on the **Middlebury Tasting Trail.**
- **EXPERIENCE:** You'll find some great stops on the way from Burlington to Middlebury. In late summer and fall, pick apples at the lakeside **Shelburne Orchards,** or explore the breathtaking **Shelburne Farms;** the rolling property is perfect for long walks, and they make cheddar and maple syrup on-site. For some non-food-related fun, soak in some culture at the **Rokeby Museum** and the **Lake Champlain Maritime Museum** in Vergennes.

Day 3: Mad River Valley

Head up and over the Green Mountains on the winding, scenic **Route 125** east to the Mad River Valley (1 hr.). Spend the night in Warren, or just up the valley in Waitsfield.

- **EAT:** Have dinner in Waitsfield at the country-punk **Mad Taco** or head just down the road to **American Flatbread** for a bonfire and a pizza.
- **DRINK:** Stop by the Waitsfield tasting room of **Mad River Distillers,** or schedule a guided tour of their Warren distillery.
- **EXPERIENCE:** Warren's **Blueberry Lake** is the perfect place to unwind, with a family-friendly swimming area and plenty of space to paddle a canoe. It also has one of Vermont's best trove of blueberry bushes. In July and August, make like a bear and fill your belly with the wild fruit.

Day 4: Waterbury and Stowe

Continue north to Waterbury, then Stowe, on **Route 100** (41 min.). Spend the night in Stowe.

- **EAT:** Especially if you're traveling with kids, you'll want to hit Waterbury's iconic **Ben & Jerry's factory.** If you can still walk after all that ice cream, snag a fresh cider doughnut at the **Cold Hollow Cider Mill,** or just go for broke at the James Beard Award-winning **Hen of the Wood** restaurant in Waterbury or **The Bench** in Stowe.
- **DRINK:** On the way to Stowe, don't bypass

foraging for wild ramps to bring into the kitchen

Mad River Distillers

Small State, Big Beer

The Green Mountain State is experiencing a golden age of brewing, with craft beers that have garnered national acclaim.

Hill Farmstead Brewery *(page 226)*

Shaun Hill claimed the **Best Brewery in the World** title in 2013 and 2015. Stop by his Greensboro brewery to see where the magic happens and fill up a growler.

Long Trail Brewing Company *(page 92)*

Those only familiar with the ubiquitous **Long Trail Ale** may be surprised by the wealth of beers on tap at this Bridgewater Corners brewpub.

Citizen Cider *(page 123)*

In the heart of Burlington, this cidery has been giving beer a run for its money. Try the **Full Nelson,** which is dry hopped with Nelson Sauvin hops.

The Alchemist *(page 176)*

This Stowe-based brewery is known for its hop-heavy canned beer **Heady Topper,** which has been twice named the **Best Beer in the World.** It's full flavored and hard to find on the shelf; seek it out at a restaurant or call local stores to find out when they receive their weekly delivery—then show up early.

Lawson's Finest Liquids *(page 170)*

A flagship IPA from this Warren microbrewery, **Sip of Sunshine** is a bright-tasting beer with wonderfully floral aromas. This microbrewery isn't open to the public, but Lawson's beer is on tap at restaurants throughout the state.

Waterbury's **"Beermuda Triangle,"** which consists of some fabulous beer stops, including **The Reservoir, Blackback Pub,** and the **Waterbury Craft Beer Cellar.** Once you've settled in at Stowe, visit the legendary **Alchemist** brewery and pick up a few growlers of cider to take home from **Stowe Cider.**

- **EXPERIENCE:** After all that food and drink, stretch your legs on a walk to **Sterling Pond** from Smugglers' Notch, the narrow pass that towers above Stowe.

Days 5 and 6: Northeast Kingdom

The landscape will grow wilder as you head north on **Route 100** then east on **Route 15** to St. Johnsbury (1 hr.), the perfect base for exploring the Northeast Kingdom.

- **EAT:** Many of the Kingdom's most memorable dining experiences are at romantic country inns. Waterford's **Rabbit Hill Inn** has long been a foodie destination, and the refined Austrian fare at the **Derby Line Village Inn** will ward off the winter chill.
- **DRINK:** Sip gin and vodka made with regional honey at **Caledonia Spirits** distillery in Hardwick, or make a beer pilgrimage to the renowned **Hill Farmstead Brewery** in Greensboro.
- **EXPERIENCE:** On your way to St. Johnsbury, take a side trip to the **Cabot Creamery,** where you can sample the state's most famous cheddar. Then visit the sheep—and the shepherds—at **Bonnieview Farm** in Craftsbury. On your second day in the Kingdom, head to Newport's **Northeast Kingdom Tasting Center,** where you can try the best of the region in tasting menus of cheeses, meats, ice cider, and beer.

Day 7: Back to Burlington

Head back toward the shores of Lake Champlain on **Route 2** west and **I-89** north (76 miles, 1.5 hours), and watch the landscape ease into rolling farmland.

- **EAT:** Try a **creemee** (soft-serve maple ice cream cone) at one of the snack bars along Burlington's waterfront, then head to

Fabulous Foliage

Autumn is Vermont's star season, when nights turn cool and the hillsides explode into a riot of color. The transformation follows the weather and begins in the north—and at higher altitudes—and moves downslope and downstate. Red- and orange-hued trees are around every bend this time of year, but the following scenic drives are some of the most spectacular places to watch the show. Don't feel like driving? Post up in the captivating **Mad River Valley** (page 195), surrounded by mountains on all sides.

It's impossible to predict exactly when Vermont's most colorful show will begin and end.

Smugglers' Notch Road *(page 190)*

Route 108 winds through the mountain pass that separates **Stowe** from Smugglers' Notch Resort (30 min.), crawling between boulders and high cliffs; trees climb precipitous slopes to the peak of **Mount Mansfield.**.

Molly Stark Trail *(page 50)*

The scenic Molly Stark Trail (Route 9) connects artsy **Brattleboro** and historical **Bennington** (1 hr.), rising up and over a mountain pass with long views of the **Green Mountain National Forest.**

Route 100 *(page 65)*

The ultimate autumn road trip, this road follows the spine of the Green Mountains the whole length of the state. Start at the intersection with Route 9, and wind through **Weston** (page 67), **Warren** (page 199), **Stowe** (page 174), and **Newport** (page 245) for a gorgeous five-hour drive that cuts through the Mad River Valley.

Winooski for dinner. Stroll through the tiny downtown, where hip bars and intimate restaurants cluster around a walkable roundabout.

- **DRINK:** Sip a locavore cocktail by a blazing fire at **Juniper Bar** in downtown Burlington, which stocks every spirit distilled in Vermont.
- **EXPERIENCE:** Take a final stroll through some farm fields at Burlington's **Intervale Center**—in July and August, don't miss **Summervale,** a weekly farm party with live music, local beer and food, and a colorful crowd of off-work farmers, families, and dancing toddlers.

Into the Green Mountains

There's a reason Vermont is named after the mountains that run the length of the state. Everywhere you look, the Green Mountains fill the horizon and offer endless opportunities for adventure in any season. This weeklong jaunt is custom made for the outdoorsy traveler. You'll spend your first night in Burlington, your second night in Middlebury, nights three through five in Stowe (with the option of a one-night detour to a paddle-in campground), and nights six and seven in the Northeast Kingdom town of East Burke.

Day 1

Start your tour in Burlington. On your first day, take a kayak or sailboat out on the waters of **Lake Champlain,** reveling in the unique vantage of the islands from the open water. Or if you are trained in scuba diving, explore the underwater shipwrecks of military and merchant vessels. For tours and equipment rentals, contact the **Waterfront Diving Center.**

Day 2

Head south down Route 7 to **Middlebury** (1 hr.), then into the **Moosalamoo Recreation Area,** 20,000 acres of pristine Green Mountain wilderness that is one of the state's best-kept secrets and offers great hiking. If you spend the night at the peaceful **Moosalamoo Campground,** keep your eyes peeled for moose!

Day 3

Hike back to the parking area, and then drive north along Route 17 through the breathtaking **Appalachian Gap,** then north along Route 100 through the Mad River Valley to **Stowe** (90 min.). Put in some recovery time at a **spa** or do your relaxing at a café in the compact downtown.

Day 4

Today it's up early to tackle the highest mountain in the state, hiking **Mount Mansfield** for a panoramic view of the mountains all around. At

Once covered with farms and fields, the Green Mountains are now thickly forested.

night, nurse sore muscles with a cocktail at one of Stowe's many après-ski pubs.

Day 5

Give your legs a rest and your arms a workout with a paddle down the scenic **Lamoille River,** lined with the red barns and cows of your pastoral dreams. For a remoter adventure, head to **Green River Reservoir,** where you can paddle in to campsites accessible only by nonmotorized boat and spend a night listening to the haunting calls of loons.

Day 6

Today, leave Stowe and head into Vermont's wild **Northeast Kingdom** with a drive north up Route 100, east on Route 15, east on U.S. 2, and north on U.S. 5 to **East Burke** (1.5 hrs.). Rent yourself a mountain bike there and set out on the **Kingdom Trails Network,** 100 miles of pristine country landscape just crying out for two-wheeled exploration.

Day 7

Spend another day on your bike, tackling the death-defying slopes of **Burke Mountain Resort.** Or stretch your legs on a hike up Mount Pisgah on the **South Trail** to commune with peregrine falcons with a view over the lovely Lake Willoughby. At night, splurge on a massage in preparation for tomorrow's trip home.

Skiing at Its Peak

TOP EXPERIENCE

Snowy Vermont shines in winter. All that powder turns the state into the perfect playground, whether that means skiing the moguls or taking in the silence on a cross-country jaunt.

Big and Bad

Killington is a behemoth—with six peaks to choose from, the resort has something for everyone, including careening double diamonds, twisting glades, and family-friendly cruisers. This southern heavyweight also attracts Vermont's most devoted party scene, which fills mammoth nightclubs all week long.

For a somewhat less crowded experience, many skiers head north to **Sugarbush,** which is second only to Killington in the number and variety of trails; it boasts a large amount of natural snowfall thanks to the storms that come in from Lake Champlain.

Tumbling down the slopes of Mount Mansfield—that's Vermont's highest peak—**Stowe** is the state's most glamorous place to hop a gondola. Tons of terrain mean that even on crowded days there's a place to ski and ride at Stowe, and the adjacent village has one of Vermont's hottest post-slope scenes.

It's hard to argue with the accessibility of **Mount Snow,** in the southern part of the state. It's a favorite of day-trippers from New York and southern New England. But for a wilder, remoter mountain experience, head north to the imposing **Jay Peak.** Its average annual snowfall—a staggering 350 inches—is the most of any ski area in the eastern United States.

Old School (and Proud of It)

If all those shiny lifts and lodges make you want to run for the hills, these resorts are for you; they've kept it real since the rope-tow era and tend to have a friendly locals atmosphere.

Skiers-only **Mad River Glen** is unapologetically crusty, with the motto "Ski It If You Can." Watch for woolen knickers, lots of plaid, and the best in-bounds telemark skiers in the state.

Everyone's welcome at Woodstock's **Suicide Six,** which is far more laid-back and family friendly than the name implies. This local hill is easy to get to and has been spinning lifts since 1936.

Burke Mountain Resort, a much larger mountain with 50 trails hidden in the Northeast Kingdom, gets buried under 250 inches of annual snowfall. Yet despite that, and despite some truly

challenging terrain at Mad River Glen

challenging upper-mountain slopes that could hold their own with any mountain in the East, it is pleasantly quiet during the week.

Family Fun

Parents can't do much better than **Smugglers' Notch,** which offers a money-back guarantee if any member of the family doesn't have a good time. Small chance of that, as three mountains, kids' and teens' programs, and an indoor activity center provide plenty to put a smile on the face of even the most recalcitrant youngster.

In southern Vermont, **Bromley Mountain** markets itself as a resort for the whole family, with nearly 50 trails for all abilities and a ski school for kids featuring mascot Clyde Catamount.

Next door to Killington, pint-size **Pico Mountain** offers inviting terrain for beginners and intermediate skiers, along with lift privileges at its big brother for the experts in the family.

Cross-Country

Many resorts have a Nordic ski area attached to the main hill, some maintained for skate skiing. For dedicated cross-country skiing, head to the rolling forest at the **Craftsbury Outdoor Center,** by a secluded lake in the heart of the Northeast Kingdom.

Another highlight for self-propelled skiers is the trail system at **Trapp Family Lodge** in Stowe, where groomers weave up and across a hillside to a warming hut in the woods (complete with fireplace and steaming mugs of hot cocoa).

Southern Green Mountains

Southern Vermont's back roads and byways

lead to picture-book villages, winding rivers, and orchards hung with heirloom fruit.

Just a few hours away from New England's biggest cities, much of southern Vermont remains rural, and the spaces between towns are filled with rolling farms and forests. The Green Mountains extend nearly from one edge to the other, rearing up between the Battenkill Valley in the west and the Connecticut River Valley that shapes Vermont's eastern border.

In the southwest, free-spirited Brattleboro is a testament to quirk that feels wholly authentic, with delightful art galleries and farm-to-table restaurants. In the 1930s, pioneering academics Helen and

Highlights

Look for ★ to find recommended sights, activities, dining, and lodging.

★ **Gallery Walk:** If you aren't lucky enough to live in an artists' colony, visiting this monthly festival in Brattleboro is the next best thing (page 32).

★ **Scott Farm:** Rudyard Kipling's Vermont home presides over a stunning apple farm that overflows with heirloom fruit and literary history (page 33).

★ **Bennington Museum:** View a peerless collection of folk art by Grandma Moses and paintings by Bennington's mid-century modernist artists (page 51).

★ **Hildene:** Robert Todd Lincoln's former home is a window into Manchester's storied past (page 58).

★ **Mount Snow and Stratton Mountain:** Stratton was Jake Burton's home back when he invented snowboarding, and along with neighboring Mount Snow, it continues to draw riders (and skiers!) from around the Northeast (page 65).

★ **The Vermont Country Store:** Browsing this old-fashioned country store can be a transporting experience; penny candy, pickles, and sundry doodads are stocked alongside flannel nightgowns and quilts (page 67).

Southern Green Mountains

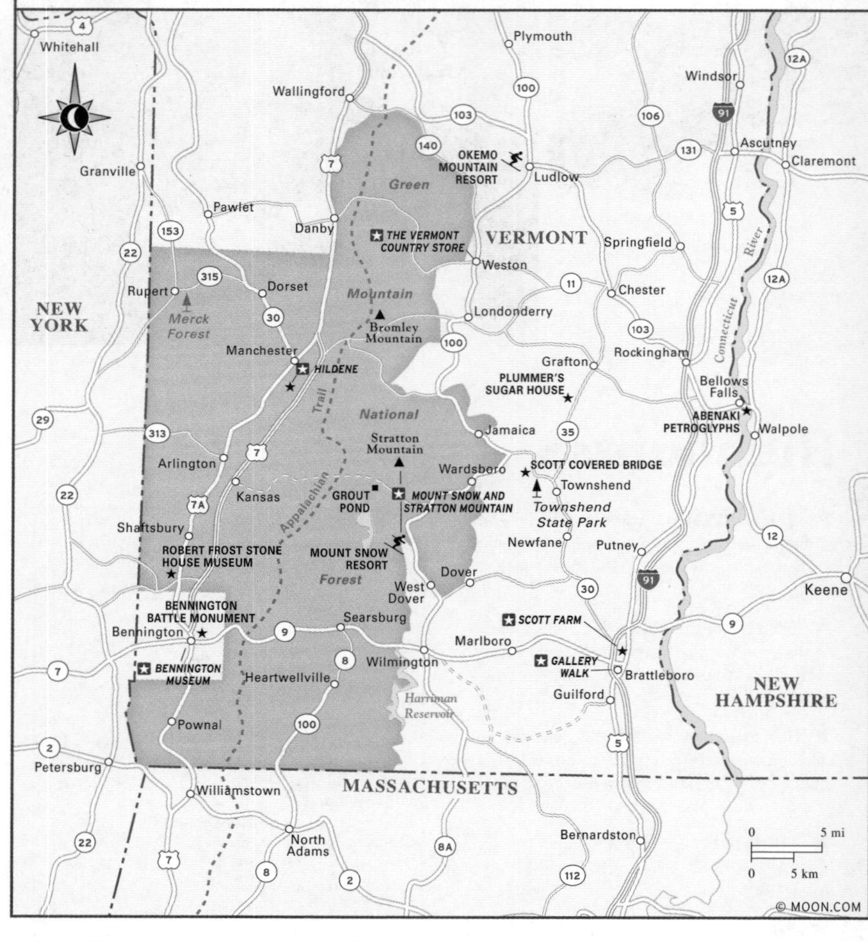

Scott Nearing settled near Brattleboro to farm, write, and live free, and the "back to the land" movement has lingering roots in the hills around town. Get a glimpse of that spirit as Brattleboro celebrates its own slow pace of life at the annual Strolling of the Heifers, Vermont's tongue-in-cheek, ambling retort to Pamplona's Running of the Bulls.

On the opposite edge of the region, Manchester is all gleaming clapboard and luxury, a destination for prosperous New Englanders since the Civil War. Now, historic golf courses and rambling mansions remain

---

Previous: sweeping views across the Green Mountains; skiing at Stratton Mountain; Brattleboro's compact downtown.

the heart of Manchester Village, a beautifully preserved gem in the dramatic shadow of Mount Equinox that extends into modern streets lined with designer outlets.

And at the foot of the Green Mountains is Bennington, a quiet, working-class town that's steeped in American history. It's the western end of the Molly Stark Trail, a warpath-turned-scenic byway named for the wife of Revolutionary general John Stark, who crossed the mountains in 1777 to defeat the British troops at the Battle of Bennington, a rebel victory that increased support for American independence. With less tourism than much of southern Vermont, Bennington is a serene final resting place for many of the soldiers who died in the battle, buried in the churchyard alongside the poet Robert Frost.

But many visitors to southern Vermont find that their most lingering impressions are of the remarkable countryside, veined with brooks and back roads that can seem unchanged by modern life. The Molly Stark Trail is a scenic passage across the mountains that turns breathtaking when fall kindles the trees, and in any season at all, Route 100 is a beautiful way to traverse the state. For adventurous travelers looking to leave the beaten path behind, drive until the pavement gives way, and discover a wandering web of smooth dirt roads that beg to be explored.

PLANNING YOUR TIME

You could breeze through slender southern Vermont in a couple of days, but to take in the sights and small-town pace, you'll need at least five. Note that on peak weekends, the winding roads can fill to capacity with poky sightseers.

The two logical bases are posh **Manchester,** set just at the edge of the Green Mountains, or funky **Brattleboro,** the beguiling, pint-size cultural mecca. For the latter, try to time your trip to take in the monthly Gallery Walk on the first Friday of the month, when the town really displays its artistic talents. If you plan ahead, you can sleep in the former home of Rudyard Kipling, set amid stunning apple orchards with views of distant peaks. The compact region lends itself to endless day trips to the Green Mountain National Forest and the many tiny villages that speckle the landscape. History buffs should be sure to spend a night in **Bennington;** for the rest of us it's an appealing day trip from Brattleboro or Manchester.

Brattleboro

Brattleboro's brick-lined center is framed by gentle mountains, lending the town a dreamy, insular feel. The Connecticut River drifts right through the heart of downtown, where locals linger in cozy cafés and farm-to-table restaurants. A heady blend of art and liberal politics infuse life here, partly driven by students that come to study everything from international development to circus skills. Maybe there's just something in the air, because even Rudyard Kipling came here to be inspired, penning some of his best-loved work at Naulakha, the quirky home that he designed and built outside of town.

For the visitor, Brattleboro is the perfect place to experience Vermont's rebellious and intellectual sides by rubbing elbows with unreconstructed hippies, professors, and aspiring clowns at one of the town's frequent community events. Strap on dancing shoes, join the lineup and do-si-do in a traditional contra dance, browse organic apples at the vibrant farmers market, or paddle a pretty stretch of the Connecticut River.

HISTORY

Starting in 1724, this region was the first part of Vermont to be settled—late compared to the rest of New England. The first permanent settlement in the state was at Fort

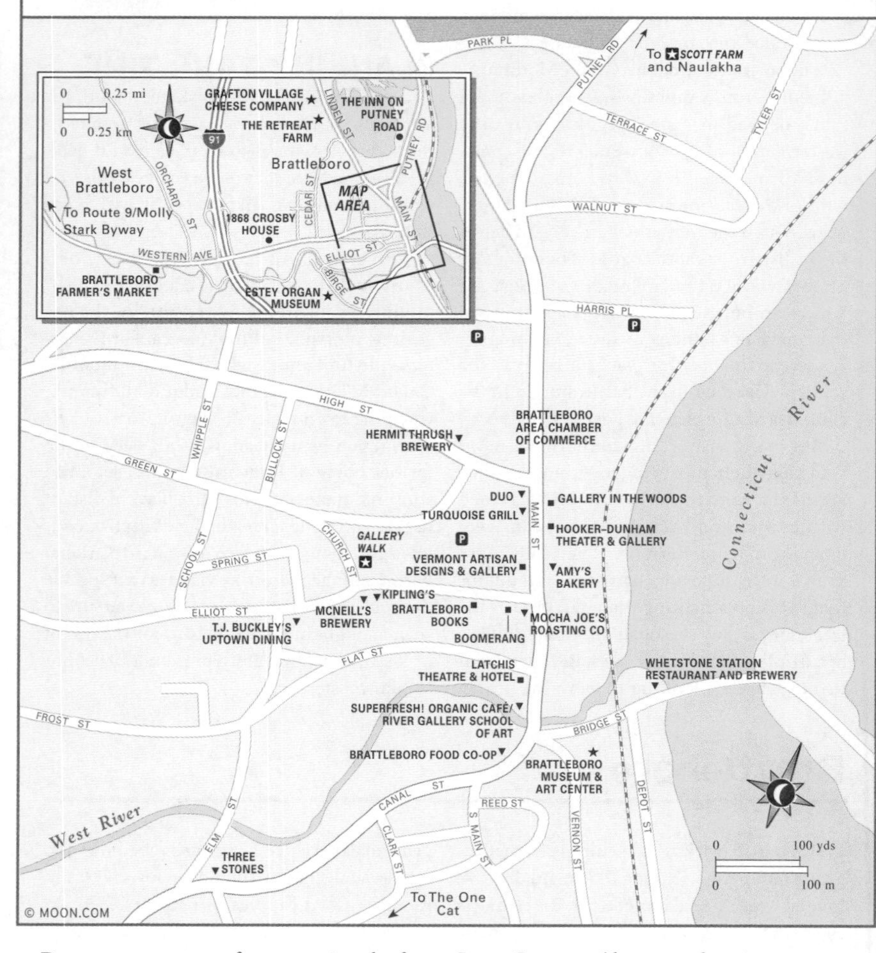

Dummer, an outpost for protecting the fertile Connecticut River Valley from the Native American peoples to the north. The fort grew steadily from a vibrant trading post to a solid base of manufacturing, eventually becoming the city of Brattleboro. In the mid-19th century, it became known as a therapeutic center, famed for a "water cure" that drew some of the country's most prominent citizens for plunges in its ice-cold springs. Later it became the "Organ Capital of the Country" for its Estey Organ Company (the comprehensive museum is mostly suited to true organ enthusiasts).

SIGHTS

★ Gallery Walk

Snow, sleet, or shine, crowds throng the center of town on the first Friday of every month for the **Gallery Walk** (802/257-2616, www.gallerywalk.org, 5:30pm-8:30pm, free), Brattleboro's signature social event. Everyone in town comes out for it, and no other experience will give you a better feel for Brattleboro's unique spirit. The streets take on a festival atmosphere as neighbors catch up on news and pore over their friends' latest creations while juggling snacks and wine. A free map and guide (available online) will help you plot a course through the 50-some venues, which are mostly concentrated on Elliot and Main Streets.

Don't miss the exquisite **Gallery in the Woods** (145 Main St., 802/257-4777, www.galleryinthewoods.com, 11am-5:30pm Mon.-Sat., noon-5pm Sun.), whose focus on the "Visionary, Surreal, Fantastic and Sacred" results in surprisingly grounded and relatable exhibits that range from folk traditions to fine art. Another gem is the **Vermont Center for Photography** (49 Flat St., 802/251-6051, www.vcphoto.org, noon-5pm Thurs.-Sun.), which hosts work by some of the region's most skilled and creative photographers. There's a broad range of mediums on display at **Vermont Artisan Designs** (106 Main St., 802/257-7044, www.vtart.com, 10am-5pm Mon.-Thurs. and Sat., 10am-8pm Fri., 10am-5pm Sun.), and it's an ideal place to browse for unique handmade gifts.

Brattleboro Museum & Art Center

Recent exhibits at the eclectic **Brattleboro Museum & Art Center** (10 Vernon St., 802/257-0124, www.brattleboromuseum.org, 11am-5pm Wed.-Mon., $8 adults, $6 seniors, $4 students, under 18 free) have included photographs of a local drag troupe and work from an experimental weaving studio in Egypt. The museum's unusual location in a renovated railway station is a draw, as are the one-off events, like yo-yo tutorials, poetry readings, and lectures. On the first Friday of the month, the galleries and gift shop stay open until 8:30pm, with free admission after 5:30pm; admission is also free 2pm-5pm every Thursday.

Estey Organ Museum

Harkening back to the past, **Estey Organ Museum** (108 Birge St., 802/246-8366, www.esteyorganmuseum.org, 2pm-4pm Sat.-Sun. mid-May-mid-Oct., $5) celebrates Brattleboro's century-long history as home to the largest reed organ-making factory in the world. The Estey Organ Company once employed more than 500 people and produced half-a-million organs. The museum occupies its former engine house, with displays of reed, pipe, and electronic organs that visitors are encouraged to play—bring your own sheet music.

The Retreat Farm

On the outskirts of town, **The Retreat Farm** (350 Linden St., 802/490-2270, www.retreatfarm.org, 10am-4pm Wed.-Sat., noon-4pm Sun. early June-Oct., $8 adults, $6 seniors and children 2-18) has a family-friendly "petting farm" with dozens of animals that range from familiar to exotic. The 475-acre property is still a working farm owned by the Windham Foundation, a private foundation dedicated to preserving Vermont's rural traditions. In the spirit of being a "gateway farm," the Retreat offers plenty of ways to interact with the resident critters, so you can scratch a pig's belly, go eye to eye with a one-ton ox, and snag a selfie with an impossibly adorable dwarf goat. The farm often opens for limited hours during school vacations.

All year round, the **Retreat Trails** are accessible from the main visitors center or from several other entry points. The network includes about nine miles of trails. One popular walk travels 1.15 miles from the farm to scenic **Ice Pond** via **Morningside Trail.** A recent addition is the **Woodlands Interpretive Trail,** a one-mile loop that is accessed at the Solar Hill trailhead off of Western Avenue; the trail has folksy, 30-minute audio guide that can be downloaded from the farm website, with idiosyncratic stories from locals.

★ Scott Farm

Just north of Brattleboro is the magnificent **Scott Farm** (707 Kipling Rd., Dummerston, 802/254-6868, www.scottfarmvermont.com, 8am-5pm daily July-Nov., farm store

Vermont's Edible Heirlooms

When a Vermont farmer's selling heirlooms, it doesn't mean she's hawking family treasures. "Heirloom" refers to old cultivars that have been passed down by generations of growers. They tend to be fruits and vegetables that didn't fit with modern agriculture's requirement that produce look shiny and fresh after three months in cold storage, but some heirloom varieties just went out of fashion.

You'll find heirloom tomatoes at every farm stand in the state, and you can fill your basket with heirloom everything, from apples to zucchini. Root aficionados shouldn't miss the **Gilfeather Turnip Festival** (Wardsboro, www.friendsofwardsborolibrary.org, late Oct.), which celebrates the town's own heirloom variety with turnip recipe contests and weigh-ins. Winning roots clock in at upward of 25 pounds, and to keep things fair for the flatlanders—non-Vermonters, that is—prizes are awarded in two categories: "grown in Wardsboro" and "grown outside Wardsboro." Root aficionados should note that the Gilfeather turnip is technically a cross between a rutabaga and a true turnip, and it has white skin, white flesh, and a sweet, rooty flavor.

Vermont's blockbuster heirlooms, though, are the hundreds of varieties of apples that are grown here, from tiny lady apples to the knobbed russet, whose lumpy exterior hides wonderfully crisp flesh.

Heirloom varieties can be found in late summer through the fall months, and if you're looking for apples, it doesn't get better than **Scott Farm,** a shrine to eclectic fruit just outside of Brattleboro that's worthy of a pilgrimage. They grow 120 kinds of apples with intriguing names such as Lamb Abbey Pearmain and Zabergau Reinette. The talented orchardist, Ezekiel Goodband, also tends other offbeat tree fruits like quince and medlar, an odd-looking fruit that makes a memorable appearance in Shakespeare's *Romeo and Juliet* and is known in French as the *fruit de trou de cul* (literally, "asshole fruit"). During harvest season, Scott Farm's produce, including medlars, is available in stores around Vermont.

Don't miss these favorite heirloom varieties:

- **Ananas Reinette:** A small, yellow apple that dates back to 16th-century France. As the name suggests, it really does taste like a pineapple.
- **Esopus Spitzenberg:** An oblong apple with red skin and a full flavor that was a favorite of Thomas Jefferson.

9am-5pm daily Sept.-late Nov.), a rolling expanse of apple trees, forest, and fields dotted with fascinating historic structures. It's a memorable experience to pick your own fruit from the trees that march up and down the hills in parallel lines, and the on-site Farm Market sells jugs of unpasteurized cider made from the farm's dozens of heirloom varieties (unlike most ciders, which are made from easier-to-grow Macintosh apples). Pick-your-own season usually extends from Labor Day through mid-September, but call ahead for apple updates.

The rambling property is also home to **Naulakha,** where author Rudyard Kipling lived from 1893 through 1896. He built the vaguely ship-shaped building on a promontory with stunning views of the Connecticut River and named it for an Indian adventure story he wrote with his brother-in-law. It proved a fertile place to work, and Kipling penned the *Jungle Book* and *Captains Courageous* at his heavy desk in the "bow." The only way to visit the home is as an overnight guest with a three-night minimum stay.

ENTERTAINMENT AND EVENTS

Bars and Breweries

The diminutive brew house at **Hermit Thrush Brewery** (29 High St., 802/257-2337, www.hermitthrushbrewery.com, 3pm-8pm Mon.-Thurs., noon-9pm Fri.-Sat., 11am-6pm Sun., tours by request Sat.-Sun., 2 oz.

- **Hubbardston Nonsuch:** A dessert apple that's red-gold, with crisp flesh and plenty of sugar.

And aside from Vermont's autumn bounty of apples, the state has a trove of old-fashioned treats that some food lovers are determined to protect. **Slow Food USA** (www.slowfoodusa.org), the stateside version of **Slow Food International** (www.slowfood.org), which was founded in Italy to protect traditional foodways, has compiled a list of endangered American foods on their Ark of Taste. Aside from the Gilfeather turnip, here are some Vermont Ark of Taste foods to watch for:

- **Boiled cider and cider jelly:** A longtime New England tradition, this sweet-tart product has roots in the 17th century, and is made by reducing fresh apple cider until it thickens. Traditionally used in baking or as a sweetener, boiled cider is rare these days, but you can pick up a jar at some co-ops and specialty stores, and it occasionally makes an appearance on a cocktail menu or cheese board.
- **Green Mountain potato:** Developed by a University of Vermont researcher as a blight-free variety in the 1840s, this oblong potato was one of America's favorite baking potatoes for decades, until it was unseated by the now-ubiquitous russet. Extremely rare.
- **Wild ramps:** One of the first things to appear in the Vermont forests after the final spring snow melts away, these are wild onions with a delicate flavor, much like that of a leek. A vogue for foraged foods in the last decade has put pressure on the wild ramp population, as overharvesting can prevent the perennial plants from returning the following spring. Look for these on farm-to-table menus in the early spring, when sautéed ramps top everything from flatbreads to handmade pasta. Should you seek them out in the woods, please pick very sparingly, ensuring that you get the entire plant.
- **Roy's Calais flint corn:** The Abenaki cultivated flint corn—a hard-kerneled variety—long before the arrival of European settlers, and this variety has roots in those early crops. Rare.
- **Randall cattle:** Blue-black cattle with a distinctive white stripe down their back, this breed was once common in New England and is named for a Vermont family that kept a "closed" herd that was never crossed with Holsteins. Rare and considered critically endangered.

samples $2) makes Belgian-inspired ales in a tiny, rustic space downtown powered by wood pellets. Try samples of their seasonal options, but don't miss the flagship Brattlebeer, a tart, refreshing sour ale brewed with 20 percent cider and aged in wine barrels. Tart, dry, and slightly fruity, it was "inspired by the town of Brattleboro." During winter months, the brewery closes one hour earlier.

With in-house craft brews on tap and a prime riverside location, **Whetstone Station** (36 Bridge St., 802/490-2354, www.whetstonestation.com, 11:30am-10pm Sun.-Thurs., 11:30am-11pm Fri.-Sat.) is a year-round favorite. Take advantage of sunny weather on the rooftop deck or the beer garden: the main restaurant serves a slightly dressed up menu of pub fare, while the beer garden serves a slightly dressed down menu of pub far.

There are bars named for Rudyard Kipling in places from Michigan to Mumbai, but **Kipling's** (78 Elliot St., 802/257-4848, 11:30am-8pm Mon.-Tues., 11:30am-2am Wed.-Fri., 3pm-2am Sat.) has a distinctively Brattleboro feel, with a mashup of Irish bar, fish-and-chips joint, local hangout, and literary mecca (try the James Joyce burger). This is the sort of bar where regulars bang out tunes on the piano and a good place to mingle with the locals.

The Arts

Jugglers, acrobats, and trapeze artists take

center stage at the **New England Center for Circus Arts** (209 Austine Dr., 802/254-9780, www.necenterforcircusarts.org, $10-20), a serious training camp for performers both silly and spectacular. Shows are held at the end of school sessions or when a visiting circus troupe is in town, with one or two performances a month from the spring to the fall. Aspiring circus performers can join the fun at one of the center's shorter, one- to three-day workshops, practicing skills from the flying trapeze to contortion and clowning.

The landmark art deco building that houses the **Latchis Theatre** (50 Main St., 802/254-6300, www.latchis.com, $9 adults, $7 children and seniors, $7 matinees) is as much a part of the show as anything on the screen. Its 750-seat main theater has an iridescent mural of the zodiac on the ceiling and frolicking Greeks along the walls. Three movie theaters show a mix of first-run and independent films. The 1938 building is also a hotel.

Just a few blocks away, the **Hooker-Dunham Theater & Gallery** (139 Main St., 802/254-9276, www.hookerdunham.org, events $5-20, gallery admission free) has a funky subterranean feel, and showcases art-house films, folk and chamber music, and avant-garde theater.

I Brake for Salamanders

It might look like a practical joke, but if you see a "Salamander Crossing" sign, don't laugh—just ease off the gas pedal and watch for slow-moving amphibians. Every spring, salamanders trek to vernal pools to lay their eggs, after spending the cold winter months in moist nooks below the frost line, often in tunnels dug by shrews and moles. When warming weather gets them moving, they start to walk to their pool of choice over the course of several rainy nights in April. But if the migration route crosses a road, entire populations risk being wiped out by passing cars.

To protect the amphibious creatures, volunteers around the state post signs to alert cars of their presence, and on the "Big Nights" when they start to migrate, an ad hoc platoon of crossing guards slow traffic and run a salamander shuttle service. The poky salamanders get scooped up one at a time, and carried to the opposite side of the road, where they can continue to mosey through forests and fields to lay their eggs. If you're in southern Vermont, you can sign up to receive updates on all things salamander from the **Bonnyvale Environmental Education Center** (www.beec.org) and even volunteer to help the adorable amphibians get to where they're going.

Events

Follow step-by-step instructions from the caller, and you'll be twirling and swinging along with a crowd at **The Brattleboro Dance** (118 Elliot St., 518/561-2594, 7pm-10pm, $8 students, $10-12 adults), a traditional contra dance with live music and a welcoming set of regulars. Beginners can show up at 6:45pm for a bit of practice, and dancers should bring a pair of clean, soft-soled shoes to change into (though you'll likely spot some bare feet in the often-woodsy crowd). Check Facebook for dates.

Each June the cows take over for the **Strolling of the Heifers** (www.strollingoftheheifers.com, early June), a parade that celebrates the area's agrarian history and draws attention to the challenges faced by local farmers. In an opening parade, the pride of the pastures saunter down the street, followed by cow floats and kids in cow costumes. During the day, a Dairy Fest features free ice cream, cheese tastings, and a "celebrity" milking contest. Events recently added to the celebration include a Green Expo showcasing environmentally sustainable products and lifestyles and a fiercely competitive Grilled Cheese Cook-off, pitting professional and amateur chefs against each other for the coveted Golden Spatula. For a true taste of country living—and some enthusiastic swing and twirls—don't miss the evening community contra dance.

SHOPPING

The **Brattleboro Farmers Market** (www.brattleborofarmersmarket.com, 9am-2pm Sat. May-Oct., 4pm-7pm Tues. June-Oct.) is the best in southern Vermont, with piles of local produce, cheese, and meat from local farms, crafters, and producers. Snap up artisanal kimchi, gelato, and pasta, among many other things. The Saturday market is on Route 9 near the covered bridge; the Tuesday market is at Whetstone pathway, on lower Main Street. Downtown Brattleboro has an eclectic mix of shops that invites leisurely browsing, like **Boomerang** (12 Elliot St., 802/257-6911, www.boomerangvermont.com, 10am-6pm Mon.-Sat., 11am-5pm Sun.), which stocks new, used, and vintage clothing for men and women and many picks with flair.

Books tower from floor to ceiling at **Brattleboro Books** (36 Elliot St., 802/257-7777, www.brattleborobooks.com, 10am-6pm Mon.-Sat., 11am-5pm Sun.), an independent store with the best selection in town, including many used and out of print copies.

FOOD

With a brightly lit industrial chic space right in the center of town, **Turquoise Grille** (128 Main St., 802/254-2327, www.turquoisegrille.com, lunch 11am-3pm Mon.-Fri., dinner 5pm-9pm daily, $14-21) beckons. The heart of the menu is Turkish, with classics like kofte and kebabs served alongside less common dishes—for something different, try the *mucver,* zucchini fritters, or *lakerda,* a Turkish-style ceviche served with greens. As a gesture to Vermont, perhaps, the menu also includes hearty burgers and salads.

The unexpectedness of ★ **Three Stones Restaurant** (105 Canal St., 802/246-1035, www.threestonesrestaurant.com, 5pm-9pm Wed.-Sat., $12-16) is enchanting. A ramshackle exterior gives way to a warm and vivid interior with a decidedly casual feel. This family-run joint prepares classic foods of the Yucatán Peninsula in southern Mexico, like *panuchos,* a stuffed, refried tortilla; *salbutes,* fried maize cakes piled high with meal and vegetables; and *cochinita adobado,* slow-cooked pork that melts in your mouth. Don't miss the *onzicil,* a sauce made from toasted pepitas and tomatoes.

Vegetable lovers who've tired of Vermont's typically meat-heavy menus should head to ★ **Superfresh! Organic Café** (30 Main St., 802/579-1751, www.superfreshcafe.com, 10am-9pm Sun.-Mon., 10am-4pm Tues., 10am-9pm Wed.-Thurs., 10am-10pm Fri.-Sat., $7-16), which serves up vibrant salads, filling sandwiches and wraps, and ample gluten-free options. You'll find plenty of smoothies, vegan "mylks," and elixirs for what ails you. The laid-back, artsy style is right at home in downtown Brattleboro, attracting a colorful crowd of locals.

The contrast between the thoughtful menus and the offbeat setting—a 1925 Worcester diner car—only heightens the experience at ★ **T. J. Buckley's Uptown Dining** (132 Elliot St., 802/257-4922, www.tjbuckleysuptowndining.com, 5:30pm-9:30pm Thurs.-Sun., open some Wed., in summer, $45), a long-standing Brattleboro favorite. There are just eight tables, so chef-owner Michael Fuller gives personal attention to each dish and offers a handful of options nightly. All of them feature bold flavor combinations, such as venison with eggplant caponata, truffle oil, and fresh currants or the quail with duck leg confit and root vegetables.

Exposed brick and an open kitchen make dining at **duo** (136 Main St., 802/254-4141, www.duorestaurants.com, dinner 5pm-9pm daily, brunch 9am-2pm Sat.-Sun. dinner $18-28, brunch $9-11) a convivial and cozy experience. Their fresh, farm-to-table menus bring diverse influences to bear on seasonal ingredients. Recent starters included fried pickled radishes and potted hot pastrami served with rémoulade, sauerkraut, and rye. The pork chop is perfectly prepared and arrives alongside cornbread, bacon, and rhubarb chowchow.

The town's unofficial meeting hall is **Amy's Bakery Arts Cafe** (113 Main St., 802/251-1071, 8am-6pm Mon.-Sat., 9am-5pm

TOP EXPERIENCE

Say Cheese!

It's only fitting that a place speckled with dairy cows should have cheese makers to match, and Vermont's got more of them per capita than any other state. Cheddar has marquee appeal, but local artisans are producing everything from richly veined blues to creamy chèvres and racking up international awards that have put Green Mountain cheese on the world stage. The Vermont Cheese Council maintains a **Cheese Trail map** (www.vtcheese.com) of the cheese makers that welcome visitors, and the truly dedicated can hopscotch across the state filling their luggage with tangy wedges.

With a factory and tasting room in Brattleboro, **Grafton Village Cheese Company** (400 Linden St., Brattleboro, 802/246-2221, www.graftonvillagecheese.com, 10am-6pm daily) is a delightful place to start. You can graze samples at the retail store, and peek through a viewing window at the cheese makers' gleaming stainless steel vats. While you're there, don't miss the **Shepsog,** a blended sheep's and cows' milk cheese that's cave aged for five months. The firm, earthy cheese has brought home a shelf full of trophies and awards for its standout flavor. (Some cheese is still made at the original location in Grafton, but with nothing to snack on, it pales in comparison with the Brattleboro shop.)

Located in a particularly pretty valley off Route 100, **Plymouth Artisan Cheese** (106 Messer Hill Rd., Plymouth Notch, 802/672-3650, www.plymouthartisancheese.com, 10am-4pm daily), which has been operating continuously since John Coolidge (father to President Calvin Coolidge) founded it in 1890. Their distinctive granular curd cheeses are made with raw cows' milk, which you can learn about and sample in the on-site museum and store. Try the **Plymouth Original** or the sharp **Plymouth Hunter.** They don't make cheese every day, so call ahead to find out when they're producing.

Up on the shores of Lake Champlain, the **Clothbound Cheddar** at **Shelburne Farms** (1611 Harbor Rd., Shelburne, 802/985-8686, www.shelburnefarms.org, cheese making 10am-3pm daily May-Oct.) gives Grafton some stiff competition. It might be the purebred herd of Brown Swiss cows, but their intensely flavored aged cheese has a rich and nutty flavor that some consider unrivalled.

If you just can't get enough of Vermont's enticing cheeses, consider planning your trip around the **Vermont Cheesemaker's Festival** (www.vtcheesefest.com, $50) that happens each July at Shelburne Farms, a daylong extravaganza of cheese and everything that complements it, notably wine and chocolate. Workshops, tastings, and demos go deep into curds and culture.

Sun., $6.50-10), where locals catch up over freshly baked bread, pastries, and coffee at tables overlooking the Connecticut River.

Tucked into a cozy basement nook, **Mocha Joe's Roasting Co.** (82 Main St., 802/257-7794, www.mochajoes.com, 7am-8pm Mon.-Thurs., 7am-9pm Fri., 7:30am-9pm Sat., 7:30am-8pm Sun.) roasts coffee that they source from around the world, with direct trade programs in Cameroon and Nicaragua. The café serves pastries and snacks, but the brews are the real focus, and the friendly, art-filled space may tempt you to while away the morning.

ACCOMMODATIONS

$100-150

Diminutive and homey, **The One Cat** (34 Clark St., 802/579-1905, www.theonecatvermont.com, $110-176) is as funky as Brattleboro itself. The two guest rooms—New England and Brighton—are named for the Anglo-American couple's homes, with according decorative flourishes, as well as televisions, DVD players, and coffeemakers. The tiny library is full of intriguing books and calls out for intimate wintertime reading. A full English breakfast is served, and a

20 percent discount is available for guests that arrive without cars.

The lobby at the **Latchis Hotel** (50 Main St., 802/254-6300, www.latchis.com, $100-190) retains art deco flourishes from its heyday in the 1930s, and for some, it doesn't get any better than a room at a downtown movie theater. Period details like terrazzo floors and chrome fixtures maintain historical cool, ongoing renovations are sprucing up the down-at-the-heels rooms, and suites with small sitting rooms are available.

$150-250

A pristine white house surrounded by meticulous gardens, **The Inn on Putney Road** (192 Putney Rd., 802/451-0335, www.vermontbandbinn.com, $160-280) is shaded by towering trees, including a wonderful Japanese maple that the innkeepers say is the largest in the United States. There's a blazing fire to warm the living room during cold months, and thoughtful perks like bath salts and baskets of snacks contribute to a general luxuriousness. A full gourmet breakfast is included.

Sweet old-fashioned rooms have romantic appeal at **The 1868 Crosby House** (175 Western Ave., 802/257-7145, www.crosbyhouse.com, $175-215). Three individual rooms each have queen-size beds and gas fireplaces, as well as televisions and air-conditioning, and breakfast is a multicourse affair. Afternoon tea is served each day, and fans of dress-up will love the special afternoon teas that the inn stages from time to time, with a selection of gloves and hats for guests, along with feathers and other accessories for decorating. The nearby Retreat Trails are perfect for morning walks.

Over $250

Slow down for a few days on the property that surrounds **Scott Farm Orchard** (707 Kipling Rd., Dummerston, 802/254-6868, www.scottfarmvermont.com), and you'll be rewarded with a sublimely peaceful retreat into scattered apple orchards and shady forests. The **Landmark Trust USA** (www.landmarktrustusa.org) maintains five historic buildings that are destinations worth planning a trip around, especially the exquisite **Naulakha** (sleeps 8, 3-night minimum stay, $430-495), Rudyard Kipling's scrupulously maintained home. The property favors historical preservation over modern-day comforts, but the grounds offer sweeping views of Wantastiquet Range, where Kipling loved to watch Mount Monadnack break the clouds "like a giant thumb-nail pointing heavenwards." The other on-site rentals include the Kiplings' charming **Carriage House** (sleeps 4, 3-night minimum stay, $245-300), a renovated sugarhouse, and two historical farmhouses. All properties must be booked in advance and have minimum stay requirements.

Camping

The actual grounds of Fort Dummer are now underwater, flooded when a dam was built along the Connecticut River. The area around it, however, has been preserved as **Fort Dummer State Park** (517 Old Guilford Rd., 802/254-2610, https://vtstateparks.com/fortdummer.html, mid-May-Labor Day, campsites $18-27). The 217-acre retreat that contains a mile and a half of gentle hiking trails through a densely wooded oak forest is home to squirrels, deer, wild turkey, and ruffed grouse. The campground has 50 wooded tent sites, as well as 10 more secluded lean-tos to accommodate overnight camping. The campground has hot showers and a dumping station, but no hookups.

Forty minutes outside of Brattleboro, **Abbott's Glen Nudist Campground** (3542 Rte. 112, Jacksonville, 802/368-2525, www.abbottsglen.com, tent sites $40 Mon.-Thurs., $60 Fri.-Sun.) might raise a few eyebrows, but it's not the only clothing-optional tent site in Vermont (there's another nudist resort and campground in Milton). The campground has shower facilities, as well as convivial bonfires on Friday nights. "Young naturists" below the age of 35 enjoy discounted rates of $35 midweek and $40 on weekends.

SPORTS AND RECREATION

Hiking and Biking

Three short, gentle nature trails leave from the **Fort Dummer State Park Campground** (517 Old Guilford Rd., 802/254-2610, https://vtstateparks.com/fortdummer.html, mid-May-Labor Day). The one-mile-long **Sunrise Trail** and the 0.5-mile **Sunset Trail** loop through the forest, and the 0.5-mile **Broad Brook Trail** leads from the southern edge of the campground loop to a river swimming hole that's a pleasantly shady haven on a hot summer day.

Brattleboro's rolling skyline is dominated by **Wantastiquet Mountain,** but the trail to the top of the 1,368-foot peak starts in New Hampshire, just across the Connecticut River. To reach the trailhead take Rte. 119 across the river from downtown Brattleboro, and turn left onto Mountain Road just after the second bridge. The trailhead is 0.9 miles from downtown Brattleboro at a small parking area on the right side of the road. The 1.5 miles of switchbacks earn you sweeping views of the Connecticut Valley from the summit, where an exposed granite slab makes an excellent picnic spot.

The 36-mile **West River Railroad** once linked Brattleboro and Londonderry, following the gentle course of the waterway that Native Americans called "Wantastiquet," which translates to "waters of the lonely way." Sections of the now-defunct railroad route have been transformed into the **West River Trail** (www.westrivertrail.org); the 3.5-mile southern section runs from Brattleboro to Dummerston and is open to walkers, bikers, and cross-country skiers. To reach the southern terminus—the Marina Trailhead—from downtown Brattleboro, follow Main Street north until it turns into Putney Road and crosses the West River, then turn left onto Spring Tree Road, which dead-ends at the trailhead. The trail is best for hybrid and mountain bikes, and it's possible to make a longer loop ride by continuing on the road when the trail ends (download the map and suggested route from the West River Trail website).

With easygoing traffic and loads of scenic country roads, Brattleboro is the perfect place to ditch four wheels for two. If you've got your own bike, the Windham Regional Commission creates a useful pdf bicycle suitability map (www.windhamregional.org/bikemap), and 21-speed hybrid bikes are available to rent at **Brattleboro Bicycle Shop** (165 Main St., 802/254-8644, www.bratbike.com, $25/day). The friendly staff are happy to suggest rides in the area, which are either flat out-and-backs in the Connecticut River Valley or hilly climbs into the Green Mountains. As is the case throughout Vermont, some of the finest riding is on unpaved dirt roads, which outnumber the nearby asphalt options three to one, and are an ideal way to escape into quiet country hollows.

Swimming

The Connecticut River looks temptingly cool as it burbles past town, but there are cleaner, more peaceful options a short drive outside of city limits. Though the river is generally too shallow for swimming, just flopping into a pool at **Stickney Brook Falls** is a delightful way to spend a hot afternoon. The series of gentle falls is on the left hand side of Stickney Brook Road; from downtown Brattleboro, drive north on Route 30, and continue 3.7 miles past the I-91 underpass. Turn left on Stickney Brook Road, and watch for cars parked along the road.

Stickney Brook is a tributary of the **West River,** which runs parallel to the Route 30 north of Brattleboro. There are excellent swimming holes all along the waterway, notably just under the West Dummerston covered

1: Rudyard Kipling's writing desk, preserved at Scott Farm near Brattleboro; **2:** Grafton's frozen-in-time architecture; **3:** Abenaki Petroglyphs in Bellows Falls

1 
1841
GRAFTON VILLAGE STORE
MKT
2
3

bridge (7.3 miles north of Brattleboro, with a sometimes strong current).

Half an hour west of Brattleboro, the sinuous **Harriman Reservoir** is pocked with pleasant spots to slip into the water. To reach the reservoir, drive west on Route 9 to the intersection with Route 100 in Wilmington. Access points and swimming beaches are on the right side of Route 100, several with picnic areas and grills. The reservoir's most famous swim spot is **The Ledges** (Ward's Beach Access Road, Wilmington, www.friendsoftheledges.com), a pristine, clothing-optional crook in the shoreline that's back in the buff after losing its nudist privileges in a hotly contested town vote. Thanks to support from groups like A.A.N.R.—that's the American Association for Nude Recreation—the vote was eventually overturned.

Boating

Canoes, kayaks, and tubes can be rented from the **Vermont Canoe Touring Center** (451 Putney Rd., 802/257-5008, www.vermontcanoetouringcenter.com; kayak from $20/hr., canoe from $25/hr., tube $20/day, reservations required) at the intersection of the Connecticut and West Rivers. The stretch of the Connecticut above Vernon Dam is wide and pleasant, with some small islands along the way for paddlers to get out and explore; the West River is smaller but similarly peaceful, though it can also offer some great Class II and III white water in the early spring when the snow melts or on one of a few release dates from the upstream dam each year.

INFORMATION AND SERVICES

The **Brattleboro Area Chamber of Commerce** (180 Main St., 802/254-4565, www.brattleborochamber.org, 9am-5pm Mon.-Fri.) runs a visitors center downtown.

The area's premier hospital is **Brattleboro Memorial Hospital** (17 Belmont Ave., 802/257-0341, www.bmhvt.org). For pharmacy needs, there's **Rite-Aid Pharmacy** (499 Canal St., 802/257-4204) and **Walgreens** (476 Canal St., 802/254-5633). For nonmedical emergencies, contact the **Brattleboro Police** (230 Main St., 802/257-7946).

Banks are found all over the downtown area, particularly on Main Street. ATMs are plentiful around retail stores, in and around hotels, and in convenience stores. Most cafés have **wireless Internet.** Computers are available for public use at **Brooks Memorial Library** (224 Main St., 10am-9pm Wed., 10am-6pm Thurs.-Fri., 10am-5pm Sat.).

GETTING THERE AND AROUND

To get to Brattleboro from Boston (115 mi., 2.25 hrs.), take Route 2 west to Greenfield, then I-91 north to exit 1. From Hartford (85 mi., 1.5 hrs.) and Springfield (60 mi., 1 hr.), Brattleboro is a straight shot north up I-91 to exit 1. From Manchester, New Hampshire (80 mi., 1.7 hrs.), take I-93 and I-89 to exit 5, and then head west along Route 9 to the Vermont border.

Just off the north-south I-91, Brattleboro is the eastern edge of Vermont's east-west Route 9, a scenic, two-lane highway that's known as the **Molly Stark Trail**, named for the wife of a Revolutionary-era general. Brattleboro is also on both of Vermont's Amtrak lines, the Ethan Allen Express from **New York City**, and The Vermonter, which travels from **Washington, D.C.** (800/872-7245, www.amtrak.com, NYC 5.5 hrs., from $65, from DC 8.75 hrs., from $135), and which now allow bicycles. **Greyhound Bus** (800-231-2222, www.greyhound.com) links Brattleboro with cities around the region, and taxi service is available from **Brattleboro Taxi** (802/254-6446, www.brattleborotaxi.com).

Metered parking is available all over downtown Brattleboro, and the town's small downtown is compact and easy to navigate. Three city bus lines connect at the Flat Street Transportation Center in downtown; rides within town are $1, buses operate Monday-Saturday, and a service map is available at www.crtransit.org.

North of Brattleboro

North of Brattleboro, the gentle foothills of the Green Mountains hold half a dozen small villages, with winding roads lined by barns and trim white houses. The towns are perfectly situated for a looping day trip that starts by heading up Route 5 to **Bellows Falls** for a glimpse into the Connecticut River Valley's industrial past, pausing for a walking tour of the town's eclectic and historic architecture.

Delve even deeper into the country on sinuous Route 121 to immaculate **Grafton,** painstakingly preserved by a private foundation that owns much of the town. Ambling through the village is a transporting experience, and Grafton is also renowned for its cheese-making company, which has contributed to the state's reputation for sharp and creamy cheddars.

From there you can take the unpaved Grafton Road to **Newfane,** a strong contender for Vermont's prettiest village. It's a straight, though slow, trip back to Brattleboro on Route 30, or you can add a drive down gorgeous Route 100 to join the Molly Stark Trail at Wilmington.

BELLOWS FALLS (ROCKINGHAM)

Known to locals as Bellows Falls, the town of Rockingham clusters around a brick Italianate clock tower that's visible from miles around. Once an important gathering place for Abenaki people, Bellows Falls became a crossroads and market town during the colonial era. When the railroad arrived in the 1850s, Bellows Falls grew into a center of industry for companies like the Vermont Farm Machine Company, which produced dairy equipment, and the Bellows Falls Cooperative Creamery, which processed cow's milk. Though the heyday is long past, a recent revival has brought independent shops and cafés to the historic downtown, which is an eclectic jumble of architectural styles. Route 5 runs directly to Bellows Falls from Brattleboro and is a more scenic alternative to the interstate.

Bellows Falls Historic District

An unexpected architectural gem, Bellows Falls has fine examples of homes of just about every architectural style in New England, including Federal, Greek Revival, Gothic Revival, Italianate, Second Empire, Stick, Shingle, Queen Anne, Colonial Revival, Dutch Colonial Revival. The town produces a **self-guided walking tour** to the **Bellows Falls Historic District** (802/463-3964, www.bellowsfallsvt.org), which is listed on the National Register of Historic Places. Highlights include the Second Empire **Wyman & Almira Flint House Masonic Temple** (61 Westminster St.) and the curious Greek Revival/Queen Anne-hybrid **Babbitt Tenement House** (11 South St.). Homes are private and not open for tours, but a walking tour of their exteriors is a pleasant way to pass an afternoon.

Abenaki Petroglyphs

According to local historians, excellent fishing once drew the Abenaki to the Bellows Falls area, and the western side of Bellows Falls is said to have been an Abenaki burial ground, where bodies were interred in a seated position with knees drawn up to the chin. And hidden beneath an unpromising, dilapidated bridge in Bellows Falls is a series of mysterious **petroglyphs,** which, depending on your view of such things, may or may not look *exactly like alien heads.*

The granite rocks along the river are etched with a series of faces turned to the west—the direction that Abenaki souls are believed to travel after death. University of Vermont professor William Haviland writes that the petroglyphs were created at some time before the 18th century, but could date back to as far as 1000 CE, with the first European description of the carvings from 1789. Over the years, settlers have speculated (baselessly) that the carvings were anything from doodles—"the work of idle hours"—to family trees, but Haviland believes they're associated with shamanism, and could be images that relate visions seen by people during trance states.

The Bellows Falls petroglyphs have been damaged by construction, erosion, and other intrusions, both well-meaning and otherwise. Haviland relates that in the 1930s, the local chapter of the Daughters of the American Revolution hired a stonecutter to re-etch the eroded petroglyphs. A few decades later, the Chamber of Commerce had them traced in bright yellow paint, which lingers to this day. With all those factors, it's hard to know which aspects of the carvings are original, but they certainly still resemble the earliest known sketches: a series of elongated heads with rays extending upward like antennae.

Reaching the petroglyphs is a bit of an adventure, requiring sturdy shoes and a willingness to get dirty. Follow Bridge Street to a dead end at the closed Vilas Bridge over the Connecticut River. When facing the bridge, a steep embankment drops to the granite rocks at the edge of the water, where you'll find two main clusters of carvings amid a scattering of trash and beer cans.

For more information about the Bellows Falls petroglyphs, including fascinating details about the use of trance states and hallucinations by Algonquin and Abenaki peoples in the region that would become New England, read Haviland's 1994 paper for the Vermont Historical Society (https://vermonthistory.org/journal/misc/BellowsFallsPetroglyphs.pdf).

Events

Every June, Bellows Falls fills with musicians from around the country for the laid-back **Roots on the River** (early June, www.vermontfestivalsllc.com, $20-155), with multiple stages in town. A highlight is always the Sunday show at the Rockingham Meeting House with singer-songwriter Mary Gauthier.

Shopping

As you pass through Putney on the way to Bellows Falls, you won't miss **Basketville** (8 Bellows Falls Rd., Putney, 802/387-5509, www.basketville.com, 9am-6pm daily) in downtown Putney. What started here as a family business more than 100 years ago has grown into a giant emporium, selling picnic baskets, step baskets, Shaker reproduction baskets, Nantucket lightship baskets, and every other conceivable form of wicker carrying apparatus.

Seek out finds as historical as the setting at **Windham Antique Center** (5 The Square, Bellows Falls, 802/732-8081, www.windhamantiquecenter.com, 10am-7pm Mon.-Sat., 10am-5pm Sun.), a multidealer shop in the center of town.

With everything from insulated curtains to pumpkin rolls, **Vermont Country Store** (1292 Rockingham Rd., Bellows Falls, 802/463-2224, www.vermontcountrystore.com, 9am-7pm daily) is the delightfully overstuffed home of the old-fashioned catalog business (there's a second home over in Weston). Even if you're not shopping, the store is undeniably impressive in person—the multiple floors overflow with reminders of the era before department stores (and Amazon). Beware though: The place tends to get incredibly crowded in tour bus season, so if you're planning on browsing or buying at a leisurely pace, it's best to get here before the lunchtime rush.

Food

A blue school bus along with a few scattered picnic tables is all that you'll find at the outdoor **Curtis' BBQ** (7 Putney Landing Rd., Putney, 802/387-5474, 10am-7pm Thurs.-Sun. Apr.-Oct., $7-25), which bills itself as the "ninth wonder of the world" and rarely disappoints. Run by transplanted Georgian Curtis Tuffs, this is where to get your fix of Southern-style pork ribs and grilled chicken, slathered with a tangy special sauce. (Just don't tell Curtis's pet Vietnamese potbellied pig what you are eating.)

Almost a century old, the **Miss Bellows Falls Diner** (90 Rockingham St., Bellows Falls, 802/463-8700, 6am-2pm Mon.-Sat., 7am-2pm Sun., $5-10) was constructed by the Worcester Lunch Car Co. and added to the National Register of Historic Places in 1983. The menu is standard diner fare; for classic filling breakfasts and a cozy seat by a local, it's just right.

If Italian-inspired, farm-to-table ★ **Popolo** (36 The Square, Bellows Falls, www.popolomeanspeople.com, brunch 10am-2:30pm Sun., lunch 11:30am-2:30pm Fri.-Sat., dinner 5pm-9:30pm Tues.-Sat., $16-23) is a sign of the times, things are looking up for Bellows Falls. Slip into a cozy booth or take a seat at the long communal table in this relaxed and modern space, which is warmed by exposed brick and vivid artwork. Start with roasted olives or warm artichoke fonduta, or just dive straight into the fennel-scented broth that envelops the Neapolitan seafood stew. Popolo also hosts concerts and movie nights.

The hip **Flat Iron Exchange** (51 The Square, Bellows Falls, www.flatironexchangevt.com, 6am-9pm daily) has perfect espresso, tea, and pastries, as well as a delightfully eclectic space with a commanding view of the action downtown.

Accommodations

There are sweeping views from the cozy common spaces at **Halladays Harvest Barn Inn** (16 Webb Ter., Bellows Falls, 802/732-8254, www.harvestbarninn.com, $99-159). Homemade cookies in the afternoon may tempt you to curl up and watch the Connecticut River drift by, and the backyard includes a pond and hiking trails that take advantage of the inn's position on a bluff. The multicourse breakfasts are a highlight, and the rooms are comfortable and well-appointed; discounts for business travelers may be available.

Information and Services

The **Great Falls Region Chamber of Commerce** (17 Depot St., Bellows Falls, 802/463-4280, www.gfrcc.org) operates a seasonal visitors center stocked with brochures, educational exhibits, and enthusiastic staff. It's adjacent to the railway station. Pharmacy services can be found at **Rite-Aid Pharmacy** (112 Rockingham St., Bellows Falls, 802/463-9910, 8am-9pm Mon.-Fri., 8am-6pm Sat., 8am-5pm Sun., pharmacy 9am-9pm Mon.-Fri., 9am-6pm Sat., 9am-5pm Sun.). ATMs are available at several locations in downtown Putney and Bellows Falls, including at branches of **Chittenden Bank** (58 Main St., Putney, or 25 The Square, Bellows Falls). Free wireless Internet access is available in the café at **Village Square Booksellers** (32 The Square, Bellows Falls, 802/463-9404, 9am-5pm Mon.-Thurs. and Sat., 9am-7pm Fri., 10am-3pm Sun.).

GRAFTON

During its heyday in the 19th century, Grafton and the inn at its heart hosted presidents and poets as they traveled through the Vermont countryside. Theodore Roosevelt, Ralph Waldo Emerson, Woodrow Wilson, and Oliver Wendell Holmes all stayed here, but by the 1960s the town's population had dwindled and the village was lapsing into dereliction.

It's a familiar story in small towns across the state, but Grafton's decline was reversed by Dean Mathey, a New Jersey investment banker with family ties to the region. In 1963 he established the Windham Foundation to "promote the vitality of Grafton and Vermont's rural communities," and it essentially bought the entire place and restored it to a high shine, including the elegant Grafton Inn, which has been in business since 1801.

The result is a company town with undeniable—if anachronistic—appeal. Grafton also boasts an extraordinary cheese-making company and a 2,000-acre recreation area, the Grafton Ponds Outdoor Center, with cross-country skiing, hiking, mountain biking, and paddling. While you could walk the length of the village in a few minutes, it's a good base for exploring the surrounding countryside or just soaking up the carefully orchestrated country charm.

Grafton Village Cheese Company

While the retail location of the **Grafton Village Cheese Company** (533 Townshend Rd., 802/843-1062, www.graftonvillagecheese.com, 10am-5pm daily) has moved to Brattleboro, it's still possible to peek into the factory to see cheddar in the making. The original, farmer-founded cooperative burned down in 1912, but the Windham Foundation rebuilt in the 1960s, with a vision of making cheese in the rural tradition, with raw milk from family farms. To get a taste of the delightfully grainy aged cheddar in town, stop by MKT, a nearby gourmet shop.

Plummer's Sugar House

Vermont's other famous foodstuff can be found down the road at **Plummer's Sugar House** (2866 Townshend Rd., 802/843-2207, www.plummerssugarhouse.com, 9am-5pm daily), where sap from 10,000 taps is turned into maple syrup when the first warm days arrive in the spring, usually between late February to early April. The proprietors, John and Debe Plummer, are happy to give tours of the syrup-making process, but it's worth calling ahead to ensure that they're "boiling," or making syrup.

Grafton Ponds Outdoor Center

A sprawling expanse of fields and forest, **Grafton Ponds** (783 Townshend Rd., 802/843-2400, www.graftonponds.com, $5/$10 for half-/full-day summer trail access, $20/$10 for winter trail passes) has nine miles of trails. During the summer months, the network is open to hikers and mountain bikers (bike rentals for $20/40 for half/full day), and it's groomed for cross-country skiing in the winter (rentals from $20/10 for adults/youth). The outdoor center also rents fat bikes and snowshoes—check the website to ensure that trails are open for fat biking.

If all that sounds a little strenuous, Grafton Ponds can just set you up with some lawn games for a more leisurely afternoon. For $50, they'll lay out bocce, badminton, or croquet for your group.

Nature Museum

Grafton is home to a small **Nature Museum** (186 Townshend Rd., 802/843-2111, www.nature-museum.org, 10am-4pm Thurs.-Fri. year-round, also 10am-4pm Sat. Memorial Day-Columbus Day, by donation), which is filled with dioramas and stuffed examples of the local fauna. While some of the exhibits are a bit mangy, the museum is worth a look for its impressive catamount, the now-extinct mountain lions in these parts.

Galleries

The diversity and high quality of work available at **Gallery Northstar** (151 Townshend Rd., 802/843-2465, www.gnsgrafton.com, 10am-5pm daily) make it one of the best in southern Vermont. Art is displayed in six rooms of an 1877 village house.

Many of the sculptures at the **Jud Hartmann Gallery** (6 Main St., 802/843-2018, www.judhartmanngallery.com, 10am-5pm daily mid-Sept.-early Nov., by appointment mid-Nov.-Memorial Day) are vivid renderings of Native Americans from northeastern tribes. They're full of life and exquisite details; particularly dynamic are those that depict Iroquois lacrosse players. The hours can vary, so call ahead to confirm that the gallery is open.

Food

A country store-turned-cafe, ★ **MKT: Grafton** (162 Main St., 802/843-2255, 7:30am-6pm Mon.-Thurs., 7:30am-7pm Fri.-Sat., 8am-6pm Sun., $6-14) turns local ingredients into superfresh salads and sandwiches and stocks a good selection of picnic-worthy cheeses, wines, and other delights. Toast comes topped with whipped ricotta and figs, or order the soup of the day and a generous salad. The sunny space is lined with local art, and the café has breathed young energy into Grafton's museum-like historic center.

The Windham-owned **Grafton Inn** (92 Main St., 802/843-2231 or 800/843-1802, www.graftoninnvermont.com) dominates the dining scene in Grafton, but fortunately for hungry visitors, they serve commendable food in both of their establishments. The more casual of the two is the **Phelps Barn Pub** (92 Main St., 5pm-8pm Sun.-Tues., 5pm-9pm Wed.-Sat., $11-30) serving comfort food that is remarkably refined for something dubbed "pub grub." Burgers and Grafton Mac & Cheese line up alongside options like sole meunière with barley and roasted fennel. The inn's fine-dining option is the **Old Tavern Restaurant** (92 Main St., 8am-10am daily, 6pm-9pm Fri.-Sat., 5:30pm-8pm Sun.-Mon., hours may be limited in winter, $22-30), whose menu overlaps with the Phelps Barn Pub, but offers a wider range of plated entrées in a beautiful dining room in keeping with the inn's historical feel.

Accommodations

Grafton's historical **Grafton Inn** (92 Main St., 802/843-2231 or 800/843-1802, www.graftoninnvermont.com, $165-420) was founded in 1801, making it one of the oldest continually operating inns in the United States, a point of pride with the innkeepers, who keep the historic furnishings in fine condition. Guests are greeted with crackers and Grafton cheddar, and the rooms add some modern-day comforts to the old-fashioned property. A full, country breakfast is included for guests, as is admission to **Grafton Ponds Outdoor Center.**

If the hustle and bustle of the village are cramping your style, head out of town to **The Inn at Woodchuck Hill Farm** (275 Woodchuck Hill Rd., 802/843-2398, www.woodchuckhill.com, $129-290), which is set high on a hill above a quiet dirt road. The 200-acre property has ample fields and forests for strolling and old-fashioned rooms with mostly modernized bathrooms. It is also the site of a **Kundalini Yoga Center,** which offers weekly classes, or you can just relax on the broad porch overlooking the yard. Somewhat confoundingly, the hotel's website notes that "if you can't find us, you can't stay here," and the inn is, in fact, rather hard to find in the dark, so it's worth planning to arrive before sunset.

Information and Services

For more information on Grafton, contact the **Windham Foundation** (802/843-2211, www.windham-foundation.org), which owns and operates many of the town's attractions, including the Grafton Village Cheese Company.

In addition to the hospital in Brattleboro, area emergency health services are provided by **Grace Cottage Hospital** (185 Grafton Rd., Townshend, 802/365-7357, www.gracecottage.org). Pharmacy services can be found across the street at **Messenger Valley Pharmacy** (170 Rte. 30, Townshend, 802/365-4117, 8:30am-6pm Mon.-Fri. and 9am-2pm Sat.).

TOWNSHEND AND NEWFANE

Completing the loop of small towns north of Brattleboro are two quiet communities that, while they have few sights to speak of, are great destinations while exploring the countryside. Filled with pristine white buildings that seem rather too grand for such a rural spot, Newfane is among the prettiest villages in Vermont. In the 19th-century, lumber mills and flour mills powered the town's economy, and a series of Greek Revival and Federalist buildings sprang up around the town green.

Five miles up the road, the village of Townshend has more the feel of a working Vermont town, with rows of homes clustered around the town green's gazebo and church. The town also boasts a classic covered bridge and a wonderful horse farm, where you can hop a sleigh for a snowy ride through the hills.

Sights

At 277 feet, **Scott Covered Bridge** (Rte. 30, west of Townshend) is one of the longest in Vermont, with an unusual latticework pattern that uses both town lattices and king posts. In all, seven covered bridges are scattered throughout the immediate vicinity, including the 118-foot-long **Williamsville Bridge** (Dover Rd., South Newfane).

The eye-catching horses at **Friesians of Majesty** (185 Maggie Ladd Rd., Townshend, 802/365-7526, www.friesiansofmajesty.com) may be descended from Middle Ages warhorses, but these perfectly groomed mounts spend their days roaming a picturesque farm. Friesians of Majesty offers dreamy sleigh rides through their snowy pastures (45 min., from $62 adult, $31 children 5-12), carriage rides to weddings and events, and even horse-drawn hearse service.

Shopping

Calling carnivores with the wafting smell of cob-smoked bacon, ham, turkey, and sausages, **Lawrence's Smoke Shop and Country Store** (653 Rte. 30, Townshend, 802/365-7372, www.lawrencessmokeshop.com, 10am-5pm Sun.-Thurs., 10am-6pm Fri.-Sat.) has been a Townshend landmark since 1964.

Food

The fare at the **Townshend Dam Diner** (Rte. 30, 2 mi. north of the Townshend Dam, 802/874-4107, 5am-8pm Wed.-Mon., $6-10) is classic: plates of roasted turkey, pork, and beef with traditional sides, served on paper place mats advertising used cars and home improvement. They say it's "the best home-cooked food for your money by a dam site," and plenty of locals are inclined to agree.

The romantic **Windham Hill Inn** (311 Lawrence Dr., West Townshend, 802/874-4080, www.windhamhill.com, 6pm-8:30pm daily in summer and fall, 6pm-8:30pm Wed.-Sun. winter and spring, $22-36) has sophisticated dining in a tranquil country setting. The refined menu includes braised local rabbit ragout and salted cod with shaved truffles, and the flourless chocolate torte is perfectly set off by spiced pistachio ice cream and brittle. The Windham Hill Inn has received awards from *Wine Spectator* magazine for their extensive cellars.

Set in Newfane's Four Columns Inn, **Artisan Restaurant and Tavern** (21 West St., Newfane, 802/365-7713, www.fourcolumnsvt.com, 5:30pm-8:30pm Tues.-Sat., 11am-2pm Sun., dinner $26-34, prix fixe brunch $17) has a cozy, refined atmosphere.

Townshend is often called one of Vermont's prettiest villages.

Being the only place in town is not the only reason to go—the chef turns out well-executed New American offerings that feature ingredients from local farms and producers. With cheeses from some of the state's best creameries, the restaurant's cheese boards are a highlight. The adjoining tavern has a more casual feel, with live music and deals on burgers every Wednesday.

Accommodations

UNDER $100

Staying at **Ranney Brook Farm** (Rte. 30, 2 mi. north of the Townshend Dam, $75-85) is like having friends with a Vermont farmhouse, complete with a dog, birds, two cats, and a hearty breakfast. The four rooms are somewhat dated and cutesy, but they're also comfortable and furnished with homemade cookies.

Another simple, homey option, the **Boardman House Bed & Breakfast** (On the Green, Townshend, 802/365-4086, $80) has just five rooms in an 1840 farmhouse. The owners, Sarah and Paul, prepare a filling homemade breakfast tailored to guests' needs, and their friendly dogs form an enthusiastic welcome committee.

OVER $200

Overflowing with updated country charm, the ★ **Four Columns Inn** (21 West St., Newfane, 802/365-7713, $200-295) has a fabulous location overlooking the center of town. The "Windham with a view" rooms have banks of windows that face the green, perfect for sipping your morning coffee as village life unspools below. Behind the inn, private hiking trails wind through an expansive, wooded property, while a brook runs through the backyard. Rates include an à la carte breakfast that's served in the inn's sunny tavern.

CAMPING

At the base of Bald Mountain, **Townshend State Park** (2755 State Forest Rd., Townshend, 802/365-7500, https://vtstateparks.com/htm/townshend.htm, late May-early Sept.) was headquarters during the Great Depression for the Civilian Conservation Corps, which built a well-appointed **campground** with stone house, picnic area, and fire tower. The campground itself is heavily wooded, offering quiet seclusion to 30 tent sites and 4 lean-to sites ($18-27/night) that are located along the back side of a gently babbling brook.

GETTING THERE AND AROUND

From Brattleboro, drive north up I-91 to exit 5 for Bellows Falls (23 mi., 30 min.), or take the smaller Route 5 (23 mi., 40 min.). From Bellows Falls, take Route 121 northwest to Grafton (14 mi., 25 min.). Continue south down Route 35 for Townshend (10 mi., 20 min.) or take the unpaved Grafton Road (10 mi., 30 min.); then head south down Route 30 for Newfane (5 mi., 10 min.). Complete the loop by continuing down Route 30 to Brattleboro (12 mi., 20 min.). Of course, the loop works just as well the other way.

The Molly Stark Trail

The **Molly Stark Trail** (Rte. 9) may be the main route between Brattleboro and Bennington (40 mi., 1 hr.), but it's a winding track through the mountains with arresting views. It's a gorgeous drive, and it's named for the wife of Major General John Stark, who led troops across these mountains on the way to the 1777 Battle of Bennington, supposedly saying: "There are the red coats! They will be ours, or tonight Molly Stark sleeps a widow." (Spoiler: the Redcoats lost both the battle and the war, while Molly kept her husband.)

Traveling from east to west, the first main stop is the scenic overlook at **Hogback Mountain,** where a pullout overlooks a 100-mile panorama that stretches to Massachusetts and New Hampshire, with the **Green Mountain National Forest** bristling away to the north.

A bit farther along, **Wilmington** makes an excellent stop for stretching your legs—a short main street is lined with shops and cafés. On the other side of town, you'll pass the northern edge of the **Harriman Reservoir,** where **The Ledges** (Ward's Beach Access Road, Wilmington, www.friendsoftheledges.com) is a favorite for nude swimming and sunbathing.

The Molly Stark Trail's not the only great drive in Vermont—the state is crisscrossed with winding roads that are often the prettiest way to get where you're going, and the distinctly un-touristy country stores and working farms they pass offer a glimpse of daily life in the state. Vermont maintains a map of designated **Scenic Byways** (www.vermont-byways.us), which are an excellent way to find your own back road through Vermont's rolling landscape.

Bennington to Manchester

A broad, north-south valley divides the Green Mountains and the Taconic Range, a low ridge of mountains on the border with New York state. In the valley floor lies a string of historic towns that extend from the working-class community of Bennington in the south to the posh community of Manchester, whose Civil War-era hotels and designer outlets read like a then-and-now of luxury vacationing. Linking the two towns is Route 7, a two-lane highway that passes through a series of small towns, with covered bridges, town greens, and the former home of poet Robert Frost.

BENNINGTON

Bennington has a long and rich history, but the town is best known for a battle that took place 12 miles to the west, just over the New York border. The Battle of Bennington is remembered as a defining moment for the American Revolutionary cause, a fascinating clash between the pro-British forces—a mixed group of German dragoons, Native Americans, Canadians, and loyalists—and a rebel force led by General John Stark and reinforced by Ethan Allen's Green Mountain Boys. (If you try to visit a Vermont library or city hall on August 16, don't be surprised if it's closed for Bennington Battle Day.)

The region has calmed down significantly since 1777, and modern-day Bennington is a tranquil former mill town with a renowned liberal arts college and a number of attractions, including an excellent art and history museum, Robert Frost's grave site, and a monument commemorating the battle. Frost came here to "plant a new garden of Eden with a thousand apple trees of some unforbidden variety," and the rolling landscape outside of town remains bucolic, despite Bennington's industry and development.

Bennington Battle Monument

It's hard to miss the **Bennington Battle Monument** (15 Monument Cir., 802/447-0550, www.benningtonbattlemonument.com, 9am-5pm daily mid-Apr.-Oct., $5 adults, $1 children), a 306-foot-tall limestone obelisk

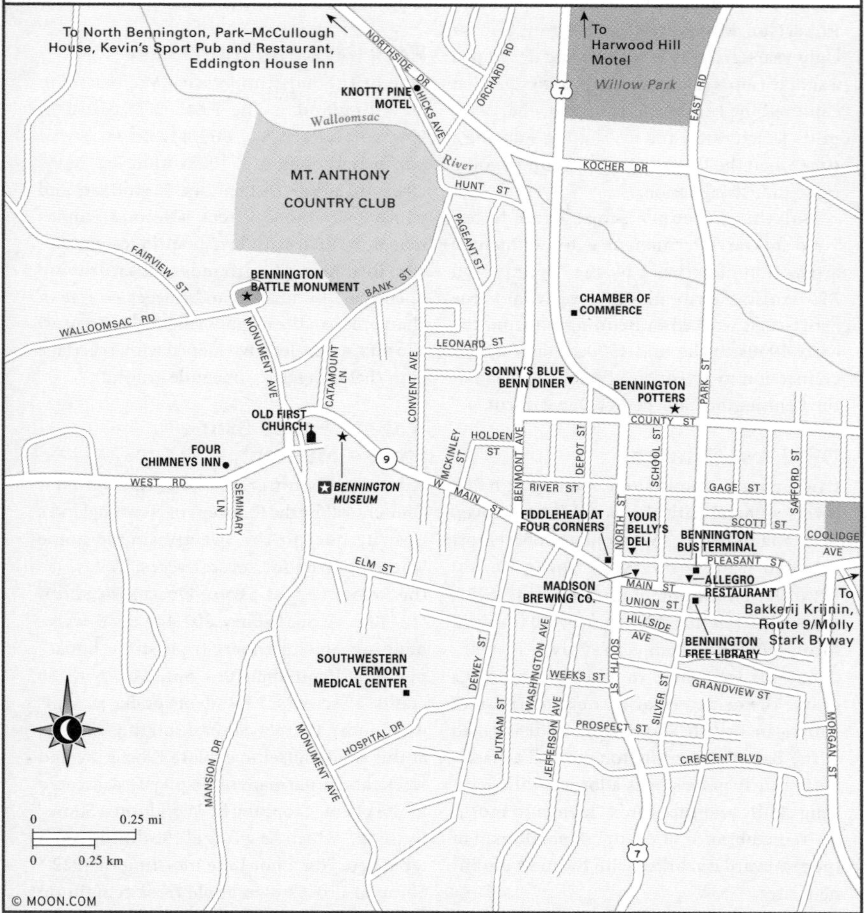

that towers over the town like a half-size version of the Washington Monument. Inside is a diorama of the second engagement of the Battle of Bennington, along with an elevator that takes visitors two-thirds of the way up for a knockout view of the Green Mountains, the Berkshires, and the Taconic Range (in Vermont, Massachusetts, and New York, respectively). Statues of the battle's heroes, John Stark and Seth Warner, strike heroic poses on the monument grounds, and the actual site of the storehouse the British had hoped to capture is now a gift shop.

★ Bennington Museum

The art-filled **Bennington Museum** (75 Main St., 802/447-1571, www.benningtonmuseum.org, 10am-5pm daily June-Oct., 10am-5pm Thurs.-Tues. Nov.-Dec. and Feb.-May, closed Jan., $10 adults, $9 students and seniors, under 18 free) is a detour-worthy destination. The museum has the largest public collection of work by folk artist Grandma Moses, along with her painting desk (itself painted on) and chair. Anna Mary Robertson Moses lived in Bennington for eight years, from 1927 to 1935 and developed a simple (some might say simplistic) style that captured the rural American past—harvests, mills, sleigh rides, and ice-skating—during a time when the United States was undergoing rapid industrialization.

But the museum's scope extends beyond folk art. Permanent exhibits include a selection of artwork by the "Bennington Modernists," a vibrant group of avant-garde artists that worked in Bennington from the early 1950s to the mid-1970s, many with a connection to artist Paul Feeley, the head of the Bennington College Art Department.

Old First Church

Laid under a simple stone reading "I had a lovers' quarrel with the world," the beloved poet (and sometimes Vermonter) Robert Frost is buried at the **Old First Congregational Church** (1 Monument Cir., 802/447-1223, www.oldfirstchurchbenn.org, 10am-4pm Mon.-Sat. 1pm-4pm Sun. July-mid-Oct., donations welcome). In addition to Frost's grave, the cemetery also contains those of American, British, and Hessian soldiers killed at the Battle of Bennington, as well as fascinating early gravestones adorned with grinning skulls and the words "memento mori," or "remembrance of death." A small map of the graveyard is marked with the most prominent sites.

Bennington Potters

The first pottery in Bennington was constructed by a Revolutionary War veteran in 1793. Since then, the town has become famous for its earthenware, a tradition that is carried on at **Bennington Potters** (324 County St., 802/447-7531 or 800/205-8033, www.benningtonpotters.com, 9:30am-6pm Mon.-Sat., 10am-5pm Sun.), which is equal parts outlet store and museum. You can browse several rooms of mugs, bowls, and plates made in the company's distinctive "speckleware" patterns and then watch artisans at work spinning clay in the potters' yard.

Park-McCullough House

One of the most impressive Victorians in New England is the **Park-McCullough House** (1 Park St., 802/442-5441, www.parkmccullough.org, 10am-4pm Fri. May-Dec., $15 adults, $12 seniors, $8 students and youth 8-17, under 8 free), a Second Empire mansion filled with lavish antiques and period furniture. The grounds and gardens are open year-round and can be accessed free of charge, as can the neighboring **Mile-Around Woods,** a forested idyll looped with a carriage path that is precisely one mile around.

Robert Frost Stone House Museum

After visiting his grave site at the Old First Church, follow the footsteps of New England's favorite poet to the sweetly simple home where he lived for several years. Today, it's the **Robert Frost Stone House Museum** (121 Rte. 7A, Shaftsbury, 802/447-6200, www.bennington.edu/robert-frost-stone-house-museum, 10am-5pm Tues.-Sun. May-Nov., $6 adults, $5 seniors, $3 students under 18, children under 10 free). Several rotating exhibits at this small museum explore Frost's life and work, and a permanent display is dedicated to the poem "Stopping by Woods on a Snowy Evening," which he wrote at the dining room table here "on a hot June morning in 1922." Some of Frost's own apple trees remain on the slightly ramshackle grounds, along with crumbling stone walls and groves of birch.

Covered Bridges

The country roads around Bennington are the perfect place to explore Vermont's distinctive covered bridges, wooden structures built to withstand harsh winter weather that became icons of the New England landscape. Start at

1: Bennington Battle Monument; **2:** Robert Frost Stone House Museum; **3:** Bennington Museum

1
Frost
House
2
3

the elegantly trussed **Silk Bridge** across the Walloomsac River, a single-lane "town lattice truss" that dates to 1840; follow Route 7 north from downtown Bennington to Route 67A, and turn left onto Silk Road (10 min., 3.9 mi. from the intersection of Route 7 and Route 9). Continue northeast on Route 67A to a left turn on Murphy Road, where the **Paper Mill Village Bridge** stretches 125 over the river (3 min., 0.2 mi.). The original bridge construction was in 1889, but the existing structure was rebuilt in 2000.

Drive across the Paper Mill Village Bridge, and continue south on Murphy Road, which loops around to **Burt Henry Covered Bridge,** another 1840 structure with town lattice trussing (4 min., 1.3 mi.). Keep an eye out for **Henry House,** to the left of the road just south of the bridge; built in 1769, it is one of the oldest surviving houses in Vermont.

The area's other two covered bridges are 15 miles north, in the village of Arlington. Cross the Burt Henry Bridge and turn right on River Road, then follow Route 67A to Route 67 and 7A north. Just before the Stewart's shop in Arlington, turn right on East Arlington Road, which turns into Sunderland Road before reaching the **Chiselville Bridge** across Roaring Branch Brook (25 min., 15.3 mi.). Set over a steep embankment, this 1870 bridge features threatening a one-dollar fine for crossing above a walking pace.

Retrace your path back to Route 7A, and go north for 0.2 miles before turning left on Route 313. Take a left onto the aptly named Covered Bridge Road after 4.2 miles, and you'll find the **Arlington Green Covered Bridge** (12 min., 6.3 mi.). With a bucolic view of West Arlington's town green and forested hills, this bridge is among Vermont's most photogenic, especially when fall colors highlight it's iconic, rust-red color. The bridge is a stone's throw from the home where artist Norman Rockwell lived and painted for 15 years, now the Inn on Covered Bridge Green.

Entertainment and Events

On August 16 of every year, Vermont celebrates its very own holiday, **Bennington Battle Day** (802/447-3311 or 800/229-0252, www.bennington.com), during which the town holds an annual parade along with battle reenactments on the monument grounds.

Set in a nondescript brick building in workaday downtown Bennington, **Oldcastle Theatre Company** (331 Main St., 802/447-0564, www.oldcastletheatre.org) has been putting on professional caliber performances since 1972. Catch shows that range from Shakespeare to show tunes and slapstick.

A few weeks later, bring your breath mints to the **Southern Vermont Garlic and Herb Festival** (802/447-3311, www.bennington.com/garlicfest), an annual Labor Day weekend celebration that offers up plenty of piquant samples of garlic spreads, garlic jellies, garlic salsas, and even garlic ice cream (don't miss the tent with garlic margaritas) at a fairground off Route 9 west of town. In between eating and not kissing, fairgoers can take in musical performances, face painting, and a hay maze.

Shopping

The shelves at **Bennington Bookshop** (467 Main St., 802/442-5059, www.benningtonbookshop.com, 10am-6pm Mon.-Sat., noon-4pm Sun.) are built for browsing, with an ample selection of children's books, beach reads, and serious literature, along with plenty of local subject matter.

Browse a fun collection of jewelry, arts, and crafts at **Fiddlehead at Four Corners** (338 Main St., 802/447-1000, 10am-5pm daily), a friendly store set into an old bank with slate-lined vault where visitors can scrawl messages in chalk. The friendly, knowledgeable owner makes this shop a local favorite, and he's an excellent source of local lore and attractions.

Food and Drink

If you don't know what to order at ★ **Sonny's Blue Benn Diner** (314 North St./Rte. 7, 802/442-5140, 6am-5pm Mon.-Tues., 6am-8pm Wed.-Fri., 6am-4pm Sat., 7am-4pm Sun., $3-12), just look up. Every inch of wall space in this prefab 1940s diner car is covered with specials. Especially to-die-for are the waffles and French toast, topped with every imaginable combination of syrups, fruits, and nuts.

Tucked into a downtown side street, **Your Belly's Deli** (100 Pleasant St., 802/422-3653, 10:30am-3pm Sat. and Mon.-Thurs., 10:30am-7pm Sun., $4-15) serves fresh plates of soups, sandwiches, and salads to a regular crowd of downtown workers. The soups, which change daily, are a real highlight, especially the rich cheesy tomato soup that reappears each week.

The dishes at **Allegro Ristorante** (520 Main St., 802/442-0990, www.allegroristorante.com, 5pm-10pm daily, $14-23) pull from all over the home country, often adapting locally produced ingredients to Italian classics. They serve a long list of pastas, with gluten-free options available, and the tiramisu has a loyal following. Dimly lit and adorned with soft-focus paintings of Italy, it's a pleasantly quiet spot to spend the evening.

Hard to pronounce and easy to love, ★ **Bakkerij Krijnin** (1001 Main St., 802/442-1001, 8:30am-5:30pm Thurs.-Sun., $3-10) combines classic pastries and breads from around Europe with Dutch favorites, like dense squares of almond-filled spice cake and apple kuchen. The bakery also has creative soups and sandwiches, including vegan options—it's hard to beat a hot drink and an oozing *stroopwafel* on a chilly day.

The convivial **Madison Brewing Company** (428 Main St., 802/442-7397, www.madisonbrewingco.com, 11:30am-9pm Sun.-Thurs., 11:30am-10pm Fri.-Sat., $11-20) serves handcrafted beers along with pub grub from around the world: Cottage pie, mezze platters, Irish lounge fries, and pork schnitzel are among the democratic offerings. The malty, smooth Old 76 Strong Ale is a standout among their brews, many of which change with the season.

Just up the road in North Bennington, **Kevin's Sport Pub and Restaurant** (27 Main St., North Bennington, 802/442-0122, www.kevinssportspubandrestaurant.com, 11am-2am daily, $8-19) is a neighborhood bar and restaurant that's fiercely beloved by locals in North Bennington, about six miles from downtown Bennington. They come for burgers, fried chicken, and steak, or just to lean an elbow on the bar and watch the whole town come and go. There's usually live music on Friday and Saturday nights, and the game is always on.

Accommodations

UNDER $100

The owners at the ★ **Harwood Hill Motel** (864 Harwood Hill Rd., 802/442-6278, www.harwoodhillmotel.com, $99-130) have spruced up their rooms with paintings by local artists and added appealing splashes of color to the simple roadside motel, which has a sweeping view over the town. All rooms have coffeemakers and refrigerators, and rollaway beds are provided for no extra charge. If you're staying for two nights and plan to take in the sights, the Arts Package is an amazing deal: $285 covers both evenings as well as admission and discounts at a laundry list of local attractions.

Just down the hill from the Bennington Battle Monument, the **Knotty Pine Motel** (130 Northside Dr., 802/442-5487, www.knottypinemotel.com, $90-110) offers good value and spotless rooms, including queens, doubles, and efficiencies with kitchenettes.

$150-250

The sweetly restored ★ **Eddington House Inn** (21 Main St., North Bennington, 800/941-1857, www.eddingtonhouseinn.com, $179-219) is full of thoughtful touches; handmade truffles, afternoon snacks, and delicious breakfasts make it a welcoming place, as do the friendly owners. The rooms are decorated with beautiful taste, antiques are atmospheric but uncluttered, and each one includes a sitting area that's perfect for curling up with a book. The Eddington House is in North Bennington, a village that's about six miles north of downtown Bennington.

You can't miss the solid brick stacks that project from the roof of **The Four Chimneys**

Inn (21 West Rd./Rte. 9, 802/447-3500, www.fourchimneys.com, $159-299), a sprawling Revolutionary-era parsonage that has been converted to an upscale bed-and-breakfast. As might be expected, many of the rooms have fireplaces, including one with a real wood-burning hearth. The white-cloth dining room has French doors looking out on the grounds and serves a menu of refined New England cuisine, with specialties such as grilled apple cider salmon and mushroom and leek risotto.

CAMPING

Eight miles outside of town, ★ **Greenwood Lodge and Campsites** (311 Greenwood Dr., Woodford, 802/442-2546, www.campvermont.com/greenwood, mid-May-late Oct., dorms $32/35 for HI members/nonmembers, private rooms $72-79) is an unbeatable deal set in a serene mountain property. Female and male dorms are four and five beds, respectively, and share a bathroom down the hall. Rustic, mountain cottage decor makes this a cozy place to relax after a day exploring the area's many hiking trails and lakes, and the hostel has a shared kitchen and common area. There is a $3 discount for travelers with their own linens and towels, and dinner supplies are available at the nearby general store.

Sports and Recreation

HIKING

The Appalachian Trail becomes the **Long Trail** when it passes into Vermont, and it intersects Route 9 5.2 miles east of Bennington (from the intersection of Route 9 and Route 7). The trail is mostly forested on either side of Route 9, but ambitious hikers can earn panoramic views of the Green Mountain National Forest from the rickety fire tower atop **Glastonbury Mountain**, 7.3 miles north of the road crossing. South of Route 9, **Harmon Hill** is a steep, but shorter option (3.7 miles round-trip). The trail switchbacks and steps its way up 1,200 feet of elevation gain to an open meadow that peers down on the town of Bennington, where the Bennington Battle Monument pokes high above the trees. For maps and information on the hike, contact the **Manchester Ranger District** (2538 Depot St./Rte. 11/30, Manchester Center, 802/362-2307, www.fs.usda.gov/greenmountain).

Information and Services

The **Bennington Area Chamber of Commerce** (100 Veterans Memorial Dr., 802/447-3311, www.bennington.com) runs a visitors center in town. Emergency medical services are handled by **Southwestern Vermont Medical Center** (100 Hospital Dr., East Bennington, 802/442-6361, www.svhealthcare.org). For medications, **Extended Care Pharmacy** (207 North St., 802/442-4600) is located in the center of town, along with a chain **Rite-Aid Pharmacy** (194 North St., 802/442-2240, 9am-9pm Mon.-Fri., 9am-6pm Sat., 9am-5pm Sun.). On the north side of town is **CVS Pharmacy** (8 Kocher Dr., 802/442-8369). For nonmedical emergencies, contact **Bennington Police Department** (118 South St., 802/442-1030).

Several banks with ATMs are located at the corner of Route 7 and Route 9, including **Chittenden Bank** (401 Main St.), **Sovereign Bank** (107 N. Side Rd.), and **Merchants Bank** (406 Main St., 802/442-8321, 8:30am-5pm Mon.-Thurs., 8:30am-6pm Fri.). Free Internet use is offered at the **Bennington Free Library** (101 Silver St., 802/442-9051, www.benningtonfreelibrary.org, 10am-7pm Mon., 10am-5pm Tues.-Wed., 1pm-7pm Thurs., 1pm-5pm Fri., 10am-1pm Sat.).

MANCHESTER

Manchester Village has been a summer destination for East Coast elites since before the Civil War, when the Equinox house drew moneyed guests to hike, ski, and fly-fish for trout in the Battenkill River. It's still easy to see the appeal—Mount Equinox makes a dramatic backdrop for the handsome village, which is set in a valley between the Taconic and Green Mountains. And the long-standing tourism here has become an attraction in

Manchester

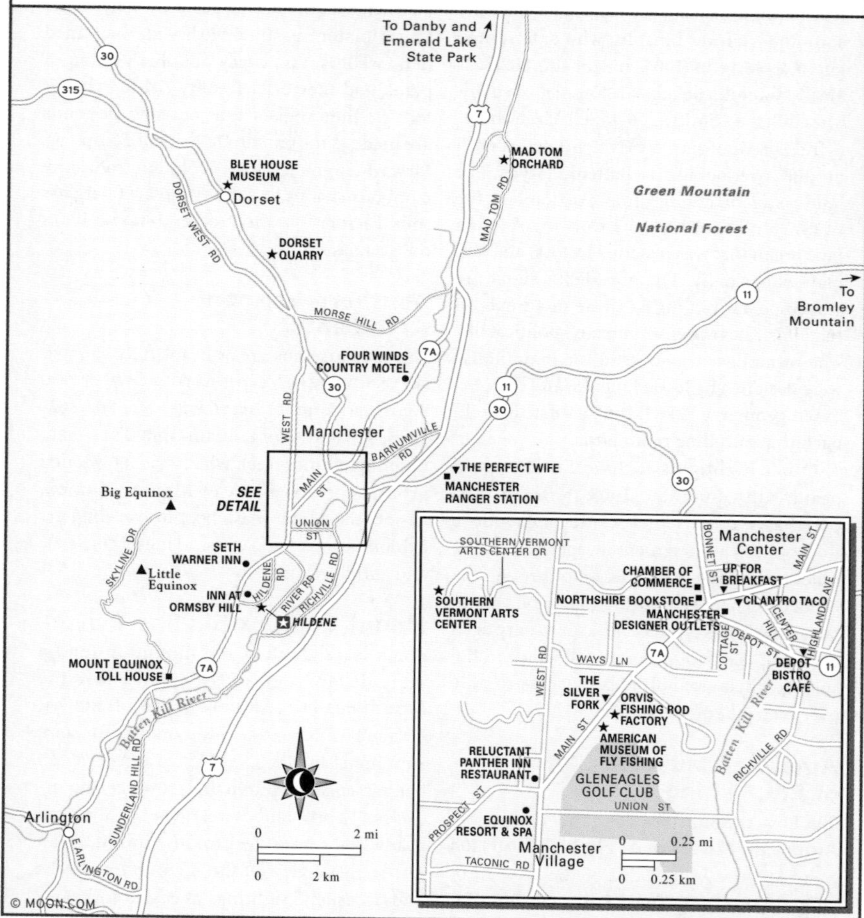

itself; it's well worth a walk down Manchester Village's streets, which are lined with 19th-century mansions set side by side like cabins at summer camp.

Many of today's attractions date to Manchester's early days, whether it's golfing on a course beloved by Robert Todd Lincoln, walking forested trails, or taking in a rejuvenating spa treatment—many visitors to the Equinox came for the invigorating mountain air and water, and would "weigh out" before leaving to be sure they'd added a bit of padding in their time up north. Just a few miles down the road, Manchester Center is another snapshot of upscale vacationing, and the winding path of Route 7 is lined with outlet shops bearing the names of top designers such as Kate Spade, Armani, and Ralph Lauren. Some visitors find the newer development unappealing, but dedicated shoppers could easily while away a weekend in the gleaming stores.

★ Hildene

Among those who once made Manchester their summer home was Abraham Lincoln's son, Robert Todd Lincoln, who entertained guests at **Hildene** (1005 Hildene Rd., 802/362-1788, www.hildene.org, 9:30am-4:30pm daily, $18 adults, $5 children 6-14, children under 6 free), a Georgian Revival mansion with grounds overlooking the Battenkill River. The house is an intriguing glimpse of domestic life in Lincoln's time. It has a working Aeolian pipe organ that was installed in 1908 and still plays songs daily. The president's signature stovepipe hat retains its shine in an exhibit that illustrates the elder Lincoln's political life. The formal gardens behind the main house were designed by Jessie Lincoln, and their ordered geometry is striking against the wild backdrop of rolling mountains.

Other highlights include **Sunbeam,** a beautifully appointed 1903 Pullman railcar that was part of President Theodore Roosevelt's campaign entourage, and the 12 miles of walking trails that loop through the property. There is a working farm on the estate whose goats produce milk for a sharp aged cheese; it is a delight to visit the herd in the spring, when gamboling baby goats tumble over each other.

American Museum of Fly Fishing

See how the masters cast and tied at the **American Museum of Fly Fishing** (4104 Main St./Rte. 7A, 802/362-3300, www.amff.com, 10am-4pm, Tues.-Sun., closed Sun. Nov.-May, $5 adults, $3 children 5-14, $10 families, donations accepted). The quaint museum showcases flies tied by Mary Orvis Marbury and other originators of the sport, along with rods owned by such celebrities as Ernest Hemingway, Babe Ruth, and George H. W. Bush.

Orvis Fishing Rod Factory and Store

Just across the parking lot from the museum, the **Orvis Store** (4189 Main St., Rte. 7A, 802/362-3750, www.orvis.com, 10am-6pm Mon.-Fri., 9am-6pm Sat., 10am-5pm Sun.) is another place of pilgrimage for fly fishers. The flagship store is filled with wide-brimmed hats, waders, and every possible version of plaid, and they offer free fly-fishing classes for first-time anglers. Find out how the goods are made at the on-site **Orvis Rod Shop** factory, where you'll see the evolution from early bamboo versions to state-of-the-art fiberglass rods. Factory tours are free, and start at 10am on weekdays.

Southern Vermont Arts Center

Few art museums are as beautifully situated as the **Southern Vermont Arts Center** (930 Southern Vermont Arts Center Dr., 802/362-1405, www.svac.org, 10am-5pm Tues.-Sat., noon-5pm Sun., free), which has its wooded grounds on the flank of Mount Equinox. Inside, the center plays host to traveling art exhibitions, jazz and classical music concerts, and author readings.

Mount Equinox Skyline Drive

For a closer look at the mountain (and a more distant view of the valley), take the **Mount Equinox Skyline Drive** (off Rte. 7A, 802/362-1115, www.equinoxmountain.com, 9am-4pm late May-Oct., $15 car and driver, $5 per passenger, children under 10 free, motorcycles $12 bike and driver). The winding toll road climbs 3,800 feet to the summit for an unparalleled view of the surrounding peaks and occasional sightings of eagles and peregrine falcons. At the top of the mountain is the **Saint Bruno Viewing Center,** which tells the story of the nearby Carthusian Monastery, the only one of its kind in North America. A half-mile hiking trail starts at the viewing center and winds around the mountaintop.

Spas

The **Equinox Resort & Spa** (3567 Main St./Rte. 7A, 800/362-4747, www.equinoxresort.com, $115-220) focuses on bringing the Green Mountains inside with an emphasis on natural ingredients such as maple sugar, mineral clay, and wildflower essences, all sourced from Vermont. Not everything here is so local, however. Among the most decadent of treatments is an "autumn ritual" drawn from Egyptian roots incorporating chamomile and mineral gold in a top-to-tail massage and exfoliation.

Shopping

The **Manchester Designer Outlets** (97 Depot St., 802/362-3736, www.manchesterdesigneroutlets.com, hours vary by store) have some 30 factory outlet stores, including such top names as Giorgio Armani, Brooks Brothers, and Coach. The best stores are along Routes 11 and 30 (take a right after you hit the town center), conveniently grouped in several strip malls.

The sweetly curated selection of bric-a-brac at **The Gold Trout** (145 Elm St., Manchester Depot, 802/366-0512, www.goldtrout.com, 11am-6pm Tues.-Fri., 10am-4pm Sat.-Sun.) is full of simple style. Find paper peonies and letterpress stationery, gorgeous jewelry and perfect hostess gifts.

The shelves at **Northshire Bookstore** (4869 Main St., 802/362-2200, www.northshire.com, 10am-7pm Sun.-Thurs., 10am-9pm Fri.-Sat.) are stocked with books on Vermont's history, culture, and natural world. This is one of the best collections of local reads in the state.

Food

The unpretentious ★ **Cilantro Taco** (5036 Main St., 802/768-8141, www.cilantrorestaurantvt.com, 11:30am-8am daily, $8-10) fills simple tacos and burritos with regionally sourced veggies and meat, along with house-made salsas. The food is excellent, the vibe is hip, and the friendly staff turn it out with a minimum of fuss.

If the rooster motif at **Up for Breakfast** (4935 Main St./Rte. 7A, 802/362-4204, 7am-12:30pm Mon.-Fri., 7am-1:30pm Sat.-Sun., $8-12) doesn't open your eyes, the hearty meals here will. It's on the second floor overlooking Main Street. The "red flannel hash" and sourdough *bâtard* French toast are perfect for fueling up before hitting the slopes or heading out for a day of hiking.

Even if the name grates on your nerves, the atmosphere is relaxed at **The Perfect Wife** (2594 Depot St./Rte. 11/30, 802/362-2817, www.perfectwife.com, restaurant 5pm-10pm Tues.-Sat., tavern 4pm-close Tues.-Sat., $20-32), which can feel more like a dinner party than a restaurant. Chef Amy Chamberlain's "freestyle cuisine" features classic dishes from home and abroad, with a twist. The adjoining tavern, **The Other Woman,** offers burgers and other pub fare, along with frequent live music.

Superfresh Turkish cuisine isn't the only draw at the ★ **Depot Bistro Café** (515 Depot St., 802/366-8181, www.depotbistro.com, 11:30am-9pm daily, $15-19), which is located inside a home furnishings shop. The effect—not unpleasant—is of dining in an Anatolian Pottery Barn, with a menu of kebabs and *kofta* to go along with the exquisite rugs and lush decor. The wood-fired brick oven also turns out flatbreads that range from straightforward pepperoni to the "Taste of Anatolia," a Turkish pita topped with lamb.

There are six tables and five bar stools at **The Silver Fork** (4201 Main St., 802/768-8444, www.thesilverforkvt.com, 5pm-9:30pm Mon.-Sat., $26-35), but if you manage to get a table, you'll have a memorable meal. The chef creates a "menu in motion" that changes constantly and draws flavors from around the globe, from plantain-crusted mahimahi to tamarind barbecue salmon. Simple, rich desserts like chocolate mousse and crème brûlée go perfectly with the selection of after-dinner drinks, from port to sauternes.

Accommodations

$100-150

Just outside of Manchester Center, the **Four Winds Country Motel** (7379 Rte. 7A, 802/362-1105, www.fourwindsmanchester.com, $119-149) is a bit faded, but clean, with decor that blends pastoral Vermont with India-inspired velvet paintings in vibrant hues. The freestanding cottage is an excellent choice for families, with kitchen facilities and room for a group; a simple breakfast is included.

The charmingly old-fashioned **Seth Warner Inn** (2353 Rte. 7A, 802/362-3830, www.sethwarnerinn.com, $145-155) is set on an expansive property at the base of Mount Equinox, and each room is furnished with care and antiques. A full breakfast is served in the dining room of the historical inn.

$150-250

When Manchester's most romantic B&B, **The Reluctant Panther Inn & Restaurant** (39 West Rd., 802/362-2568, www.reluctantpanther.com, $199-759), was gutted by fire several years back, owners Liz and Jerry Lavalley took the occasion to renovate with even more upscale amenities. Each room in the antique-filled home now has at least one fireplace (some have two) and a Jacuzzi-style tub (most large enough to fit two people). A carriage house and a pair of older buildings on the grounds feature wood-burning fireplaces and private porches. Despite the heavy emphasis on couples, some rooms do allow small dogs or small children. An on-site restaurant offers upscale continental and American regional cuisine with a view of Mount Equinox. You may be reluctant to leave.

More intimate, but no less luxurious, is ★ **The Inn at Ormsby Hill** (1842 Main St./Rte. 7A, 802/362-1163, www.ormsbyhill.com, $240-425), a Revolutionary-era mansion named after a captain of the Green Mountain Boys. The inn, which underwent a renovation in 2008, prides itself on individual attention to guests and a lavish decor calling to mind an English drawing room (complete with carved mantelpieces and wood-beaded ceilings). Innkeeper Chris Sprague is an imaginative breakfast cook, along the lines of bacon-and-egg risotto and eggs Benedict bread pudding.

The delightfully eccentric ★ **Wilburton Inn** (257 Wilburton Dr., 802/362-2500, www.wilburtoninn.com, $185-325) is high on its own hill, a sprawling property covered with art and run by the intriguing Levis family. The central mansion is furnished with luxuriant antiques, chaise lounges, and velvet drapes, and the windows frame broad views of the countryside. The property also includes several self-contained houses available for rent. On-site is the **Museum of the Creative Process,** curated by psychiatrist and paterfamilias Albert Levis, whose sculpture and art installations explore creativity and relationships, using imagery from diverse mythological traditions. Other Levis family members include an excellent bread baker (whose loaves appear at the full breakfast) and a farmer; the inn offers a "Farmers' Package" that includes a workshop on sustainable farming.

OVER $250

Much has changed at the **Equinox Resort & Spa** (3567 Main St./Rte. 7A, 800/362-4747, www.equinoxresort.com, $149-799) since the late 19th century, when East Coast elite—including the Lincoln family—came to shed city stress by fishing, golfing, and breathing Vermont's clean country air. Behind the brilliant white facade, the hotel is tastefully modern, though the almost 200 rooms can have a slightly generic, corporate feel. But the staff are impeccably professional, and the resort's 1,300-acre spread is designed to satisfy every whim: a comprehensive, world-class spa, walking trails, excellent restaurants, even a school where guests can learn the aristocratic sport of falconry.

CAMPING

Fifteen minutes north of Manchester **Emerald Lake State Park** (65 Emerald Lake Ln., East Dorset, 802/362-1655, https://vtstateparks.com/emerald.html, tent sites $18-20, lean-tos $25-27) has a maze of forested sites at the head of a long, slender lake. The appealing valley that shelters the campground also retains noise from the nearby road, so it can get rather loud, but the sites are stocked with fire pits for marshmallow toasting, and the lake's sandy beach is great for cooling off on hot days. Hot showers are coin operated, and boats are available to rent on-site.

Information and Services

The **Manchester and the Mountains Chamber of Commerce** (5046 Main St., 800/362-4144, www.manchestervermont.net) runs a small information booth on the town green on Route 7A. Manchester has several pharmacies in the town center, including **Rite-Aid Pharmacy** (4993 Main St., 802/362-2230, 8am-9pm Mon.-Sat., 9am-6pm Sun., pharmacy 9am-9pm Mon.-Fri., 9am-6pm Sat.-Sun.).

Free Wi-Fi is available at **Spiral Press Cafe** (15 Bonnet St., 802/362-9944, 7:30am-7pm Mon.-Wed., 7:30am-9pm Thurs.-Sat., 8:30am-7pm Sun.), right at the corner of Routes 15 and 30 and attached to Northshire Bookstore. In an emergency, contact the **Manchester Police Department** (6041 Main St., 802/362-2121, www.manchesternh.gov).

DORSET

A few miles north up the mountains from Manchester, the town of **Dorset** claims the contested title of "birthplace of Vermont." (Tiny Windsor, over in the Connecticut River Valley, is the main competitor.) During the days of disputed land claims, the leaders of the New Hampshire Grants met twice at a local tavern, signing the Articles of Association to declare themselves an independent territory. The association didn't last long, however, as the easterners declared their own independence a few years later. The pretty little town now has many fine examples of colonial buildings, as well as Victorian homes from its 18th-century heyday as a resort town and artists' colony.

Dorset is also pocked with deep holes, excavations that began when marble was discovered here. The town claims the first commercial marble quarry in the United States, stone that would build the New York Public Library, but the marble drills and chisels have gone quiet (and at least one quarry has been turned into a stellar swimming hole).

Dorset Quarry

A flooded marble quarry that stays cool on the hottest days, the **Dorset Quarry** (Rte. 30 at Kelly Rd.) is among the best swim spots in Vermont. The marble walls drop cleanly into the deep water, with jumping spots that range from knee-high to vertiginous. Though it can get crowded on hot days, the quarry has more than enough room for dozens of swimmers, along with cliffs for diving and human sculptures carved into the rock. There's usually a portable toilet in the parking lot here, but you'll need to bring your own water.

Bley House Museum

One of the better local historical museums in Vermont, the Dorset Historical Society's **Bley House Museum** (Rte. 30 at Kent Hill Rd., 802/867-0331, www.dorsethistory.com, 10am-4pm Wed.-Fri., 10am-2pm Sat., donations welcome) oozes evidence of the care and hard work of its volunteer curators. Exhibitions include a collection of coins—minted in nearby Rupert—from the days when Vermont was an independent republic (1776-1791), as well as artifacts relating to the marble, stoneware, and textile industries and several fine examples of paintings from the days in the early 20th century when the town was an artists' community. The historical society also provides a tape for a self-guided walking tour of many of the historical homes in the village, including the Dorset Inn, which was built on the site of Kent Tavern, where the Republic of Vermont was arguably born.

Mad Tom Orchard

Some thought Tom Smith crazy when he decided to restore his father's old mountainside apple orchard in 1999. But he persisted, and the fruits of his labor can be seen (and picked) at **Mad Tom Orchard** (2615 Mad Tom Rd., East Dorset, 802/366-8107, www.madtomorchard.com, 9am-5:30pm Tues.-Sun. July-Oct.). Guests can pluck McIntosh and Cortland apples from venerable 60-year-old trees and hunt among the raspberry bushes with a view of the mountains all around. Call to confirm harvest dates.

Entertainment and Events

"Summer people" and year-rounders alike fill the aisles for the **Dorset Theatre Festival** (104 Cheney Rd., 802/867-2223 Sept.-May or 802/867-5777 June-Aug., www.dorsettheatrefestival.org), an acclaimed summer stock festival that has been producing both classics (Tennessee Williams, Oscar Wilde) and new playwrights for 30 years. During the rest of the year, the playhouse gets turned back to the **Dorset Players** (802/867-5777 www.dorsetplayers.org), the amateur theater troupe that built the playhouse in the 1920s and performs excellent theater in its own right.

Food

It doesn't get much more historical in atmosphere than in the dining room of **Barrows House Inn & Restaurant** (3156 Rte. 30, 802/867-4455, www.barrowshouse.com, 5:30pm-close Wed.-Sun., $15-29). The green walls are hand-painted with a mural of Dorset historical landmarks, so you're literally surrounded by the village's highlights. The menu does its part to outshine them, however, with specials like baked haddock with a cracker crumb and parmesan-and-hazelnut-encrusted pork loin.

Information and Services

For more info, stop by the **Dorset Village Public Library** (corner of Rte. 30 and Church St., 802/867-5774, www.dorsetlibraryinfo.org, 10am-5pm Mon.-Fri., 10am-3pm Sat.) or contact the **Dorset Chamber of Commerce** (802/867-2450, www.dorsetvt.com). There is an ATM at **Berkshire Bank** (23 Church St., 802/867-2234).

SPORTS AND RECREATION

Equinox Resort

The **Equinox Resort** (3567 Main St./Rte. 7A, Manchester, 800/362-4747, www.equinoxresort.com, $314-469) offers a range of posh country pursuits. Perhaps the most impressive is the **Green Mountain Falconry** (www.greenmountainfalconryschool.com, greenmountainfalconry@comcast.net, classes start at $130 pp for 45-min. lesson), which will teach you how to hunt quail, pheasants, and other game birds with your very own Harris hawk. Another option is the affiliated **Land Rover Experience Driving School** (802/362-0687, www.equinoxresort.com, $250/1-hr. lesson, $1,200/full-day program). If you harbor images of chewing up mud and rock while you whiz around curves in your Land Rover, however, be forewarned that the driving school is more of an exercise in technology than skill—the truck does most of the work through its impressive array of dashboard settings that can take on snow, sand, mud, or any other terrain. Your job is to mostly keep your hands on the wheel and try not to scratch the paint job as you slowly maneuver through the course. If you are a gearhead, you'll love it; if not, you might find yourself wishing for a bit more control.

Hiking

Near Bennington is the start of the **Long Trail,** Vermont's predecessor to the Appalachian Trail, which wends its way along the spine of the Green Mountains from Massachusetts to the Canadian border. You can find information about day hikes along the trail as well as other hiking paths from the **Green Mountain Club** (802/244-7037, www.greenmountainclub.org).

For those who would like to see Vermont at a pace set by their legs, the Green Mountain Club maintains some 70 campsites along the Long Trail from Bennington to the Canadian border. Most of the sites are primitive in nature, accommodating anywhere from 8 to 20 people, and are first-come, first-served and free (some with a caretaker ask a small fee). All of the sites have a water source, and some are built out with lean-tos or fully enclosed lodges.

Hikers interested in venturing forth on the Long Trail would do well to pick up a copy of the *Long Trail Guide*, available in any bookshop or outdoor store in the area (and often at pharmacies and convenience stores as well), or through the Green Mountain Club's website.

For day hikers, the hills around Manchester and Bennington are filled with many more hiking trails, which start from several of the most popular sights. The **Manchester Ranger Station** (2538 Depot St./Rte. 11/30, Manchester Center, 802/362-2307, www.fs.usda.gov/greenmountain) offers a free (if rudimentary) trail map of day hikes within Green Mountain National Forest that range from easy to difficult, with distances up to 11 miles. A favorite among many hikers is the hike to **Lye Brook Falls,** a four-mile round-trip hike (2.5 hrs.) to one of the highest waterfalls in Vermont. The trailhead is on the Lye Brook access road, and detailed directions are available on the Green Mountain National Forest website.

If that whets your appetite to climb **Mount Equinox** itself, you can find a trail map at the tollhouse for Skyline Drive. Trails on the mountain vary, from a short hike up to a panoramic view of Manchester at Lookout Rock to a strenuous four-mile hike to the summit 3,848 feet above sea level. The trail climbs out from a dark forest of oak, maple, and birch into sweet-smelling balsam trees where you can occasionally spot peregrine falcons. That's all a prelude to one of the best—if not the best—views in southern Vermont, surrounded on all sides by the green peaks of the Taconic Range. The 5.8-mile round-trip takes 4-5 hours, and the trail is marked with blue blazes.

Skiing and Riding

In the winter months, Manchester becomes a playground for cross-country skiers, who have several trail systems to choose from. Several miles of groomed and tracked trails can be found at the **Hildene Touring Center** (Rte. 7A, Manchester, 802/362-1788, www.hildene.org, 9:30am-4:30pm Dec.-mid-Mar., trail pass $20 adults, $5 youth, Nordic ski or snowshoe rental $15, lessons $30), where the estate's carriage barn is turned into a warming hut and rental shop.

The south-facing slopes of **Bromley Mountain** (3984 Rte. 11, Peru, 802/824-5522, www.bromley.com, $80 adults, $70 youth 13-17, $53 youth 6-12, children under 6 free) make it one of Vermont's sunniest for downhill skiers. The terrain is less extreme than the surrounding mountains, and Bromley is known for family programs, including a kids' ski school with animal friends Alex the Alligator and Clyde Catamount. Check the website before showing up to the mountain, as it's often cheaper to purchase lift tickets online.

Biking

The rolling terrain around Manchester and Bennington makes for excellent cycling, though even some small roads may be thoroughfares and heavily trafficked. In Manchester, you can rent wheels at **Battenkill Sports Bicycle Shop** (1240 Depot St., 802/362-2734, www.battenkillsports.com, 9:30am-5:30pm daily, full-day rental $40/road bike, $30/hybrid or mountain bike). The shop stocks plenty of maps and suggestions for great day rides; one favorite follows back roads for 11 miles to Arlington, where you can fill up on fudge before heading home. More cycling resources and ride suggestions can be found at www.bikemanchestervt.com.

Fishing

The **Equinox Resort & Spa** (3567 Main St./Rte. 7A, Manchester, 800/362-4747, www.equinoxresort.com, $314-469) is also home to the **Orvis Fly Fishing School** (866/531-6213, $489 two-day course), which carries on the tradition of Frank Orvis by offering

THE VERMONT COUNTRY STORE
THE ORTON FAMILY BUSINESS
the INN at WESTON
LUXURIOUS ACCOMMODATIONS
FINE DINING
Open To The Public
LIVE PIANO MUSIC
TONIGHT
1
2
3

close instruction on snaring brook trout on the Battenkill.

For a more flexible itinerary, contact **Young's Fly Fishing** (673 Crow Hill Rd., Arlington, 802/375-9313, www.youngsflyfishing.com), whose proprietor, Bob Young, is a veteran instructor for the Orvis school and will instruct you in your choice of fly-fishing or spin fishing, with or without a boat.

Chartered bass fishing on nearby lakes is offered by **Green Mountain Fishing Guide Service** (593 Rte. 140, Tinmouth, 802/446-3375, http://greenmtnguide.com), whose bass master, Rod Start, has 25 years of experience on the fishing tournament circuit.

Boating

If your vision of enjoying the river doesn't include a fishing rod, **BattenKill Canoe** (6328 Rte. 7A, Arlington, 802/362-2800, www.battenkill.com) rents canoes and leads package canoe tours with stays in country inns along the rivers.

Horseback Riding

A few miles up Route 7, the **Chipman Stables** (Danby Four Corners, 802/293-5242, www.chipmanstables.com) takes visitors on guided horseback rides, as well as hayrides and sleigh rides depending on the season.

GETTING THERE AND AROUND

To get to Bennington, drive west along Route 9 from Brattleboro (40 mi., 1 hr.). Drive north up Route 7 from Bennington for Shaftsbury (10 mi., 15 min.), Arlington (15 mi., 25 min.), Manchester (25 mi., 40 min.), Dorset (30 mi., 45 min.), or Danby (35 mi., 50 min.).

Buses run by **Greyhound Bus Lines** (800/231-2222, www.greyhound.com) stop at **Bennington Bus Station** (126 Washington Ave., 802/442-4808). The **Green Mountain Express** (802/447-0477, www.greenmtncn.org), has bus service that connects Manchester to Bennington and Rutland, along with a useful list of ways to connect to other regional bus services.

Route 100

Halfway between Brattleboro and Bennington, Route 100 veers off toward the north, and the twisting highway is on the short list of the most scenic in New England. Moving from south to north, the road passes Mount Snow and Stratton Mountain ski resorts in quick succession and then travels through a series of villages set in verdant farmland. With a sweet town center and the landmark Vermont Country Store, Weston is a popular destination for tour buses, then Route 100 skirts around the base of Mount Okemo on its way through hills sprinkled with secluded mountain resorts.

1: The Vermont Country Store in Weston; 2: Inn at Weston; 3: Hildene, Robert Todd Lincoln's former home, in Manchester

★ MOUNT SNOW AND STRATTON MOUNTAIN

These two ski hills are just 15 miles apart, and both are popular destinations from Boston and New York. They're also steeped in winter sports history: Jake Burton invented snowboarding at Stratton Mountain and started the world's first snowboarding school here in 1983. Mount Snow built the first snowboarding terrain park in the East in 1992. More recently, Stratton has been the home base for some of the winningest skiers in the United States, including the Nordic powerhouses Jessie Diggins and Sophie Caldwell, who both train at the Stratton Mountain School.

While both have appealing accommodation options, Stratton has a more established town, with plenty of dining and nightlife to keep it lively after the lifts have closed for

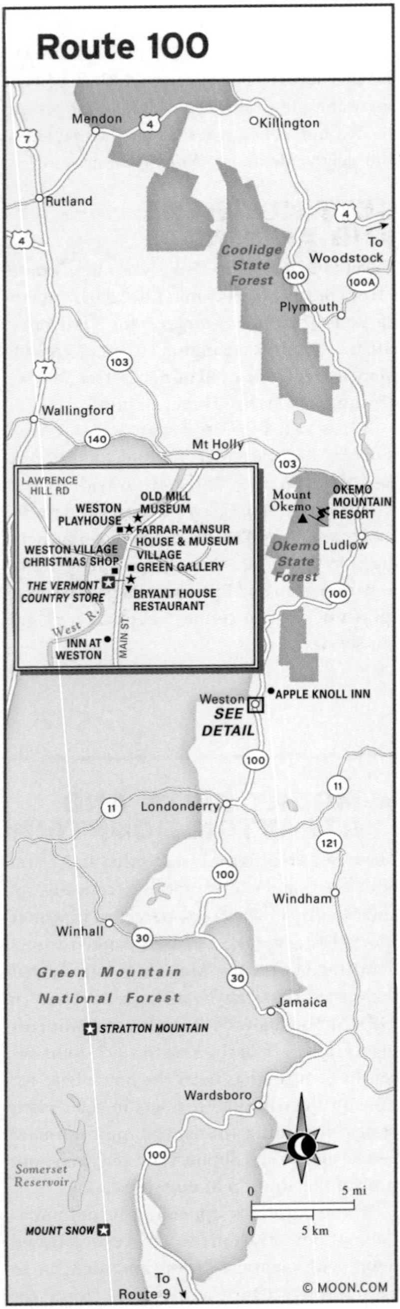

Route 100

the day. Both resorts make a huge amount of snow, and so can weather the freezes and thaws of northeastern skiing with a ride-able base intact. In the summer, both resorts open their trails to lift-served mountain biking.

Mount Snow (Mt. Snow Rd., West Dover, 800/245-7669, www.mountsnow.com, $100 adults, $80 youth 7-17 and seniors, $5 children under 7) has a vertical drop of 1,700 feet and 80 trails: About three-quarters of them are intermediate, with the remainder split between beginner and expert options. The mountain is divided into four faces including the recently redeveloped Carinthia, whose 12 terrain parks sport a minipipe and a superpipe with staggering 18-foot-high walls. Check the resort website before visiting, as buying tickets online is often cheaper than walking up to the ticket window.

You'll get an extra 300 feet of vertical at **Stratton Mountain** (5 Village Lodge Rd., Stratton Mountain, 800/787-2886, www.stratton.com, $115 adult, $90 youth 7-17 and seniors above 70, $10 children under 7), and the mountain features some lengthy rides: It's three miles to the bottom if you take **Mike's Way** down to **Wanderer** trail. There are more options for novices than at Mount Snow, with around 40 percent beginners' trails and another 31 percent intermediate, making it a good choice for families.

These two peaks aren't your only options for snow sports in the area. Ludlow's **Okemo Mountain Resort** (77 Okemo Ridge Rd., Ludlow, 800/786-5366, www.okemo.com, $100 adults, $88 youth 13-18 and seniors 65-69, $76 children 7-12 and seniors 70 and above, children under 7 free) is another family-friendly option.

Food

If you're headed to the mountain, it's worth stopping at **Sticky Fingers Bakery** (210 Rte. 100, West Dover, 802/464-9463, www.stickyfingersvermontbakery.com, 7am-4pm Thurs.-Mon., $3-7) to pick up a cinnamon roll the size of a small mogul. Danishes, cookies, and other crumbly delights also make excellent snacks on the gondola.

The interior of **The Last Chair Bar & Grill** (267 Rte. 100, West Dover, 802/464-1133, www.lastchairvt.com, 4pm-close Mon.-Fri., 11:30am-close Sat.-Sun, $12-28) is all rustic wood and cozy booths, with a lineup of comforting food like nachos, tacos, and ribs, as well as pizzas and pasta. The wait can be considerable on weekend nights, so call ahead.

Laid-back **Mulligans** (11B Village Square, Stratton, 802/297-9293, www.mulligans-vt.com, 11am-10pm Sat.-Thurs., 11am-10:30pm Fri., $13-29) is always bustling with skiers and snowboarders refueling on hearty pub food. They've got the classics: poutine, burgers, and steaks, with a vast beer selection and a game room for the kids. The bar has great specials that could tempt you away from catching the last lift (cheap wings and nachos from 3:30pm until 6pm).

The thoughtful, refined food at ★ **Verdé** (19 Village Lodge Rd., Stratton, 802/297-9200, www.verdestratton.com, lunch 11:30am-2:30pm Fri.-Sun., dinner 5pm-9pm Mon.-Thurs. and Sun., 5pm-10pm Fri.-Sat., $19-33) isn't your average après-ski fare. On a recent evening, pappardelle pasta came with luscious chicken confit and hen of the woods mushrooms, and seared scallops were accompanied by a striking swath of black rice and roasted beets. The menu changes frequently but is consistently of a very high quality. While modern plating, romantic lighting, and efficient service may convince you to swap ski bibs for real pants, the restaurant remains Vermont casual.

Named for a Stratton Mountain icon, **Fire Tower Restaurant and Tavern** (5 Village Lodge Rd., Stratton, 802/297-2000, www.firetowerstratton.com, 4pm-10pm Mon. and Thurs., 3pm-10pm Fri., 11:30am-10pm Sat.-Sun., $11-34) serves flatbreads, burgers, and hearty main plates centered around local cuts of meat.

Accommodations

With a convenient mountainside location, **Black Bear Lodge** (30 Middle Ridge Rd., Stratton, 802/297-2200, www.stratton.com, $84-215) offers basic but decent accommodations with the best prices in the area. The rooms and common spaces show their age despite some recent renovations, but it remains a fine place to shack up when you're headed to the snow. A free shuttle bus to the ski area runs every 10-15 minutes.

The serenity of ★ **Yoga BnB** (11 Founders Hill Rd., Stratton, 802/431-0017, www.yogabnb.com, $150-250, suite $500) is remarkable, given that it's just walking distance from the base of the mountain. The smaller rooms are a bit cramped, but each is decorated with individualized style. The common areas are lovely, and guests can opt for a traditional, raw, or vegetarian breakfast. Most days yoga classes are held in the on-site studio and open to guests by donation.

Right by the slopes at Mount Snow is the **Grand Summit Resort Hotel** (89 Grand Summit Way, Dover, 800/245-7669, www.mountsnow.com, $145-340), with an on-site spa and recently updated rooms making it a convenient and comfy place to land. Studios with kitchenettes and condos are also available. Call the reservation line to get discounted lift tickets with your accommodations.

WESTON

The Green Mountains really take flight as Route 100 continues north, undulating between ridgelines and snug valleys. Tucked into one of them is the tiny village of Weston—blink and you'd miss the entire downtown, but it's worth a stop to explore the overflowing shelves at the Vermont Country Store. The entire town is on the National Register of Historic Places, and there's a fascinating priory whose Benedictine monks sing in each day's sunrise and sunset with traditional tunes.

★ The Vermont Country Store

Back in the day, when roads between villages were long and the snow would block mountain passes for months, the country store had to be all things to all people, packing foodstuffs, medicines, clothes, hardware, and everything else the family needed to prosper. Over time, stores specialized, and the country store literally fell by the wayside. That is, until it was revived by Vrest Orton, who opened the original restored **Vermont Country Store** (657 Main St., 802/824-3184, www.vermontcountrystore.com, 9am-6pm Mon.-Sat.) on Weston Common in 1946. The shop was so successful that it has spawned countless imitators and expanded many times over the past decades. Now the store is a Vermont vision of a country mall, with everything from local foods to novelty aprons.

If you haven't yet found that perfect block of cheddar cheese or a tin of maple syrup, you'll find it here. But this is not just another tacky souvenir shop; the proprietors—still members of the Orton family—have gone out of their way to closely evoke the old-time rural character of the state, taking requests from customers to stock hard-to-find beauty products, medicinal balms, and rugged clothing items they remembered from yesteryear but despaired of ever finding again. Especially poignant for some customers are the children's toys and candy thought to have vanished long ago. For the true spirit of old-time Vermont, this is one-stop shopping.

Weston Priory

At **Weston Priory** (58 Priory Hill Rd., 802/824-5409, www.westonpriory.org), a monastery set up on a steep hill on the way out of town, Benedictine monks sing plainsong in a peaceful setting several times a day with wind and insects joining in for counterpoint. The public is invited to attend, and the beautiful setting and music make it a worthwhile experience regardless of belief. The community closes to the public on retreat days, so check the website for details.

Farrar-Mansur House Museum

Situated on the town common in Weston, the Federal-style **Farrar-Mansur House Museum** (Rte. 100, 802/824-8194, www.weston-vermont.com, 10am-4pm Sat., 1pm-4pm Sun. and Wed., July 5-Labor Day, free) was completed in 1797, a homestead that featured a tavern, ballroom, and ladies' parlor that must have been the toast of the town at the turn of the 18th century. It is now filled with antique New England furniture, portraits, and household goods, and careful restoration work has retouched the elaborate stenciling around the ballroom.

Old Mill Museum

Run by the Weston Historical Society, the **Old Mill Museum** (Rte. 100, 802/824-8194, www.weston-vermont.com, 10am-4pm Sat., 1pm-4pm Sun. and Wed., July 5-Labor Day, free) is a glimpse of just how labor-intensive early Vermont life must have been. Originally built as a sawmill in 1780, the mill used river power to pare down trees culled from the surrounding forest; after burning down in 1900, it was converted into a gristmill run by the Orton family, who would eventually found the Vermont Country Store. A look at the original turbine is a thrill for gearheads, and there's a working tinsmith shop on the first floor.

Entertainment and Events

When the **Weston Playhouse Theatre Company** (703 Main St., 802/824-5288, www.westonplayhouse.org, late June-early Sept., $15-48) opened in 1935, a *Boston Globe* theater critic called it "the most beautiful theatre in New England," and though it was rebuilt after a devastating 1962 fire, the Greek Revival building is a bright spot of elegance in the Vermont countryside. In addition to Broadway musicals and stage classics, the company performs a cabaret-style review nightly after each main performance.

The **Weston Antiques Show** (802/824-5307, www.westonantiquesshow.org) has been recognized as one of the best in New England. It takes place every year in the beginning of October, when the foliage is at its height.

Shopping

Lovers of year-round yuletide, take note:

Weston Village Christmas Shop (660 Main St., 802/824-5477, www.westonvillagestore.com, 10am-5:30pm daily) keeps the comfort and joy flowing with a store that's piled high with Christmas collectibles, ornaments, and every imaginable form of glimmering, shimmering fake snow.

The art-centric **Village Green Gallery** (661 Main St., 802/824-3669, www.thevillagegreengallery.com, 9:30am-5pm Thurs.-Tues.) features photographs of snow, foliage, and fences that are a cut above the usual Vermont-made images, as well as furniture and crafts from Vermont artisans. Maybe that's because photographer and proprietor Nobu Fuji'i spent 30 years shooting modern architecture in Japan and brings a uniquely geometric eye to his shots.

Food

An antique soda fountain and 1885 barroom lend the **Bryant House Restaurant** (Rte. 100, 802/824-6287, 11am-3:30pm daily, dinner 4pm-8:30pm Fri.-Sat., $13-20) an old-fashioned charm, with food that blends classic Yankee meals with contemporary items (such as salads, which were not a major player on early Vermont tables). If you've been craving a pot roast, or Indian pudding, this is the place to go. The restaurant is next door to the Vermont Country Store, and you might need to wait for a seat on busy days—if you plan to browse in the interval, they'll call you over the intercom. The adjoining **Mildred's Dairy Bar** (11am-6pm daily, $3-7) dishes up classic Vermont "snack bar" fare throughout the summer—think fries, hamburgers, and creemees—with outdoor seating.

The romantic ★ **Inn at Weston** (630 Main St./Rte. 100, 802/824-6789, www.innweston.com, 5:30pm-close, June to New Year's, $25-35) serves contemporary food using plenty of local ingredients: Duck-confit risotto and ravioli with a star anise carrot reduction were standouts on a recent menu, but the lineup of dishes changes seasonally. Their cellar won them a *Wine Spectator* Award of Excellence, and dinners are often accompanied by music from a pianist who does lovely versions of classic melodies and show tunes (he also takes requests). In summer months, try to snag a table in the flower-filled gazebo; the best cold-weather spot is right by the wood fire.

Accommodations

$100-150

The **Colonial House Inn & Motel** (287 Rte. 100, 802/824-6286 or 800/639-5033, www.cohoinn.com, $70-130) brings the hospitality of a bed-and-breakfast to a quaint, quirky motel property, which includes a comfy main house and more traditional motel units. Breakfast is a spread of granola, pastries, and coffee cakes from Grandma Millers in Londonderry, served alongside made-to-order omelets and hot cereals. The owners often serve guest dinners on Friday and Saturday nights for $30 per person, but it's worth giving them advance notice, especially for large groups.

The sweet and tranquil **Apple Knoll Inn** (815 Rte. 100, 802/824-0051, www.appleknollinn.com, $125-155) is just outside of town, on a rolling property that abuts conservation land. Rooms are furnished with old-fashioned charm, from embroidered curtains to patchwork quilts. There's a two-night minimum, and rates include an extravagant cooked breakfast. No children.

$150-250

Right in the heart of the village, the ★ **Inn at Weston** (630 Main St./Rte. 100, 802/824-6789, www.innweston.com, $185-325) is among the most romantic in the state. Rooms are thoughtfully furnished with comfy seating, beds are topped with pretty quilts, and some include in-room woodstoves and whirlpool tubs. The welcoming innkeepers, Bob and Linda, are the real highlight, and serve a multicourse breakfast each morning in the sunlit dining room. Bob is also an orchid expert and for years tended one of the largest private collections in the Northeast; the 2015 winter and a heating failure wiped them out, but it's worth checking back, as plans are in place to restore the greenhouse to its former glory. The inn's delightful restaurant is worth a stay on all its own, but plan to book your table as soon as possible (the table by the fire is especially nice on winter evenings).

LUDLOW

Situated at the base of Okemo Mountain Resort, Ludlow can't compete with Weston's cuteness, but there are far more services to keep you fed and rested. It's a tried-and-true ski town, with great riding at Okemo, though with easily accessible hiking and exploring in the surrounding hills, Ludlow would also make a worthwhile home base for exploring the region and Route 100.

Okemo Mountain Resort

The slopes at **Okemo Mountain Resort** (77 Okemo Ridge Rd., 800/786-5366, www.okemo.com, $100 adults, $88 youth 13-18 and seniors 65-69, $76 children 7-12 and seniors 70 and above, children under 7 free) have the highest vertical drop in southern Vermont, but Okemo's mostly established a niche as a family mountain. Fun and accessible programs keep kids motivated on the slope, with reasonably challenging runs to keep more experienced skiers entertained. There's significant snowmaking coverage, so Okemo remains rideable even through a shaky winter, and experts can test themselves against challenging glades, a superpipe, and eight terrain parks.

Food and Drink

A classic Irish bar down to the creaking floorboards, **The Killarney** (4 Pond St., 802/228-7797, www.killarneyludlow.com, 3pm-2am Mon.-Fri., noon-2am Sat.-Sun., dinner $5-17) is the place to come rub elbows with Boston tourists, construction workers, and your goggle-tanned ski instructor from earlier in the day. Seemingly every surface is decked with badges and memorabilia from local firefighters and military, and aside from the full lineup of Irish whiskeys and beers, there's a hefty pub menu that ranges from a very respectable fish-and-chips to buffalo wings. The normally friendly restaurant scene in Ludlow gets deadly competitive when it comes to wings, and chefs go wing-to-wing at an annual informal competition—the kitchen at The Killarney has proudly taken top honors in several recent years.

Run by a female chef-sommelier duo, ★ **Stemwinders** (46 S. Depot St., 802/228-5200, www.stemwindervt.com, 5pm-9pm Tues.-Sat., bar opens at 4pm Fri.-Sat., $15-25) is convivial and comfortable, in a colorful space that makes for free-flowing conversation. There's a mix of flatbreads and small plates, and even familiar dishes—such as brisket tacos or roasted beets—manage to surprise with bursts of intense flavor. The wine is truly a bright spot, with truly lovely pours available by the bottle or by the glass (if you find a favorite, most are stocked in the adjoining wineshop, which is run by the co-owner).

Don't let the name fool you. **The Downtown Grocery** (41 South Depot St., 802/228-7566, www.thedowntowngrocery.com, 5:30pm-close Mon. and Thurs.-Sat., 10:30am-1:30pm and 5:30pm-close Sun., $20-32) is a locally driven fine-dining restaurant with tempting mains like roasted eggplant *arancini* with house-made ricotta, and braised pork belly with watermelon. The atmosphere is casual, but the food makes for a special night out.

Based at the hostel of the some name, **Homestyle Hostel** (119 Main St., 802/975-0030, www.homestylehostel.com, 5pm-9pm Thurs.-Sun., $18-25) has an excellent restaurant in its own right. Shared plates make for a friendly atmosphere, and the unassuming menu keeps the pub-style fare fresh and appealing. As with Main and Mountain Bar, from the same owners, cocktails are excellent.

For a sugary jolt of après-ski energy, it's hard to beat a slice from **The Southern Pie Company** (28 Main St., 802/875-7437, www.thesouthernpiecompany.com, 11am-5pm Sun. and Wed.-Thurs., 11am-6pm Fri.-Sat., $3-7), a sweet little store front that doles out classics like chocolate chess pie, bourbon pecan pie, and key lime pie, along with savory chicken potpie.

Set in a chic, modern space, ★ **Main and Mountain Bar** (112 Main St., 802/242-1608, www.mainandmountain.com, 5pm-close Thurs.-Sun., $3-12) has some of the best drinks in town. The cocktail menu is fresh and innovative, blending classic cocktails with ad hoc creations by the creative bartender.

Accommodations

UNDER $100

Friendly and casual, ★ **Homestyle Hostel** (119 Main St., 802/975-0030, www.homestylehostel.com, dorms $40-60, private rooms $75-150) is a hospitable place to land, even for travelers who are decades away from their last hostel experience. The rooms, which include a queen suite and a private room with bunk beds, are simple but thoughtfully designed, some with shared baths and others with en suite. Six-bunk dorm rooms, while fairly spare and simple, are sparkling clean and airy. Rates include a breakfast of homemade granola with yogurt and coffee, common spaces are stocked with board games, and guests are welcome to use the kitchen during morning hours. The on-site restaurant is great.

$150-250

A welcome addition to southern Vermont's woodsy, old-fashioned inns, the owners of **Main and Mountain** (112 Main St., 802/242-1608, www.mainandmountain.com, $159-250) took an old-school motel and made the rooms airy and stylish. The overall effect is appealingly minimalistic: Headboards are carved from massive slabs of lumber, plaid accent blankets are spread across the beds, and some rooms have whispy trees stenciled on the walls. The "invisible service" means checking yourself in with a code, and while it's always possible to reach staff by phone, not every guest feels entirely comfortable with the tech.

There's a time-warp quality to a stay at **Echo Lake Inn** (2 Dublin Rd., 802/228-8602, www.echolakeinn.com, $115-290), a historic property that's housed guests from Thomas Edison to Calvin Coolidge. The decor is nicely worn in and old-fashioned, and on chilly nights, the innkeeper kindles a blazing fire in the living room, which is stocked with games and comfy couches. Set on the edge of Echo Lake, the inn's property includes a winding network of trails.

CAMPING

On the shores of Echo Lake—just across the water from the Echo Lake Inn—**Camp Plymouth State Park** (2008 Scout Camp Rd., 802/228-2025, https://vtstateparks.com/plymouth.html, tent sites and lean-tos $18-27, cottages $97/night) was a farm, gold-mining operation, and summer camp before its transformation in to a pretty, wooded state park. It's a pleasant place to stay, with swimming beaches, canoes and kayaks to rent, and picnic areas, and **gold panners** still come to try their luck in Buffalo Brook. There's often someone in the area renting out gold-panning equipment during the summer months—ask the ranger on-site.

Information and Services

For more information on the Okemo area, contact **Okemo Valley Regional Chamber of Commerce** (802/228-5830, www.okemovalleyvt.org), which runs information booths at the clock tower in Ludlow. **Chittenden Bank** (213 Main St., 802/228-8821, 9am-5pm Mon.-Thurs., 9am-6pm Fri.) has an ATM right in downtown Ludlow. In the same plaza is a **Rite-Aid Pharmacy** (213 Main St., 802/228-8477, 8am-7pm Mon.-Sat., 9am-5pm Sun., pharmacy 8am-7pm Mon.-Fri., 9am-6pm Sat., 9am-5pm Sun.). In the event of emergency, contact **Ludlow Police** (19 W. Hill St., 802/228-4411).

SPORTS AND RECREATION

Hiking

A short walk leads to great views on the summit of **Mount Okemo**, which is accessible by car from late spring through the fall, when it's a gorgeous spot for checking out the foliage. To reach the top, follow Okemo Mountain Road past Okemo Lodge, continuing on to a private drive that's open to the public during the snow-free months. After four or five miles of switchbacks, you'll reach a parking lot, then can continue on foot for roughly 20 minutes to the fire tower that the Civilian Conservation Corps built between 1932 and 1934. The fire tower was manned by a lookout until the 1970s, and is now on the National Historic Lookout Register (yes, such a thing exists).

To make a longer day of it, climb Mount Okemo on the **Healdville Trail** (https://vtstateparks.com/assets/pdf/okemo_sf_trails.pdf), a six-mile round-trip hike that follows an old logging road, then narrows into a path through the Okemo State Forest. The trail follows blue blazes, climbing 1,943 feet from the trailhead to the summit, leapfrogging a brook, ascending into a mixed forest of birch and evergreen trees, and ending at the CCC fire tower. To reach the trailhead from Ludlow, follow Route 103 west from the junction of Route 100 and Route 103, then turn left onto Station Road after 2.7 miles. Stay left after the railroad tracks, and the gravel road will end in a parking lot. (Detailed trail notes and a map are downloadable from the Vermont State Parks website.)

Swimming

The favorite local swim spot is at **Buttermilk Falls** (Buttermilk Falls Rd., Ludlow), a burbling series of drops and pools in Branch Brook. To reach the falls, drive north out of Ludlow on Route 100/Route103/Pond Road, then turn left (west) to stay on Route 103. Turn right onto Buttermilk Falls Road, and follow it to the end, where you'll find parking for the easy, 200-yard walk to the falls, a trail that leaves to the right of the road.

GETTING THERE AND AROUND

Route 100 starts from Route 9 at Wilmington, 20 miles west of Brattleboro and 20 miles east of Bennington. From Wilmington, Route 100 passes Mount Snow (7.6 miles, 15 min.) and then the turnoff for Stratton Mountain resort 6 miles later. It merges with Route 30 through Jamaica, and then heads north again traveling through Weston (40 miles, 1 hr. from Wilmington), Ludlow (50 miles, 1.25 hrs. from Wilmington), and Plymouth (60 miles, 1.25 hrs. from Wilmington), before joining Route 4, with access to Woodstock, Killington, and Rutland. As in much of rural Vermont, there are few public transportation options, and a car is the best way to move between places.

Along Route 4

Route 4 spans just 66 miles, but traverses a cross section of quintessential Vermont landscapes and cultures.

The path was already well established by the time the railroad line was laid across the state, connecting the Connecticut River Valley with the burgeoning metropolis of Rutland. Early explorers couldn't have chosen a prettier way, and the road follows the twists and turns of the Ottauquechee River.

If you travel from east to west, you'll start in White River Junction, an unassuming town at the confluence of major rivers, railways, and roads; it remains a memorial to the changing face of transportation in the Northeast. Nearby Windsor and Norwich are thriving villages that

Highlights

Look for ★ to find recommended sights, activities, dining, and lodging.

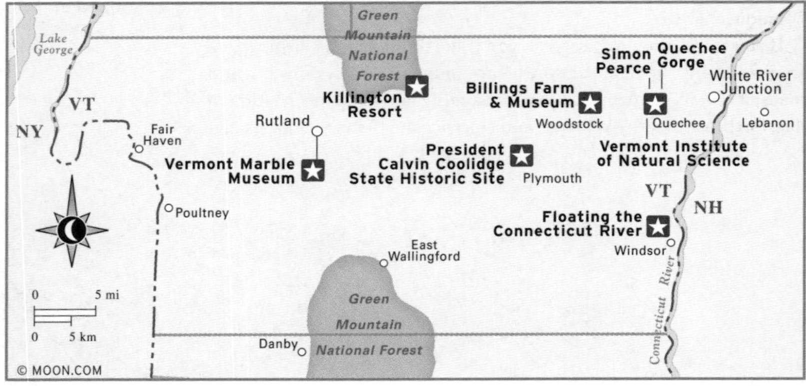

★ **Floating the Connecticut River:** Drift below covered bridges and leafy canopies on a leisurely trip downstream (page 85).

★ **Quechee Gorge:** Stroll around or swim in the cool depths of a glacially carved gorge, the deepest in Vermont (page 87).

★ **Vermont Institute of Natural Science:** Catch a thrilling raptor show, walk trails through a tranquil forest, and go eyeball-to-eyeball with a snowy owl (page 87).

★ **Simon Pearce:** Watch wineglasses take shape at this fascinating glassblowing workshop, then visit the posh shop where the glassware is sold (page 87).

★ **Billings Farm & Museum:** The farm that single-handedly saved Vermont's dairy industry now has exhibits about all aspects of agriculture (page 91).

★ **President Calvin Coolidge State Historic Site:** The former president's birthplace is a back-road gem, with beautifully preserved historical buildings, campsites with sweeping views, and its own artisanal cheese factory (page 92).

★ **Killington Resort:** The six mountains of Killington provide the biggest and baddest skiing around (page 98).

★ **Vermont Marble Museum:** Learn about the story of the Rutland marble industry and the thousands of immigrants who once labored there (page 107).

Along Route 4

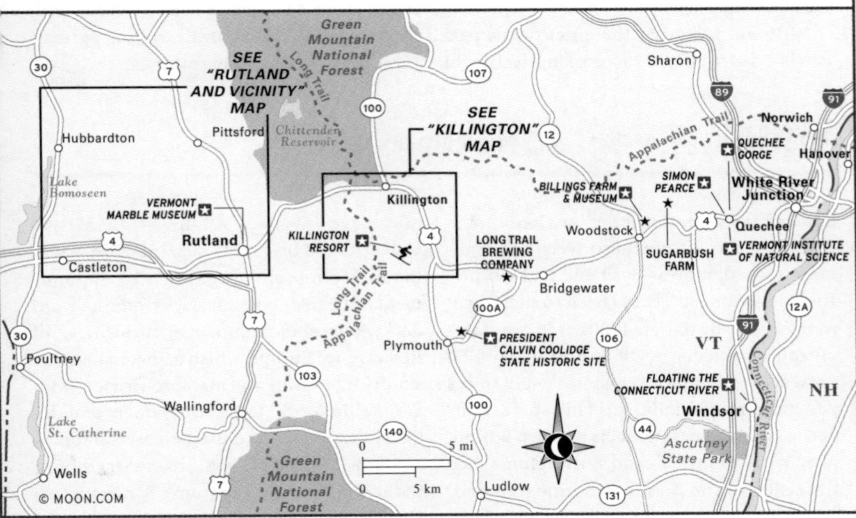

are steeped in Yankee history, with charming downtowns stocked with white steeples and redbrick homes.

Heading west, the road hews closely to the river, which still powers the renowned glassblowing studios of Simon Pearce. A bit farther along, even the highway slows down to go through Woodstock, a favorite getaway that's one of New England's most fetching small towns.

When the road rises up and over the spine of the Green Mountains, it winds through valleys that ignite during foliage season, past the behemoth Mount Killington, which presides over the peaks around and supports an adrenaline-fueled resort culture at the "Beast of the East."

As Route 4 begins to roll downhill, it sinks into quarrying country, where faded towns are graced with marble flourishes from a time when Rutland drew immigrants speaking French, Italian, and Polish who came with masonry tools. Just past the city's scattered outskirts, the road passes through one of Vermont's quietest corners, a tranquil landscape whose Holstein cows preside over historical sites and forest-ringed lakes.

PLANNING YOUR TIME

Route 4 can serve as a day trip, splitting up a journey between the northern and southern part of the state, or it can be a road map for several days of exploring, especially during winter or foliage season. Tranquil **Woodstock** makes an excellent base, with appealing accommodation options and memorable restaurants; the region surrounding it is webbed with slow-traffic country roads and whistle-stop villages. If you're skiing or snowboarding, diminutive Suicide Six is just 10 minutes away, and you can reach Killington's high-speed gondola in 30. But for dedicated riders, it's hard to beat a room slope-side at

Previous: Hubbardton Battlefield State Historic Site; Killington, one of Vermont's most popular resorts; President Calvin Coolidge State Historic Site.

Killington, where you can join the winter-long raucous party and still get first tracks in the morning.

With an extra day, the quiet towns past **Rutland** provide a taste of daily life in Vermont, which continues to be the most rural of the United States. It may be most blank space on the map, but it's filled with pristine lakes, hiking trails, rolling agricultural land—and very few tourists.

White River Junction Area

Situated at the confluence of the Connecticut River and two of northern New England's main thoroughfares—I-89 and I-91—White River Junction has always been something of a crossroads. By the late 1800s, it was the largest railroad center north of Boston, with 50 passenger trains and even more freight trains passing through daily, carrying stone, lumber, wool, and dairy products between Boston, New York, Montréal, and Burlington. Once the center of the Boston & Maine Railroad, White River Junction faded into a backwater when highways replaced railways, though recent years have brought new energy to the brick-lined downtown.

The villages dispersed around White River Junction remain a draw: historical Windsor with a stately downtown, neighboring Norwich, Vermont, and Hanover, New Hampshire, where Dartmouth's college campus presides over a serene setting.

WHITE RIVER JUNCTION

Despite its prominent location, White River Junction is a locale that most visitors to the state journey through, not to. After the decline of the railway, "WRJ" grew into an ugly industrial sprawl that didn't provide the most inviting introduction to the state. An economic base of manufacturing industries has provided steady employment to many neighboring residents, however, and recently the city's downtown has started to come back to life with a slow influx of artists and young people.

Sights

A museum of oddities as Lewis Carroll may have invented it, the **Main Street Museum** (58 Bridge St., 802/356-2776, www.mainstreetmuseum.org, tours by appointment only, free) takes its cues from the *wunderkammern*, or "cabinets of curiosities," of Renaissance Europe, which gathered together sundry interesting and macabre artifacts from around the world to the amazement and delight of viewers. The museum's several rooms contain "a piece of wood from Strasbourg Cathedral," "an egg cup from a San Francisco Hotel in the Great Fire of 1907," "pressed poppies from Napoleon's Grave," and a thousand or so equally random artifacts.

Speaking of quirky, one of the more unusual accredited educational institutions in Vermont is the **Center for Cartoon Studies** (94 S. Main St., 802/295-3319, www.cartoonstudies.org, call to arrange visit), which offers a two-year master of fine arts degree, as well as one- and two-year certificates for developing cartoonists. Exhibit space on campus often showcases student work, and the school sometimes hosts visiting writers or cartoonists such as Myla Goldberg and Garry Trudeau. To get a better idea of the center's cartooning philosophy, visit their website to read *The World Is Made of Cheese: The Applied Cartooning Manifesto,* which like many of the world's best cartoons, breaks down subtle concepts with an adorably drawn critter.

Entertainment and Events

Lovers of serious theater, lighthearted productions, and children's musicals should investigate the ever-changing productions at **Northern Stage** (Briggs Opera House, 4 S.

Main St., 802/291-9009, www.northernstage.org). Considered one of the state's best, the company also stages many national and regional premieres.

Anyone with an inner—or actual—three-year-old should take the express train to **Glory Days of the Railroad Festival** (802/295-5036, www.vtglorydaysfestival.com, early Sept., free), a one-day celebration of steamies, diesels, and engineers that brings model railroad enthusiasts young and old down to the train station (102 Railroad Row, White River Junction) for music and family-friendly attractions.

Shopping

Give your wardrobe a blast from the past at **Revolution** (26 N. Main St., 802/295-6487, www.revolutionvintage.com, 10am-7pm daily), modeled after urban thrift stores and packed with excellent-condition vintage wear and creative reconstructed clothing, not to mention an espresso bar and a make-your-own T-shirt counter.

Take a love of landscapes and mix it with classic lighting and you've got **Lampscapes** (77 Gates St., 802/295-8044, lampscapesvt.wordpress.com, 10am-5pm Tues.-Sat.), a store filled to its brim with lamps that have been painted with one-of-a-kind designs by artist Ken Blaisdell.

Food

Both laid-back and high energy at once, **Thyme** (85 N. Main St., 802/295-3312, www.thymevermont.com, 11:30am-2:30pm and 5pm-9pm Tues.-Sat., $19-25) is a great blend of bistro and coffeehouse. At lunchtime the sunny spot serves sandwiches and soups, and at night it brings the candlelight out alongside entrées like the refined house specialty, pork and ginger meat loaf.

Stylish and modern, **Tuckerbox** (1 S. Main St., 802/359-4041, www.tuckerboxvermont.com, 7am-5pm Mon., 7am-9pm Tues.-Thurs., 7am-10pm Fri.-Sat., 10:30am-9pm Sun., $8-28) is a cheerful synthesis of modern coffeehouse (granola, lattes, exposed brick) and authentic Turkish café (kebabs, *börek*, baklava). While some of the menu will be familiar to aficionados of Mediterranean cuisines, other gems include *güveç*, smoky Turkish casseroles baked in earthenware bowls, and *künefe*, a dessert that blends sweet cheese with pastry similar to shredded wheat.

With Instagram-ready lighting and decor, **Piecemeal Pies** (5 S. Main St., 802/281-6910, www.piecemealpies.com, 8am-4pm Tues.-Thurs., 8am-8pm Fri., 10am-3pm Sat.-Sun., $4-13) also has savory pies and sweet treats that are easily worth getting off the highway for. This is the place to see WRJ's creative set over house-made sodas and strong cups of coffee, and ingredients for the excellent salads are culled from local farms.

Accommodations

With 30 guest rooms—each with private bathrooms, wireless Internet service, TVs, and phones, and many with queen-size or double beds—**Hotel Coolidge** (39 S. Main St., 802/295-3118, www.hotelcoolidge.com, $99-169) is one of the area's better deals. The hotel started as a junction house for the local railroad in the 1850s and, thanks to the decor, still retains much of that historical flavor. One wing is set aside as a Hostelling International hostel, with single beds, shared bathrooms, and a basic kitchenette for $49 ($3 discount for HI members).

Information and Services

For information about White River Junction and the surrounding area, contact the **Upper Valley Chamber of Commerce** (802/295-6200, www.uppervalleychamber.com), which staffs an information booth (100 Railroad Row) at the railroad station in downtown White River Junction. WRJ has several pharmacies, including **Corner Drug** (213 Maple St., 802/295-2012). Banks clustered around the intersection of Routes 4 and 5 include **People's United Bank** (190 Maple St., 802/295-5701) and **Mascoma Bank** (263 Maple St., 802/295-5456). In emergencies, contact the **Town of Hartford Police Department** (802/295-9425).

NORWICH AND HANOVER, NEW HAMPSHIRE

Settled in 1765 by residents of Norwich, Connecticut, **Norwich** is one of Vermont's oldest towns, but the explorers' taste for novelty clearly didn't extend to brainstorming new names. A serenely pretty village, it is now better known as the site of two very different tourist attractions—the Montshire Museum of Science and the flagship store for King Arthur Flour.

Norwich bleeds across the river into its sister village of **Hanover,** founded the same year in what would later become New Hampshire. Dartmouth College was established four years later, and today it's difficult to separate the two: The college is the town's main source of economy and attention, and the town is considered by the college to practically be an extension of its campus. That perennial student energy ensures that there is plenty to do and see around town, from shopping to loafing around in the cafés on Main Street.

Sights

Take a stroll around the gracious campus of **Dartmouth College** (Rte. 10A, Hanover, 603/646-1110, www.dartmouth.edu), which was founded in 1769. Sign up for a guided tour at the admissions office (www.admissions.dartmouth.edu), or download the school's app, which includes a detailed campus map and information. Highlights of the tour include **Dartmouth Hall,** the original location of the college, and the sumptuous libraries. Stop by the **Sanborn Library,** the home of the English department, which has reading nooks for paging through Oxford editions of every major and minor English and American author. The Sanborn Library has hosted an afternoon teatime for almost a century, and every weekday afternoon at 4pm students, faculty, and visitors stop by for tea and cookies—still priced at 25 cents.

At the **Hood Museum of Art** (4 E. Wheelock St., Hanover, 603/646-1110, www.hoodmuseum.dartmouth.edu, 10am-5pm Tues. and Thurs.-Sat., 10am-9pm Wed., noon-5pm Sun., free), an excellent college art museum, the building itself is impressive—an award-winning postmodern design by architects Charles Moore and Chad Floyd. The collection inside is like a survey course of the world's art, presenting European and American painting alongside a particularly strong collection of art from the Near East and Africa. Among the highlights are a spectacular 9th-century bas-relief from an Assyrian palace and a collection of art from Indonesia and the South Pacific that is among the most important in the country. As of the time of writing, a significant expansion was underway adding a series of new galleries to house collections that haven't been a part of the regular exhibits, including Australian Aboriginal art, Native American art, and modern art.

An ambitious and sprawling riot of wildlife, astronomy, and physics, the large **Montshire Museum of Science** (1 Montshire Rd./I-91 exit 13, Norwich, 802/649-2200, www.montshire.org, 10am-5pm daily, $15 adults, $12 children 2-17, children under 2 free, prices increase $2 in summer) is home to both a leaf-cutter ant colony and a 250-foot watercourse. Outdoors is a scale model of the solar system, along with several easy-grade nature trails.

Entertainment and Events

On campus, the **Spaulding Auditorium** (Dartmouth College, Hanover, 603/646-2422, www.hop.dartmouth.edu) at the Hopkins Center for the Arts is the place to catch plays, concerts, and dance shows put on by visiting artists as well as students.

A tradition since 1911, Dartmouth's biggest event each year is **Winter Carnival** (603/646-3399, www.dartmouth.edu, early Feb.), a four-day celebration of the season with athletic (and not-so-athletic) competitions, giant ice and snow sculptures, and hot chocolate-induced merriment.

Shopping

Bakers will need to be dragged away from the gift shop at **King Arthur Flour Baking Store and Baking Education Center** (135 Rte. 5 S., Norwich, 802/649-3361, www.kingarthurflour.com, 7:30am-6pm daily) where they can stock up on flour, cookbooks, baking pans, and kitchen doodads of all sorts. Pick up a loaf of bread or a pastry at the café (this is one of the few places in the region to get a slice of authentic *Bienenstich,* the Bee Sting Cake that is the apple pie of Germany), and eat it while watching the professionals whip out perfectly-shaped croissants behind glass windows.

Go green—quite literally—with a little help from the stock at **Dartmouth Co-op** (21 S. Main St., Hanover, 800/643-2667, www.dartmouthcoop.com, 9:30am-6pm Mon.-Sat., 9:30am-4pm Sun.). Here, everything from golf hats and tote bags to sweatshirts and sleepwear comes emblazoned with the school's logo. All profits from the store go directly to the college.

One could spend hours rifling through the aisles of **Left Bank Books** (9 S. Main St., Hanover, 603/643-4479, 9:30am-5pm Mon.-Sat., 11:30am-3:30pm Sun.), which carries loads of fiction (classic and contemporary), poetry, how-tos, and kids' books. This is the place to stock up on all the books you need.

Food

There's a classic diner vibe and breakfast served all day at **Lou's Restaurant** (30 Main St., Hanover, 603/643-3321, www.lousrestaurant.net, 6am-3pm Mon.-Fri., 7am-3pm Sat.-Sun., $8-13), which is the stuff of nostalgia for generations of Dartmouth students. You can get filling sandwiches, salads, and shakes, along with sweet treats from the on-site bakery, which also boxes up care packages to send over to campus. Lou's Cruller French Toast takes doughnuts over the edge by battering and grilling them, and freshly made corned beef hash has inspired odes since the restaurant opened in 1947.

Tucked into the refined Hanover Inn, **PINE Restaurant** (2 E. Wheelock St., Hanover, 603/646-8000, www.pineathanoverinn.com, 6:30am-11pm Sun.-Thurs., 6:30am-midnight Fri.-Sat., breakfast $9-15, lunch $13-22, dinner $17-36) gives an Italian twist to farm-to-table cuisine. Dinner features a mix of seafood, meat-focused dishes, and some standout vegetarian options; try roasted swordfish or ravioli with hen of the wood mushrooms. It's a lively spot when it fills with students and visiting parents.

Head chef Bruce MacLeod was classically trained in France and did stints all over the world before taking over the kitchen at **Carpenter & Main** (326 Main St., Norwich, 802/649-2922, www.carpenterandmain.com, 5:30pm-10pm Wed.-Sat., 5:30pm-9pm Sun., $12-26). His diverse, French-influenced background shows in the sophisticated menu, with offerings such as Moroccan lamb meatballs with spicy tomato glaze, duck confit with mustard vinaigrette, and wild bass with red pepper relish.

Peeking inside the elegant Norwich Inn is a perk when you eat at **Jasper Murdock's Alehouse** (325 Main St., Norwich, 802/649-1143, www.norwichinn.com, breakfast 8am-10:30am Fri.; brunch and lunch 11:30am-2pm Fri., 8am-2pm Sat.-Sun.; pub menu 3pm-5pm Mon.-Fri., 2pm-5pm Sat.-Sun.; dinner 5pm-close daily; $11-14), which is also the home to a tiny brewery that produces English-style ales. Seating is available in the congenial pub or in the larger, more buttoned-up dining room, but both share a menu of burgers, wings, and notably, eggplant fries. The beers on tap rotate constantly, but don't miss the house-made Whistling Pig Red Ale, a sweet, malty Irish red. Reservations are accepted for the dining room only.

If you're craving something a bit less Yankee, trek over to **Base Camp Café** (3 Lebanon St., Hanover, 603/643-2007, www.basecampcafenh.com, 11am-9pm Sun.-Thurs., 11am-10pm Fri.-Sat., $13-23) where very nicely done Nepalese specialties are served in a casual environment. The *momos* (dumplings) are especially beloved, as are the

Vermont's Distilling Revival

Vermont has had a fraught relationship with alcohol—the state went dry more than once in the 19th century, long before nationwide prohibition. Throughout the 1920s, Canadian booze came in by boat, car, and horse-drawn wagon, but these days, domestic distillates are all the rage. In the years since Vermont Spirits opened their doors in 1999, craft liquor has had something of a renaissance, and tiny alembic and towering column stills are turning out high-quality hard alcohol around the state. You could easily shape a tour around dropping by each one for a taste, and The Distilled Spirits Council of Vermont links them up on their **Tasting Tour Passport** (www.distilledvermont.org), which you can pick up at any of the participating distilleries.

Not all of the distilleries listed with the Tasting Tour are open for regular visits all year, so it's important to call ahead to confirm. And if you can't tag every still in the state, it's worth asking about local spirits if you stop by a bar or liquor store; don't miss the **Backwoods Reserve Rum** from **Dunc's Mill** in St. Johnsbury, which is closed to the public. It's an extraordinarily rich and flavorful sipping spirit aged in Hungarian oak.

These are some distilleries worth a visit:

ALONG ROUTE 4

Quechee's **Vermont Spirits** (5573 Woodstock Rd., Quechee, 802/281-6398, www.vermontspirits.com, 10am-5pm daily, free samples) is a great place to start, with a sample of **Vermont White Vodka** made from whey. Just 25 minutes south is the shiny new distillery at **SILO Distillery** (3 Artisans Way, Windsor, 802/674-4220, www.silodistillery.com, 11am-6pm Sun.-Thurs., 11am-7pm Fri.-Sat. May-Sept., 11am-5pm daily Oct.-Dec., 11am-5pm Thurs.-Mon. Jan-Apr., free samples) where the **SILO Bourbon Whiskey** has been racking up awards and is a standout among a solid selection of everything from lavender vodka to barrel-aged gin.

CHAMPLAIN VALLEY

Try a Vermont take on calvados at **Mad River Distillers** (137 St. Paul St., Burlington, 802/489-5501, www.madriverdistillers.com, noon-6pm Sun.-Wed., noon-8pm Thurs., noon-10pm Fri.-Sat.), whose apple brandy is a bracing spirit made from local apples; don't miss their First Run Rum, a richly flavorful cane sugar rum with a bit of caramel sweetness from charred American oak barrels.

tarkaris, spicy curries that come stocked with everything from plantain to shrimp.

FARMERS MARKET

If you're visiting between May and October, try to catch the **Norwich Farmers' Market** (Rte. 5 S., 1.5 miles south of exit 13, www.norwichfarmersmarket.org, 9am-1pm Sat.) where maple syrup, pastries, vegetables, meat, and cheese stream in from area farms and kitchens.

Accommodations

$150-250

The Victorian **Norwich Inn** (325 Main St., Norwich, 802/649-1143, www.norwichinn.com, $140-290) opened in 1890 and has undergone several upgrades in the decades since. Today its 37 guest rooms and suites come stocked with all the modern necessities: TV, telephone, air-conditioning, hairdryers, irons and ironing boards, and free wireless. The front porch's comfy rocking chairs are a pleasant place to while away the afternoon with a beer from the inn's on-site brewery.

A Westin-run chain hotel with an environmentally friendly ethos and modern style, **Element Hanover-Lebanon** (25 Foothill St., Lebanon, 603/448-5000, www.elementhanoverlebanon.com, $170-240) is a great option if the area's old-fashioned bed-and-breakfasts just aren't your thing. There's a fitness center and saline pool, business center, and outdoor seating, and the breakfast

In a stylish mod-industrial facility, **Stonecutter Spirits** (1197 Exchange St., Middlebury, 802/388-3000, www.stonecutterspirits.com, noon-8pm Thurs., noon-6pm Fri.-Sat.) opened in 2015 and has racked up awards for a barrel-aged gin is made with plenty of juniper, cardamom, and orange peel. Try it straight or in a cocktail, and then move on to the spicy and smooth cask-aged whiskey.

NORTHERN GREEN MOUNTAINS

Way up in the mountains, **Smugglers' Notch Distillery** (276 Rte. 108 S., Jeffersonville, 802/309-3077, www.smugglersnotchdistillery.com, 11am-5pm daily, tastings $5) makes award-winning vodka that's smooth as can be, as well as bourbon, rum, and an unusual gin infused with hops. Stop by their distillery in Jeffersonville, or just sample the goods in their Waterbury Center tasting room (2657 Waterbury Stowe Rd., Waterbury Center, 802/309-3077, www.smugglersnotchdistillery.com, 11am-5pm daily, tastings $5).

NORTHEAST KINGDOM

The wild and scenic Northeast Kingdom is speckled with stills (some of them unofficial), but the extraordinary **Caledonia Spirits** (46 Log Yard Dr., Hardwick, 802/472-8000, www.caledoniaspirits.com, 10am-5pm Mon.-Sat., 11am-3pm Sun., free samples) is aboveboard; they infuse grain spirits with juniper berries and raw honey to make **Barr Hill Gin,** one of the best drinks in the state.

Even farther-flung is **Elm Brook Farm** (250 Elm Brook Rd., East Fairfield, 802/782-5999, www.elmbrookfarm.com, email or call ahead to visit) where David and Lisa Howe make **Literary Dog Vodka** and **Rail Dog** maple spirit from sap that they gather from their on-site sugar bush. (One devoted customer flies in on a private plane whenever his stock runs low.) The remarkable spirits are named for the equally appealing Braque Français dogs that have their run of the place. On Saturday and Sunday, the Howes go to farmers markets, but if you email in advance (ebf@elmbrookfarm.com), they welcome visitors to the farm and distillery during the week. East Fairfield is a 45-minute drive northeast from Burlington. It is a bit out of the way, but you can pick up a bottle at many area liquor stores, and the distillers offer samples on Saturday at the **Burlington Farmers' Market.**

buffet has an unusually appealing selection of healthy food.

OVER $250

Facing the Dartmouth College green, **The Hanover Inn** (2 S. Main St., Hanover, 603/643-4300, www.hanoverinn.com, $259-309) manages country elegance despite feeling vast. Guest rooms are furnished with handmade quilts and wingback chairs, and the common areas have been recently renovated, adding a contemporary flair to the classic style. Another recent addition is PINE, a refined farm-to-table restaurant that offers breakfast, lunch, and dinners.

Set on 16 acres of beautiful grounds, **The Trumbull House Bed & Breakfast** (40 Etna Rd., Hanover, 800/651-5141, www.trumbullhouse.com, $219-344) is welcoming and comfortable, with six old-fashioned rooms with enough modern updates to feel luxurious. Breakfast starts with fruit, then fortifies guest with house-baked sweets and entrées that are made to order from a short menu. Footpaths on the property link up with the Appalachian Trail.

Information and Services

The **Hanover Area Chamber of Commerce** (603/643-3115, www.hanoverchamber.org) runs an information booth on the green. Free Wi-Fi is available at **Howe Library** (13 South St., Hanover, www.howelibrary.org, 10am-8pm Mon.-Thurs., 10am-6pm Fri.,

10am-5pm Sat., 1pm-5pm Sun.). Pharmacies include **Eastman Pharmacy** (22 S. Main St., Hanover, 603/643-4112) and **CVS Pharmacy** (79 S. Main St., Hanover, 603/643-3178, 24 hours daily, pharmacy 8am-10pm Mon.-Fri., 9am-6pm Sat.-Sun.). There's a **Bank of America** (63 S. Main St., Hanover, 603/643-1057) and a **Citizens Bank** (44 S. Main St., Hanover, 603/640-1150, 8:30am-5pm Mon.-Fri., 9am-noon Sat.), along with a smattering of other banks with ATMs. In an emergency, contact the **Hanover Police Department** (46 Lyme Rd., Hanover, 603/643-2222).

WINDSOR

Claiming to be no less than "the birthplace of Vermont," Windsor served as headquarters for the state militia during the time of the Revolutionary War. As the storm clouds of war swirled around Lake Champlain to the west, the leaders of New Connecticut—as the young territory was then called—gathered around a table in Elias West's tavern and slapped together a state constitution based on that of Pennsylvania. Not that it was a carbon copy: The new constitution was the first to abolish slavery, and it also granted suffrage to men who did not hold property. Somewhere in the course of negotiations, the delegates took the name of Vermont, a combination of the French words for "green" and "mountain"—and the rest, as they say, is history. The town center has retained its historical character, with many fine examples of Federal-style architecture well worth a walk around; if it's too hot for that, you can simply take to the river in an inner tube, kayak, or canoe.

Historical Windsor Walking Tour

Windsor is justifiably proud of its place in the history of the republic and has created an informative and engaging **walking tour of downtown** (www.tappt.net/windsor/tour, free), which you can follow on the website or by scanning QR codes installed at six locations downtown: at The Robbins & Lawrence Armory (196 Main St.), the Old South Church (Main St. at River St.), Court Square (Court St.), Windsor House (54 Main St.), Old Constitution House (16 N. Main St.), and Depot (Depot Ave.).

A mandatory stop is **Old Constitution House** (16 N. Main St., 802/672-3773, www.historicsites.vermont.gov, 11am-5pm Sat.-Sun. late May-mid-Oct., $3 adults, children 14 and under free), the tavern where the state constitution document was hammered out. The tavern has since been restored to its Revolutionary-era glory. A permanent exhibition looks at the state's struggle for statehood with period artifacts and decor.

Later in Windsor's history, the town took advantage of the swift-flowing Connecticut River to become a center of manufacturing. That era is preserved in the **American Precision Museum** (196 Main St., 802/674-5781, www.americanprecision.org, 10am-5pm daily late May-Oct., $8 adults, $5 students, children under 6 free, $20 family). If you've never thought about how people actually make the objects—from furniture to computer chips—that we use every day, you will after seeing the fascinating exhibits here, which include one of the world's largest collections of machine tools, as well as antique sewing machines, typewriters, rifles, and a "Machine Tool Hall of Fame" enshrining the ingenious inventors of modern manufacturing.

Windsor-Cornish Bridge

The granddaddy of Vermont covered bridges is actually in New Hampshire. That's because the state line is drawn on the *west* bank of the Connecticut River, thereby leaving all of the 450-foot Windsor-Cornish Bridge solidly in Granite State airspace. No matter—it's still a beaut. The longest covered bridge in the United States, it was built in 1866 from heavy spruce timber. Still open to traffic, it remains a testament to 19th-century engineering. A word of warning is posted for equestrian visitors: Dismount before crossing the bridge, or you may face a $2 fine.

SILO Distillery and Harpoon Brewery

It may not have started in Vermont, but **Harpoon Brewery** (336 Ruth Carney Dr., 802/674-5491, www.harpoonbrewery.com, 10am-6pm Sun.-Wed., 10am-9pm Thurs.-Sat., four samples free) has made itself right at home. The Windsor brewery has a little enclosure where you can watch the action and an expansive dining room with a hearty menu of pub food that may help you absorb a few of the 20 beers on tap. They've got all the flagship beers—like their IPA, which is now almost ubiquitous at bars around New England—but the real prizes are the limited releases that you won't find anywhere else. Despite being one of the big names in craft brewing, Harpoon has kept in touch with its small-scale roots and has a standing offer to reimburse employees for the ingredients they use in their home-brewing projects, just to keep the ideas flowing.

And just across the parking lot is **SILO Distillery** (3 Artisans Way, 802/674-4220, www.silodistillery.com, 11am-6pm Sun.-Thurs., 11am-7pm Fri.-Sat. May-Sept., 11am-5pm daily Oct.-Dec., 11am-5pm Thurs.-Mon. Jan-Apr., free tastings) where you can sample vodka, gin, whiskey, and special runs that are often collaborations with Vermont producers. Corn, rye, and wheat are sourced from a local farm.

Events

Especially good times to visit the Harpoon Brewery are during the **Harpoon Championships of New England Barbecue** in late July—where you can discover how very well ale goes with ribs and grilled chicken—and **Harpoon Octoberfest** in early October, when the eponymous beer is released.

Shopping

Challenge yourself to find the flaws in the "seconds" at the **Simon Pearce Factory Outlet** (109 Park Rd., 802/230-2402, www.simonpearce.com, 10am-5pm daily), which is stocked with the gorgeous glassware and pottery from up the road in Quechee. Glassblowers and potters are on-site.

Food

Housed in Windsor's historical railway depot, **Windsor Station Restaurant and Barroom** (26 Depot Ave., 802/674-4180, www.windsorstationvt.com, 4:30pm-9pm Tues.-Sat., 4:30pm-10pm Sat.-Sun., bar open until 2am, $9-23) serves hearty American fare like burgers—beef or veggie—alongside Italian mains. Clams and linguine or pork chop Milanaise are right at home in the warm interior. Chat with friendly regulars at the tin-sheathed bar, or slide into a cozy banquette. Wood floors and walls make this a haven in the wintertime, and the cocktail list is fabulous.

There's more than just beer at the **Harpoon Brewery** (336 Ruth Carney Dr., 802/674-5491, www.harpoonbrewery.com, 10am-6pm Sun.-Wed., 10am-9pm Thurs.-Sat. May-Oct., 10am-6pm Sun. and Tues.-Wed., 10am-9pm Thurs.-Sat. Nov.-Apr., $8-13)—there's lots of things to go with beer. Bar snacks like handmade pretzels and wings share the menu with hearty sandwiches and a few salads. The IPA beef and bean chili is a hearty treat.

Surely the only sports-themed espresso bar in the state, **Boston Dreams** (7 State St., 802/230-4107, www.bostondreams.com, 7:30am-6pm daily, $2-9) is decked with photos of Beantown's great sports heroes. Even if Red Sox memorabilia leave you cold, it's an excellent stop for coffee, ice cream, or a light lunch; the menu has waffles, soups, and excellent panini that ooze Vermont cheddar cheese.

Accommodations

The proud, brick building that houses **The Snapdragon Inn** (26 Main St., 802/779-9131, www.snapdragoninn.com, $148-210) was once owned by Max Perkins, a celebrity editor who is credited with "discovering" the authors Hemingway, Fitzgerald, and Thomas Wolfe, among many others, and rooms are stocked with volumes that Perkins edited.

1
2
3

Literary history aside, the inn is a beautiful and romantic place to stay. Nine rooms have featherbeds and radiant floor heating, while some offer perks like claw-foot bathtubs. Rates include a continental breakfast, and there are plenty of places to lounge: Play board games by the fire in the library or take a spin on the tree swing. Spa services are available on-site. An elegant property sitting on 14 acres, the **Windsor Mansion Inn** (153 Pembroke Rd., 802/674-4112, www.windsormansioninn.com, $189-250) is surprisingly grand, from the be-columned facade to the rooms' dark-hued wood furniture. A hot breakfast is served each day in the great room, and the tavern has puzzles and board games that are perfect for long winter evenings. Views stretch across the Connecticut River Valley to Mount Ascutney, a scene that's especially dramatic in the fall.

Information and Services

For information, contact the **Windsor/Mt. Ascutney Chamber of Commerce** (802/674-5910). The regional hospital for the Upper Valley area, **Mount Ascutney Hospital and Health Center** (289 County Rd., 802/674-6711, www.mtascutneyhospital.org) handles both emergency and routine care. For pharmacy needs, turn to **Rite-Aid Pharmacy** (52 Main St., 802/674-2334). For banking needs, visit **People's United Bank** (50 N. Main St., 802/674-2131, 9am-5pm Mon.-Fri.). Free public Wi-Fi is available at the **Windsor Public Library** (43 State St., 802/674-2556, www.windsorlibrary.org, 10am-7:30pm Mon., 10am-5:30pm Tues.-Fri., 10am-3pm Sat.).

SPORTS AND RECREATION

★ Floating the Connecticut River

When the weather gets muggy, it's impossible to imagine an activity more alluring than floating down the Connecticut River in an inner tube. Windsor-based **Great River Outfitters** (36 Park Rd., 802/674-9923, www.greatriveroutfitters.com) has you covered and will shuttle you upriver with a tube, canoe, kayak, or raft; a three-hour float is $25/$35 for children/adults, eight hours is $80/$60. The five-mile section of the river from Sumner Falls to Windsor is among the most scenic and takes 2.5-3 hours. Conveniently, the take-out point is right next door to the Harpoon Brewery, where you can refuel after all that paddling.

Hiking and Camping

Hikers will find plenty of trails at **Ascutney State Park** (1826 Back Mountain Rd., Windsor, 802/674-2060, https://vtstateparks.com, mid-May-mid-Oct.). Two trails in particular leave from separate parking lots on Route 44 to climb the summit of 3,143-foot Mount Ascutney. The 3.2-mile **Brownsville Trail** makes a detour to an abandoned granite quarry, and the 2.7-mile **Windsor Trail** includes a small waterfall a mile into the hike. Both trails then include several viewing spots on their way up the mountain and join before the best views at the granite ledges of Brownsville Rock, a popular launching pad for both hawks and hang gliders. On the summit itself, a fire tower offers panoramic views of the surrounding mountains. Those not up for a strenuous hike can also drive up to the summit via the 3.7-mile Mount Ascutney Parkway. The park also has 49 campsites, including both tent sites and lean-tos ($18-27/night). The campsite has bathrooms and showers as well as a dump station for RVs, but no hookups. If possible, request one of the sites to the right of the entrance road, which tend to be more widely spaced and private.

Another nice day hike in the area is **Moose Mountain,** across the Connecticut River in Hanover. A favorite hike for Dartmouth students, the 1.7-mile trail to the 2,300-foot peak of South Moose Mountain is part of the

1: Old South Church in Windsor's historic downtown; **2:** Quechee Gorge; **3:** floating the Connecticut River

Appalachian Trail. Several decades ago, an airplane crashed on the peak, and the summit was cleared of vegetation to facilitate helicopter landings to help clear the debris. Subsequently, a caterpillar infestation killed the remaining trees, leaving a bald and open view of downtown Hanover, Dartmouth College, and the surrounding Connecticut River Valley.

To find the trailhead, from The Green in Hanover take East Wheelock Street four miles to the village of Etna; turn left on Two Mile Road, right on Rudsboro Road, and left on the dirt Three Mile Road. There's a small dirt parking lot near the trailhead. The trail up to South Moose Mountain is a two-mile hike through a variety of terrain, including marshland and hemlocks. For a day hike, you can continue back down the way you came; for an overnight hike, you can proceed north another half mile to the Moose Mountain Shelter, maintained by the **Dartmouth Outing Club** (603/646-2429, www.dartmouth.edu), which sleeps eight on a first-come, first-served basis, with a tent site for overflow. From there, a 1.5-mile loop takes you back to the parking area.

GETTING THERE AND AROUND

To drive to White River Junction from Boston, take I-93 to I-89. After crossing the Vermont border, take I-91 north to exit 11 (2 hrs. total). For Norwich and Hanover, take I-91 north from WRJ to exit 13 (5 mi., 10 min.). For Windsor, take I-91 south to exit 9, then Route 5 south (12 mi., 20 min.).

Amtrak (800/872-7245, www.amtrak.com) runs its Vermonter Service to White River Junction (100 Railroad Row) and Windsor (26 Depot Ave.). In summer months, the **White River Flyer** (800/707-3530, www.rails-vt.com) offers a round-trip train from WRJ to the Montshire Museum in Norwich.

Advance Transit (802/295-1824, www.advancetransit.com) runs regular free bus service around White River Junction, Norwich, and Hanover. **Connecticut River Transit** (802/885-5165, www.crtransit.org) offers bus service between WRJ and Windsor.

Quechee

This village is perched at a sweeping bend in the Ottauquechee River, which winds through the deepest gorge in Vermont, carved 13,000 years ago by glaciers. When Tropical Storm Irene swept through the state in 2011, Quechee was devastated by the waterway that has always been its lifeblood. Flooding dissolved roadways and destroyed the village's historical covered bridge, thought to be among Vermont's prettiest. The bridge has since been rebuilt, and while it lacks the jewel-box charm of neighboring Woodstock, Quechee remains an appealing place to spend an afternoon exploring hiking trails, a glassblowing studio, and locally crafted spirits. Quechee is officially a village of the town of **Hartford,** so depending on the source you may find street addresses listed as either location.

SIGHTS

Vermont Spirits

In an unassuming cluster of commercial buildings on Route 4, Vermont's oldest existing distillery produces a handful of carefully crafted spirits that offer unique twists on classic Vermont flavors. **Vermont Sprits** (5573 Woodstock Rd., 802/281-6398, www.vermontspirits.com, 10am-5pm daily, free samples) has been firing their stills and making booze from unexpected ingredients since 1999. Their smooth-as-can-be Vermont White Vodka is made from whey, the sugars that occur naturally in cow's milk; the equally silky Vermont Gold Vodka is made from maple sap. The bright tasting room gives great views of the working distillery, and free samples are available.

★ Quechee Gorge

The views of the **Quechee Gorge** (5800 Woodstock Rd., 802/295-2990, https://vtstateparks.com) are lovely from the road, but the 651-acre state park that envelops the dramatic stretch of river offers an afternoon's worth of wandering shady trails. Part of the appeal of the narrow, rocky canyon is the way it comes across Route 4 so suddenly, plunging 165 feet down into the Ottauquechee River racing below. The gorge was formed some 13,000 years ago, when waters from a glacial lake cut inch by inch through tough bedrock schist. There's a short and scenic walk along the river from the visitors center, which also has exhibits illustrating the geological and natural history of the area.

To reach the best swimming area here, take the trail from the visitors center, then turn left (downstream) as the Quechee Gorge Trail turns upstream, then follow the river for roughly 0.5 mile to a broad swimming hole.

★ Vermont Institute of Natural Science

The mission of the **Vermont Institute of Natural Science** (VINS, Rte. 4 just west of Quechee Gorge, 802/359-5000, www.vinsweb.org, 10am-4pm daily Nov.-mid-Apr., 10am-5pm daily mid-Apr.-Oct., $15.50 adults, $14.50 seniors, $13.50 children 4-17, children 3 and under free) is to rescue and rehabilitate birds of prey, including hawks, owls, and eagles, and display them for the education of visitors. Watching the raptors watch you is an unforgettable experience. The birds are released when fully healed, but one visit included a great horned owl, merlin falcons, and other fiercely captivating creatures.

Try to time your visit with one of the raptor educational programs, held at 11am, or their feeding time at 2:45pm. VINS puts on other educational programs throughout the day and also has an hour-long interpretive nature trail that winds through the forested property.

★ Simon Pearce

Even if you're not in the market for their high-end glassware, **Simon Pearce** (1760 Main St., the Mill at Quechee, 802/295-2711, www.simonpearce.com, 10am-9pm daily) is a fascinating stop. Located in an old mill building run entirely by hydroelectric power, the studio is open to the public, and in the downstairs area glassblowers blow bubbles into glowing orange balls of 2,400-degree silica (the glassblowing room is especially pleasant in winter). It's an extraordinary sight, especially the way

See rescued birds of prey up close at the Vermont Institute of Natural Science.

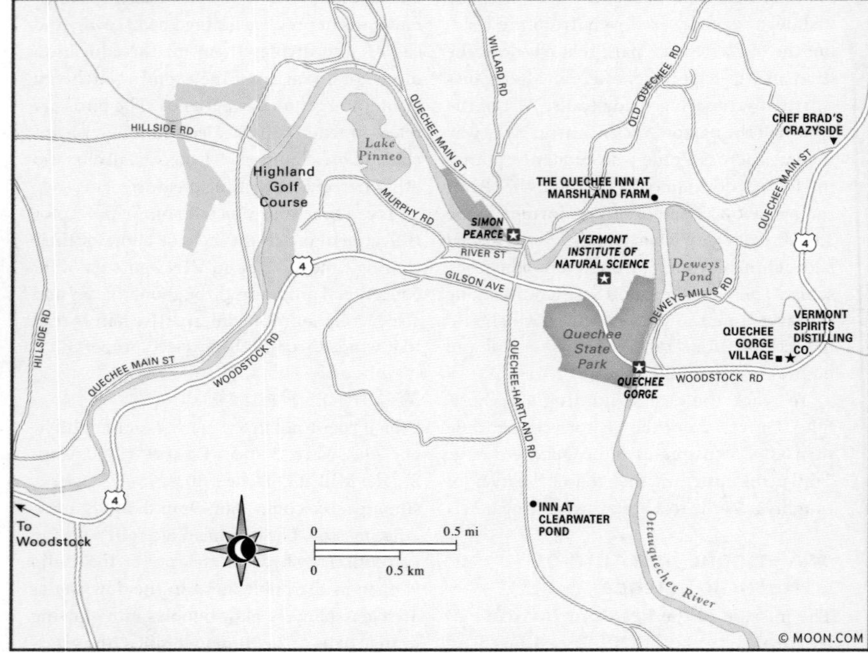

multiple craftspeople coordinate individual components of a delicate wineglass, with precise timing and handiwork. If they slip up, of course, that's one more glass for the shelf of perfect-seeming "seconds" available for purchase at somewhat lower prices.

If you're in the market, the majority of seconds are on display at the **Simon Pearce Factory Outlet** (109 Park Rd., Windsor, 802/230-2402, www.simonpearce.com, 10am-5pm daily) in Windsor. The Quechee location also has an excellent on-site **Simon Pearce Restaurant** (11:30am-2:45pm and 5:30pm-9pm daily, $14-18 lunch, $28-33 dinner), which serves meals that are as refined and creative as everything else they do, in a gorgeous dining room overlooking the river. To find the Mill at Quechee (coming from I-89), cross Quechee Gorge and take a right at the first blinking light.

EVENTS

Colored canvas lights up the sky above Quechee Gorge at the annual **Quechee Hot Air Balloon, Fine Arts, Craft & Music Festival** (802/295-7900, www.quecheeballoonfestival.com, June), a tradition for more than 35 years. The event features musical performances, kids' games, and—of course—rides "up, up, and away" in more than two dozen brightly colored balloons.

FOOD

With seating in a colorful school bus and a kitchen in a converted trailer, **Chef Brad's CrazySide** (1 Quechee Main St., 802/295-6400, www.chefbrads.com, 12:30pm-2:30pm and 5pm-7:30pm Thurs.-Sun., $5-12) is a delightful stop when you're ready for a break from quaint inns and farm-to-table cuisine. Fish tacos are stars of the menu, but there are burgers, sandwiches, and even some Caribbean fare, and almost everything arrives wrapped in newsprint. There's an outdoor fridge full of desserts that runs on the honor system—just drop your cash into the bucket and grab a cupcake or popsicle. At the time of writing, an indoor space was under construction.

The charming **Quechee Inn at Marshland Farm** (1119 Quechee Main St., 800/235-3133, www.quecheeinn.com, 6pm-9pm daily, $25-34) is in a 1794 farmhouse and has atmosphere in spades. Their on-site restaurant is a treat, with excellent value three-course prix fixe menus for $25 per person on Wednesday nights, and a Friday night special that's $55 for two including wine. The slow-roasted duck with wild-rice pilaf is a perennial favorite, as is the indulgent maple crème brûlée.

Truly memorable meals can be found at ★ **Simon Pearce Restaurant** (1760 Main St., 802/295-1470, www.simonpearce.com, 11:30am-2:45pm and 5:30pm-9pm daily, $14-18 lunch and $28-33 dinner). Settle into the elegant and sunny room overlooking the rushing Ottauquechee River and its dam, and dig into plates of horseradish-crusted cod, crisp confit duck with orange sauce, and beef and Guinness stew with paprika potatoes. As part of the Simon Pearce building, the kitchen serves everything on pottery and glassware literally made downstairs.

ACCOMMODATIONS

The Quechee Inn at Marshland Farm (1119 Quechee Main St., 800/235-3133, www.quecheeinn.com, $109-257) was once the home of Vermont's first lieutenant governor, Colonel Joseph Marsh. It still treats those who stay here like VIPs, with pretty, individually decorated rooms decked out with antiques, cable TV, and air-conditioning—and many with terrific views of the Ottauquechee River. The inn has an excellent restaurant on-site.

On a back road south of Quechee, the romantic **Inn at Clearwater Pond** (984 Quechee-Hartland Rd., 802/295-0606, www.innatclearwaterpond.com, $175-325) offers all the classic amenities of fine bed-and-breakfasts, like fluffy towels, elegant furnishings, and a sumptuous breakfast. What sets this inn apart is a game assortment of activities, like llama treks, hot air ballooning, croquet, bocce, and on-site massage therapy (advance notice required). The swimming pond and sweeping outdoor spaces make this an especially appealing destination in the summer.

Simon Pearce glassmaking studio

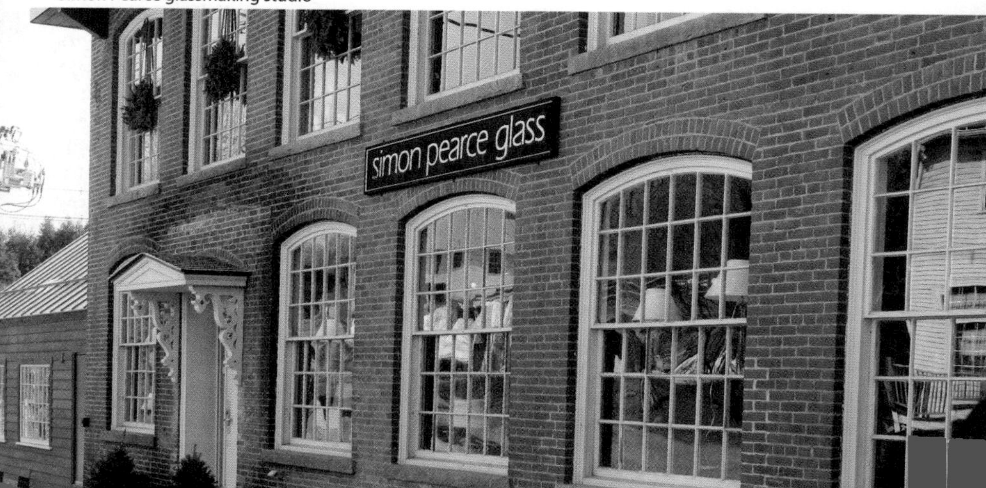

Camping

Quechee State Park (5800 Woodstock Rd., 802/295-2990, https://vtstateparks.com/htm/quechee.htm, mid-May-mid-Oct.) has some excellent spots for river swimming near a bustling, friendly **campground,** with lean-tos and 45 RV and tent sites along a forested loop (tents $18-24, lean-tos $25-29). There is a dump station, but no hookups; fully powered sites in this area are limited, and the closest option is 2.6 miles farther east, at the **Quechee/Pine Valley KOA** (3700 E. Woodstock Rd., White River Junction, May-mid-Oct., tents $28-36, RVs $45-70).

SPORTS AND RECREATION

Hiking

Quechee State Park (5800 Woodstock Rd., Hartford, 802/295-2990, https://vtstateparks.com/htm/quechee.htm, mid-May-mid-Oct., free) has a pleasant 2.2-mile round-trip trail into Vermont's deepest gorge, which was carved by retreating glaciers. While the park's self-nomination as "Vermont's Little Grand Canyon" might set visitors up for a disappointment, the walk is lovely. The **Quechee Gorge Trail** hike takes about an hour, and starts from the visitors center.

INFORMATION AND SERVICES

The racks at **Quechee Gorge Village** (Rte. 4, 802/295-1550, www.quecheegorge.com, 9:30am-5:30pm daily) are stuffed with brochures on the town and surrounding area. For more information, contact the **Hartford Area Chamber of Commerce** (802/295-7900, www.hartfordvtchamber.com).

GETTING THERE AND AROUND

From White River Junction, head west on Route 4 for Quechee (8 mi., 12 min.).

Advance Transit (802/295-1824, www.advancetransit.com) runs regular free bus service around White River Junction, Norwich, Hanover, and Quechee.

Woodstock

This gracious village has a bit of starch and a lot of history. It is the eastern terminus to the sinuous path that Route 4 carves through the mountains and provides a tony counterpoint to Rutland, which is an hour's drive west and a world away. While Rutland's past is defined by the working landscape and blue-collar immigrants, Woodstock has always drawn an affluent set of families from Connecticut and Massachusetts, who built and preserved one of the prettiest town centers in all of New England. Names like Rockefeller, Billings, and Marsh continue to define today's landscape of elegant inns and ski areas. In fact, the conservational efforts of those families are largely responsible for the nostalgic charm of the area, a legacy that is on display at the Marsh-Billings-Rockefeller National Historical Park, which also reflects on the nature of conservation around the world.

In part due to its carefully maintained past, Woodstock continues to attract transplants from urban areas around the East. This blend of new and old lends an unusual vitality to the small town, where upscale restaurants, art galleries, and boutiques cheerfully coexist with covered bridges and a quirky "town crier," a community blackboard listing contra dances and church suppers. Nestled into the base of the Green Mountains, it is alluring in the winter months and makes an ideal base for skiing, particularly if you prefer your après-ski dining with white tablecloths and a good wine list. In summertime, there are farms to visit, and endless back roads invite lazy drives with no destination. Anytime at all, this is one of Vermont's most romantic getaways.

SIGHTS

★ Billings Farm & Museum

One of Woodstock's most successful native sons was Frederick Billings, who made his money as a San Francisco lawyer in the heat of the gold rush. In the 1870s he returned to Woodstock and bought the old Charles Marsh Farm, which he transformed into a model dairy farm complete with imported Jersey cows. Today visitors to the grounds of the **Billings Farm & Museum** (53 Elm St., 802/457-2355, www.billingsfarm.org, 10am-5pm daily Apr.-Oct., 10am-4pm Sat.-Sun. Nov.-Feb., $16 adults, $14 seniors, $9 students 16 and above, $8 children 5-15, $4 children 3-4, children under 3 free) can tour the property in wagons drawn by Percheron draft horses, meet the well-groomed herd of milking cows, and churn fresh cream into butter. The farm produces two varieties of cheddar from a herd of all Jersey cows: full-flavored and creamy sweet cheddar and butter cheddar that is slightly salty with a rich, melting texture.

Next door, **Marsh-Billings-Rockefeller National Historical Park** (54 Elm St., 802/457-3368, www.nps.gov/mabi, 10am-5pm daily Memorial Day-Oct., $8 adults, $4 seniors, children 15 and under free) frames the mansion built by natural philosopher Charles Marsh between 1805 and 1807 and bought by Billings in 1861. The mansion, open for tours by advance reservation, has a Tiffany stained-glass window and an extensive collection of American landscape paintings. In 1934, Billings's granddaughter married Laurance Rockefeller, and they donated the land to the National Park Service in 1992. The main visitors center is the former Carriage Barn, which houses a permanent exhibit about conservation history, a reading library, and bookstore. **Combination tickets** ($21 adults, $16 seniors) include two-day admission to both Billings Farm and Marsh-Billings-Rockefeller National Historical Park.

Sugarbush Farm

Cows and other farm animals can be found at **Sugarbush Farm** (591 Sugarbush Rd., 802/457-1757, www.sugarbushfarm.com, 9am-5pm daily), which produces excellent cheddar cheese and keeps their maple sugar shack open all year (though syrup is typically made in March and April). Set atop a scenic hill, the farm also produces maple syrup, mustards, and jams—all of which are free to sample. To get here, take a right across the covered bridge at the small village of Taftsville and follow the signs to the farm. Call ahead for road conditions in winter and early spring.

Dana House Museum

For a glimpse into Woodstock's nonagricultural past, visit the **Dana House Museum** (26 Elm St., 802/457-1822, 1pm-5pm Wed.-Sat., 11am-3pm Sun. June-late Oct., free), a Federal-style home once owned by a prosperous local dry goods merchant. Now a museum run by the Woodstock Historical Society, it contains period rooms full of fine china, antique furniture, kitchen instruments, and children's toys.

Art Galleries

It's easy to visit the town's vibrant art galleries on foot, as they're in a compact cluster at the center of town, on Elm and Center Streets.

Start at the town green, then walk to **The Woodstock Gallery** (6 Elm St., 802/457-2012, www.woodstockgalleryvt.com, 10am-5pm Mon.-Sat., 11am-4pm Sun.), where the imagery is closer to home. Fine and folk artists offer their takes on the New England landscape and other themes, and the gallery stocks a good selection of work by **Sabra Field,** a beloved Vermont artist who has captured the spirit of the state with striking woodblock prints.

Turn left on Center Street for a short stroll to **Collective—the art of craft** (46 Central St., 802/457-1298, www.collective-theartofcraft.com, 10am-5pm Mon.-Sat., 11am-4pm Sun.), where a small group of local artists and artisans display their work in an old stone mill. Handwoven fabrics, blown woodwork, and metalwork are y high quality.

turn and head back up the street **on the Green** (1 The Green, 6, www.galleryonthegreen.com, Mon.-Fri., 10am-6pm Sat., 11am- , which has an extensive collection of sweetly pastoral paintings by Chip Evans, as well as other fine examples of the New England "red barns and Holsteins" genre.

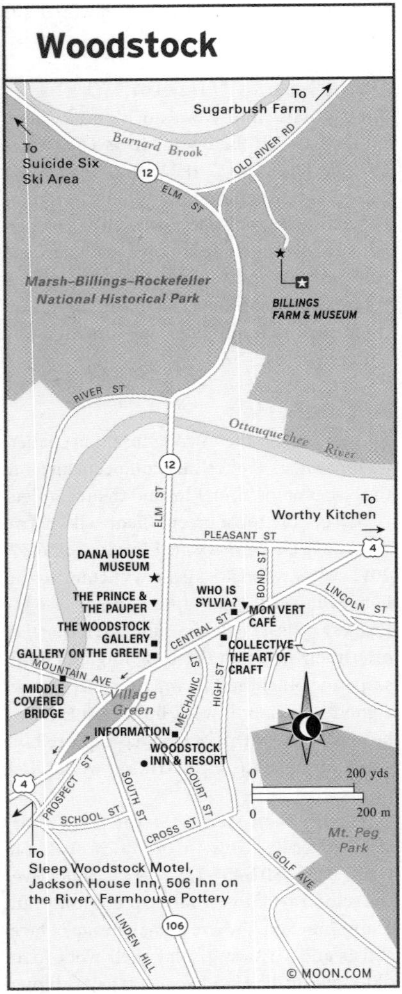

Around Woodstock

LONG TRAIL BREWING COMPANY

Back before there was a craft brewery in almost every village, there was **Long Trail Brewing Company** (5520 Rte. 4, Bridgewater Corners, 802/672-5011, www.longtrail.com, 10am-7pm daily, free), 15 minutes west of Woodstock. Long Trail started filling kegs in 1989, and their flagship amber ale is now ubiquitous in Vermont. If that's the only Long Trail brew you've tried, you'll be astounded by the selection at the brewery, which keeps around 13 beers on tap. Standouts include the barrel-aged triple bag, but the bartenders are through-and-through beer geeks who can help guide your selection. The brewery also has a menu of pub food served 11am-7pm, featuring wings, burgers, and other beer-friendly meals. A raised walkway overlooks the bottling and brewing facility, giving you a fascinating bird's-eye view of the action.

★ PRESIDENT CALVIN COOLIDGE STATE HISTORIC SITE

One of the best presidential historic sites in the country, the **President Calvin Coolidge State Historic Site** (3780 Rte. 100A, Plymouth, 802/672-3773, www.historicsites.vermont.gov/directory/coolidge, 9:30am-5pm daily late May-mid-Oct., $9 adults, $2 children 6-14, children under 6 free, $25 family pass) is situated on the grounds of the 30th president's boyhood home, a sprawling collection of houses, barns, and factories in a mountain-ringed valley. The exhibits inside give a rare intimate look into the upbringing of the president known as "Silent Cal" for his lack of emotion, but who restored the dignity of the office during a time of widespread scandal. The family parlor preserves the spot where Coolidge was sworn into office—by his father, a notary public. Even in 1924, when Calvin Coolidge ran for re-election, the homestead swearing-in must have seemed like a scene from a simple, earlier time—one radio

1: one of the resident goats at Billings Farm;
2: quaint downtown Woodstock

1
2

campaign ad described it in heavily nostalgic terms, pitching Cal as a rustic counterpoint to Washington, D.C.'s modernity and urban sophistication.

Plymouth is 14 miles southwest of Woodstock.

PLYMOUTH ARTISAN CHEESE

Plymouth Artisan Cheese (106 Messer Hill Rd., Plymouth Notch, 802/672-3650, www.plymouthartisancheese.com, 10am-4pm daily) was founded in 1890 by John Coolidge, Calvin Coolidge's father. Their granular curd cheeses were once relatively common in the United States, but are now rare. Learn about the cheesemaking process at the on-site museum, then sample everything from squeaky-fresh cheese curds to granular aged cheeses that have been hand dipped in wax.

Plymouth Notch is 15 miles southwest of Woodstock and a mile southwest of Plymouth.

EVENTS

Billings Farm sponsors many special events throughout the summer, including **Cow Appreciation Day** every July, which includes a judging of the Jerseys, ice cream and butter making, and (always gripping) dairy trivia, as well as a **Harvest** celebration in October with husking competitions and cider pressing. In late July, Woodstock gets wordy during **Bookstock** (www.bookstockvt.org), a festival that attracts an intriguing lineup of writers.

SHOPPING

Downtown Woodstock

Handmade pottery with a gorgeously modern aesthetic is the main draw at **Farmhouse Pottery** (1837 Rte. 4, 802/774-8373, www.farmhousepottery.com, 10am-5pm daily) where you can watch the artisans at work. The store also stocks maple rolling pins, candles, and a seemingly endless array of beautiful things.

Not your average vintage store, **Who Is Sylvia?** (26 Central St., 802/457-1110, 11am-5pm Sun.-Mon. and Thurs., 11am-6pm Fri.-Sat.) stocks flapper dresses, pillbox hats, brocade jackets, and other hard-to-find items dating back more than a century.

Bridgewater Mill Mall

Six miles west of Woodstock on Route 4, **Bridgewater Mill Mall** is filled with studio space for artisans and craftspeople. A highlight is **Shackleton Thomas** (102 Mill Rd., Bridgewater, 802/672-5175, www.shackletonthomas.com, 10am-5pm

Traditional methods are used at Plymouth Artisan Cheese.

Tues.-Sat., 11am-4pm Sun.), where Charles Shackleton—a distant relation of Antarctic explorer Ernest Shackleton—crafts simple but elegant Shaker and modern-style furniture. It's fascinating to watch the woodcarvers, who train for years, and the display room is also stocked with eclectic gifts with unusual charm.

FOOD

Dining on mostly fried, salty fare at a "snack bar" is a quintessential summer experience in Vermont, and **White Cottage** (863 Woodstock Rd., 802/457-3455, www.whitecottagesnackbar.com, 11am-10pm daily May-Oct., $3-22, cash only) is a fine place to get your fix. Golden mounds of fried clams come with tartar sauce and lemon, maple creemees are piled high on sugar cones, and hamburgers are simple and to-the-point. Snack bar food doesn't vary much from place to place, but White Cottage's outdoor tables, riverside location, and friendly staff make it a favorite—and you can wade in the river while you wait for your order.

Along with excellent espresso, **Mon Vert Cafe** (28 Central St., 802/457-7143, www.monvertcafe.com, 7:30am-5:30pm Mon.-Thurs., 7:30am-6:30pm Fri.-Sat., 8am-5:30pm Sun., breakfast $7-13, lunch $9-12) has fresh breakfast and lunch in a sunny and stylish spot. Breakfast burritos and baked goods give way to a lunch menu of sandwiches and panini. The café also prepares food to go, which makes for great road-tripping supplies.

Sedate and sophisticated in an old-fashioned way, **The Prince & The Pauper** (24 Elm St., 802/457-1818, www.princeandpauper.com, 5:30pm-8:30pm Sun.-Thurs., 5:30pm-9pm Fri.-Sat., $18-25) serves fine-dining classics—don't miss the restaurant's signature *carré d'agneau royale*, a tender dish of lamb, spinach, and mushrooms wrapped in puff pastry—in a candlelit country setting. Think high-backed wooden booths, exposed beams, and local art for sale on the wall. It's an ideal date setting, though families and groups are also welcome.

If you're looking for farm-to-table food that comes without a white tablecloth, ★ **Worthy Kitchen** (442 E. Woodstock Rd., 802/457-7281, www.worthyvermont.com, 4pm-9pm Mon.-Thurs., 4pm-10pm Fri., 11:30am-10pm Sat., 11:30am-9pm Sun., $8-15) is a "farm diner" that has a hearty selection of pub food with flair, from fried chicken to poutine. Burritos, nachos, and burgers are other favorites, and there's an excellent beer selection scrawled on chalkboards above the bar.

Pick up supplies at the confusingly named **Woodstock Farmers' Market** (979 W. Woodstock Rd., 802/457-3658, www.woodstockfarmersmarket.com, 7:30am-7pm Tues.-Sat.), which turns out to be a specialty food shop that stocks plenty of locally made treats, cheese, beer, wine, and everything else you might need for a showstopping picnic on the road.

ACCOMMODATIONS

Woodstock has some of the most appealing accommodations in the state. Prices tend to be higher than elsewhere and rise dramatically during peak foliage season, while off-season prices may be significantly lower than those listed.

$100-150

There's nothing fancy about **Sleep Woodstock Motel** (4324 W. Woodstock Rd., 802/332-6336, www.sleepwoodstock.com, $88-178, 2-bedroom suite $250-450), but a 2017 renovation has revitalized the property, which is a total bargain for the area. The roadside motel was built in 1959, and rooms retain a retro feel, but bathrooms are new and everything feels fresh and sunny. The motel is a short drive west of the center.

$150-250

Elegant, well-appointed rooms at the ★ **Jackson House Inn** (43 Senior Ln., 802/457-2065, www.jacksonhouse.com, $189-339) manage to avoid fussiness. Quarters in the main house are somewhat more in keeping with the old-fashioned style of the place, but new additions come with perks like massage tubs. Each one is different, so peek into a few before making your choice. The crackling fire is an appealing place to thaw, but in summer months the broad porch entices. The congenial owners, Rick and Kathy, are devoted to local food, and Rick prepares sumptuous breakfasts with ingredients from area farms.

The **506 on the River Inn** (1653 Rte. 4, 802/457-5000, www.ontheriverwoodstock.com, $139-379) was renovated in 2014 and has an appealingly updated take on Woodstock's genteel country style. Throw pillows are emblazoned with folksy Vermont expressions, antiques are used with restraint, and welcome extras include a game room, library, and toddler playroom. Breakfast is well prepared and lavish, served in a dining room and bar that open to the public at night. The inn's bistro menu covers classed-up pub food and child-friendly diner standbys like mac and cheese. If you're traveling with kids, ask at the front desk about borrowing their collection of child-size books, binoculars, telescopes, and microscopes.

Over $250

You can't miss the grand ★ **Woodstock Inn & Resort** (14 The Green, 802/457-1100 or 800/448-7900, www.woodstockinn.com, $235-820), which dominates the green in the heart of the village. The rooms and facilities are some of the prettiest in Vermont, full of thoughtful touches and design. This location has been a tourist destination since a tavern with accommodations was established in 1793, but Laurance Rockefeller built the current structure in the 1970s. There are seemingly endless facilities: spa, fitness center, cruiser bikes for exploring the town, organic gardens, and a celebrated 18-hole golf course. You can come take courses on farming and falconry, or just watch the weather from the glassed-in conservatory.

The exquisite and extravagant **Twin Farms** (452 Royalton Turnpike, Barnard, 800/894-6327, www.twinfarms.com, $1,450-2,800) is the former home of journalist Dorothy Thompson and Nobel laureate Sinclair Lewis, who was known for his stirring critiques of capitalism and materialism. Even he might be tempted by this alluring and romantic resort, where the rooms are kitted out with four-poster beds, fireplaces, whirlpool tubs, rare woods, and museum art, with views over a breathtaking property. Twin Farms is all-inclusive and offers an impressive suite of activities, along with remarkable food and drink.

Camping

Perched on the side of a valley, the campground at **Coolidge State Park** (855 Coolidge State Park Rd., Plymouth, 802/672-3612, https://vtstateparks.com, tent sites $18-22, lean-tos $25-29) has 26 wooded sites, some of which command excellent mountain views. Though the campground is rather more basic than other Vermont state park campgrounds, there are coin-operated hot showers in the restrooms, and most sites have fireplaces and grills that can (theoretically) be used for cooking.

SPORTS AND RECREATION

Hiking

In addition to the exhibits at **Marsh-Billings-Rockefeller National Historical Park** (54 Elm St., 802/457-3368, www.nps.gov/mabi, 10am-5pm daily Memorial Day-Oct., $8 adults, $4 seniors, children 15 and under free), the preserve has 20 miles of walking trails, which are accessible from the park entrance on Route 12 and a parking lot on Prosper Road. The roads circle around the slopes of Mount Tom, which is forested with old-growth hemlock, beech, and sugar maples. Popular hikes include the 0.7-mile loop around the mountain pond called **The Pogue** and the gentle, 1-mile climb up to the **South Summit** of Mount Tom, which lords over Woodstock and the river below. No mountain bicycles are allowed on the trails; in the winter, they are groomed for cross-country skiing.

It's also possible to walk 2.75 miles

round-trip to the summit of **Mount Tom** starting at the centrally located **Middle Covered Bridge** on Mountain Avenue. Cross the bridge and follow Mountain Avenue as it curves around to the left along a rock wall. An opening in the rock wall leads to the **Faulkner Trail** at Faulkner Park, where it begins to switchback up the gentle south flank of the peak. The last 300 feet of the trail get a bit steeper, giving wide views of the Green Mountains. Allow an hour for the hike.

Swimming

There's an actual swimming pool inside the **Woodstock Recreation Department** (54 River St., 802/457-1502, www.woodstockrec.com, 6am-8pm Mon.-Fri., 8am-2pm Sat., 9am-1pm Sun.), but the real treat is a dip in the **Ottauquechee River**. There's a short path that leaves from right behind the Rec Department, descending to a gentle swimming area that's suitable for families. On the very hottest days, the finest place to swim is in the **Quechee Gorge**, where the water seems to stay cool through the heat of the summer. To reach the best swimming area, take the trail from the visitors center, then turn left (downstream) as the Quechee Gorge Trail turns upstream, then follow the river for roughly 0.5 mile to a broad swimming hole.

Skiing and Snowshoeing

If you've had enough of the ruckus at Killington, the smaller, family-friendly **Suicide Six Ski Area** (802/457-6661, www.woodstockinn.com/ski-area, lifts operate 9am-4pm daily, $35/72 weekday/weekend adults, $30/55 weekday/weekend seniors and children 6-15, under 6 $10) might be just the thing. Now owned and operated by the Woodstock Inn, the resort is served by two chairlifts and a J-bar, and has two dozen trails, equitably split between beginner, intermediate, and advanced options. Children who are guests at the Woodstock Inn ski for free every day; adults, on weekends, peak dates excepted.

Also affiliated with the inn, the **Tubbs Snowshoe & Fischer Nordic Adventure Center** (Rte. 106/Cross St., 802/457-6674, www.woodstockinn.com, for day/half-day tickets are $25/20 adult, $18/13 youth and senior) has more than 18 miles of groomed trails; the first 6.2 miles cross an undulating meadow, before the trail weaves up and around Woodstock's two mountains, Mount Tom and Mount Peg. Don't miss the log cabin warming hut, where you can thaw out by a wood fire. The center also grooms trails for snowshoeing and winter hiking and has skis and snowshoes for rent.

INFORMATION AND SERVICES

The **Woodstock Area Chamber of Commerce** (888/469-6378, www.woodstockvt.com) runs a welcome center (3 Mechanic St., 802/432-1100, 9am-5pm daily) and an information booth (on the green). The well-stocked, independent **Woodstock Pharmacy** (19 Central St., 802/457-1306) is conveniently located in the center of town, as are the ATM machines at **People's United Bank** (2 The Green, 802/457-2660) and **Citizens Bank** (431 Woodstock Rd., 802/457-3666, 9am-5pm Mon.-Fri.). In an emergency, contact the **Woodstock Police** (454 Rte. 4, 802/457-1420).

GETTING THERE

To get to Woodstock from Boston, take I-93 to Concord (70 mi., 1.25 hrs.), then I-89 to White River Junction (70 mi., 1.25 hrs.), before exiting onto Route 4 west for another 10 miles (20 min.). The total trip from Boston to Woodstock is about 150 miles (2.75 hrs.).

Killington

Following the Ottauquechee River through the southern Green Mountains, Route 4 rolls right to the foot of the imposing Killington Peak. It's been a ski resort since 1958 and was ambitious from the first chair—Killington strung lift after lift on the neighboring peaks and became one of the first mountains to install snowmaking equipment. (It's still known as the first resort to open and last to close each year, though early- and late-season skiing may require dodging patches of grass.)

The mountain's very size and popularity led to some unattractive development on its flank—and the long, twisting Killington Road is now a very un-Vermont stretch of hotels, restaurants, and nightclubs extending up to the summit. Local may roll their eyes, but for some it's a welcome bit of civilization and fun in the middle of the woods.

The mountain can get crowded on big winter weekends, though Killington's scale offers notable advantages: varied terrain, 3,000 feet of vertical drop, and their unique "good snow guarantee." If you don't like the conditions, you can return your lift ticket. In recent years, Killington has added a popular downhill mountain biking area, with lift service and Vermont's most challenging terrain.

★ KILLINGTON RESORT

The mountain that gives Killington its name is only one of six peaks that make up **Killington Resort** (4763 Killington Rd., 800/621-6867, www.killington.com, $105 adults, $89 seniors, $81 youth 7-18, under 6 and over 80 ski free), a massive ski resort that boasts more than 200 trails. But the main event is still Killington Peak, where most of the toughest trails start their descent. The peak is accessible from the express gondola from the K-1 Lodge at the top of Killington Road.

Ten minutes west of Killington, the co-owned **Pico Mountain** (Rte. 4, 2 mi. west of Killington Rd., 866/667-7426, www.picomountain.com, $79 adults, $61 seniors, $67 youth 7-18, under 6 and over 80 ski free) is a quieter and less crowded mountain with 50-some trails and a family-friendly reputation. Pico is closed Tuesday and Wednesday outside of peak skiing weeks.

As might be expected, skiing is not the only way to hit the hill. **Killington Snowmobile Tours** (802/422-2121, www.snowmobilevermont.com) offers one-hour gentle rides along groomed ski trails ($99 single/$139 double), as well as a more challenging 25-mile, two-hour backcountry ride through Calvin Coolidge State Forest ($154/$199).

Both skate and classic skiers will love the gentle terrain at **Mountain Meadows Cross Country Ski and Snowshoe Center** (Rte. 4 at Rte. 100, 802/775-7077, www.xcskiing.net, $19 adult, $16 senior, $8 youth, under 6 free) where you can rent skis and snowshoes.

In the summer months, Killington has **mountain biking** on trails served by the K-1 Express Gondola, and the Snowshed Express Quad, that ranges from relatively approachable beginner trails to serious and challenging downhilling. A full day of lift and trail access is $60 for adults and $45 for youth, or you can sweat your way up the hill and ride the trails for $20. The resort also rents protective gear and full-suspension bikes.

ENTERTAINMENT AND EVENTS

Nightlife

For 50 years, the classic Killington spot has been **The Wobbly Barn** (2229 Killington Rd., 802/422-6171, www.wobblybarn.com, 8pm-2am daily Nov.-Apr., $20 cover for events) where there's a consistently boisterous crowd watching live music and dancing.

Toward the bottom of the access road, **JAX Food & Games** (1667 Killington Rd., 802/422-5334, www.supportinglocalmusic.

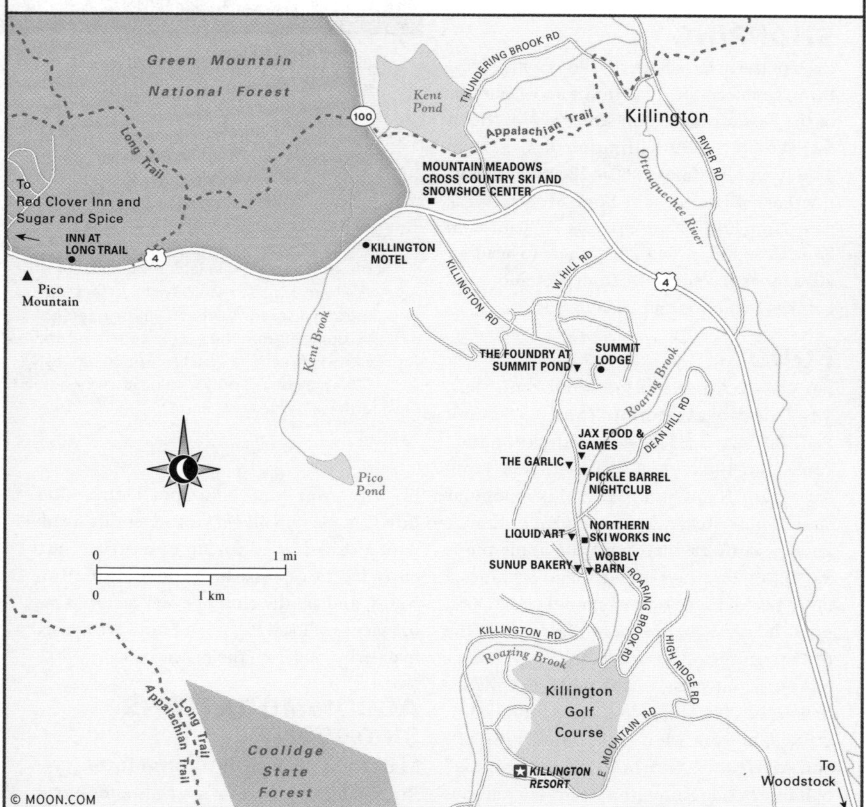

com, 3pm-2am daily) is a fun venue with plenty of live music and a game room with air hockey, arcade games, and pool. The **Pickle Barrel Night Club** (1741 Killington Rd., 802/422-3035, www.picklebarrelnightclub.com, 8pm-2am Thurs.-Sun. Oct.-Apr., $20) has three levels of dancing space, each with its own bar and loud music, and tends to attract a young party crowd.

Festivals and Events

Most months feature at least one or two festivals at Killington, so check the resort's **Events Calendar** (www.killington.com). Every summer, the **Killington Music Festival** (802/773-4003, www.killingtonmusicfestival.org) stages a series of classical music events called "Music in the Mountains," with musicians from around the country. The weekend before Labor Day, a thousand motorcyclists invade town for the **Killington Classic Motorcycle Rally** (518/798-7888, www.killingtonclassic.com). Events include a cycle rodeo and bike judging.

The **Killington Foliage Weekend** and **Brewfest Weekend** (802/422-6237, www.killington.com) overlap in the town center and on the local slopes every year, getting underway in late September and early October. Family activities, from hayrides to gondola tours, are a highlight, as are the handcrafted beers served.

SHOPPING

Each of the resorts have ski shops with everything you need for a day in the snow, but one of the best off-mountain stores is **Northern Ski Works** (2089 Killington Rd., next to The Wobbly Barn, 802/422-9675, www.northernski.com, 8am-8pm Mon.-Thurs., 8am-11pm Fri., 7:30am-9pm Sat., 7:30am-8pm Sun., closed May-Sept.). It's where to head for all manner of equipment, from snowshoes and helmets to boards and, of course, skis.

FOOD

For classic American fare done with flair, **The Foundry at Summit Pond** (63 Summit Path, 802/422-5335, www.foundrykillington.com, 3pm-10pm Mon.-Fri., 11:30am-11pm Sat., 11am-10pm Sun., $18-50) is a popular spot. Their steaks are superlative, there's an appealing raw bar, and the apple pie is a delight. The Tavern bar menu includes a more relaxed selection of sandwiches. Don't miss their ice-skating pond, just beside the restaurant.

You won't miss **Liquid Art** (37 Miller Brook Rd., 802/422-2787, www.liquidartvt.com, 8am-9pm Mon.-Fri., 7am-9pm Sat.-Sun. May-Nov., $4-10) in an eye-catching blue building beside Killington Road. They always open an hour before the lifts and have a hearty breakfast menu and locally roasted coffee. The menu is available all day, and the sandwiches and light fare include the most plentiful vegetarian options in town.

With a cozy feel and a popular bar, **The Garlic** (1724 Killington Rd., 802/422-5055, www.thegarlicvermont.net, 5pm-10pm daily, $10-30) serves Italian classics like osso bucco and pasta puttanesca that are perfect for a post-ski meal. It's cozy, dim, and the closest that Killington's eateries get to subdued.

The cheerful early birds at **Sunup Bakery** (2250 Killington Rd., 802/422-3865, www.sunupbakery.com, 7am-5pm Mon.-Fri., 6:30am-5pm Sat.-Sun. Nov.-Apr., 7am-3pm Fri.-Sun. May-June, 7am-3pm Thurs.-Mon. July-Oct., $3-8) will get you adventure-ready with a carb-loaded lineup of pastries (seriously, try the espresso bread pudding muffin), soups, and sandwiches of every stripe. They use plenty of local ingredients and are housed in a perky chalet on the main road.

And Everything Nice . . .

Breakfast fiends come from all over to dig into the groaning platters of truly excellent pancakes cooked up at **Sugar and Spice** (Rte. 4, Mendon, 802/773-7832, www.vtsugarandspice.com, 7am-2pm daily, $6-11), a working sugar shack turned restaurant that's 10 miles west of Killington. Feather-light and studded with juicy blueberries, the specialties are a thing worthy of addiction—especially under a pour of the house-made maple syrup. In fact, during sugar season waitstaff will draw off hot syrup right from the evaporation tank and bring it directly to your table upon request. (This may be the only breakfast spot where artificial syrup costs extra.)

ACCOMMODATIONS

$100-150

The rooms at the **Killington Motel** (1946 Rte. 4, 800/366-0493, www.killingtonmotel.com, $119-240) are clean and comfortable, and the owners, Robin and Steve, are friendly enough to inspire a loyal following who return year after year. The place has an unselfconsciously retro vibe and is one of the best places for value in the area. Steve roasts coffee beans on-site, and wintertime rates include an appealing breakfast.

Several generations of Saint Bernards have greeted guests at the **Summit Lodge** (200 Summit Rd., off Killington Rd., 800/635-6343, www.summitlodgevermont.com, $99-219), which is as famous for its canine companions

1: ski lift at Killington Resort; **2:** Michael's Toy Company in downtown Rutland

1

2

as it is for its congenial staff. Even though the lodge is only a few minutes away from Killington Resort, its position at the top of a steep hill makes it feel secluded. Rooms are nothing fancy but are quiet and clean, with friendly service. A pool and reading room offer extra relaxation.

$150-250

Twenty minutes away from the ski lifts, the **Red Clover Inn** (7 Woodward Rd., Mendon, 802/775-2290, www.redcloverinn.com, $199-340) feels a world away from Killington's bustling scene. Set on a rambling property that once housed a goat farm, the guest rooms retain a country charm and quiet that are enhanced by the lack of in-room televisions. The inn's restaurant and diminutive bar are enough to keep you in for the evening, with local beers, cocktails, and a well-crafted menu that makes the dining room a destination.

Over $250

If you book a slope-side room at the **Killington Grand Resort Hotel** (228 E. Mountain Rd., 802/422-5001, www.killington.com, $350 and up), you can spend your evening watching the grooming machines crawl up and down the mountain like glowworms. The comfortable rooms include access to the excellent health club, and there's a spa and restaurant on-site.

Camping

Gifford Woods State Park (34 Gifford Woods Rd., 802/775-5354, https://vtstateparks.com) has 4 cabins, 22 tent sites, and 20 lean-tos for overnights (campsites $18-29/night, cabins $48-50/night). The northern tent loop is much more secluded than the southern one. Several "prime" lean-tos are especially secluded in one of Vermont's only old-growth hardwood forests, made up of giant sugar maple, white ash, and beech trees.

SPORTS AND RECREATION

Hiking

In addition to the hiking trails at Killington, a popular short trek is the one up to the scenic overlook on Deer Leap Mountain, located in **Gifford Woods State Park** (34 Gifford Woods Rd., 802/775-5354, https://vtstateparks.com). The trail starts behind the Inn at Long Trail on Route 4 and is two miles round-trip to fantastic views of Pico Peak and Killington Mountain.

To summit the main attraction, trek the **Bucklin Trail** to the top of Killington Peak. The 7.2-mile out-and-back starts from the Bucklin Trailhead (20 Wheelerville Rd., Mendon), and follows a west-facing ridgeline for 3.3 miles before intersecting with the Long Trail. A 0.2 mile spur from the Long Trail leads to the rocky, exposed peak, where you can see all the way to Mount Mansfield on a clear day.

Swimming and Fishing

The Appalachian Trail runs right past **Kent Pond** (access on Thundering Brook Rd., off of Rte. 4), but you don't have to be a "thru-hiker" to enjoy the scenic swimming spot. The pond is ringed by low mountains and stocked with both brook and rainbow trout.

INFORMATION AND SERVICES

The **Killington Chamber of Commerce** (2026 Rte. 4, 802/773-4181, www.killingtonchamber.com) operates a visitor information center at the intersection of Route 4 and Killington Road. Near the same intersection is a branch of **Lake Sunapee Bank** (1995 Rte. 4, 802/773-2581). Additional ATMs are available at **Merchants Bank** (286 Rte. 7 S., Rutland, 802/747-5000, 9am-5pm Mon.-Thurs., 9am-6pm Fri.) as well as at Killington Resort's base lodge. For condos and hotel reservations, you can also try the helpful **Killington Resort's Central Reservations**

(800/621-6867), which is especially useful for large groups.

GETTING THERE AND AROUND

Killington is a 20-mile (30-min.) drive down Route 4 from Woodstock. For such a popular destination, public transport options are limited. It's possible to schedule pickup service with **Killington Transportation** (802/770-3977) from Rutland or White River Junction. Within Killington, the resort offers shuttle bus service between the various base lodges and nearby lodging.

Rutland and Vicinity

Vermont's second-largest city is tucked into a valley between the Green Mountains and the Taconic Range, but the scenic location is overshadowed by some ugly sprawl and a downtown that's looking rather worn, despite a few interesting places to pause and explore. Most visitors pass through here on their way to somewhere else, which means that Rutland's main accommodation options are chain hotels spread out along Route 7, universally seen by locals one of Vermont's least appealing stretches of road. Here, as elsewhere in Vermont, it's worth finding the slow way to wherever you're going: The scrappy outskirts of town turn to forests and fields dotted with intriguing historical sites and are shot through with cobalt lakes and rivers. The surrounding countryside has several appealing bed-and-breakfasts and two museums—maple and marble—that illustrate the history of this working landscape. As in other quarrying regions in Vermont, the cemeteries are worth a stop; they're full of elaborate headstones commemorating the stoneworkers who came here from around the globe, when Rutland was sending marble to grace some of the world's grandest facades.

RUTLAND

A 19th-century world leader in marble production, this working-class town has been down and out for generations. Once quarrying slowed, the Marble City lacked the transportation infrastructure to grow alternative commerce, the interstate passed it by, and the once-bustling railroad station was replaced by a Wal-Mart. Even normally polite Vermonters are hard on Rutland, giving it the mocking and somewhat mystifying nickname of "RutVegas," which supposedly refers to Rutland's sprawled out "strip."

But there is a threadbare charm to the once resplendent downtown, to the grand faded houses ringed by elegant porches, and the brick facades with art deco flourishes. Rutland is dotted by magnificent marble installations made by the skilled masons—mostly Italian, Irish, Polish, French Canadian—who lived and worked here, and there are pockets of upstart vibrancy, too. Downtown has a growing collection of tempting cafés and art galleries maintained by dedicated locals, and if you came here believing the bad rap on Rutland, you may find that its charm is only heightened by being unexpected.

Sights

For 15 years, artist Norman Rockwell lived and painted in nearby Arlington. On the eastern outskirts of Rutland, the small **Norman Rockwell Museum** (654 Rte. 4, 802/773-6095, www.normanrockwellvt.com, 9am-5pm daily, $6.50 adults, $6 seniors, $2.50 children ages 8-17, children under 8 free), located just across the Rutland city line on Route 4, doesn't contain any original work by the artist. It does, however, present an impressive overview of his career via several thousand original magazine covers, books, and reproductions—from Rockwell's beginnings in the 1910s as art editor of *Boys' Life* magazine to the illustration of Johnny Carson he made for

Rutland and Vicinity

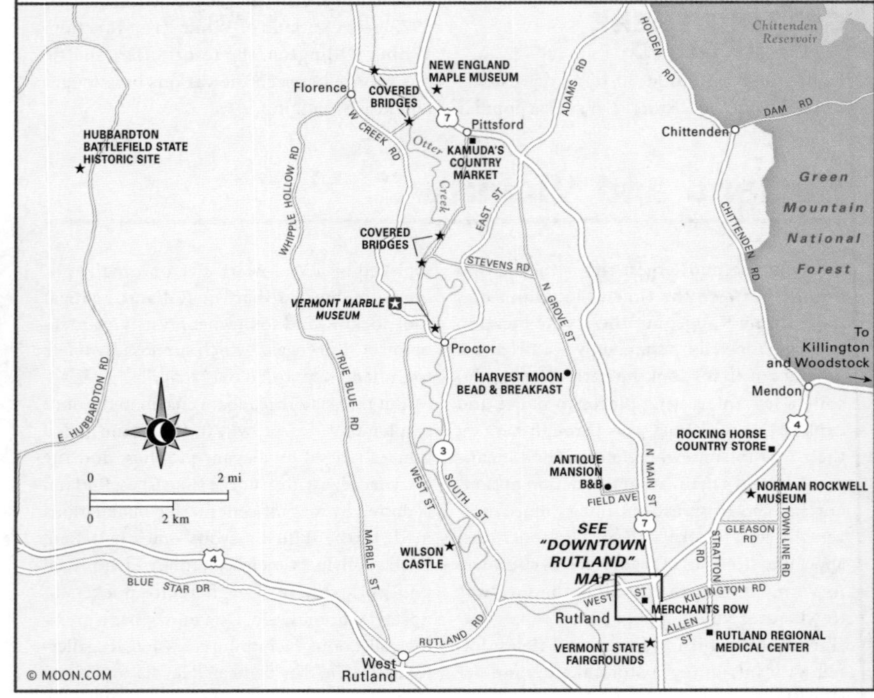

TV Guide shortly before his death in 1978. A sizable gift shop has both original covers and reproduction posters.

Artwork by local students and artists fills the **Chaffee Art Center** (16 S. Main St., 802/775-0356, www.chaffeeartcenter.org, open only for scheduled exhibits), housed in a gorgeous 1896 Queen Anne mansion that gives visitors a backdrop for imagining Rutland's glory days. Their centrally located **Chaffee Downtown** (75 Merchants Row, 10am-5pm Mon.-Fri., 9am-3pm Sat.) has rotating exhibits; a recent show featured the work of the Vermont Pastel Society.

Entertainment and Events

Once upon a time, the **Paramount Theatre** (30 Center St., 802/775-0570, www.paramountvt.org) drew top names such as Harry Houdini, Groucho Marx, and Sarah Bernhardt. The interior has been restored to the Victorian splendor that was retro even when it was built 100 years ago, and it now hosts a lively lineup of movies, music, and dance.

Every September since 1846, the **Vermont State Fair** (175 S. Main St., 802/775-5200, www.vermontstatefair.net, $5-10 adults and youth, $4-5 seniors, children under 12 free) lights up the Vermont sky with a Ferris wheel and other thrilling midway rides and hosts the state's premier agricultural competitions. One recent fair included the state championship demolition derby, equestrian harness races, and musical performances by country legends Randy Travis and Charlie Daniels. Throughout the year, the fairgrounds play host to other agricultural and musical events.

Rutland

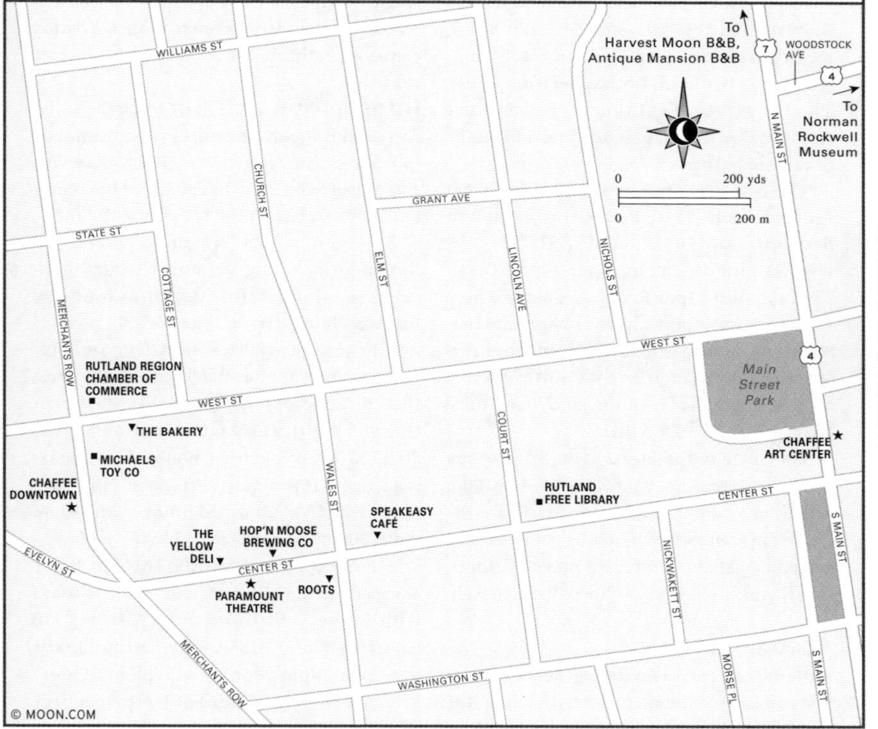

Shopping

A play-ready collection of handcrafted wooden trucks and whimsical toys fills the shelves at **Michael's Toy Company** (64 Merchants Row, 802/773-3765, www.michaelstoys.com, 9am-5pm Mon.-Fri., 9am-4pm Sat.), which is packed to the gills with time-warp treasures. It's sweetly quirky, and well worth a browse even if you're not shopping for pint-size fire engines; the wheels on the race cars are cut from "blanks" that Michael collects from a nearby baseball bat factory.

Food

For inspired local fare in Rutland, the clear choice is ★ **Roots** (51 Wales St., 802/747-7414, www.rootsrutland.com, 11am-9pm Tues.-Thurs. and Sun., 11am-10pm Fri.-Sat., $17-23) with options ranging from shrimp and sausage risotto to the adventurous chimichurri emu. The colorful dining room is intimate and lively.

You can get food for thought along with your soup, salad, or sandwich at **The Yellow Deli** (23 Center St., 802/775-9800, www.yellowdeli.com, open 24 hours Mon.-Thurs., midnight-3pm Fri., noon-midnight Sun., $6-8), which is more hippie than hipster and a project of the collective Christian community Twelve Tribes, which some have accused of cultlike practices. The psychedelic interior feels a world (and a few decades) away from downtown Rutland, and the outgoing group maintains a hiker's hostel for "thru-hikers" on the Long Trail.

More mainstream fare is available at **The Bakery** (122 West St., 802/775-3220, www.rootsrutland.com, 6am-5pm Mon.-Fri., 6am-4pm Sat., $3-10), run by the chef from Roots. They've got excellent sandwiches on their freshly baked bread, pastries, and a full suite of caffeinated brews.

The best pizza in town happens to be at Rutland's only brewpub, the **Hop'n Moose Brewing Co.** (41 Center St., 802/775-7063, www.hopnmoose.com, 4pm-10pm Tues.-Thurs., noon-11pm Fri.-Sat., $8-12) where you can nurse a pint while watching the flatbreads slide into a wood-fired oven. The beers are constantly changing, so it's worth ordering a flight to get the lay of the land, but a local favorite is the Rutland Red.

The coffee and ambience at the **Speakeasy Café** (67 Center St., 802/747-3325, 7am-6pm Mon.-Fri., 8am-4pm Sat.-Sun., $2-5) are the hippest in town, with cheerfully painted walls, art, and a gleaming espresso maker. Bridget, the friendly owner, bakes the pastries herself.

Accommodations

Rutland has surprisingly few accommodations aside from the chain hotels that line "the strip" along Route 7, but there are a couple of gems right in town.

Harvest Moon Bed & Breakfast (1659 N. Grove St., 802/773-0889 www.harvestmoonvt.com, $95-130) is just 10 minutes away from downtown Rutland, but the historical farmhouse is a different world altogether. The friendly owners have created a homey atmosphere with just two guest rooms and serve homemade vegetarian breakfasts that use some ingredients from their organic garden. The broad view across the valley is extraordinary all year.

The aptly named **Antique Mansion B&B** (85 Field Ave., 802/855-8372, www.antiquemansionbb.com, $129-139) channels Rutland's glory days in a stately home surrounded by trees and rolling lawns. Breakfasts are a highlight, as are the owner's outgoing cats. The Arabella Rose Room has single occupancy rates of $109, and the spacious Fletcher Suite comes with a dreamy claw-foot bathtub.

Information and Services

Rutland Region Chamber of Commerce (50 Merchants Row, 802/773-2747, www.rutlandvermont.com) has plenty of brochures and maps and a helpful, friendly staff.

Emergency services are centered in Rutland—including Vermont's second-largest hospital. **Rutland Regional Medical Center** (160 Allen St., 802/775-7111) offers a full range of services, inpatient and outpatient. Several pharmacies are in the area, though none operate all night. Most central are **Walgreens** (10 Woodstock Ave., 802/773-6980, open 24 hours daily, pharmacy 8am-10pm Mon.-Fri., 9am-5pm Sat.-Sun.) and **CVS** (31 N. Main St., 8am-10pm daily, 802/775-6736).

A number of banks with ATMs line Route 4, especially on either side of the crossroads with Route 7. **Rutland Free Library** (10 Court St., 802/773-1860, www.rutlandlibrary.org, 10am-7pm Mon.-Wed., 10am-5:30pm Thurs.-Fri, 10am-5pm Sat.) provides free Wi-Fi to patrons.

State troopers can be found at **Vermont State Police** (124 State Pl., 802/773-9101), and local authorities are at **Rutland Police** (108 Wales St., 802/773-1816).

SOUTH OF RUTLAND

Clarendon Gorge

The Long Trail passes right over a series of swimming holes that are a 15-minute drive south of Rutland. To reach the **Clarendon Gorge,** follow Route 7 south from town, then turn east on Route 103. Look for the Long Trail parking lot on the right side of the road after 2.2 miles. From the trailhead, follow the Long Trail south for five minutes, then descend to the river after crossing the suspension bridge.

Sugaring Off

Spring in Vermont is better known as "mud season," when frozen back roads melt into quagmires, and precipitation falls as a slushy wintry mix. But the period from mid-March until early April is also **sugaring season,** when a precise cycle of alternating freezes and thaws kick-starts the sugar maples' vascular systems and causes sap to flow. When that happens, sugar makers collect the slightly sweet liquid by drilling tapholes into each tree and collecting the runoff in metal buckets or plastic tubing that runs through the forest like spiderwebs.

Once they have enough sap, sugar makers boil it in a wide, shallow pan called an evaporator, usually heated by wood gathered in the surrounding hills, and cook it down until it turns thick and golden—the ratio of sap to syrup varies from tree to tree but averages around 40:1.

Sugaring is a social event in Vermont, and neighbors have a sixth sense for when someone's boiling. Over the course of an evening in the sugarhouse, friends will drop by for beer and conversation, along with shots of hot, fresh syrup, right out of the pan. Everyone's got a favorite sugaring snack, from hot dogs boiled in sap to syrup poured over vanilla ice cream. You can discover yours at the yearly Maple Open House Weekend (www.vermontmaple.org, mid-Mar.) when sugarhouses around the state open their doors to visitors and prepare all the traditional treats. Don't miss sugar-on-snow: Syrup is cooked to a taffy-like consistency and served with a pickle.

PROCTOR AND PITTSFORD

North of Rutland, the Green Mountains relax into classically pastoral scenery, in a wide, rolling valley flanked by foothills. The landscape is punctuated by marble flourishes, like **Proctor**'s gracefully arched bridge and fascinating cemetery, complete with Greek Revival crypts. The legacy of the valley's agricultural and industrial past lives on in two museums, one dedicated to maple, the other to marble. North of Proctor, get off of Route 7 to explore the back roads of **Pittsford,** a colonial-era village known for its concentration of covered bridges.

New England Maple Museum

Vermont bottles an estimated 500 million gallons of maple syrup each year—accounting for more than a third of the output of the entire country. It's a remarkable process that depends on precise weather conditions and sugar makers who tend to their trees all year. Learn a bit of syrup's poetry and production at the **New England Maple Museum** (Rte. 7, just north of Pittsford, 802/483-9414, www.maplemuseum.com, call for hours, $5 adults, $1 children, under 6 free) north of Rutland. The roadside museum itself has the feeling of an artifact, with timeworn dioramas and displays, but the exhibits are informative, and they've got a great collection of antique syrup jugs. Once you grasp the vast amount of work that goes into turning 40 gallons of sap into a jug of syrup, you may find it tastes even sweeter.

★ Vermont Marble Museum

On the grounds of an abandoned quarry, the **Vermont Marble Museum** (52 Main St., Proctor, 800/427-1396, www.vermontmarble.com, 10am-5pm daily mid-May-Oct., $9 adults, $7 seniors, $4 children 6-18, children under 6 free, purchase tickets in advance for a $1 discount on adult admission) is filled with exhibits and photographs that tell the story of the Rutland marble industry and the thousands of immigrants who once labored in the quarries. A grand gallery contains marble bas-reliefs of all of the nation's presidents, along with other marble statuary carved over the years. Modern-day marble carver Allen Dwight, the museum's artist-in-residence, gives demonstrations on the craft.

Wilson Castle

Near the Vermont Marble Museum is **Wilson Castle** (2909 W. Proctor Rd., Proctor,

802/773-3284, www.wilsoncastle.com, 9am-5pm daily late May-mid-Oct., $12 adults, $11 seniors and AAA members, $6 children 6-12, children under 6 free), built in the late 19th century by a doctor with a taste for extravagance. Now rather in need of repairs, the five-story mansion is a mishmash of European styles, with 19 proscenium arches, a turret, a parapet, and a balcony. Inside, the building is filled with antiques from around the world, including Chinese scrolls, Tiffany chandeliers, and a Louis XVI crown jewel case. Guided tours lasting 45 minutes are given throughout the day. (Last tour leaves at 5pm.) If you can, time your visit for a Sunday morning, when an electronic organ fills the art gallery with church music, or selected evenings in October, when nighttime "haunted tours" amplify the castle's creepy grandeur.

Covered Bridges

One of the more attractive covered bridges in the state, the 144-foot **Gorham Bridge,** is just north of Proctor center, where Gorham Bridge Road crosses Otter Creek. Farther down the same road, take a turn onto Elm Street to find the **Cooley Bridge,** a 53-foot bridge over Furnace Creek. North of Pittsford, take Kendall Hill Road to view **Hammond Bridge,** a 139-foot bridge similar in design to Gorham Bridge, though closed to traffic. As you continue to Depot Hill Road, the 121-foot **Depot Bridge** also crosses Otter Creek, with the road continuing on back to Route 7.

Events

The **Proctor Fall Festival** (Main Street Park, Proctor, 802/770-7223, mid-Sept.) features fall foliage train rides, a pumpkin pie competition, and sales of marble gifts.

Shopping

An almost daily stop for many locals, **Kamuda's Country Market** (Rte. 7 between Rutland and Brandon, Pittsford, 802/483-2361, 7am-7pm Mon.-Fri., 7am-6pm Sat., 7am-1pm Sun.) is where to find tasty made-to-order sandwiches, souvenirs, greeting cards, and a bevy of Vermont-made specialties to take home.

Food

If knocking back samples at the New England Maple Museum left you hungry for more, head to **JR's Eatery** (4601 Rte. 7, Pittsford, 802/483-2318, 6am-2pm Sat.-Wed., 6am-8pm Thurs.-Fri., $5-12), where the Formica bar and country curtains feel like your grandparents' living room, with food to match. Piles of buttermilk pancakes—with or without blueberries—drip syrup and butter, and specials like shepherd's pie are filling comfort food at its best.

SOUTHWESTERN LAKES REGION

The sleepy swath of farmland and villages west of Rutland isn't on the way to anywhere, and tourists often overlook it entirely. General stores and clapboard churches don't look overly shined up here, and their parking lots tend to be full of pickup trucks with local plates. But the hilly landscape invites leisurely drives and contemplation, and it's stippled with lakes, including Lake Bomoseen and Lake Saint Catherine, two of the prettiest in the state. In fact, these hills are part of the Taconics, a geologically distinct mountain range that continues south through New York state. While most villages don't have many "sights" to speak of, the downtowns of **Castleton** and **Poultney** are both on the Register of Historic Places for their profusion of Federal-style architecture.

Hubbardton Battlefield State Historic Site

Early on in the Revolutionary War, the Americans at Fort Ticonderoga and Mount Independence were outflanked by the British and made a hasty retreat south through Vermont. The British, under General "Gentleman Johnnie" Burgoyne, caught up with them near the hamlet of Hubbardton. There, a rear guard of more than a thousand troops led by Green Mountain Boys colonel Seth Warner stayed back to delay the Redcoats by setting up defenses on a hilltop and repulsing repeated attacks. The action, one of the most successful rearguard actions in history, headed off the British advance as Burgoyne stayed behind for several days to bury dead and rest his troops, allowing American general Arthur St. Clair to escape with his men and eventually return victorious at the Battle of Saratoga.

Today, the **Hubbardton Battlefield State Historic Site** (5696 Monument Rd., Bomoseen, 802/759-2412, www.hubbardton.net, 10am-5pm Wed.-Sun. late May-mid-Oct., $3 adults, children under 15 free) includes a visitors center with relics of the battle, along with a three-dimensional map with fiber-optic lighting that takes visitors inside the heat of the engagement.

Events

The highlight of the year in these parts is the annual **Frosty Derby** (Poultney, 802/287-9742, www.poultneyareachamber.com, early Mar.), an ice-fishing contest on Lake Saint Catherine that brings residents out for fierce competition for bass, perch, and pike as well as general winter merriment.

Shopping

For souvenirs that bridge the gap between strange and spot-on, the **Original Vermont Gift Shop** (163 Main St., Poultney, 802/287-9111, www.originalvermontstore.com, 10am-5pm Wed.-Sat., 11am-3pm Sun.) is one-stop shopping. Think pineapple motifs on home accessories, slate hangings, old-fashioned homemade jams, children's books, and maple cookies, along with delectable fudge.

Or jump back in time with a walk through **East Poultney General Store** (11 On the Green, East Poultney, 802/287-4042, 7:30am-7pm Mon.-Sat.). The 1830s country store sells lots of snacks, candy, toys, and crafts and even houses its own post office. The other old-fashioned spot to shop is **Otto's Cones Point General Store** (3816 Rte. 30, Poultney, 802/287-9925, www.ottosconespoint.com, 6am-9pm Sun.-Thurs., 6am-10pm Fri.-Sat., $3-14), a market that also offers ice cream and a menu of sandwiches and burgers. Call 48 hours ahead, and you can pick up a whole coconut cream pie or a cake.

Food

A favorite for breakfasts is **Perry's Main Street Eatery** (253 Main St., Poultney, 802/287-5188, 6am-7pm Mon., 6am-8pm Tues.-Thurs., 6am-9pm Fri.-Sat., 6am-2pm Sun., $9-16) where the memorable French toast is made with house-made bread, but the

reliving Revolutionary history at the Hubbardton Battlefield State Historic Site

chicken and biscuits and burgers might bring you back for dinner.

For more classic American fare, **Tot's Diner** (84 Main St., Poultney, 802/287-2213, 7am-noon Sun.-Fri., 8am-1pm Sat., $6-12) is a great place to mix with locals and fill up on big stacks of pancakes, club sandwiches, and heaping slices of pie.

Excellent sandwiches come with German potato salad or coleslaw at **Sissy's Kitchen** (10 West St., Middletown Springs, 802/235-2000, www.sissyskitchen.com, 9am-6pm Thurs.-Sat., 9am-4pm Sun., $6-13), a laid-back little spot that's more or less in the middle of nowhere. Breakfast features waffles, egg sandwiches, and house-made corned beef hash, and many menu items are made from locally sourced, organic ingredients. One great bonus—whether you're camping or have a spot with a kitchen—is that there's a cooler stocked with dinner items that are easy to prepare and completely delicious.

Accommodations

Steps away from Green Mountain College, **The Bentley House Bed & Breakfast** (399 Bentley Ave., Poultney, 802/287-4004, www.thebentleyhouse.com, $107-148) pampers with soft comforters and a country aesthetic. The Queen Anne home is graced with lots of stained-glass windows, period antiques, and a wraparound porch that's perfect for relaxing.

An country inn with a backdrop of forested hills, the **Pond Mountain Inn** (1955 Saw Mill Hill Rd., Wells, 802/325-2829, www.pondmountaininn.com, 1-2 adults $179-199, 3-5 adults $199-219) has an apartment and guest cottage that are well appointed and comfortable. The rooms are equipped with kitchens, and guests have access to the outdoor barbecue, decks, and other comfortable spaces to lounge. A rare, rural spot that's easy to reach by train, the inn is 15 minutes from the Castleton Amtrak station, and the innkeepers offer free pickup.

CAMPING

There's a campground wrapped around a peaceful pond at **Half Moon Pond State Park** (1621 Black Pond Rd., Hubbardton, 802/273-2848, https://vtstateparks.com, campsites $18-29, cabins $48-50), an area within Bomoseen State Park. It's clean, quiet, and family oriented, and the campers-only swimming area means that there's always an uncrowded place for a dip on hot days.

Also popular is the campground at **Lake St. Catherine State Park** (3034 Rte. 30, Poultney, 802/287-9158, https://vtstateparks.com, campsites $18-29), which has 50 tent/trailer sites and 11 lean-tos located in a mix of grassy and wooded sites. The prime spots are the five tent sites along the lakes and the dozen or so located in a wooded loop by Parker Brook. The park is a great one for kids, with a play area, two sandy beaches, a snack bar, and a large grassy field to get out their energy. Unlike Bomoseen, Lake St. Catherine doesn't have a lot of hiking trails, but it does have a one-mile nature trail through the famed "Big Trees" of St. Catherine (enormous red oak and other species), which includes a stunning view of nearby Birdseye Mountain.

Information and Services

For information on the area, contact the **Poultney Area Chamber of Commerce** (802/287-2010, www.poultneyvt.com). **Drake's Pharmacy** (188 Main St., Poultney, 802/287-5281) is conveniently located downtown.

SPORTS AND RECREATION

Hiking and Biking

There are several scenic hikes in **Bomoseen State Park** (22 Cedar Mountain Rd., Fair Haven, 802/265-4242, https://vtstateparks.com), including the moderate 1.5-mile **Bomoseen Hiking Loop,** which takes hikers through an overgrown early 20th-century farm. Look out for apple trees, where deer, fox, and other wildlife are wont to congregate for a snack. The more strenuous **Glen Lake Trail** stretches for more than four miles of beaver ponds, slate cliffs, and meadows; the highlight is a 100-meter-high overlook with spacious views of Glen Lake. The park has 56 tent sites and 10 lean-tos in a mix of wooded and grassy spots. The most desirable are the 5 lean-tos located directly on the lakeshore (ask for Deer, Porcupine, Coyote, Squirrel, or Moose). The campground is a busy one, with a snack bar concession stand and boat rentals on the beach.

Within the **Lake St. Catherine State Park** (3034 Rte. 30, Poultney, 802/287-9158, https://vtstateparks.com), a mile-long nature trail passes towering stands of red oak and other deciduous trees.

Cross the road from Lake St. Catherine to find a few more miles of hiking trails at **Endless Brook Trails** (975 Endless Brook Rd., Poultney, www.slatevalleytrails.org), which are designed for hiking and easy mountain biking. The longest of the trails is 1.9 miles, but by linking together the different loops, you can spend half a day winding through the forest. Trail maps are available for download on the Slate Valley Trails website.

Boating and Fishing

A boat ramp at the southern end of **Lake St. Catherine State Park** (3034 Rte. 30, Poultney, 802/287-9158, https://vtstateparks.com) offers access to the lake's crystal clear water. For those without their own craft, the park rents canoes. Boat rentals including kayaks, canoes, rowboats, and paddleboats are also available at the campground at **Bomoseen State Park** (22 Cedar Mountain Rd., Fair Haven, 802/265-4242, https://vtstateparks.com, $7.50-15/hr., $20-32/half day, $35-50/full day). Bomoseen and St. Catherine are also famed for their vigorous population of rainbow trout, pike, and largemouth and smallmouth bass.

If you're out for a paddle, you can peer at the privately owned **Neshobe Island,** which was once the property of writer Alexander Woollcott, who visited throughout the 1920s and '30s with other members of the Algonquin Round Table, a group of New York intellectuals and creative types. The island is the setting for the fictionalized satirical book *Entirely Surrounded* by Charles Brackett.

Horseback Riding

A 2,000-acre horse ranch outside Castleton, **Pond Hill Ranch** (1373 Rte. 4, East Castleton, 802/468-2449, www.pondhillranch.com, $40 pp for hour-long ride, appointments necessary) leads daily horseback rides on backcountry trails; ponies are available for the kids.

Rock Climbing

An 8,000-square-foot gym with dozens of rope stations on 25-foot climbing walls is just the beginning at the **Green Mountain Rock Climbing Center** (223 Woodstock Ave., Rutland, 802/773-3343, www.vermontclimbing.com, $18 adults, $15 youth, $10 children under 6). Owner Steve Lulek, who once served as head instructor at the military's Mountaineering School, also leads a full range of mountaineering classes and guided tours of Deer's Leap and other nearby cliff faces through his companion outfit, **Vermont Adventure Tours** (www.vermontadventuretours.com).

GETTING THERE AND AROUND

Rutland is 15 miles (20 min.) west of Killington on Route 4 and 35 miles (45 min.) north of Manchester or 15 miles (20 min.) south of Brandon on Route 7. From Rutland, Castleton is 15 miles (20 min.) west on Route 4, while Poultney is another 8 miles (15 min.) south on Route 30.

In terms of public transportation, Rutland is a major transportation hub. Continental's CommutAir flies routes from Boston to **Rutland Airport** (802/747-9963, www.flyrutlandvt.com) starting at around $150 round-trip. **Amtrak** (800/872-7245, www.amtrak.com) runs trains to Rutland with its Ethan Allen service from New York City, stopping at the Rutland Depot behind Wal-Mart. **Vermont Transit Lines** (800/642-3133, www.vttranslines.com) runs buses to Rutland's bus station (102 West St., 802/773-2774). **Marble Valley Regional Transit** (802/773-3244) runs bus routes throughout the Rutland area.

rlington and e Champlain Valley

Lake Champlain is New England's grandest lake,

with a meandering shoreline that offers expansive views of the mountains that line its flanks.

The whalebones and shipwrecks beneath the lake's surface are clues to its former lives as an inland sea, trading hub, and site of fierce naval battles during the Revolutionary War. Lake Champlain joins the Hudson River to the St. Lawrence and is the gateway to the far north; a stick dropped into Burlington Bay could drift all the way to Newfoundland's chilly shores. The water that rose and fell though the Champlain Valley's glaciations left behind rich clay soils that now support thriving farms—and dairy cows that graze with views of two mountain ranges.

Highlights

Look for ★ to find recommended sights, activities, dining, and lodging.

★ **Burlington's Waterfront Park:** Everyone comes out for sunset at the city's lakefront, lining up for maple creemees and watching the sun sink behind the Adirondack Mountains (page 116).

★ **Pine Street Breweries:** Sample Burlington's best beer and cider at the walkable cluster of breweries in an artsy neighborhood south of downtown (page 123).

★ **Burlington Bike Path:** A lakeside bike path runs right through downtown Burlington, then continues into the middle of Lake Champlain on a slender raised causeway (page 129).

★ **Paddling Lake Champlain:** The best view of the lake is a close-up, from a kayak, canoe, or stand-up paddleboard (page 137).

★ **Shelburne Museum:** "Eclectic" doesn't do justice to this sprawling, fascinating collection of Americana and art (page 139).

★ **Farm Visits and Dinners:** Get back to the land, dine and dance alongside dairy cows, or snuggle a baby lamb (pages 127 and 140).

★ **Lake Champlain Maritime Museum:** The lake's dramatic naval past comes alive at a museum that will intrigue boat lovers and history buffs (page 143).

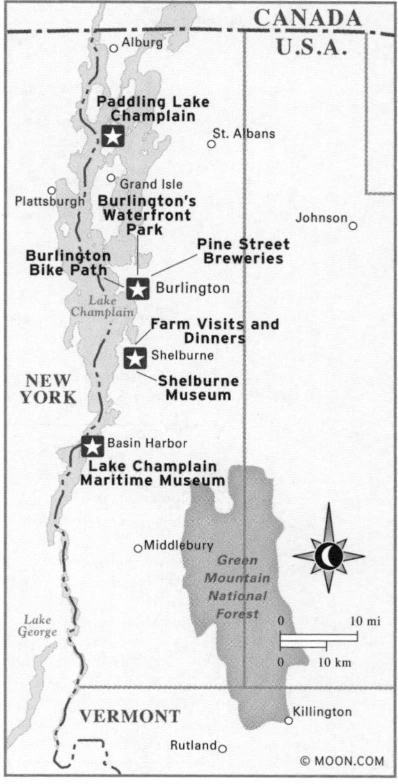

Burlington and the Champlain Valley

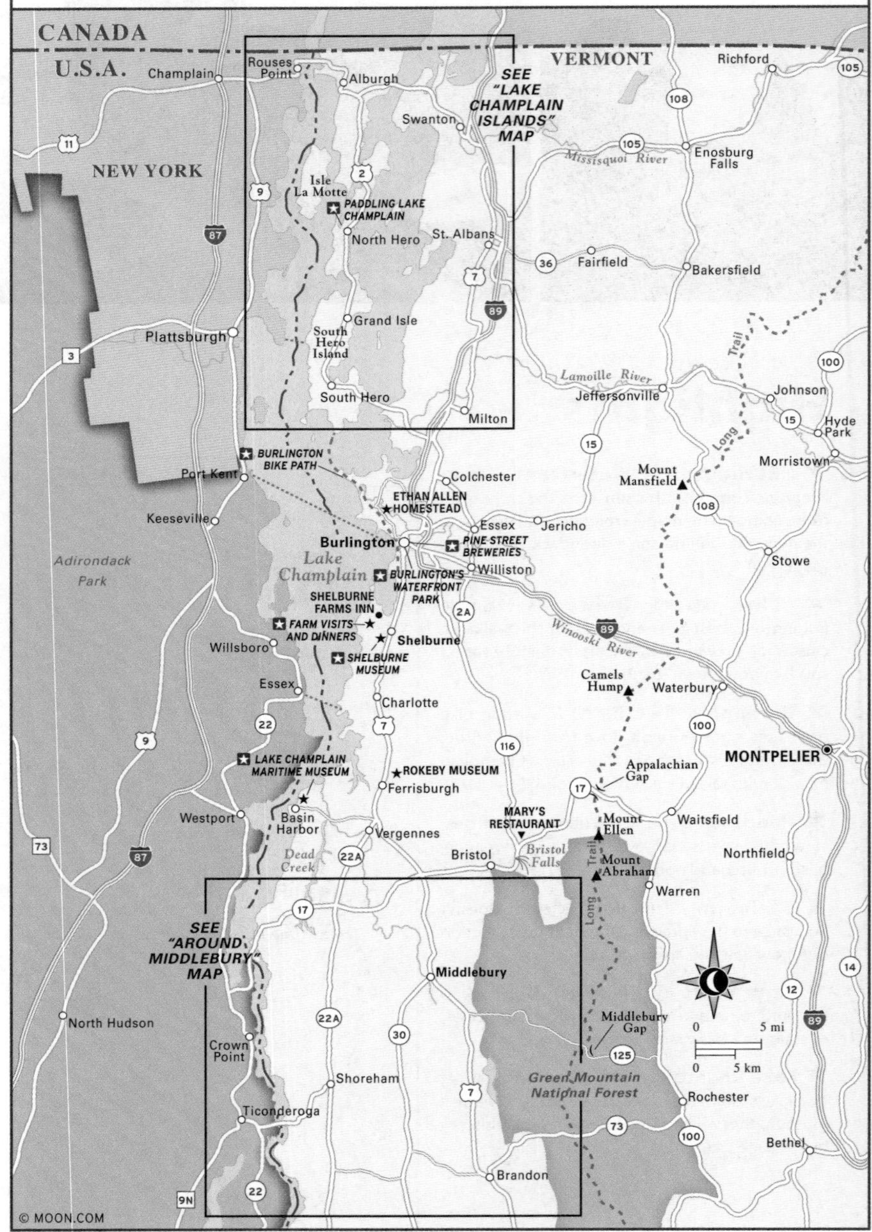

It's easy to see why this was one of the first areas of New England that Europeans settled in—three hundred years ago it was less arduous to traverse the heavily forested northeast by water than by land, and the Champlain Valley enjoys relatively mild weather compared to the mountainous spine of the state. Many early explorers and trappers were French, starting with the adventurer-navigator Samuel de Champlain, and that heritage is still woven into the culture of the region. Some older locals spoke only French until they entered public school, and their grandchildren still call them "mamie" and "papie," likely descended from the French Canadian terms *mémère* and *pépère*.

While the lake is no longer a major point of entry to the United States, the Burlington area retains a port town's cosmopolitan bustle and is a vibrant hub of Vermont's culinary, musical, and artistic culture. With 42,000 residents, it's Vermont's largest city, and though emblematic, it is also distinct from the rest of the state. Much of the city's young, progressive population is from "away," but Vermont's characteristic energy has always been tied to an influx of immigrants and idealists, from 18th-century homesteaders to 1960s hippies and the recent resettlement of refugees from around the globe.

This dynamic blend makes the Champlain Valley a fascinating place to explore. Here it's easy to weave between Vermont's many guises: the subdued, pastoral beauty of the islands, Middlebury's Yankee charm, and Burlington's world-class breweries and restaurants.

PLANNING YOUR TIME

You'll need at least three days to take in this area's highlights, and you easily could spend that time in **Burlington** alone. The Queen City's appealing accommodations and walkable downtown make it a good base for exploration, and while relatively subdued, the nightlife is the best in the state.

If you're staying in Burlington, the **Champlain Islands** are an easy day trip for bike rides, vineyards, and apple picking, or you can head south into the **Champlain Valley**'s agricultural heart.

Middlebury is another prime place to start a trip to the Champlain Valley. Its historical bed-and-breakfasts are steeped in New England's staid charm, and the small downtown has a growing number of hip bars and restaurants. Mountains rise up dramatically to the east of town, and this area's winding roads, trails, and small towns call out for a meandering adventure.

By and large, restaurants in the cities and the islands stay open with regular hours year-round, but in farther-flung places they may close periodically. Call first if you're planning ahead.

Burlington

This lakefront community is Vermont's largest city, beloved by residents who are drawn to its unusual juxtaposition of urban and rural life. There are forested trails, organic farms, and rocky coastlines within the city limits, and on snowbound winter mornings you can spot cross-country skis lined up outside of coffee shops. Downhill enthusiasts can choose from a handful of resorts within an hour's drive, or opt for pond skating, ice fishing, or fat biking right in town.

On hot afternoons the waterfront fills with sailboats and kayaks, and locals ditch work to cool off at their favorite swimming spots. The summer months are a frenzy of activity in Burlington, and almost-weekly festivals flood

Previous: Shelburne Farms; view from the Burlington Bike Path; paddling Lake Champlain.

the town with music, art, and food lovers. It's no surprise that the Queen City makes regular appearances on "best-of" lists based on indices of quality of life and health.

In recent years, a strong economy has helped energize downtown, and '90s-era Phish-loving hippies have given way (or turned into) a progressive and professional population. They're a key to the success of Vermont's local food renaissance, and downtown has a great bar and restaurant scene that has garnered national attention. On warm evenings, many venues throw open the windows and explode onto the sidewalks, and an alfresco table is a great vantage point for watching the town drift by.

Perched above it all is the stately campus of the University of Vermont, whose 12,000 students swell the population by almost 30 percent. The school was founded in 1791 by Ira Allen—that's Ethan's brother—and academic life remains an important source of energy for the town. This is not a place with a town-gown divide: On a Saturday night in Burlington you can raise a glass or cut a rug with sugar makers, sociologists, and senators.

SIGHTS

★ Waterfront Park

A few decades of renovations have turned the **Burlington Waterfront** (1 College St., 802/864-0123), once a bustling lumber port, into a pedestrian-friendly park filled with art and native plants. The view is dramatic when the sun sets over the Adirondacks, so bring a picnic and watch as sailboats, paddleboards, and kayaks drift by. The bike path runs right through the middle of things, so if you've got two wheels or want to rent them, the waterfront is a great starting point. While you're exploring, see if you can find the statue of **The Lone Sailor** tucked behind the **ECHO Leahy Center for Lake Champlain.** The monument was cast with bronze from eight U.S. Navy ships, a fitting tribute on the shores of Lake Champlain, which saw key naval battles in the Revolutionary War and the War of 1812.

On summer days when the city is stifling, the best seat in town may be at the easy-to-miss **Splash at the Boathouse** (0 College St., 802/658-2244, www.splashattheboathouse.com, 11am-sunset daily May-Oct., $8-22) at the end of a dock on the waterfront. Snag an Adirondack chair for a stellar sunset view.

ECHO Leahy Center for Lake Champlain

With ancient coral reefs, whale skeletons, and a mythical monster in its depths, Lake Champlain is one of the most distinctive bodies of freshwater in the world. The scientists behind the **ECHO Leahy Center for Lake Champlain** (1 College St., 802/864-1848, www.echovermont.org, 10am-5pm daily, $14.50 adults, $12.50 seniors and students, $11.50 children 3-17, children 2 and under free) have done a great job of making the geology and fauna of the lake accessible and family-friendly. Hands-on exhibits at this small science center keep kids engaged (and wet) while they learn about river currents or pull critters out of lake pools. There is plenty for nature-loving adults, too, like aquarium tanks full of the fish, turtles, snakes, and frogs that live beneath the surface of Lake Champlain. ECHO is a nonprofit organization with a mission to use education to further the goal of lake conservation and to develop environmental stewardship values in the community.

Lake Tours

Check out Burlington from the water (and with a voiceover) on the ***Spirit of Ethan Allen III*** (Burlington Boathouse, 1 College St., 802/862-8300, www.soea.com, 10am, noon, 2pm, and 4pm daily May-Oct., $22.15 adults, $8.45 children 3-11), whose narration covers local history and landscapes, with snacks are available for purchase onboard.

And if you prefer to hit the lake under sail, consider a trip on the beautiful gaff-rigged sloop ***Friend Ship*** (1 College St., 802/825-7245, www.whistlingman.com, May-Oct., $50 adults, $35 children under 12), which offers three daily sailing cruises as well as two-, four-, and eight-hour private charters. It's a

Burlington

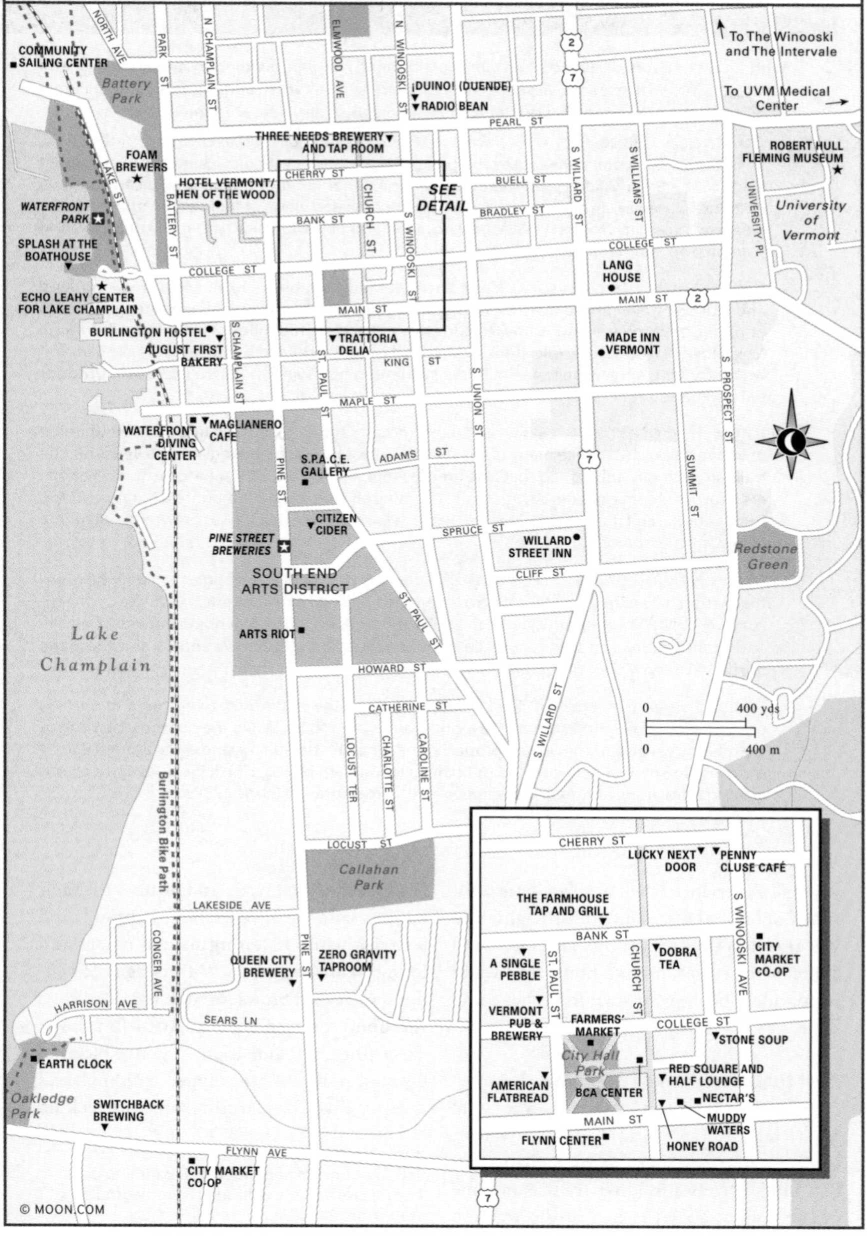

COMMUNITY SAILING CENTER
Battery Park
FOAM BREWERS
WATERFRONT PARK
SPLASH AT THE BOATHOUSE
ECHO LEAHY CENTER FOR LAKE CHAMPLAIN
BURLINGTON HOSTEL
AUGUST FIRST BAKERY
HOTEL VERMONT/ HEN OF THE WOOD
THREE NEEDS BREWERY AND TAP ROOM
¡DUINO! (DUENDE)
RADIO BEAN
SEE DETAIL
To The Winooski and The Intervale
To UVM Medical Center
ROBERT HULL FLEMING MUSEUM
University of Vermont
LANG HOUSE
MADE INN VERMONT
TRATTORIA DELIA
WATERFRONT DIVING CENTER
MAGLIANERO CAFE
S.P.A.C.E. GALLERY
CITIZEN CIDER
PINE STREET BREWERIES
SOUTH END ARTS DISTRICT
ARTS RIOT
WILLARD STREET INN
Redstone Green
Lake Champlain
Burlington Bike Path
Callahan Park
QUEEN CITY BREWERY
ZERO GRAVITY TAPROOM
EARTH CLOCK
Oakledge Park
SWITCHBACK BREWING
CITY MARKET CO-OP

NORTH AVE
PARK ST
N CHAMPLAIN ST
ELMWOOD AVE
N WINOOSKI ST
PEARL ST
CHERRY ST
BANK ST
CHURCH ST
S WINOOSKI ST
BUELL ST
BRADLEY ST
S WILLARD ST
S WILLIAMS ST
UNIVERSITY PL
COLLEGE ST
LAKE ST
BATTERY ST
MAIN ST
KING ST
S CHAMPLAIN ST
ST. PAUL ST
S UNION ST
S PROSPECT ST
MAPLE ST
ADAMS ST
PINE ST
SUMMIT ST
SPRUCE ST
CLIFF ST
HOWARD ST
CATHERINE ST
LOCUST TER
CHARLOTTE ST
CAROLINE ST
LOCUST ST
LAKESIDE AVE
CONGER AVE
HARRISON AVE
SEARS LN
FLYNN AVE
2
7

0 400 yds
0 400 m

CHERRY ST
LUCKY NEXT DOOR
PENNY CLUSE CAFÉ
THE FARMHOUSE TAP AND GRILL
BANK ST
A SINGLE PEBBLE
ST. PAUL ST
CHURCH ST
DOBRA TEA
S WINOOSKI AVE
CITY MARKET CO-OP
VERMONT PUB & BREWERY
FARMERS' MARKET
COLLEGE ST
STONE SOUP
City Hall Park
RED SQUARE AND HALF LOUNGE
AMERICAN FLATBREAD
BCA CENTER
NECTAR'S
MUDDY WATERS
MAIN ST
FLYNN CENTER
HONEY ROAD

TOP EXPERIENCE

Biking in Vermont

With a vast network of dirt roads, a vibrant community of trail-building mountain bikers, and plenty of off-road bike paths, Vermont is a great place to be a cyclist. Burlington's got some great rides, but there's destination-worthy pedaling across the state. Here are some top picks:

- **Burlington Bike Path, Burlington:** Eight miles of paved, off-road path (www.enjoyburlington.com) connect several parks that are perfect for picnicking, with a spur that leads to the Ethan Allen Homestead. At the far northern end of the path, you can continue onto the Causeway, an elevated path that has unparalleled views of the lake. On most summer weekends you can catch a bicycle ferry from the end of the Causeway that will drop you and your bike on South Hero Island (page 129).
- **Kingdom Trails Network, East Burke:** Mountain bikers from across New England and Québec travel to the Northeast Kingdom's tiny East Burke, where a unique patchwork of public and private land is now traced with more than 100 miles of trail. The rides range from flowy, swooping single-track to the kind of rocky riding the northeast is known for, with a thriving après-ride scene at Burke swimming holes and the town's seasonal outdoor tiki bar (page 229).
- **Cady Hill Forest, Stowe:** Fun and flowy mountain bike trails wind up and down the side of Stowe Valley, and unlike many of the free-to-access mountain biking areas in Vermont, the trails are well-enough signed that first-time visitors can explore without a local guide. For bikers, Stowe's charm goes far beyond Cady Hill, though: There's great mountain biking at Trapp Family Lodge, and the Stowe Recreation Path is a leisurely ride that passes brewpubs and prime picnic spots (page 187).
- **Lamoille Valley Rail Trail, Lamoille Valley:** New England's longest rail trail will eventually stretch 93 miles east to west across Vermont, linking Lake Champlain with the Connecticut River Valley. Thirty-three miles of the trail are now open, with great riding between Danville and St. Johnsbury, and another excellent section that joins Morristown and Cambridge in the northern Green Mountains (pages 194 and 227).
- **Millstone Trails, Barre:** The landscape around the stone-quarrying town of Barre is pocked with gaping holes where Vermont granite used to be. While the quarries themselves are off-limits—they're still private property, and fenced—the rolling landscape around Barre's quarries has some of Vermont's most technical mountain biking, which includes some teeth-gritting rides along ledges and over piles of discarded granite (page 173).

sublime experience when a steady breeze allows Captain Mike to shut off the engine and you travel to the sounds of water and wind alone. The cruises are two hours and water is provided; bring your own food, beer, and wine.

Burlington Farmers' Market

The outdoor **Burlington Farmers' Market** (City Hall Park, www.burlingtonfarmersmarket.org, 8:30am-2pm Sat. May-Oct.) is a foodie paradise and one of the biggest social events of the week in the Queen City. Locals and visitors fill their baskets with fresh vegetables, hot food, and pastries while listening to live music and lounging on the grass. With dozens of vendors, you could browse all day, but don't miss the home-brewed soda at **Rookie's Root Beer** (the Dark Side is an addictive blend of espresso and root beer topped with molasses cream). If you're planning a picnic, pick up

1: Burlington Farmers' Market; **2:** paddling by lakeside cliffs near Burlington; **3:** Burlington's Waterfront Park

Garlic
Scapes
$3 Per Bunch
1
2
3

some excellent goat cheese at **Doe's Leap** to go with rye bread from **Slow Fire Bakery** or savory biscuits from **Barrio Bakery.** There are lots of sweet treats to choose from, but on a hot day you can follow the lines to **Adam's Berry Farm** for popsicles made from organic fruit or to **The Farm Between** for what may be the world's best snow cones—try the black currant.

BCA Center

Contemporary art with a Vermont theme is the purview of the **BCA Center** (135 Church St., 802/865-7166, www.burlingtoncityarts.org, noon-5pm Tues.-Thurs. and Sun., noon-8pm Fri.-Sat. in summer; noon-5pm Tues.-Thurs., noon-8pm Sat.-Sun. in winter, free), which pushes the envelope with multimedia and interactive exhibitions in oversize gallery spaces. Some of its shows are more successful than others; all are provocative. A recent exhibit, for example, looked at perspectives from Iraq vets-turned-artists working in media, including U.S. currency and flags and their own uniforms, to come to grips with their experiences in war.

University of Vermont and the Fleming Museum

University of Vermont (194 S. Prospect St., 802/656-3131, www.uvm.edu) educates some 12,000 students on a stately campus filled with historical brick buildings. Chartered in 1791 by a group of Vermonters including Ira Allen, it was the fifth college in the country (after Harvard, Yale, Dartmouth, and Brown). For visitors, its main attraction is the **Robert Hull Fleming Museum** (University of Vermont, 61 Colchester Ave., 802/656-0750, www.uvm.edu, 10am-4pm Tues., Thurs., Fri., 10am-7pm Wed., noon-4pm Sat.-Sun., $5 adults, $3 students and seniors, $10 family, children 6 and under free), an art and archaeology museum with mummies, Buddha images, Mesoamerican pottery, and other artifacts from some of the world's great civilizations, presented in an up-to-date style that avoids the paternalism of many archaeology museums. It also has a small collection of American and European paintings. The museum also features three rotating exhibits, which are thoughtfully curated and engaging.

Ethan Allen Homestead

Today, Ethan Allen's name recalls the furniture company that was named for him in 1932. But Allen was also one of the most colorful—and enigmatic—characters of early Vermont history. His modest Cape Cod-style home, known as the **Ethan Allen Homestead** (1 Ethan Allen Homestead Way, 802/865-4556, www.ethanallenhomestead.org, 10am-4pm daily May-Oct., $10 adults, $6 students, children 5 and under free), has been restored to the period, though only his kitchen table and a few other small Allen artifacts survive. The homestead offers a low-budget film exploring the conflicting accounts of the man himself as well as a guided tour of the property.

Although the exhibits relating to Allen aren't particularly in-depth, the tour guides are spirited in their evocation of Vermont's larger-than-life founding father. And Allen aside, the restored home is an excellent lesson in how early Americans lived.

ENTERTAINMENT AND EVENTS

The best place to find out what's happening in the Queen City's nightclubs, theaters, and concert halls is in the free weekly paper ***Seven Days*** (www.7dvt.com) or on the **Lake Champlain Region Chamber of Commerce website** (www.vermont.org).

Bars

The last several years have seen an explosion of craft cocktail culture in Vermont, as creative bartenders bring the "farm-to-table" approach to mixing drinks using locally distilled spirits, artisanal bitters, and fresh ingredients of all kinds. Some of the best cocktail bars are also restaurants, like the superb **Juniper Bar at Hotel Vermont** (41 Cherry St., 802/651-0080, www.hotelvt.com, 7am-midnight daily), which stocks every single spirit made

Ethan Allen

Revolutionary and farmer Ethan Allen once worked a riverside property in Burlington.

Colonial mountain man Ethan Allen looms large over the history of Vermont. Depending on which account you believe, he was an American Robin Hood, a war hero, a traitor, or a drunk. Born in Litchfield, Connecticut, Allen came to Vermont before the Revolutionary War with his brother Ira to start a farm near Bennington on a land grant received from New Hampshire governor Benning Wentworth. When King George found out that Wentworth was giving out grants under his nose (without paying duties to the Crown), he declared them void and gave the governor of New York rights to the same land. Caught in the middle, Allen and other landowners weren't about to give up without a fight. They defied the courts with a hastily arranged militia called the Green Mountain Boys, which helped enforce the New Hampshire Grants by persuasion, threat, and force, and eventually led to the founding of Vermont as a separate state.

The Boys achieved legitimacy through valiant fighting in the Revolution, where they played key roles in the battles of Hubbardton and Bennington. After leading the capture of Fort Ticonderoga in the beginning days of the war, however, Allen himself took little part. He was captured by the British during an ill-planned raid on Montréal and lived out the war as a prisoner in England and New York.

After the war, he was briefly named the general of the Army of Vermont, and then he became fabulously wealthy through the Onion River Land Company, a holding company that bought up and distributed much of the land in Vermont. Though his brother entered into politics, Ethan Allen preferred to influence government behind the scenes—such as his controversial role in the ill-fated attempt to return Vermont to the British in 1782.

By the time he built the homestead on the Onion River near Burlington in 1787, he was spending most of his time walking his land with surveyor's tools and a hip flask. He lived in the home for only two years before he was killed in a sledding accident on Lake Champlain (the hip flask was no doubt involved). Almost as soon as he died, the arguments began about the role he played in early Vermont history. Only one thing is for sure: If it weren't for him, Vermont probably wouldn't exist as a state today. You can visit his former home, the Ethan Allen Homestead, in Burlington.

in Vermont and blends them into thoughtful drinks. With modern, Scandinavian design and an open hearth, it's a wonderful place to sip a drink on a snowy evening. For a broader look at local cocktail and spirits culture, join the monthly **Cocktail Walk** (www.cocktail-walk.com, $45), which visits three creative cocktail bars in Burlington and neighboring Winooski for drinks and snacks with Vermont distillers and bartenders.

And though beer lovers could easily confine their tippling to Burlington's breweries, it would be a shame to miss the suds at **The Farmhouse Tap & Grill** (160 Bank St., 802/859-0888, www.farmhousetg.com, 11am-11pm Mon.-Thurs., 11am-midnight Fri., 10am-midnight Sat., 10am-11pm Sun.) a gastropub with 24 taps and 160 bottled beers. In summertime the outdoor beer garden is a shady haven, and in winter months you can warm up by the fire in the ultra-cozy subterranean parlor.

There is something transporting about a lazy afternoon at **Splash at the Boathouse** (0 College St., 802/658-2244, www.splashattheboathouse.com, 11am-sunset daily May-Oct.) where generic tropical bar decor complements the best views in town. Since Splash is built on a floating dock, you can drink your beer with your toes in the water, while watching bare-chested yachties maneuver their powerboats in the marina's close quarters. The menu of mostly fried foods isn't particularly memorable, but the beer list does include a few local favorites.

Breweries

Vermont has more breweries per capita than any other state, and many of its award-winning craft beers are only available locally. It's a source of pride to beer-loving residents, who are always ready to debate the finer points of hop varieties and snap up tickets to Burlington's **Vermont Brewers Festival** (third weekend of July, www.vtbrewfest.com, $43) fast as a case of Heady Topper (a notoriously hard-to-find canned beer made in Stowe).

Conveniently, the downtown breweries are next door to one another, and the **Pine Street Arts District** is home to a cluster of young breweries that are easily reached by car or bus from the center. If all the options leave you thinking that you'd like a tour guide (and chauffeur), you can hop on the bus with **Burlington Brew Tours** (261 S. Union St., 802/760-6091, www.burlingtonbrewtours.com, $70), whose itineraries take you behind the scenes at some of the best breweries in town.

DOWNTOWN

When Greg Noonan founded his laid-back brewpub, **The Vermont Pub & Brewery** (144 College St., 802/231-2037, www.vermontbrewery.com, 11:30am-1am daily), in 1988, most Vermonters had never heard of craft beer. Today, many cutting-edge brewers cite Noonan's influence—and influential book—as key to their own learning. It remains one of the mainstays of the local beer scene, with plenty of beers on tap, solid pub grub, and a convivial scene that's popular among students.

The wide, wooden bar at **Zero Gravity Craft Brewery** at American Flatbread (115 St. Paul St., 802/861-2999, www.zerogravitybeer.com, 11:30am-close daily) is the perfect place to watch locals coming for some of Burlington's best pizza and beer. The scene at Flatbread is a bit more grown-up than next door at the Vermont Pub & Brewery, and on Friday and Saturday nights, it can be hard to find a place to rest your elbow. Lean through the friendly crowd to order a beer and get a glimpse of the singular tap handles, made to order by local artists. Zero Gravity's flagship beer is the **Conehead,** a single hop wheat India pale ale that's brewed with aromatic Citra hops.

Continue a few more blocks to the waterfront to **Foam Brewers** (112 Lake St., 802/399-2511, www.foambrewers.com, noon-9pm Mon.-Wed., noon-10pm Thurs., noon-11pm Fri.-Sat., 11am-7pm Sun.), a newer arrival to Burlington's beer scene. Founded by former Switchback brewers, Foam pours an ever-changing lineup of creative beers that lean towards IPAs, and in 2017, was named by RateBeer as one of the world's best new breweries. The funky, industrial space hosts frequent musical events, and the bar serves tasty cheese and charcuterie platters

★ PINE STREET

The Pine Street neighborhood, just south of downtown, is Burlington's funky, creative hub, with artist studios, eye-catching murals, and a walkable cluster of hip breweries. These taprooms fill up with a friendly, after-work crowd and are the perfect introduction to Burlington's thriving beer scene. Switchback Brewing Co.'s stylish tasting room is a bit of a hike from the main Pine Street corridor, but it's an ideal stopover if you're headed to Oakledge Park for a swim.

Branch out from beer at **Citizen Cider** (316 Pine St., 802/448-3278, www.citizencider.com, 11am-10pm Mon.-Sat., 11am-7pm Sun.), which serves many varieties made from Vermont apples in a beautifully designed taproom. Tours tend to be impromptu but are a fascinating glimpse of the cider-making process. The five-glass flights are an excellent introduction to these unusual ciders: The sweetest of the bunch is the flagship **Unified Press,** but the ginger-spiked **Dirty Mayor** has a passionate following, as does the **Lake Hopper,** which is dry hopped with local Cascade hops to give it a beer-like edge.

Queen City Brewery (703 Pine St., 802/540-0280, www.queencitybrewery.com, noon-8pm Tues.-Wed., noon-10pm Thurs.-Sat., noon-7pm Sun.) makes European-style beers in a nondescript industrial building. The tasting room has more charm and is lined with old beer cans and historical images of Burlington. Try the hugely popular **Yorkshire Porter,** an English dark ale that's rich and full-bodied, or **Argument,** an English India pale ale that's brewed true to style: strong and bitter.

The sunlit industrial-chic **Zero Gravity Taproom** (716 Pine St., 802/497-0054, www.zerogravitybeer.com, noon-9pm Sun.-Thurs., noon-10pm Fri.-Sat.) opened in 2015. Here you can sip their beers away from the crush of downtown American Flatbread. The clientele is the young and hip crowd that lingers in south end bars after work, nibbling handmade pretzels and mustard and sampling the brews. The taproom has the same house-made beers as the downtown location. If you're on your way back from Oakledge Park's beach, you can't do better than a tall pour of the **Green State Lager,** a refreshing pilsner with noble hops and a clean taste.

In 2014, **Switchback Brewing Co.** (160 Flynn Ave., 802/651-4114, www.switchbackvt.com, 11am-8pm Mon.-Sat., 11am-7pm Sun.) opened a taproom a short distance off Pine Street. The wood and glass tasting room is stylish and casual, and the knowledgeable bartenders are happy to guide your tasting of the beers on tap. Free tours are offered on Saturday at 1pm and 2pm; call for reservations. Their flagship beer is a highly drinkable reddish amber ale **Switchback Ale,** which is almost ubiquitous in Vermont, but a brewery visit may be your only chance to try their more eclectic offerings like the **Slow-Fermented Brown Ale.**

SOUTH BURLINGTON

From Switchback, you can continue 2.5 miles south to **Magic Hat Brewing Company** (5 Bartlett Bay Rd., South Burlington, 802/658-2739, www.magichat.net, 11am-7pm Mon.-Sat., noon-5pm Sun.), where their **Artifactory** has 48 beers on tap, including some Vermont exclusives. The taproom is decorated in Magic Hat's trippy and offbeat style, and there's plenty of merch to take home with you. The popular **#9** is a "not quite pale ale" that's lightly fruity and crisp, and the **Circus Boy** hefeweizen is a hazy, unfiltered brew that's smooth and a little bit sweet.

Live Music and Dancing

You can find something to shimmy to every of the week in Burlington, where most bars stay open until 2am. There's always a full lineup at **Radio Bean** (8 N. Winooski Ave., 802/660-9346, www.radiobean.com), a bar and coffee shop packed with hipsters watching acts that range from traditional Irish to experimental jazz. **Honky Tonk Night** (10pm Tues.) is a good bet for swinging neo-country music.

On weekend nights, **Church Street Marketplace** is thronged with a lively college crowd that heads to **Red Square** (136 Church St., 802/859-8909) or **Nectar's** (188 Main St., 802/856-4771, www.liveatnectars.com) to shake it off to DJ and live music. The diminutive **Half Lounge** (136½ Church St., 802/865-0012, www.halflounge.com) attracts a slightly older crowd with tapas, cocktails, and a nice wine list to go with turntable sets and local singer-songwriters.

It's always worth checking the lineup of high-quality indie groups that play at **Signal Kitchen** (71 Main St., 802/399-2337, www.signalkitchen.com) and **ArtsRiot** (400 Pine St., 802/540-0406, www.artsriot.com), who further their mission of "destroying apathy" by cooking up great shows and tasty, creative pub food. When bigger acts come through Burlington, though, they usually land at **Higher Ground** (1214 Williston Rd., South Burlington, 802/652-0777, www.highergroundmusic.com).

The Arts

A former vaudeville house, the **Flynn Center for the Performing Arts** (153 Main St., 802/863-5966, www.flynncenter.org) was restored to its art deco grandeur in 2000. It now serves as the cultural hub of the city, with musicals, dance performances, and shows by mainstream jazz and country acts from Diana Krall to Pink Martini. Meanwhile, the **Vermont Symphony Orchestra** (2 Church St., Ste. 3B, 802/864-5741, www.vso.org) is all about playing the masters, from Tchaikovsky to Strauss. The group plays at numerous venues around the state throughout the season but can be found most frequently at its home base in Burlington.

The **South End Arts District** (802/859-9222, www.seaba.com) is home to many collective studios and galleries. They throw open their doors for the **First Friday Art Walk** (802/264-4839, www.artmapburlington.com) each month, which is free to attend; most galleries stay open between 5pm and 8pm. Don't miss the **S.P.A.C.E. Gallery** (266 Pine St., Ste. 105, 802/578-2512, https://spacegalleryvt.com, noon-5pm Thurs.-Sat.).

Events

Burlington hosts a festival almost every weekend during the summer, and it's worth booking far ahead during those times, as hotels fill up quickly. For 10 days in early June, music lovers from around the region flock to the **Burlington Discover Jazz Festival** (www.discoverjazz.com, June). The town is filled with tunes, from ticketed events featuring big-name artists to free daily jazz sets in many restaurants, bars, and parks. And if you prefer brews to blues, don't miss the **Vermont Brewers Festival** (802/760-8535, www.vtbrewfest.com, July) when a who's who of local and regional brewers set up shop right in the Waterfront Park. If you'd like to attend, check the website well in advance of your trip, as tickets often sell out the day they go on sale (usually in May).

One of the most energetic days on the lake is the picturesque **Dragon Boat Festival** (802/999-5478, www.ridethedragon.org, Aug.), a boat race in which teams of 20 paddle 40-foot brightly painted canoes to raise money for local charities. The winner is invariably the team that works the best together, not necessarily the strongest.

The summer wraps up with the **Grand Point North** (www.grandpointnorth.com, mid-Sept.) festival, put on by hometown musical heroes **Grace Potter and the Nocturnals**. Two days of music feature an impressive lineup of bands on open-air stages on the **Burlington Waterfront**, and Sunday's final show is usually attended by a flotilla of kayaks and sailboats getting their tunes for free.

SHOPPING

Church Street Marketplace (2 Church St., 802/863-1648, www.churchstmarketplace.com, noon-4pm Mon.-Fri.) is the pedestrian heart of Burlington, lined with restaurants, bars, and a blend of local and national stores. There's a handful of excellent outdoor gear stores, like **Outdoor Gear Exchange** (37 Church St., 802/860-0190, www.gearx.com, 10am-7pm Mon.-Thurs., 10am-8pm Fri.-Sat., 10am-6pm Sun.), which sells new and used equipment for every adventure imaginable, and the **Ski Rack** (85 Main St., 800/882-4530, www.skirack.com, 10am-7pm Mon.-Sat., 11am-5pm Sun.), both of which carry rental gear of many kinds.

Downtown Burlington also has two excellent locally owned bookstores: **Crow Bookshop** (14 Church St., 802/862-0848, www.crowbooks.com, 10am-9pm Mon.-Wed., 10am-10pm Thurs.-Sat., 10am-8pm Sun.) has a nice collection of used books and many local authors. **Phoenix Books** (191 Bank St., 802/448-3350, www.phoenixbooks.biz, 10am-9pm Mon.-Sat., 11am-6pm Sun.) has a broader selection of new books, including many options for regional travel.

FOOD

Casual

Before opening on the site of a national hamburger chain, **The Farmhouse Tap & Grill** (160 Bank St., 802/859-0888, www.farmhousetg.com, 11am-11pm Mon.-Thurs., 11am-midnight Fri., 10am-midnight Sat., 10am-11pm Sun., $17-25) asked the community to suggest names, and then held a vote on their favorites. The winner was "The old McDonalds Farmhouse." Now known simply as The Farmhouse, this farm-to-table gastropub is popular for creative and comforting fare. The burgers are celebrated, but the starters, like the beef tartare with freshly made potato chips, are often standouts.

Zabby & Elf's Stone Soup (211 College St., 802/862-7616, www.stonesoupvt.com, 7am-9pm Mon.-Fri., 9am-9pm Sat., $7-12), an intimate, sunlit café, serves hearty soups, salads, and excellent sandwiches on their own bread, along with an eclectic buffet with plenty of vegan and gluten-free options. The large front window is made for people-watching and there's a decent wine and beer selection. When you add in one of their almond macaroons, you've got all the ingredients for a perfect afternoon.

The food is as whimsical as the hosts are at ★ **Penny Cluse Cafe** (169 Cherry St., 802/651-8834, www.pennycluse.com, 6:45am-3pm Mon.-Fri., 8am-3pm Sat.-Sun., $6-14.50), named for the owner's childhood dog and decked out with an ever-rotating collection of posters and local art. Dig into gingerbread pancakes at breakfast, or hang out until lunch and order up Baja fish tacos and a Bloody Mary.

Lucky Next Door (163 Cherry St., 802/399-2121, www.luckynextdoor.com, 9am-5pm daily, $5-10) is just the thing for a light lunch or emergency infusion of chocolate and espresso. The menu at this sweetly simple café changes seasonally, but "things on toast" are a mainstay: favorites include sardines and avocados.

★ **Butch + Babes** (258 N. Winooski Ave., 802/495-0716, www.butchandbabes.com, 5pm-9pm Mon. and Wed., 5pm-10pm Thurs.-Sat., 9:30am-2pm and 5pm-9pm Sun., $14-18) blends the Chicago roots of the owner with ingredients and techniques from across Asia; the pub-inspired menu pulls from those sources willy-nilly. The results are surprisingly harmonious and refreshingly laid-back, in an atmosphere that channels the vitality and diversity of the Old North End neighborhood where it's located.

The folks at **American Flatbread** (115 St. Paul St., 802/861-2999, www.americanflatbread.com, 11:30am-3pm and 5pm-11:30pm Mon.-Fri., 11:30am-11:30pm Sat.-Sun., pizzas $12-20) bought local before it was cool. This beloved pizza joint still serves thin crust pizza topped with cheese, veggies, and meats from area farms. The specials are always worth a try, but the basic menu is filled with excellent options like the Punctuated

Winooski: The Brooklyn of Burlington?

Just a couple of miles away from downtown Burlington, it would be easy to mistake **Winooski** for another neighborhood, but the city has a spirit all its own. In recent years, it's also become a favorite destination for food and drink, with a few truly great restaurants and bars wrapped around the city's roundabout.

Dine with views of the Winooski Falls at ★ **Waterworks** (20 Winooski Falls Way, 802/497-3525, www.waterworksvt.com, brunch 10am-3pm Sun., lunch 11:30am-2pm Mon.-Sat., dinner 5pm-9pm Sun.-Thurs., 5pm-10pm Fri.-Sat., $22-32), whose glass-walled dining room juts out over the river. In warm months, outdoor riverside seating is a lovely place for evening drinks, and the indoor ambience—dim lighting, an open dining room that never seems too loud—is among the most pleasant in the area. There's an appealing list of mains, but many come for the flatbreads and small plates, which include delightfully crispy chicken wings. A menu of drinks ranges from classic cocktails to creative, esoteric creations, with a beautifully chosen selection of beers and wines.

Try some of Vermont's most creative and thoughtful dishes at the James Beard-nominated ★ **Misery Loves Co.** (46 Main St., 802/497-3989, www.miserylovescovt.com, 3pm-10pm Tues.-Fri., 10am-10pm Sat., 10am-2pm Sun., $15-35), which serves delicious and sometimes delightfully odd meals alongside superlative cocktails. The small space has an open kitchen and a casual feel, but it's truly a special place to eat: Try squid ink pasta topped with sea urchins, fried oysters wrapped in crisp lettuce shells, or the delightful family-style fried chicken. The plates of house-pickled vegetables and fresh cheese are a must.

Casual and friendly, **Tiny Thai** (24 Main St., 802/655-4888, www.tinythairestaurant.net, 11:30am-2:30pm and 4:30pm-9:30pm Mon.-Fri., 11:30am-9:30pm Sat., 4:30pm-9:30pm Sun., $10-18) has some of the Burlington area's best Thai food, with a menu inspired by street food and family dinners. Tiny Thai is BYO, so if you'd like something to drink with your meal, head up the street to the **Beverage Warehouse of Vermont** (1 East St., 802/655-2620, www.beveragewarehousevt.com), which has an excellent selection of beer and wine. (This is also a key destination for anyone wishing to bring home hard-to-find Vermont beers.)

More of a craft beer destination than a restaurant, **Mule Bar** (38 Main St., 802/399-2020, www.mulebarvt.com, 11am-1am Sun.-Thurs., 11am-2am Fri.-Sat.) does have an appealing menu of pub food, including burgers and hand-cut fries piled under poutine toppings, nacho cheese, and pecorino romano. For beer lovers, this is a great stop, and the bartenders usually have encyclopedic knowledge of Vermont breweries.

Like every other Winooski listing, **Scout & Co.** (1 E. Allen St., www.scoutandcompanyvt.com, 7am-6pm Mon.-Fri., 8am-6pm Sat.-Sun.) has a prime spot on the roundabout, and the sunny coffee shop is a favorite hangout for locals. House-made ice cream and excellent coffee are the main draws, but the pastry case is stocked with treats from local bakers.

Winooski is two miles northeast of downtown Burlington. By car (6 min.), take Pearl Street east, which crosses a bridge to Winooski's roundabout. By bus (11 min.), take Route 9 Riverside/Winooski from the Cherry Street bus station, which leaves every 30-60 minutes ($1.25). The Champlain Mill stop is central to all attractions.

Equilibrium, with olives, red peppers, and goat cheese. Wait times can get long on weekend nights, but if you can wedge yourself into the crowd at the bar, it's a convivial place to while away an evening.

On evenings that call for low light and house-made banana ketchup, atmospheric **¡Duino!(Duende)** (10 N. Winooski Ave., 802/660-9346, www.duinoduende.com, 4pm-11:30pm Mon.-Thurs., 4pm-midnight Fri., 10am-midnight Sat., 10am-3:30pm Sun., $10-15) beckons. Their concept of "International Street Food" is interpreted loosely and with a taste for cultural mashups: Korean tacos with kimchi and coconut rice is a standout example. Duino is connected by an internal door to the **Radio Bean** bar, so check the music lineup before settling in for dinner.

Fine Dining

Hen of the Wood (55 Cherry St., 802/540-0534, www.henofthewood.com, 5pm-10pm daily, $22-35) is the second location of Eric Warnstedt's award-winning restaurant, and both turn out inspired, thoughtful food that draws diners from around the region. Warnstedt blends a refined aesthetic with a serious throw down of New England flavors. He places agriculture front and center and has been awarded a "Snail of Approval" by Vermont's Slow Food Organization (www.slowfoodvermont.org). The menu changes frequently, but oysters are a standout, as is the house-made charcuterie.

Shortly after opening ★ **Honey Road** (156 Church St., 802/497-2145, www.honeyroadrestaurant.com, 4pm-9pm Sun.-Thurs., 4pm-10pm Fri.-Sat., small plates $4-18) chef Cara Chigazola Tobin snagged a James Beard nomination for best chef in the Northeast, and another for best new restaurant. Tobin serves an eclectic lineup of Mediterranean small plates that bounce from Morocco to Turkey and Lebanon. The desserts and cocktails are a delight.

Taiwanese chef Duval brings her fresh, local approach to cooking classic and regional Chinese dishes at this excellent restaurant, **A Single Pebble** (133 Bank St., 802/865-5200, www.asinglepebble.com, dim sum 11:30am-1:45pm Sun., lunch 11:30am-1:45pm Mon.-Fri., 11:30am-3pm Sat., dinner 5pm-late daily, $10-25), to ongoing acclaim. This is a favorite for special occasions and holidays, and the mock eel is legendary.

Regional, thoughtfully prepared Italian takes center stage at **Trattoria Delia** (152 Saint Paul St., 802/864-5253, www.trattoriadelia.com, 5pm-10pm daily, $18-38), with an excellent wine list and an emphasis on freshly made pastas and authentically cooked high-quality meats.

Cafés and Bakeries

Like many cloudy locales, Burlington has a thriving café culture with plenty of hip spots to sip coffee and tea, whatever the weather. The creative crowd tends to settle in at minimalist **Maglianero** (47 Maple St., 802/861-3155, www.maglianero.com, 7am-6pm Mon.-Fri., 8am-5pm Sat.-Sun.) whose bicycle theme includes a bike repair station, while the philosophical set goes for **Dobra Tea** (80 Church St., 802/951-2424, www.dobrateavt.com, 10am-11pm Thurs.-Sat.,10am-10pmSun.-Wed.) where you can sit on the floor and order tea from a whimsical menu.

There's a bit of leftover hippie spirit alive at the convivial **Muddy Waters** (184 Main St., 802/658-0466, 7:30am-10pm Tues.-Fri., 7:30am-11pm Sat., 8:30am-10pm. Sun., 7:30am-6pm Mon.), which also serves beer and hosts shows by local bands. Wash down your coffee with a pastry at **August First Bakery** (149 S. Champlain St., 802/540-0060, www.augustfirstvt.com, 7:30am-4pm daily), which made national headlines for banning laptops, but whose Hungarian sweet rolls are even more newsworthy. In the Old North End neighborhood, **Scout & Co.** (237 North Ave., www.scoutandcompanyvt.com, 7am-5pm Mon.-Fri., 8am-6pm Sat.-Sun.) serves excellent espresso alongside creative house-made ice cream in an airy space equipped with a browsing library of esoteric cookbooks.

Food Shopping

At **City Market Co-op** (82 S. Winooski Ave., 802/861-9700, www.citymarket.coop, 7am-11pm daily), you'll find lots of local cheeses, beers, and wines along with plenty of regular ol' groceries. The staff here are very knowledgeable about their products and always happy to help you find something special. The made-to-order sandwiches are ideal for a picnic.

★ Farm Visits and Dinners

When flying into Burlington's airport, the city looks tiny, a tidy cluster of buildings surrounded by farms. It's worth getting out to one, because agriculture continues to be the cultural and financial mainstay of the state, and once you meet a few farmers, you'll notice their names on menus all over town and leave with a deeper sense of place. Dairy continues to be the most significant agricultural product in the Champlain Valley, but locavore culture has made this fertile ground for a thriving community of small farmers who cultivate everything from grapes to grains.

In July and August the urban farming nonprofit **Intervale Center** (180 Intervale Rd., 802/660-0440, www.intervale.org) hosts **Summervale,** an agricultural hoe-down each Thursday with music and food. They also organize free monthly tours of the on-site organic farms (call for details). For six Fridays during the summer, the organic **Bread and Butter Farm** (200 Leduc Farm Dr., Shelburne, 802/985-9200, www.breadandbutterfarm.com) throws festive and family-oriented **Burger Nights,** with kid-oriented music, burgers (veggie and beef), hot dogs, and fixin's from their cows and gardens. Their gorgeous spread is a 15-minute drive south of downtown Burlington, and tickets to Burger Night must be booked in advance.

ACCOMMODATIONS

Downtown Burlington has some great places to land, but many are for travelers looking to spend $200 and up. Splitting the difference may mean heading to the burbs and serviceable if unremarkable hotels that line Route 2 and Route 7 on the way out of town. Another good option is **Airbnb:** Walkable **downtown,** the young and diverse **Old North End,** and the tranquil **South End** area are all great neighborhoods to stay in, or you can head across the river to **Winooski.**

Under $100

A notable exception to the lack of budget offerings downtown is the **Burlington Hostel** (50 Main St., 802/540-3043, www.theburlingtonhostel.com $40 pp). It's no-frills but clean, safe, and walking distance from everything. Three of the eight-bed dorms are single gender, and several four-bed dorms are set aside for groups and families. There's on-street parking, Wi-Fi, a public computer, 24-hour reception, and a coin laundry just around the block. Weekly rates are available, and a waffle breakfast is included, but if that doesn't appeal, try the moreish Hungarian sweet rolls at the excellent bakery around the corner.

$150-250

The Willard Street Inn (349 S. Willard St., 802/651-8710, www.willardstreetinn.com, $155-305) is as beautiful inside as it is outside; the sprawling Victorian manse lays claim to impeccably decorated rooms. Each is filled with thoughtful details—a hand-carved antique chest here, a gas fireplace with antique mosaic tile there. Terry bathrobes and a full breakfast served in the marble-floored solarium come with every stay. Children over 12 are welcome.

One of a Kind BNB (53 Lakeview Ter., 802/862-5576, www.oneofakindbnb.com, $175-275) is in a sweet residential neighborhood overlooking the lake but still walking distance from downtown. The owner, artist Maggie Sherman, has thoughtfully renovated the home and the relaxed breakfasts are full of local options. There's no television or air-conditioning, but there is a friendly cat, an excellent garden, and a backyard tree swing.

Over $250

The newest, chicest digs in town are surely at ★ **Hotel Vermont** (41 Cherry St., 802/651-0080, www.hotelvt.com, $299), an urban oasis that blends a rustic aesthetic with Scandinavian-influenced modern style. From woolly blankets to rough-hewn granite, seemingly everything you touch here is sourced regionally and with beautiful taste. The friendly staff includes a Beer Concierge and an Outdoor Activities Director, and there are bicycles, snowshoes, and even an ice fishing shack available for guest use.

★ **Made INN Vermont** (204 S. Willard St., 802/399-2788, www.madeinnvermont.com, $289 and up) is perched on a hill above downtown, a bed-and-breakfast that's a temple of curated quirk with artistic flair and a contemporary sensibility. Owner Linda Wolf has filled her historical home with curiosities and comforts, and rooms are stocked with cans of Heady Topper, chalkboard walls, and views of the lake below. Atop the peaked roof and equipped with a telescope, the enclosed widow's walk is where you can watch stars and sails drift by. Breakfast is sumptuous. And well-behaved pets are welcome.

Camping

Sites are available for everything from tents to RVs at **North Beach** (60 Institute Rd., 802/862-0942, $37-45), where you'll have excellent lake access, fire pits, and bathrooms. The open-plan campground doesn't allow for much privacy between sites, but the central location makes it a perennial favorite, so it's worth reserving in advance for busy weekends.

SPORTS AND RECREATION

★ Burlington Bike Path

Burlington is a great place to be a cyclist. If you've got wheels, the logical place to start is the **Burlington Bike Path** (Burlington Parks and Recreation, 802/864-0123, www.enjoyburlington.com), an eight-mile path that runs along the river and connects several parks perfect for picnicking. A spur leads off to **Ethan Allen Homestead** (1 Ethan Allen Homestead Way, 802/865-4556, www.ethanallenhomestead.org), where cyclists with dirt-appropriate tires can follow paths to the **Intervale,** a cluster of 11 organic farms strung out along the Winooski River.

At the far northern end of the path you can continue onto the **Causeway,** an elevated path that has unparalleled views of the lake. On most summer weekends you can catch a **bicycle ferry** from the end of the causeway that will drop you and your bike on **South Hero Island.** For more information about the ferry, or to rent bikes, contact the nonprofit **Local Motion** (1 Steele St., 802/861-2700, www.localmotion.org, 10am-6pm Fri., weekends, holidays May 25-June 10 and Sept. 10-Oct. 8, 10am-6pm daily June 15-Sept. 3), which is a great source of cycling maps, gear, and advice on where to ride.

Walking Trails

You could stroll around downtown all day, but if you want to get your feet on some dirt, there are some excellent natural areas right in town. **The Rock Point Center** (20 Rock Point Rd., 802/658-6233, www.rockpointvt.org, donations accepted) is owned by the Episcopal Church, which invites visitors to stroll around their forested property that juts dramatically out into the lake, making for showstopping sunsets. Stop by the diocese office for a free pass.

Rock Point's main rival for sunset watching is **Red Rocks Park** (Central Ave., South Burlington, 802/846-4108), which has well-maintained trails with great lake views. But in springtime, at least, you won't take your eyes off the ground, which is carpeted in wildflowers: Look for Dutchman's-breeches, trillium, and columbine. For more information about parks, visit the **Burlington Parks and Recreation Department** website (www.enjoyburlington.com).

Boating

On sunny summer days the lakefront fills with a cheerful flotilla of kayaks, canoes, and stand-up paddleboards, as locals and tourist alike head for the water. It's a wonderful way to explore the ins and outs of the shoreline, like the crags at Lone Rock Point and the forested peninsula just to the north of **North Beach** (60 Institute Rd., 802/862-0942). Look carefully at the rocks on the northern side of the outcropping and you'll see a clear divide between the pale, smooth dolomite rock that makes up the top of the cliff and the dark, crumbling shale at the base. It's an exposed thrust fault, where continental plates are colliding. You can rent a kayak or paddleboard right on the beach from **Umiak Outfitters** (802/651-8760, 11am-6pm daily mid-June-Labor Day, $25-35/2 hrs.).

Closer to downtown, the **Community**

Lake Champlain Shipwrecks

On a dark night in December 1876, the canal schooner *General Butler* lost its steering and crashed headlong into Burlington Harbor, sinking just as the crew jumped to safety. It is now one of hundreds of ships that line the bottom of the lake, one of the best surviving collections of shipwrecks in the world. Many of them are remnants of the 3,000 schooners built to haul timber, iron ore, and coal across the lake in the active shipping trade of the 19th century. Currently, nine vessels are open to those with scuba gear and the wherewithal to explore this unique state park. In addition to the *Butler,* which rests under 40 feet of water in the harbor, other ships include a canal boat loaded down with granite blocks, a rare horse-powered ferryboat, and two long side-wheel steamboats.

For underwater tours and equipment rentals, visit **Waterfront Diving Center** (214 Battery St., 802/865-2771, www.waterfrontdiving.com). Basic scuba classes are $295, while two- and three-day summer trips are around $300 per person. The shop also works with a local charter company for day trips at $40 a head. All divers are required to register with a dive shop or the **Burlington Community Boathouse** (1 College St., 802/865-3377).

You don't have to be a diver to experience the wrecks, however. The **Lake Champlain Maritime Museum** (4772 Basin Harbor Rd., Vergennes, 802/475-2022, www.lcmm.org, tours $40 adults, $25 12 and under) offers dry-foot tours of the deep on selected Sundays in July, August, and September. Visit the wreck of steamboat *Champlain II* in a one-hour tour from their Basin Harbor location aboard a cruise boat that uses an ROV (remotely operated vehicle) equipped with a camera to view the wreck virtually on a video screen mounted onboard. The experience is the next-best thing to viewing it through a diving mask, and the guides tell the stories of the boat as well, bringing alive the final hours of the wreck in lurid detail. If interested, be sure to book well in advance.

Sailing Center (505 Lake St., 802/864-2499, www.communitysailingcenter.org, May-Oct., hours vary, $30-60/hr.) has kayaks, paddleboards, and sailboats for use in Burlington Bay and offers private and group classes if you want to brush up on your boat handling. Yogis ready to take their boat pose out for a spin should consider attending "Floating Yoga" classes taught on paddleboards (call for dates, $35).

Swimming

Midsummer can get downright muggy and would be miserable without a place to cool off in the lake. First and foremost is **North Beach** (60 Institute Rd., 802/862-0942), whose sandy beach, volleyball nets, and grills can seem more like Malibu than Vermont. There's a $6 fee for parking at the beach, or you can take a bus to Burlington High School, then walk in for free. The beach is also easily accessible from the Burlington Bike Path.

Another good option is **Oakledge Park** (Flynn Ave., 802/864-0123) on the other end of town, where you can swim off the beach or off the rocks just to the south. Be sure to wear shoes on the rocks to protect your feet from razor-sharp zebra mussels.

INFORMATION AND SERVICES

The **Lake Champlain Chamber of Commerce** (802/863-3489, www.vermont.org) runs an information booth during summer months on Church Street at the corner of Bank Street. Also look for a copy of the **Blue Map,** a detailed tourist map of downtown and the Greater Burlington Area.

For emergency and hospital services, head to **UVM Medical Center** (111 Colchester Ave., 802/847-0000), but **UVM Children's Hospital** (111 Colchester Ave., 802/847-0000) is equipped to handle younger patients' needs. Fill prescriptions at **Lakeside Pharmacy** (242 Pearl St., 802/862-1491, 8:30am-7pm

Mon.-Fri., 9am-4pm Sat., 9am-noon Sun.) or **Rite-Aid** (158 Cherry St., 7am-11pm Mon.-Fri., 8am-11pm Sat., 9am-9pm Sun., 802/862-1562), which also offers faxing services and has a second location (1024 North Ave., 802/865-7822). A handful of banks are in the downtown blocks of Burlington's retail area along Church Street. In that same area, ATMs seem to be on every block. In nonmedical emergencies, contact the headquarters for the **Burlington Police Department** (1 North Ave., 802/658-2704).

Internet access is offered at almost all cafés and at the **Fletcher Free Library** (235 College St., 802/863-3403, www.fletcherfree.org, 10am-8pm Tues.-Wed., 10am-6pm Thurs.-Sat. and Mon., noon-6pm Sun.). **FedEx Office Center** (199 Main St., 802/658-2561, 7am-10pm Mon.-Fri., 8am-8pm Sat., 10am-8pm Sun.) also offers fax services and shipping services.

GETTING THERE AND AROUND

Car

The easiest driving route to Burlington is I-89 across Vermont, a two-hour trip (90 mi.) from White River Junction. The more scenic route is to take winding Route 7 up from Rutland along the foothills of the Greens (65 mi., 1.75 hrs.).

Air

Flights from many major cities land at **Burlington International Airport** (BTV, 1200 Airport Dr., South Burlington, 802/863-2874, www.btv.aero), which is served by half a dozen airlines. Reservation desks for major rental car companies are available at the airport.

Bus and Train

Amtrak (800/872-7245, www.amtrak.com) sells ticket for trains to Burlington, but the station is 20 minutes away in Essex Junction (29 Railroad Ave.). **Greyhound Bus Lines** (800/231-2222, www.greyhound.com) runs buses to Burlington from Montréal and Boston that arrive at the airport, and **Megabus** (www.us.megabus.com) has regular service to several cities around the Northeast including Boston and New York City. Book ahead for low fares. The Burlington station is by the University of Vermont's Royal Tyler Theater (116 University Pl.).

Chittenden County Transportation Authority (802/864-2282, http://ridegmt.com) has bus routes throughout Burlington and the surrounding area, including buses downtown from the airport and train station. To get to downtown from the airport, take bus route 12, which arrives every 25-30 minutes (last bus is at 9:30pm Mon.-Fri., 9:20pm Sat., 7:05pm Sun.). Get off at the University Mall, and change to any bus toward downtown (ask the driver for a transfer). From the train station in Essex Junction, take bus route 2, which takes approximately 40 minutes to make the trip between Essex Junction and Cherry Street. Bus fare is $1.25.

Taxi

Taxi stands are also available at the airport and the train station; to call a cab from other locations, contact **Green Cab VT** (802/864-2424, http://greencabvt.com). Burlington is also served by **Uber** (www.uber.com), a mobile app service connecting riders with private drivers/vehicles.

Ferry

From New York, it's possible to get to Burlington via ferry from Port Kent. Several boats a day are run by **Lake Champlain Transportation** (King Street Dock, 802/864-9804, www.ferries.com, mid-June-late Sept., $8 adults, $3.10 children, children under 6 free, $30 vehicle and driver one-way), which take about an hour to cross the lake. The round-trip threading through the lake's islands is also one of the most economical ways to enjoy Champlain's scenery.

Lake Champlain Islands

With more shoreline than any other part of Vermont, this cluster of islands at the northern end of the Champlain Valley feels entirely separate from the rest of the state—if not the world. There's water on every end, along with farms, storm-weathered homes, and residents who lift their hands in a lazy wave as they pass on back roads. **South Hero** has the bulk of the landmass and is connected by bridge to the wasp-waisted **North Hero,** whose bustling general store is the islands' social hub. By contrast, the most secluded of the islands is the haunting **Isle La Motte,** home to a Catholic pilgrimage site and former site of the first settlement in the state. La Motte offers tranquil views of the lake all the way to the New York coast. Confusingly, **Grand Isle** is not an island, but a town on South Hero, and also the name of the county that contains it.

The islands' colonial story began when Samuel de Champlain arrived here about 400 years ago, and they're good for those seeking history as well as a little R&R. New England's oldest log cabin is somehow still standing in Grand Isle, and each island's individual historical societies showcase artifacts from early settlers. All that said, besides a handful of other sights of note, there isn't much else to do here—which is precisely how many visitors would have it.

SOUTH HERO

Snow Farm Vineyard

Vermont's oldest winery, **Snow Farm Vineyard** (190 W. Shore Rd., 802/372-9463, www.snowfarm.com, 11am-5pm daily May-Dec.) has won multiple awards for its delicate pinot noirs and vidal blanc ice wines. Free tours of the winery are offered daily at 11am and 2pm. During the summer the vineyard sponsors a free Music in the Vineyard series on Thursday nights, so bring a blanket and lounge in the grass. The tunes begin at 6:30pm, but for prime picnicking, snag a patch of grass at 5pm.

Allenholm Farm

The best place to get in touch with the agricultural ambience of the islands is **Allenholm Farm** (150 South St., 802/372-5566, www.allenholm.com, 9am-5pm daily May-Dec.), which has a petting paddock full of animals, including two donkeys, a Scotch Highland cow, and a fat ewe with a taste for peppermints. The farm grows over 20 varieties of apples, which you can pick yourself or buy by the peck.

Hyde Log Cabin

Built by hand in 1783, the compact **Hyde Cabin** (Rte. 2, just north of Hyde Road, Grand Isle, 802/828-3051, $3) is said to be among the oldest log cabins in the United States, and volunteer docents—often costumed—enthusiastically share stories and facts from Vermont's early days. Hours are limited and a bit unpredictable, so it's worth calling before making a special trip.

Food

With a relaxed atmosphere and a regular crowd of locals, the kitchen at the **Blue Paddle Bistro** (316 Rte. 2, 802/372-4814, www.bluepaddlebistro.com, 5pm-close Tues.-Sat., $18-27) turns out well executed, "globally inspired" meals. Terrific gorgonzola-stuffed meat loaf is a long-standing favorite, but there's also filet mignon, pork tenderloin, and plenty of seafood mains (it's an island, right?). The bar is crowned with a full-size canoe, and unlike many island establishments, the bistro is open all year.

Tucked into an unprepossessing converted home in Grand Isle, ★ **Cook Sisters** (308 Rte. 2, Grand Isle, 802/372-0101, 11am-8pm Mon.-Sat., lunch $9-12, dinner $12-15) is casual and welcoming. Sunny days draw diners

Lake Champlain Islands

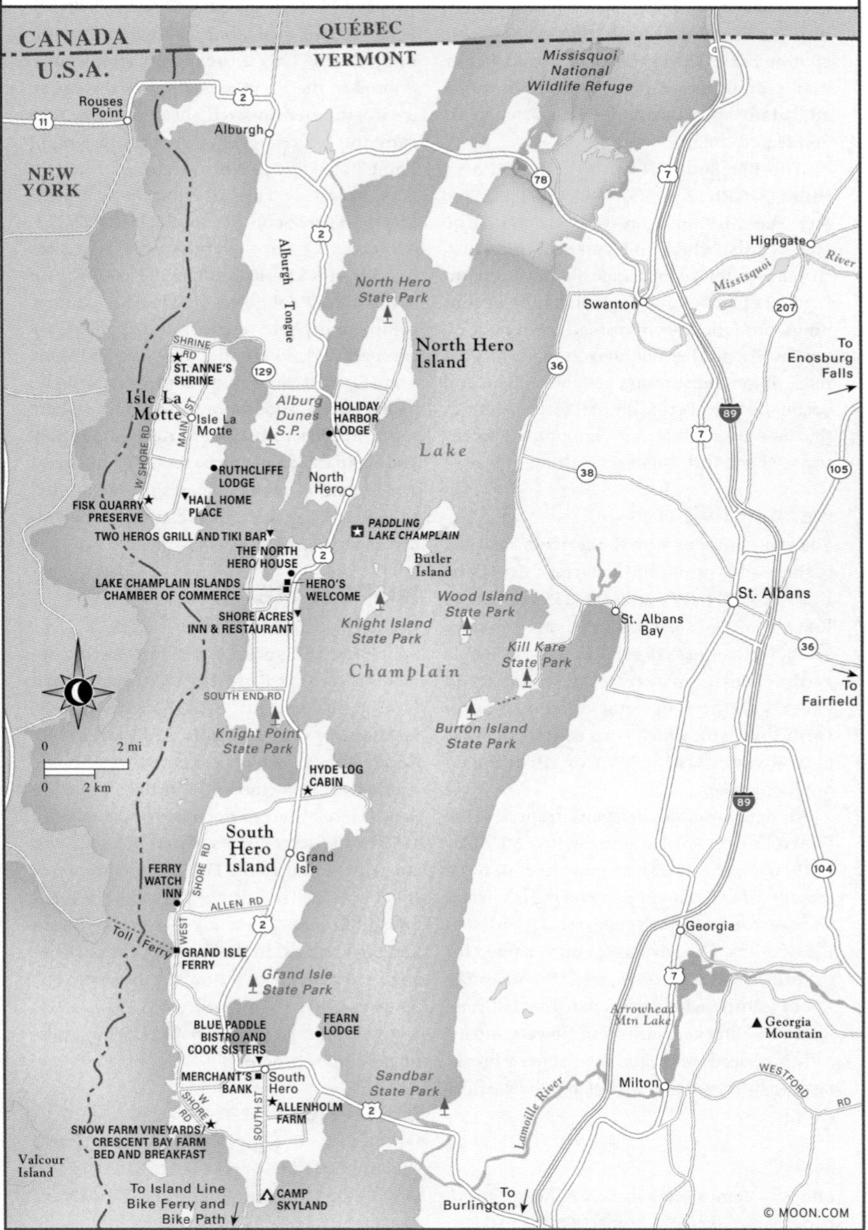

onto the deck, and the restaurant's occasional events—wine and painting, trivia nights—have become gathering places for the community. It's the food, though, that keeps people coming back: The lunch menu's sandwiches, salads, and soups are just great, and dinner adds daily specials along with pasta, steak, and seared tuna.

Another South Hero favorite is **Pan's Pizza** (326 Rte. 2, 802/372-4279, 4:30pm-7pm Sun.-Tues., 4:30pm-8pm Wed.-Sat., $11-30, no credit cards), which offers takeout thin crust, so you won't have to change out of your bathing suit. They've got the usual suite of toppings, but for a lesson in small town politics, try the Town Meeting: mayonnaise, mozzarella, onion, mushroom, artichoke, feta, and bacon. Like the actual annual town meetings that take place all around Vermont, the eccentric pie has a little bit of everything.

Accommodations

You can commune with the agricultural spirit of the islands on a working farm at **Crescent Bay Farm Bed & Breakfast** (153 West Shore Rd., 802/324-5563, www.crescentbaybb.com, $150), which raises pigs and produces maple syrup. The rooms are old-fashioned and sweet, and the proprietors also own Snow Farm Vineyard, which is an easy stroll away, ideal if you're tasting wine or attending an outdoor concert.

All dark wood and elegant draperies, the **Fearn Lodge** (50 Lighthouse Rd., 802/370-3028, www.fearnlodge.com, $250-300) has a magnificent 10 acre property on the lakefront, and just two guest bedrooms. The grandest of the two, The Equestrian Room, is named for the owners quarter horses, while the Victorian Room features a luxurious claw-foot bathtub. Rooms are stocked with fresh flowers and locally produced treats, and the elaborate breakfast can be served on the back porch on sunny days.

CAMPING

Loops of campsites, cabins, and lean-tos occupy prime lakefront property at **Grand Isle State Park** (36 East Shore Rd. South, Grand Isle, 802/372-4300, mid-May-mid-Oct., tent sites $18-22, lean-tos $25-29, cabins $48-50), where there's also a boat launch and swimming beach. This is the most-visited campground in the Vermont state park system, so it's worth reserving well ahead of time. Your camping fee also gets you access to Knight Point State Park on North Hero.

A privately run alternative is **Camp Skyland** (398 South St., South Hero, 802/372-4200, www.campskylandvt.com, tent sites $32, RV sites $35-40, cabins $500-600/wk.) on South Hero's southern tip, where a summer camp atmosphere reigns in the open, grassy campground, where sites are basic and short on privacy. The campground has a private, pebble beach, and it's the kind of place where some families return year after year. Simply and compact cabins can be rented by the week, and amenities include horseshoe pits, rental canoes and kayaks, and a reading room with board games.

NORTH HERO

Knight Point State Park

Sprawling lawns are rimmed by towering deciduous trees at **Knight Point State Park** (44 Knight Point Rd., 802/372-8389, https://vtstateparks.com, $4 adults, $2 children 4-13, under 4 free), which covers North Hero's southern tip. North Hero was once linked to South Hero by ferry, which was operated until 1892 by the descendants of John Knight, who started the shuttle in 1785. There are a few short walking trails in the park, but the main attraction here is a sandy swimming beach and boat rentals. In the summer, the park becomes a dramatic backdrop for the **Vermont Shakespeare Company** (877/874-1911, www.vermontshakespeare.org), which performs outdoors here.

North Hero State Park

Quieter than Knight Point State Park, the unstaffed **North Hero State Park** (3803 Lakeview Dr., 802/372-8727, https://vtstateparks.com, $4 adults, $2 children 4-13,

Lake Champlain's Monster

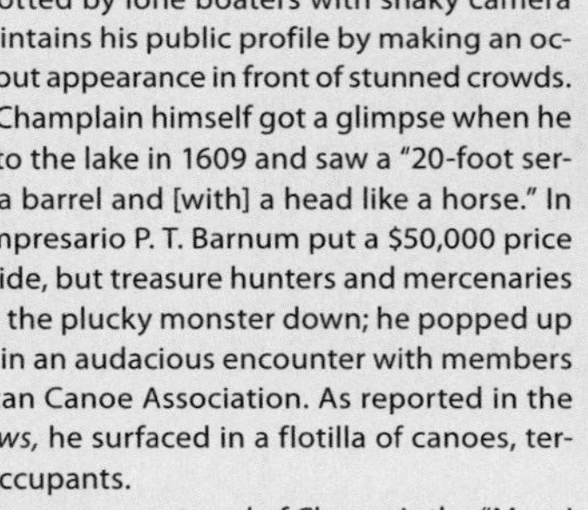

Did you just see something in the water? Like the Loch Ness in Scotland, Lake Champlain is supposed to be home to an endemic monster. The Abenaki referred to him as Tatoskok and believed he ate humans, but these days he's thoroughly nonviolent and affectionately known as Champ. Generally quite shy, Champ is most frequently spotted by lone boaters with shaky camera hands but maintains his public profile by making an occasional blowout appearance in front of stunned crowds.

Champ can easily be spotted at Burlington baseball games.

Samuel de Champlain himself got a glimpse when he first traveled to the lake in 1609 and saw a "20-foot serpent thick as a barrel and [with] a head like a horse." In 1873, circus impresario P. T. Barnum put a $50,000 price on Champ's hide, but treasure hunters and mercenaries couldn't keep the plucky monster down; he popped up again in 1892 in an audacious encounter with members of the American Canoe Association. As reported in the *Burlington News,* he surfaced in a flotilla of canoes, terrifying their occupants.

The best image ever captured of Champ is the "Mansi Photo," taken in the summer of 1977, which gives a clear profile of a slender neck and wide shoulders. Theories abound as to Champ's origins and range from the idea that he's a dinosaur that was left behind, or that he's an enormous, thick-bodied eel. If you go to find out by yourself, keep your distance; both Vermont and New York have laws on the books making it illegal to harm the (maybe) mythical monster.

Champ might be elusive in the wild, but he can always be spotted at the games of Burlington's minor-league baseball team, the Vermont Lake Monsters.

under 4 free) is mostly used as a launching point for boaters, but there's a pleasant swimming beach here, as well.

Shopping

Retail is sparse among the islands: Most folks here seem more interested in forgetting the rest of the world than buying something from it. There is, however, a prime example of a Vermont general store at **Hero's Welcome** (3537 Rte. 2, 802/372-4161, www.heroswelcome.com), which stocks Adirondack chairs, books on and maps of the area, squall jackets, and assorted gadgets. Hours are 6:30am-7pm Monday-Thursday, 6:30am-7pm Friday, 7am-7pm Saturday-Sunday mid-June-Labor Day; 6:30am-6pm Monday-Friday, 7am-6pm Saturday, 8am-5pm Sunday Labor Day-October; 6:30am-5pm Monday-Friday, 7am-5pm Saturday, 8am-5pm Sunday November-March; 6:30am-6pm Monday-Friday, 7am-6pm Saturday, 8am-6pm Sunday April-mid-June.

Food and Accommodations

Far from both the tropics and the sea, Vermont nonetheless has three tiki bars, including one in downtown Burlington and another in the mountain bike hub of East Burke. It's only fitting that the third is on an actual island, and **Two Heros Grill and Tiki Bar** (2253 Pelots Point Rd., 802/372-3900, 3pm-9pm Fri., 11am-9pm Sat.-Sun. mid-May-Sept., $9-13) makes a fine place to unwind after a day on the water. The basic menu of vaguely maritime-themed bar food includes a few grilled options, but this destination is mostly about cold beer and the

Island Camping with Mainland Access

Some of the most intriguing and secluded camp spots on Lake Champlain's smaller islands are accessible from the mainland side, like the former agricultural island that is now **Burton Island State Park** (St. Albans Bay, 802/524-6353, https://vtstateparks.com, late May-early Sept., campsites $18-37). Take a ferry to the campground, swimming, and recreation area; a resident naturalist even gives deer-spotting tours. Ferry service is available several times a day from **Kill Kare State Park,** southwest of St. Albans center. The island itself has 17 tent sites in a loop near the ferry landing and 26 lean-tos, most directly on the shore, within a relatively comfy campground offering hot showers and Wi-Fi. Canoes and rowboats are also available for rent.

If even that's too much civilization for you, bring your own boat to **Woods Island** (St. Albans Bay, 802/524-6353, https://vtstateparks.com, late May-early Sept., campsites $18-25), a primitive getaway that lives up to its name. A so-called "remote area" campground, the facilities here are delightfully simple—just five carry-in/carry-out campsites along the beach, each with only a simple fire ring and basic latrine. Permits are available through Burton Island State Park. Despite the hassle of arranging a stay here, the experience of a remote wilderness only a few miles from Vermont's largest city is unbeatable, and the spring wildflowers are a delight. Ask for site #4 if possible, which has a fire ring on a slender peninsula and a commanding view of the lake.

occasional blended drink. Oh, and there's boat parking.

The view from **Shore Acres Inn and Restaurant** (237 Shore Acres Dr., 802/372-8722, www.shoreacres.com, 5pm-8pm Mon.-Sat., meals $20-40, rooms $127-256) is delightful, and the traditional mains—such as pot roast and filet mignon—get happy reviews. Other simple but flavorful dishes include homemade grilled polenta and roasted rack of lamb in port-rosemary sauce. Rooms feel fairly basic and generic for the price, but it's the location and property that are the real draw. Adirondack chairs are great for sunsets on the lawn, there are kayaks and croquet sets available for use, and guests can swim and play tennis, golf, shuffleboard, and horseshoes. Rates include a continental breakfast from mid-April through mid-June, then late August through the beginning of December.

Another island option with an excellent vantage point, ★ **The North Hero House** (3643 Rte. 2, 802/372-4732, www.northherohouse.com, meals $18-33, rooms $140-350) has expansive lake views and old-fashioned charm. The colonial-style inn has 26 lovely and individually decorated rooms, most with antique beds, floral linens, and some with a private balcony. The semiformal on-site restaurant also overlooks the water and has a seasonally changing menu of classic dishes: Think salmon, pasta, and steak, with a few more basic options.

A great, affordable find with a waterfront location, **Holiday Harbor Lodge** (8369 Rte. 2, 802/372/4722, www.holidayharborlodge.com, rooms $125, lake views $165) has rooms with rustic, log cabin decor. Most of the simple lake-view rooms are motel style, with a screened porch, fridge, microwave, grill, and picnic table, though a few offer kitchenettes. The lakeside rooms, which have either one or two bedrooms and are generally booked weekly during the summer season, have full kitchens, a living room, and gas fireplace. With the tagline "where fish live," the lodge is all about fishing, and anglers come to drop a line in summer and winter.

ISLE LA MOTTE

Fisk Quarry Preserve

The legacy of Lake Champlain's prehistoric sojourn in the tropics is on view at the **Fisk Quarry** (West Shore Rd., 802/862-4150, www.lclt.org). Poking out of the quarry walls are the fossilized remains of the 480-million-year-old Chazy Coral Reef, the oldest known coral reef in the world. Its stony sides are visibly embedded with stromatoporoid, ancient ancestors of modern-day sea sponges. The preserve is just to the south of Fisk Farm (3849 West Shore Rd.).

St. Anne's Shrine

Situated at the far northern end of Lake Champlain, the Isle La Motte is all sparse forest and windswept solitude. It must have seemed even more desolate in 1666, when the first European settlement in Vermont, Fort St. Anne, was built by French explorers under the command of Pierre de St. Paul, Sieur La Motte. They also erected a shrine to St. Anne, staffed by Jesuit priests who accompanied the expedition. Four hundred years later, **St. Anne's Shrine** (West Shore Rd./Shrine Rd., 802/928-3362, www.saintannesshrine.org, 9am-7pm daily mid-May-mid-Oct., tours every half hour, $2 adults) still exists as a Catholic pilgrimage site, though the current building dates only from the late 19th century. In addition to the main building, where mass is still said regularly in season, the picturesque lakeshore is dotted by various grottoes filled with religious statues, including a 15-foot gold-leaf statue of the Virgin Mary rescued from a Burlington cathedral. Up the hill, a rectory and cafeteria have a small museum full of relics dating back to the French occupation in the 17th century. The lake itself is fittingly graced by a statue of the man who discovered it in 1609, explorer Samuel de Champlain, sculpted by F. L. Weber for the Montréal Expo in 1967.

Alburg Dunes State Park

A peninsula juts down from Canada into the midst of the Lake Champlain islands, and Alburg is worth a stop even if it's not *entirely* surrounded by water. With rolling sand dunes and a long, natural beach of soft sand **Alburg Dunes State Park** (151 Coon Point Rd., Alburg, 802/796-4170, https://vtstateparks.com, $4 adult, $2 children 4-13) is a great place to swim and enjoy summer sun; shallow water that extends from the shoreline makes it a favorite for younger families. Since the park faces southwest, this is a particularly nice place to watch the sunset.

Food and Accommodations

If you're looking for something simple and satisfying on Isle La Motte, the **Hall Home Place** (4445 Main St., 802/928-3091, 7:30am-2:30pm Fri., 8:30am-2:30pm Sat.-Sun. May-June, 7:30am-2:30pm Sat.-Sun. July-Sept., $5-8) may be just the thing (and the café has, admittedly, very little competition on the rural island). Sandwiches, home-baked treats, and coffee are on the menu at this sweet spot that's right in an orchard. In addition to the café, Hall Home Place makes truly delightful **ice cider,** a sweet, alcoholic cider that is made by fermenting fresh apple cider concentrated by freezing—the technique was invented in Québec in the 1990s and evokes traditional ice wines.

A simple, lakeside motel with an on-site Italian restaurant, **Ruthcliffe Lodge** (1002 Quarry Rd., 802/928-3200, www.ruthcliffe.com, rooms $142-152, dinner 5pm-8pm Thurs.-Sat. $29-40) has six simple and somewhat dated rooms with notably firm beds on the eastern shore of Isle La Motte. Views are lovely from the lawn, which is scattered with chairs and hammocks, and there are kayaks and canoes available to rent. The reservation-only restaurant, which is a bit pricey for the casual feel and open from May through September, gets solid reviews for its classic Italian American mains, and an outdoor patio is especially nice on warm summer evenings.

SPORTS AND RECREATION

★ Paddling Lake Champlain

Given that the islands are home to more shoreline than anywhere else in Vermont, this is an ideal place to take to the water in your choice of craft. Kayaks and canoes are perfect for nosing around the islands' many crannies and nooks, and in warm weather you can take a stand-up paddleboard for a spin. As with many things on the islands, a good place to start is **Hero's Welcome** (3537 Rte. 2, North Hero, 802/372-4161, www.heroswelcome.com), where kayaks, paddleboards, canoes, and rowing sculls are available starting at $25/$33 for a half/full day. The hours for Hero's Welcome are 6:30am-7pm Monday-Thursday, 6:30am-7pm Friday, 7am-7pm Saturday-Sunday mid-June-Labor Day; 6:30am-6pm Monday-Friday, 7am-6pm Saturday, 8am-5pm Sunday Labor Day-October; 6:30am-5pm Monday-Friday, 7am-5pm Saturday, 8am-5pm Sunday November-March; 6:30am-6pm Monday-Friday, 7am-6pm Saturday, 8am-6pm Sunday April-mid-June.

Experienced paddlers can pack their camping gear and head out to the remote boat-in campsites that make up the **Lake Champlain Paddlers' Trail** (www.lakechamplaincommittee.org, 802/658-1414). There are 41 sites on the lake, spaced out by a day's paddle of 8-10 miles.

If you'd prefer that someone else steer, you'll be safe in the hands of Captain Holly, the skipper at **Driftwood Tours** (3643 Rte. 2, North Hero, www.driftwoodtoursvt.com, 802/373-0022, $40/$60 for one-/two-hour trip) whose boat heads out from the dock at the **North Hero House.** Or you can hop on the **Grand Isle Ferry** (1268 Gordon's Landing, South Hero, 802/864-9804, www.ferries.com, $4.50 adults, $2.25 children 6-12, $10.75 driver and vehicle) for the 15-minute crossing to Plattsburgh, New York. The ferry runs 24 hours a day, all year.

Biking

Lake Champlain Bikeways (1 Steele St., #103, Burlington, 802/652-2453, www.champlainbikeways.org) distributes a pamphlet titled *Champlain Island Bikeways,* which details five loops around the islands taking in sand dunes, a log cabin, and the quirky stone castles built by a Swiss gardener.

Bicycle rentals are available at **Hero's Welcome** (3537 Rte. 2, North Hero, 802/372-4161, www.heroswelcome.com, $23/$27 for half/full day). You can also snag wheels at **Allenholm Farm** (150 South St., South Hero, 802/372-5566, www.allenholm.com, 9am-5pm daily May-Dec., $20/$25 for half/full day).

Swimming

If you're sweaty and spontaneous enough, you can hop in the lake wherever you'd like, but for a great swimming beach, you can't beat the sand at **Knight Point State Park** (44 Knight Point Rd., North Hero, 802/372-8389, https://vtstateparks.com, 10am-sunset Memorial Day-Labor Day, $3 adults, $2 children), which also has boat rentals, picnic areas, and grills for cooking.

INFORMATION AND SERVICES

There's a **Merchants Bank** (301 Rte. 2, Grand Isle, 802/372-4222, 9am-4pm Mon.-Thurs., 9am-5:30pm Fri.) right before the bridge to North Hero.

GETTING THERE AND AROUND

From Burlington, most of the Champlain Islands are accessible by highway. Take I-89 to exit 7, then U.S. 2 north to North Hero (30 mi., 45 min.). If arriving on a summer weekend, one option is to ride the **Burlington Bike Path** north across the Lake Champlain Causeway, then catch the bicycle-only ferry to South Hero. There is no public transportation to the islands.

Lower Champlain Valley

You're never far from the lake or mountains that border this rolling swath of farmland. It's easy to weave between dairy farms and mountain towns, and you could spend a few grand days exploring back roads, picking apples and blueberries, or following the footsteps of escaped enslaved people, Revolutionary War soldiers, and agricultural aristocrats.

SHELBURNE

A sweet cluster of inns and shops, it would be easy to miss Shelburne entirely, but beyond the picturesque downtown is a gracious landscape of well-kempt farms and vineyards. The sprawling Shelburne Farms is a grand example of a historic agricultural estate, with walking trails and barns, while Shelburne Museum is a trove of art and ephemera. And even without visiting the major sites, it's a pleasant place to spend a fall day picking apples and tasting wine.

★ Shelburne Museum

The **Shelburne Museum** (5555 Shelburne Rd., 802/985-3346, www.shelburnemuseum.org, 10am-5pm daily May-Oct., limited exhibits 10am-5pm daily Nov.-Dec., limited exhibits 10am-5pm Wed.-Sun. Jan.-Apr., $25 adults, $14 youth 13-17, $12 child 5-12, children under 5 free, $65 family day pass) is less a museum than a city-state founded by a hoarder with exquisite taste. Its 38 buildings are full of extraordinary art and historical gewgaws, not to mention a Lake Champlain steamship and its own covered bridge. This is the work of art collector Electra Havemeyer Webb, who relocated buildings from across the country to display her collection, opening the museum in 1947. The buildings are as intriguing as their contents, and include a 19th-century jailhouse, a Methodist meeting house, and a beautifully restored round barn, one of just two dozen built in Vermont.

Webb's own home was a Greek Revival mansion that now holds first-rate paintings by Cassatt, Degas, Monet, Corot, and Manet, including the first impressionist painting brought to America, a Monet painting of a drawbridge, which was purchased by Webb in Paris for $20.

The Shelburne Museum features thousands of figurines.

TOP EXPERIENCE

Farm Visits

Though agriculture no longer dominates the Vermont economy as it once did, farming and agricultural life remain at the core of the state's identity. On warm, summer weekends, families pick fruit at their local berry farms, dinners are held in barns and fields, and fall harvest feels like a statewide celebration. The farms range from elegant historic properties to down-home orchards, and there are dozens of ways to experience the bounty in the Champlain Valley. Shelburne, south of Burlington, is home to two favorite spots: Shelburne Farms and Shelburne Orchards.

THE INTERVALE

A mile and a half north of downtown Burlington, **The Intervale** (180 Intervale Rd., Burlington, 802/660-0440, www.intervale.org) is a collection of organic farms within the city limits, occupying the floodplains that surround the Winooski River. The nonprofit **Intervale Center** helps nurture young farmers and "incubator farms," addressing the challenges and high start-up costs of establishing a farm on your own (Adam's Berry Farm was once at the Intervale). It's worth heading down to the Intervale to walk the dirt road that passes between the farms, and on Thursdays in July and August, **Summervale** is a celebration of all things local with food tastings, wood-fired pizza, music, and plenty of farmers enjoying beers after a day in the fields. From April through October, **free tours** of the Intervale take place on the fourth Friday of the month 10am-11am (reserve your place by calling the center or emailing Carolyn Zeller: carolyn@intervale.org).

BREAD AND BUTTER FARM

Bread and Butter Farm (200 Leduc Farm Dr., Shelburne, 802/985-9200, www.breadandbutterfarm.com) produces grass-fed beef and organic, no-till vegetables in the rolling country between Burlington and Shelburne. Stop by their on-farm **Blank Page Café** (8am-2pm Mon.-Fri., 8am-1pm Sat.) for great coffee and farm-fresh treats, or just come by the fabulous **Burger Nights** held on six Fridays during the summer, with music and food served family-style. (Visit the website for Burger Night reservations; tickets must be booked in advance.) The farm is a 15-minute drive south of downtown Burlington.

SHELBURNE FARMS

Shelburne Farms (1611 Harbor Rd., Shelburne, 802/985-8686, www.shelburnefarms.org, 9am-5:30pm daily mid-May-Oct., $8 adults, $7 seniors, $5 children 3-17, children under 3 free) is a bewitching property that's a wonderful stop for a stroll through the wooded paths and rolling farm fields, past elegant barns with patinated copper roofs. The farm was the country retreat of

Shelburne Vineyard and Fiddlehead Brewing

Lines of grapevines welcome visitors to **Shelburne Vineyard** (6308 Shelburne Rd., 802/982-8222, www.shelburnevineyard.com, 11am-6pm daily May-Oct., 11am-5pm daily Nov.-Apr.), which produces award-winning wines from cold hardy varieties. The $7 tastings include a souvenir wineglass and a sampling of 8-10 wines that you can choose from a list of available options; don't miss the award-winning Marquette Reserve.

Just across the street is **Fiddlehead Brewing** (802/399-2994, www.fiddleheadbrewing.com, 11am-9pm Sat., noon-9pm Sun.-Fri.), which offers free tasting of their beers on tap as well as growler and growlette fills. Their flagship is the hoppy and rather austere (for Vermont) Fiddlehead IPA, which appears alongside the Webb family, and if you find it inspires hazy historical fantasies about roaming the estate with members of the American aristocracy and their glamorous guests, you're not the only one.

These days, though, you're more likely to bump into schoolkids than scions, as Shelburne Farms is now a non-profit that works for sustainability in the food system. All income from the property goes to education and conservation efforts, including those from the inn and on-site restaurant. Sights change with the season: Spring means maple sugaring and lambing—stopping by the farm to snuggle baby lambs is a yearly pilgrimage that's not to be missed—and you can bundle up for horse-drawn sleigh rides in the winter. The on-site cheese-making operation is active year-round, and the welcome center is well-stocked with samples.

Shelburne Orchards

SHELBURNE ORCHARDS

Shelburne Orchards (216 Orchard Rd., Shelburne, 802/985-2753, www.shelburneorchards.com, 9am-6pm Mon.-Fri., 9am-5pm Sat.-Sun. Sept.-late Oct.) is lined with undulating rows of trees that produce over a dozen varieties of apples, and it's a marvelous experience to visit in the early fall when the air is heavy with the scent of ripe fruit. The trees keep their own timetables, so before coming to pick fruit, call ahead to see what's available. Not all of Shelburne Orchards' joys are so terribly healthy: The house-made cider doughnuts are delightful in a crust of cinnamon sugar, and the charismatic owner distills remarkably good apple brandy from his pressed apples.

ADAM'S BERRY FARM

Adam's Berry Farm (985 Bingham Brook Rd., Charlotte, 802/578-9093, www.adamsberryfarm.com, 9am-6pm daily in season, early June through first frost in September, cash only) brings crowds of families for pick-your-own organic blueberries, raspberries, and strawberries on a beautiful property in Charlotte, which is a 15-minute drive from Shelburne, or a half-hour drive south of downtown Burlington. After you've stained your fingers blue (or red), head to the farm stand to pick up popsicles made with their own fruit as well as quince paste, jams, and sorbets.

their even hoppier Second Fiddle at bars around the state. It's worth stopping by to try their more experimental varieties, too, which often blend in seasonal ingredients from the area.

Vermont Teddy Bear Company

The **Vermont Teddy Bear Company** (6655 Shelburne Rd./Rte. 7, 802/985-3001, www.vermontteddybear.com, 9am-6pm daily mid-June-early Sept., 9am-5pm daily early Sept.-mid-Oct., 10am-4pm daily mid-Oct.-mid-June, $4 adults, $3 seniors, children 12 and under free) succeeds at a challenging task—to display the mechanics of a production-oriented toy factory while infusing the process with creativity and magic. Even for nonbelievers, they do a darn good job, and there's little point in resisting the charm. The gift shop is stocked with bears and bear things, from children's books to artwork and tiny gift boxes of "bear poo."

Or you can create your own toy at the "Make a Friend for Life" station, where you select a bear body, then fill it with fluff from a machine whose settings include Joy, Giggles, and Imagination.

Events

Past performers at the **Concerts on the Green** (5555 Shelburne Rd., 802/985-3346, www.shelburnemuseum.org) music series include Willie Nelson, Emmylou Harris, and Crosby, Stills, and Nash. Musicians play on select summer weekends on the grounds of the Shelburne Museum.

Shelburne Farms hosts the annual **Vermont Cheesemakers Festival** (1611 Harbor Rd., 866/261-8595, www.vtcheesefest.com, mid-Aug.), where you can sample the state's best wedges all in one place. Along with ample time to graze, the festival includes cheese-making demos, cooking demos, and workshops.

Shopping

You can find something to read by the lake at **The Flying Pig Bookstore** (5247 Shelburne Rd., 802/985-3999, www.flyingpigbooks.com, 10am-6pm Mon.-Sat., noon-5pm Sun.), which has a wide range of general-interest books and an excellent children's section. For groceries stop by **Shelburne Supermarket** (20 Shelburne Shopping Park, 802/985-8520, 8am-8pm Mon.-Sat., 8am-7pm Sun.), which carries many products by local bakers, cheese makers, and other artisans.

Food

As renowned for the food and drinks as for the setting, the ★ **Inn at Shelburne Farms** (1611 Harbor Rd., 802/985-8498, mid-May-mid-Oct., brunch $11-18, dinner $29-40) is worth a trip to the area. The inn's restaurant prepares beautiful meals with ingredients grown organically on-site, and it's worth coming early to enjoy a drink in an Adirondack chair on the lawn. If you'd like to experience the inn without splashing out for a full dinner, the Sunday brunch is an excellent, affordable option. Reservations are essential. Shelburne Farm's very own food truck, the **Farm Cart** (11am-3pm daily mid-May-mid-Oct.), serves lunch food made from the farm's organic ingredients. Find the farm cart parked beside the Farm Barn, and try grilled cheese sandwiches, grass-fed burgers, and hearty salads.

In the village center, **Rustic Roots** (195 Falls Rd., 802/985-9511, www.rusticrootsvt.com, 9am-3pm Wed.-Sun., 6pm-7:30pm Fri.-Sat., $14-25) serves thoughtful food with European flair in a restored home, using many local ingredients. And for a coffee with something sweet, **Village Wine and Coffee** (5288 Shelburne Rd., 802/985-8922, www.villagewineandcoffee.com, 7am-6pm Mon.-Sat., 8:30am-4pm Sun.) is a favorite stop by the town's main intersection.

Head to the southern edge of town to find **Folino's Pizza** (6305 Shelburne Rd., 802/881-8822, www.folinopizza.com, noon-9pm daily, $10-18), which serves crisp, wood-fired pizza with views of the vineyard next door. Try the rhapsody-inspiring flatbread with bacon, scallops, and lemon zest. They're strictly BYO, but they've got a freezer full of pint glasses and share a building with **Fiddlehead Brewing** (802/399-2994, www.fiddleheadbrewing.com, 11am-9pm Sat., noon-9pm Sun.-Fri).

Accommodations

The gorgeously preserved ★ **Inn at Shelburne Farms** (1611 Harbor Rd., 802/985-8498, mid-May-mid-Oct., rooms $160-530) is situated right on the lake and, with an expansive lawn and formal gardens, may well have the best sunset views in the Champlain Valley. Once the home of the William Seward and Lila Vanderbilt Webb, the inn is full of historic charm, from the guest bedrooms to the wonderfully old-fashioned library. Rates include breakfast, and the opportunity to spend your days wandering the expansive farm.

The **Heart of the Village Inn** (5347

Shelburne Rd., 802/985-9060, $230-430) is housed in a sweet Victorian in the center of town and charms with thoughtful touches like locally made chocolates. The homemade breakfasts are sumptuous, with hot and cold options available daily.

CAMPING

In addition to a great hiking trail, **Mount Philo State Park** (5425 Mt. Philo Rd., Charlotte, 802/425-2390, https://vtstateparks.com, $18-27) has a small campground of 10 sites and lean-tos that are well worth snagging in advance. RVers and tenters can set up shop at the **Shelburne Camping Area** (4385 Shelburne Rd., Shelburne, 802/985-2540, www.shelburnecamping.com, $34-50), whose serviceable sites are conveniently located.

Information and Services

The **Shelburne Museum** (5555 Shelburne Rd., 802/985-3346, www.shelburnemuseum.org, 10am-5pm daily May-Dec., 10am-5pm Wed.-Sun. Jan.-Apr.) has a visitor information center stocked with maps and brochures; no admission required.

A **Rite-Aid Pharmacy** (30 Shelburne Shopping Park, 802/985-2610, 8am-8pm Mon.-Fri., 9am-6pm Sat., 9am-5pm Sun., pharmacy closed Sat.-Sun.) is in the center of downtown. Free Wi-Fi is available at **Bruegger's Bagel Bakery** (2989 Shelburne Rd., 802/985-3183, 5:30am-5pm Mon.-Fri., 6am-5pm Sat.-Sun.). In an emergency, contact the **Shelburne Police** (5420 Shelburne Rd., 802/985-8051).

VERGENNES AND FERRISBURGH

Vergennes is the smallest city in Vermont, and with just 2,600 residents, even the word "city" can seem aspirational. But little Vergennes has been the backdrop for key historical dramas: During the War of 1812, it was the home base for a shipyard that heroically built a fleet to defeat the British on the lake—one of the few bright spots in a disastrous war. Just up the road, tiny **Ferrisburgh** was a key stop in the journeys of many African Americans fleeing slavery.

That history is on display at the extraordinary Lake Champlain Maritime Museum, which makes a fascinating stop for history buffs and boat lovers, and the Rokeby Museum, one of the best-preserved Underground Railroad sites in the country. And modern-day Vergennes is a lovely place to stop for a meal or to explore the tiny downtown, which is full of boutiques and cafés and overlooks the tranquil Otter Creek.

★ Lake Champlain Maritime Museum

The **Lake Champlain Maritime Museum** (4472 Basin Harbor Rd., Vergennes, 802/475-2022, www.lcmm.org, 10am-5pm daily late May-mid-Oct., $14 adults, $12 seniors, $8 students 5-17, children under 5 free, admission good for two consecutive days), just a few miles from the lakeshore, does an exceptional job of bringing alive the scope of the lake's domestic and military history, with a hands-on boatbuilding workshop, an exhibit on the more than 200 shipwrecks that line the lake bottom, and an interactive display on the lake's importance in the Revolutionary War.

Perhaps the biggest surprise is the story of patriot-turned-traitor Benedict Arnold, who led a heroic defense of the lake in the early years of the war. Arnold commissioned a fleet of gunships to be built at the lake's southern end in Skenesborough and fought a hopeless battle with the British off the shore of Valcour Island, a few miles up from Basin Harbor. The engagement scuttled British plans for invasion in 1776, leaving another year for the Americans to plan their defenses. In 1997, the museum undertook the mammoth task of rebuilding one of Arnold's gunboats, the *Philadelphia II*, which now floats in the harbor.

Bixby Memorial Library

The imposing Greek Revival facade of **Bixby Memorial Library** (258 Main St., Vergennes, 802/877-2211, www.bixbylibrary.

org, 12:30pm-7pm Mon., 12:30pm-5pm Tues. and Fri., 10am-5pm Wed., 10am-7pm Thurs., 9am-2pm Sat., free) is only the beginning of its charms. Inside, the library has one of the largest collections of artifacts in the state, with exhibits of native arrowheads, antique maps, stamps, and documents relating to the early history of the region, including the Revolutionary and Civil Wars.

Rokeby Museum

By the time escaped enslaved people arrived in Ferrisburgh, freedom and Canada must have seemed a hair's breadth away. The **Rokeby Museum** (4334 Rte. 7, Ferrisburgh, 802/877-3406, www.rokeby.org, tours 11am and 2pm Fri.-Mon., $10 adults, $9 seniors, $8 students, children under 5 are free, free Tues. 1pm-5pm) remembers their struggle and the Quaker family who opened their home as a part of the Underground Railroad network that assisted their flight. Exhibits give life to both the former slaves and the Robinson family. Letters and documents elucidate the Robinsons' beliefs—both religious and humanitarian—and put them into the context of a turbulent time period.

Round Barn Merinos

The **Round Barn** (4263 Rte. 7, Ferrisburgh, 802/877-6544, noon-5pm Thurs.-Sat., free) has triggered double takes for years, as one driver after another asks: "Did I just see a camel?" Oliver the camel is truly eye-catching beside the historical round barn and keeps company with a flock of gorgeously soft merino sheep. It's worth a stop just to say hello, but you can also buy hand-dyed yarn from their wool, along with hats, scarves, and blankets to keep you cozy as a Green Mountain camel.

Entertainment and Events

In its 100-year history, the **Vergennes Opera House** (120 Main St., 802/877-6737, www.vergennesoperahouse.org) has seen many permutations, from a grand classical music hall to a moving-picture theater to a condemned old building. In 1997, the town raised money to restore the hall to its Victorian splendor, and it now serves as a cultural hub with an impressive array of entertainment offerings.

Vergennes also hosts Vermont's largest **Memorial Day** parade (11am-1:30pm, www.vergennesdowntown.org), an eclectic lineup of classic cars, Shriners, high school bands, and seemingly every piece of heavy equipment in the area, from fire trucks to tractors. It's a blast, and people from around the area show up for the fun.

The annual **Tour de Farms** (www.acornvt.org) is a leisurely, 30-mile bike ride that leaves from downtown Vergennes and visits a series of local farms for snacks and drinks. It's great fun, and a good way to meet farmers that don't usually open their properties to the public.

Shopping

The compact downtown is just made for a mosey—but don't walk too quickly, or you'll reach the end in 15 minutes. Much of the action is on Main Street, but Green Street is where you'll find **Daily Chocolate** (7 Green St., Vergennes, 802/877-0087, www.dailychocolate.net, 11am-5:30pm Tues.-Fri., 11am-4pm Sat.) whose handmade chocolates include black rum caramels and crisp toffee.

Food

Once a bakery famed for its French pastries and unpredictable hours, ★ **Vergennes Laundry by CK** (247 Main St., Vergennes, 802/870-7157, http://vergenneslaundry.net, 8am-2pm and 5pm-9pm Wed.-Sat., 10am-3pm Sun., $5-12, prix fixe dinner $39) has been reborn under new ownership. Brunch and lunch include classics such as a Monte Cristo sandwich and savory grits, as well as rich French toast that's bathed in locally produced maple syrup. The fixed price dinner is three courses: Choose from several options

---

1: wine grapes ripening at Shelburne Vineyard; **2:** downtown Vergennes, full of old-fashioned charm; **3:** Stonecutter Spirits, part of Middlebury's Tasting Trail; **4:** waterfall in Moosalamoo Recreation Area, near Middlebury

1
2
Park
SQUEEZE
3
STONECUTTER
SPIRITS
SINGLE
BARREL
GIN
4

that change with the season and retain a French flair, concluding the night with one of the restaurant's delightful desserts.

Just down the block is the equally Francophile **Black Sheep Bistro** (253 Main St., Vergennes, 802/877-9991, www.blacksheepbistrovt.com, 5pm-8:30pm daily, $22), where the duck appetizer is a longtime standout. Other favorites in the moody, darkly furnished restaurant include escargot and steak.

For satisfying egg breakfasts, sandwiches, and salads, head to the casual **3 Squares Café** (221 Main St., Vergennes, 802/877-2772, www.threesquarescafe.com, 8am-8pm daily, $10-14) a homey place that's often packed with a friendly local crowd. The French toast is a strong contender for Vermont's best.

Small batches of ice cream have big flavor at **Lu Lu** (185 Main St., Vergennes, 802/777-3933, www.luluvt.com, 1pm-9pm Wed.-Mon., $3-7), which has some of the best artisanal scoops in the state. Salted caramel, curried peanut, and straight-up chocolate win raves, and the ice cream maker—which is a sister company of Mary's Restaurant—was voted Vermont's best ice cream.

Accommodations

An old-fashioned family resort set on a 700-acre wooded cove of Lake Champlain, **Basin Harbor Club** (4800 Basin Harbor Rd., Vergennes, 802/475-2311, www.basinharbor.com, May-Oct., $195-550) has been owned and hosted by the same family for four generations. From May through October, it swarms with families (who can stay in either individual rooms or cabins), and there's a long roster of activities—from waterskiing and tennis to hiking, Pilates, bonfires, and fishing. There are also a number of restaurants—the tavern-style Red Mill, the more formal Main Dining Room (with a classic menu and deep wine list), and alfresco buffets on the North Dock. Pets are welcome for a $10 surcharge.

Set in a historic home across Otter Creek from downtown Vergennes, the **Strong House Inn** (94 W Main St., Vergennes, 802/877-3337, www.stronghouseinn.com, $125-390) has beautiful grounds and old-fashioned rooms that are updated with modern comforts. The hearty, fresh-cooked breakfast is a highlight for many guests, and the inn offers plenty of places to lounge, from the outdoor gazebo to the well-appointed great room, where tea, coffee, and cookies are always available.

CAMPING

There are 70 tent and lean-to sites covering a grassy, lakeside camping area at **Button Bay State Park** (5 Button Bay Rd., Ferrisburgh, 802/475-2377, https://vtstateparks.com/htm/buttonbay.htm, $18-27), about four miles west of Vergennes. Located on the site of a tropical coral reef that remains from the time when Lake Champlain was attached to the ocean, the 1.5-mile walk passes by limestone deposits embedded with sea snail fossils. There's a pool that's great for kids, and strong swimmers can paddle across a short section of open lake to an intriguingly creepy island with some mysterious abandoned structures.

Information and Services

For more information on Vergennes, contact or visit the **Addison County Chamber of Commerce** (93 Court St., Middlebury, 802/388-7951, www.addisoncounty.com). Pharmacy needs can be taken care of downtown at **Marble Works Pharmacy** (187 Main St., Vergennes, 802/877-1190, 9am-6pm Mon.-Fri., 9am-1pm Sat.). In an emergency, contact the **Vergennes Police** (120 Main St., 802/877-2201).

BRISTOL

This tiny bucolic town is perched in the foothills at the edge of the Champlain Valley, and boasts the longest, continually running Fourth of July celebration. While you can see downtown in the time it takes to eat a maple creemee, don't be surprised if you find yourself lingering to enjoy the slow pace of life here. Keep going past Bristol, and you'll be going up into the Greens, past swimming holes in the New Haven River, through the ramshackle town of Lincoln (a rumored energy vortex), and onto the impossibly steep stretch of road that brings you over the Lincoln Gap to the Mad River Valley.

Sights

There's a lot to see in Bristol, but not many "sights" to speak of. And on hot summer days, you might find the downtown deserted because everyone's already gone to the **Bristol Falls** (Lincoln Rd.), an undeveloped swimming area in the New Haven River, where the water forms a series of pools as it drops from the mountains to the valley floor. Driving up Lincoln Road from Highway 116 there's a series of pullouts on the right-hand side of the road, and many paths down to the river; be considerate and park completely off the road, and remember that because of yearly shifts in the river's flow, even popular swimming holes can be dangerous. You could while away a beautiful afternoon by the river, so bring a picnic and settle in.

Events

The town of Bristol started its **Fourth of July Parade** (www.bristol4th.com) in 1785, which makes theirs the oldest continuous celebration in the United States. Locals keep up the tradition in grand style, with marching bands, floats, pageants, and even an award for whichever former Bristol-ite has traveled the farthest to attend the event. In the weeks leading up to the big day, there are concerts and events. From mid-June to Labor Day the **Bristol Band** (802/453-7378, www.discoverbristolvt.com) holds evening concerts in the downtown park each Wednesday evening. Bring a picnic, and enjoy a show that's been held in this gazebo since just after the Civil War.

Shopping

Pick up local artwork at **Art on Main** (25 Main St., 802/453-4032, www.artonmain.net, 11am-5pm Tues.-Sat., 11am-3pm Sun.), a cooperative community art center brimming with watercolors, oils, and acrylics, plus hand-carved walking sticks, quilts, and stained-glass kaleidoscopes. Potter Robert Compton and wife Christine are the forces behind **Robert Compton Pottery** (2662 N. Rte. 116, 802/453-3778, www.robertcomptonpottery.com, 10am-5pm "most days"), a showroom and studio filled with pieces the artist has created with a salt glaze—a special process that introduces salt into the kiln at extremely high temperatures.

Food

The best of local fare tends to be tied to the area's farms—like the fresh produce and goods at **Almost Home Market** (28 North St., 802/453-5775, www.almosthomemarket.net, 7:30am-5:30pm Mon.-Fri., 8am-3:30pm Sat., $7-9). Half country store, half café, it whips up fresh-baked breads and pastries, plus sandwiches and snazzy meals like lavender-roasted chicken with lemon and garlic or salmon teriyaki.

Even closer to the source is ★ **Mary's Restaurant** (1868 N. Rte. 116, 888/424-2432, www.innatbaldwincreek.com/marys, 5pm-9pm Wed.-Sat., brunch 10:30am-2pm Sun., $13-37), located at the Inn at Baldwin Creek, where much of the menu comes straight from the property's farm and other area farms. (Don't miss the legendary cream of garlic soup.) The dining room blends farmhouse charm with laid-back elegance, a pleasing mix of white tablecloths and old wood that is a special occasion destination for food lovers throughout the region.

Don't forget to make a reservation for the English-style **Bobcat Cafe** (5 Main St., 802/453-3311, www.bobcatcafe.com, 4pm-9pm Sun.-Thurs., 4pm-9:30pm Fri.-Sat., $12-20), which gets packed with regulars for the burgers made from locally raised beef; other hearty entrées include grilled pork chops and roasted chicken with rice pilaf.

If it's hot, the odds are good that anyone not at the Bristol Falls is hanging around the **Village Creemee Stand** (41 West St., 802/453-6034), a name that comes up frequently in the ongoing, heated debates about who makes the best maple creemees in Vermont.

Accommodations

Simple and romantic, the **Inn at Baldwin Creek** (1868 N. Rte. 116, 888/424-2432, www.baldwincreek.net, $210-295) appoints its spacious rooms with four-poster queen beds, gas-fired woodstoves, and TVs with VCRs or DVD players. Most overlook the property's gardens, and all come with free wireless Internet access, CD players, and fluffy bathrobes—not to mention a three-course breakfast and afternoon snacks (think chocolate chip cookies, blackberry scones, or apple and cheddar cheese fondue). One suite has trundle beds, ideal for families, and there's an outdoor heated swimming pool. The on-site restaurant, Mary's, is renowned for its dinners of local farm specialties.

And right in the center of town is friendly **Bristol Suites** (19 Main St., 802/453-4065, www.bristolsuites.com, doubles $125, 3-bedroom suites $255), which is especially attractive for groups, as the suites have kitchenettes and homey living room areas.

CAMPING

A grassy expanse at the foot of a forested hill, **Green Mountain Family Campground** (4817 S. Rte. 116, 802/453-3123, www.greenmountainfamily.com, tent sites $25, RV sites $37-42, lean-to or bunkhouse $30) features vacation-ready swimming pools, horseshoes, grills, badminton, and volleyball. Most sites pick up a Wi-Fi signal, and the owners allow friendly dogs (though prohibit some breeds, including pit bulls).

Information and Services

The **Bristol Parks Arts & Recreation Department** (1 South St., 802/453-5885, www.bristolrec.org) runs an information center during the summer at the Howden Hall Community Center (19 West St.). For more information on Bristol, contact or visit the **Addison County Chamber of Commerce** (93 Court St., Middlebury, 802/388-7951, www.addisoncounty.com).

SPORTS AND RECREATION

Hiking

One of the best views of the lake is the sweeping panorama from **Mount Philo State Park** (5425 Mt. Philo Rd., Charlotte, 802/425-2390, https://vtstateparks.com, $4 adults, $2 children 4-13, children 3 and under free). The 968-foot mountain sits all by itself on the shore, affording drop-dead views west to the Adirondacks. The heights, which can be reached on the 1.9-mile Mount Philo Trail, are capped by a picnic area and small campground with just 10 sites ($18-27 nightly base rate).

A favorite place for a stroll along Lake Champlain is **Button Bay State Park** (5 Button Bay Rd., Ferrisburgh, 802/475-2377, https://vtstateparks.com/htm/buttonbay.htm, $4 adults, $2 children 4-13, children 3 and under free), about four miles west of Vergennes. This is also a stop on the Lake Champlain Paddlers' Trail and a convenient location for launching a canoe or kayak.

It's hard to miss **Mount Abraham,** which at 4,006 feet towers above the valley below. The hike to the peak is strenuous but offers sweeping views of the lake and the Adirondacks from the summit. The final stretch of trail is a scramble up a rocky slope. This is a great place to see one of Vermont's fragile and fascinating alpine areas and to try out your hiking muscles on a section of the **Long Trail,** which runs the entire length of Vermont. The hike is 5.7 miles round-trip, and you should budget at least four hours and bring food, water, and plenty of extra clothing. To get to the trailhead, turn up Lincoln Gap Road from Highway 116, and continue until the very top, where there's a dirt parking lot on the right. The trailhead is on the other side of the road, and the path is indicated with white blazes.

When traveling to Mount Abraham from Bristol, you'll pass through the town of Lincoln, which is believed by many Vermonters to be an "energy vortex" that's especially rich in spiritual forces. Keep your windows down and soak it in!

Biking

The farm country around Vergennes is a dream for cycling, with miles of back roads and rolling terrain studded with farm stands, country stores, and stunning views of the lake and Adirondack Mountains on the western shore. The **Lake Champlain Bikeways** (802/652-2453, www.champlainbikeways.org) website is a great resource for riding itineraries: Check out **The Rebel's Retreat Trail,** a 42-mile loop through the rolling farmlands around Vergennes. If you don't have your own wheels, stop by **Little City Cycles** (10 N. Main St., Vergennes, 802/877-3000, www.littlecitycycles.com, bikes $20/day), where you can also pick up maps of the area and tips on where to ride.

GETTING THERE AND AROUND

Shelburne is a short drive south down Route 7 from Burlington (7 mi., 15 min.). From Shelburne, Vergennes is another 15 miles down the road (25 min.). Alternatively, you can reach Shelburne by driving north on Route 7 from Middlebury (10 mi., 15 min.). From Vergennes, drive east on Route 17 to reach Bristol (15 mi., 20 min.). Or to drive to Bristol from the highway, leave I-89 at exit 9 and take Route 100B and then Route 100 south through Waitsfield; then head west along Route 17 through the breathtaking Appalachian Gap (95 mi., 2.5 hrs. from White River Junction).

Addison County Transit Resources (802/388-2287, www.actr-vt.org) runs buses between Middlebury (Exchange St. or Merchants Row), Bristol (Town Green, 30 min., $1), and Vergennes (Main St. and Green St., 30 min., $1), and some routes continue to Burlington (Pine St. and Lakeside, 1.5 hrs., $2). From New York, **Lake Champlain Transportation Company** (802/864-9804, www.ferries.com) runs car ferries from Essex, New York, to Charlotte, halfway between Vergennes and Shelburne.

Middlebury

This dignified town exerts a nostalgic pull, from downtown's decorated brick facades to the stately grace of the Middlebury College campus. In fact, the entire place can feel like a New England college movie set, complete with cafés full of students and bookstores stocked with serious tomes, and Middlebury continues to have a vibrant cultural life that makes it the social hub of the lower Champlain Valley.

The college was founded in 1800 by Gamaliel Painter, one of the town's first settlers and a profoundly religious man who wanted to safeguard the spiritual education of local farmers' sons against the secularism of the University of Vermont in Burlington. Buoyed by the college and a variety of industries, including grist and woolen mills and marble quarrying, Middlebury became the largest community west of the Green Mountains by the mid-19th century, surpassing Bennington, Manchester, Rutland, and even Burlington.

These days, Middlebury's 8,000 residents enjoy a compact downtown full of shops and galleries, along with several excellent museums. It is also home to several excellent breweries and distilleries, along with a beloved vineyard. Active visitors can explore the 18-mile Trail Around Middlebury, which links up a series of paths to make a giant loop around the town, or head for the hills—the winding road to Middlebury Gap leaves right from downtown.

SIGHTS

Middlebury College

Few college campuses are as visually harmonious as that of **Middlebury College** (802/443-5000, www.middlebury.edu), which consists of

Middlebury Tasting Trail

Local purveyors of liquid pleasures created the **Middlebury Tasting Trail** (www.middtastingtrail.com), which hops from north to south through town. There are eight stops on the trail that range from locally pressed wine to hard cider, including the following:

- Family-run **Lincoln Peak Vineyard** (142 River Rd., New Haven, 802/388-7368, www.lincolnpeakvineyard.com, 11am-5pm Sat., other days by appointment or "chance") makes diverse wines from the grapes grown at their 12-acre vineyard. The aromatic **La Crescent** is a refreshing white, and even those who avoid sweet wines may fall for **Firelight,** a dessert unto itself.
- In a stylish mod-industrial facility, **Stonecutter Spirits** (1197 Exchange St., 802/388-3000, www.stonecutterspirits.com, noon-8pm Thurs., noon-6pm Fri.-Sat.) opened in 2015 and is the most recent addition to the tasting trail. Their barrel-aged gin is made with plenty of juniper, cardamom, and orange peel—try it straight or in a cocktail—and the cask-aged whiskey is spicy and smooth.
- The solar-powered **Appalachian Gap Distillery** (88 Mainelli Rd., 802/388-3000, 1pm-5pm Mon.-Sat.) creates a wide-ranging list of spirits, from a biting unaged whiskey to aged rum and kaffevän, a smooth, coffee-infused liqueur. Tastings are free, and lucky visitors will be guided through the spirits by the enthusiastic and creative distiller.
- While **WhistlePig** (52 Seymour St., 802/897-7700, www.whistlepigwhiskey.com, 11:30am-5:30pm Thurs.-Sat., 11:30am-4pm Sun.) stirred up controversy for marketing "Vermont rye" that was sourced in Canada, there's no denying they pour some of the world's finest rye whiskey. The distillery and aging facility is in Shoreham, and not open to visitors, but they've set up a tasting table in the Danforth Pewter shop that's well worth a stop for a sip.
- The southern end of the trail is **Drop-In Brewery** (610 Rte. 7 S., 802/989-7414, www.dropinbrewing.com, 11am-7pm Mon.-Sat., noon-5pm Sun.), where you shouldn't miss the beloved **Heart of Lothian,** a full-flavored Scottish ale.

a collection of granite and marble academic halls capped with white spires and cupolas arranged around a wide central quad. For a stroll around campus, park in the visitors' lot behind the admissions office on South Main Street.

A campus highlight, the **Middlebury College Museum of Art** (S. Main St./Rte. 30, 802/443-5007, www.middlebury.edu/arts/museum, 10am-5pm Tues.-Fri., noon-5pm Sat.-Sun., free) is a Met in miniature, with terra-cotta Greek urns, Roman marble reliefs, Chinese ceramics, Japanese woodcuts, and European paintings—many of which are used in the college's various art classes. Upstairs, a large open gallery displays changing exhibits of modern art and photography.

Vermont Folklife Center

Since 1984 the **Vermont Folklife Center** (88 Main St., 802/388-4964, www.vermontfolklifecenter.org, 10am-5pm Tues.-Sat., free) has been dedicated to preserving Vermont's cultural traditions, and their work has created a staggering archive of recordings and images from all over the state. If you'd like to browse them, you can schedule a visit with the archivist, but otherwise, it's a worthwhile stop to browse their most recent exhibit, as well as the gift shop stocked with handicrafts made by Vermonters, including recent arrivals from around the world. The exhibits vary but share an appreciative perspective on local lives and color.

Henry Sheldon Museum of Vermont History

The culture and history of all of Vermont are on display at the **Henry Sheldon Museum of Vermont History** (1 Park St., 802/388-2117, www.henrysheldonmuseum.org, 10am-5pm Tues.-Sat. year-round and 1pm-5pm Sun. June-Aug., $5 adult, $4.50 senior, $3 youth 6-18, children under 6 free, $12 family), which has a rich collection of furniture and portraits stretching back more than 100 years. Rather than concern itself with battles and politicians, the museum sets out to demonstrate how the common people lived: One of its most affecting exhibits, "A Glimpse of Christmas Past," displays antique decorations and toys every year during the holiday season.

UVM Morgan Horse Farm and Pulp Mill Covered Bridge

When George Custer was defeated at the Battle of Little Bighorn, the only survivor was a Morgan horse named Comanche. Praised for their strength, versatility, and athleticism, the Morgan breed has long been associated with Vermont, where it has been bred since the late 1700s. That tradition continues at the **UVM Morgan Horse Farm** (74 Battell Dr., Weybridge, 802/388-2011, www.uvm.edu/morgan, 9am-4pm daily May 1-Oct. 31, $5 adults, $4 youth 12-18, $2 children 5-12, free under 5), which is recognized as having one of the best bloodlines for breeding and competition. A tour of the farm describes the scrupulous care and training the Morgan horses receive and is especially fun in springtime, when spindly-legged foals wander the property. On your way to the farm is the **Pulp Mill Covered Bridge,** which is the oldest in Vermont, though its exact age is up for debate; estimates range between 1808 and 1850.

ENTERTAINMENT AND EVENTS

Nightlife

Middlebury gets pretty quiet at night, but when residents of the surrounding villages "go into town," this is where they head. In summer months, it's impossible to beat a comfy seat on the balcony at **The Lobby** (7 Bakery Ln., 802/989-7463, www.lobbyrestaurantvt.com, 11am-2:30pm and 5pm-close daily, $12-28), which overlooks Otter Creek. The interior is hip and painted black, and the menu of eclectic pub fare complements the creative cocktails and extensive beer list. Or you can try the lively **Two Brothers Tavern** (86 Main St., 802/388-0002, www.twobrotherstavern.com, 11:30am-2am daily, $11-17), which hosts trivia and open-mic nights in an archetypical college town pub.

Just north of town, **Lincoln Peak Vineyard** (142 River Rd., New Haven, 802/388-7368, www.lincolnpeakvineyard.com) has a Friday night music series that features excellent local bands and singer-songwriters in their tasting room. Check the website for updated schedules.

The Arts

The college's various musical and theater groups perform at the **Middlebury College Center for the Arts** (S. Main St./Rte. 30, 802/443-3168, www.middlebury.edu/arts), a 100,000-square-foot facility housing an intimate black-box theater, a dance studio, and large recital hall.

Events

Some towns have a daylong festival; others party for a weekend. Middlebury goes for a whole week's worth of musical and family events in its summertime **Festival on the Green** (802/462-3555, www.festivalonthegreen.com, mid-July). Each day of the event features several free musical performers in "brown bag" lunchtime shows and evening performances. The festival culminates with a Saturday jazz block party.

North of Middlebury in New Haven, the **Addison County Fair and Field Days** (1790 Field Days Rd., New Haven, 802/545-2557, www.addisoncountyfielddays.com, early Aug.) is one of the largest county fairs in Vermont. In addition to the usual lineup of midway rides and tractor pulls, it features

Middlebury

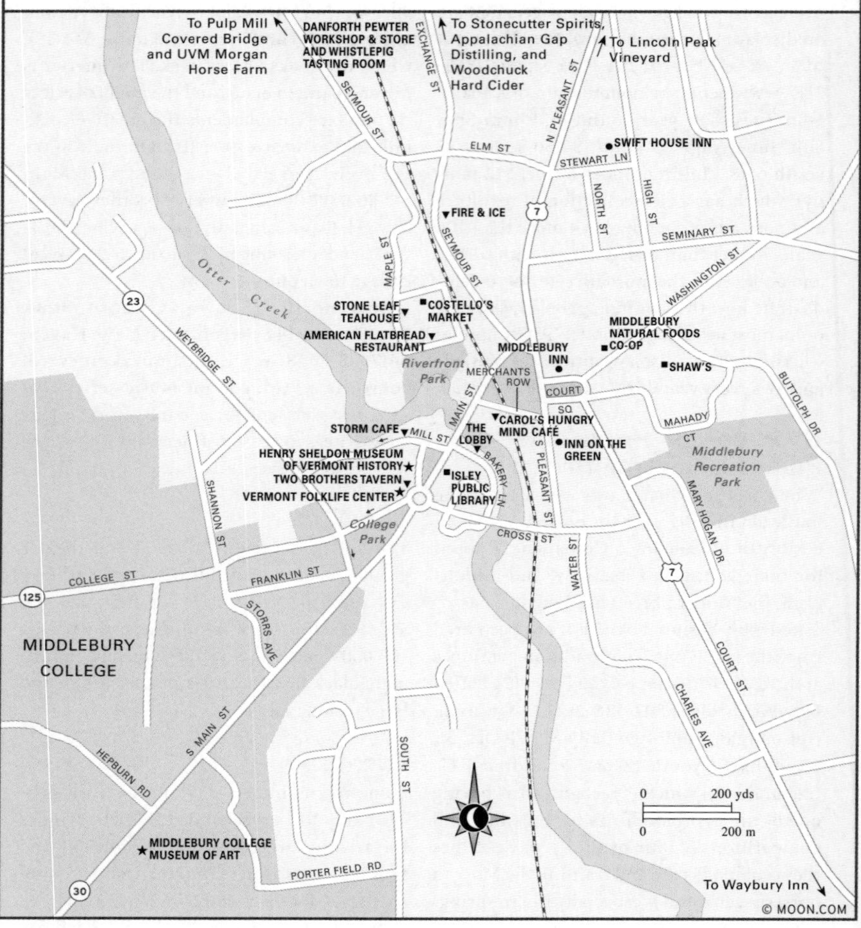

a milking barn and "dairy bar" that dispenses fresh local ice cream.

SHOPPING

Original and gleaming gifts fill the studio of **Danforth Pewter Workshop & Store** (52 Seymour St., 802/388-0098, www.danforthpewter.com/workshop, 9:30am-5:30pm Mon.-Sat., 11am-4pm Sun.), which makes vases, holiday ornaments, and baby gifts with heft. Arrive before 3pm on a weekday to watch the artisans at work. (This is also the home of the WhistlePig rye whiskey tasting room.)

FOOD

★ **Stone Leaf Teahouse** (111 Maple St., 802/458-0460, www.stoneleaftea.com, 11am-6pm Tues.-Sat., 11am-5pm Sun., cash only) offers a broad selection of teas that the owner brings back from yearly trips across Asia. The knowledgeable staff can guide you through the menu, and they also sell the best loose teas in the state. For espresso drinks, fresh pastries, and a strong dose of student life stop by **Carol's Hungry Mind Café** (24 Merchants Row, 802/388-0101, www.carolshungrymindcafe.com, 7am-5pm Mon.-Fri., 8am-5pm Sat.-Sun.), which has plenty of space to read a book or check your email.

As much a museum as it is a restaurant, every inch of the upscale (but family-friendly) **Fire and Ice** (26 Seymour St., 802/388-7166, www.fireandicerestaurant.com, 5pm-9pm Mon.-Thurs., noon-9pm Fri.-Sat., 1pm-9pm Sun., $12-28) is covered with old photographs, books, Victorian lamps, and map covers. A warren of interlocking rooms, the friendly, dimly lighted establishment focuses on classic American dishes—the likes of hand-cut steaks, boiled lobster, and broiled salmon. The homemade carrot cake is a local legend.

Its name notwithstanding, the **Storm Cafe** (3 Mill St., 802/388-1063, www.thestormcafe.com, 9am-2:30pm and 5pm-8pm Tues.-Sat., 9am-2pm Sun., $10-28) is a peaceful spot in a former stone mill that's right on the river. The dinner menu leans Italian, with penne carbonara and risotto, but lunch is more about salads and sandwiches, as well as soup-sandwich combo meals that are lovely for the price.

Locals and tour groups alike sidle up to the counter at **Rosie's** (Rte. 7 S., 802/388-7052, www.rosiesrestaurantvt.com, 6am-9pm daily, $5-23), a longtime favorite that serves homey and unpretentious food just south of town. Homemade hot-turkey sandwiches are served at lunch along with macaroni and cheese and apple crumb pie.

Deli sandwiches don't usually inspire odes, but ★ **Costello's Market** (99 Maple St., Ste. 13A, 802/388-3385, www.costellosmarket.com, 10am-6pm Tues.-Fri., 10am-5pm Sat., $7-10) is not most delis. They stack freshly baked rolls with Italian classics—or anything else that comes to mind. The caponata is a legend among road-tripping Vermonters, and on sunny days you can enjoy your spread on picnic tables by the river.

Another outpost of Vermont's bohemian pizza minichain, **American Flatbread** (137 Maple St., 802/388-3300, www.americanflatbread.com, 5pm-9pm Tues.-Sat., $16-19) is a beloved institution that turns out wood-fired pizzas using plenty of local ingredients. The locally made maple-fennel-sausage pizza with caramelized onions and Vermont mozzarella is alone worth the trip.

ACCOMMODATIONS

$100-150

If you remember, and are looking for, the Vermont of Bob Newhart's dreams, look no further than the **Waybury Inn** (457 E. Main St., 802/388-4015 or 800/348-1810, www.wayburyinn.com, $140-335), just out of town on the road to Ripton. The exterior was used at the beginning of the show *Newhart,* which ran from 1982 to 1990. The interior is just as picturesque: Guests lounge in suites enjoying views of the lush lawns and mountains. Some rooms have four-poster beds and whirlpool tubs. Several rooms are located in private cabins. A quiet, elegant restaurant is on-site, and the inn maintains beautiful gardens.

$150-250

And at the heart of it all is the historical ★ **Middlebury Inn** (14 Court Sq., 802/388-4961, www.middleburyinn.com, $135-180), with a stately front porch facing downtown and an elegant interior full of flourishes from almost 200 years of hospitality. Modern comforts include access to a fitness center and flat-screen televisions, but the real charm is in the old-time details—antique tub fixtures in the tiled bathrooms, afternoon tea in wingback chairs, and above all, a ride in the 1926 Otis elevator.

An 1814 home-turned-inn (once belonging to Vermont judge and governor John Stewart), ★ **Swift House Inn** (25 Stewart Ln., 866/388-9925, www.swifthouseinn.com, $130-299) is actually three buildings, each renovated and appointed with ornate stained glass and luxury furnishings. Pristine and individually decorated rooms, many outfitted in subtle florals, come with claw-foot tubs, quilt-covered wood or iron-wrought beds, or working fireplaces.

The Federal-style **Inn on the Green** (71 S. Pleasant St., 802/388-7512, www.innonthegreen.com, $150-260) overlooks the Middlebury town green. With a handful of suites, plus rooms with twin and queen beds, it's perfect for families (or couples looking to relax—the kitchen serves breakfast in bed). Rooms are cheerfully decorated with bright color, bay windows, and high-quality country wooden furniture—some antiques.

Camping

Ten miles south of Middlebury, Lake Dunmore is a scenic gem wrapped with steep hills, which are dramatic in the fall when they're illuminated by foliage. Much of the lake is developed, and the shoreline is dotted with vacation houses, but it's a convivial and relaxing place with two appealing campgrounds.

The privately run **Kampersville** (1457 Lake Dunmore Rd., Salisbury, 802/352-4501, www.kampersville.com, Apr.-Oct., $29-50) has a maze of sites, some of which are just across the road from the campground's private beach. In addition to spots for everything from tents to RVs, there are a few family cabins and paddleboats, canoes, and kayaks for rent. Some sites are a long walk from the lake; consult the campground map before choosing yours.

On the eastern shore of the lake is **Branbury State Park** (3570 Lake Dunmore Rd., Salisbury, 802/247-5925, https://vtstateparks.com, $18-27), which has 37 campsites, laid out at the base of Mount Moosalamoo. Campers and day visitors can cool on the great, family-friendly swimming beach, and there are coin-operated showers for use.

INFORMATION AND SERVICES

For more information on Middlebury and the surrounding area, contact the extremely helpful regional tourism office, **Addison County Chamber of Commerce** (93 Court St., 802/388-7951, www.addisoncounty.com), which runs a visitors center across from the Vermont Folklife Center. For Middlebury proper, you can also contact the **Middlebury Business Association** (802/377-3557, www.bettermiddleburypartnership.org), which produces a helpful map of the town.

Middlebury is a regional hub, with hospital services at **Porter Medical Center** (115 Porter Dr., 802/388-4701, www.portermedical.org). Several pharmacies are located along Route 7, including **Kinney Drugs** (38 Court St., 802/388-0973) in the center of town and **Rite-Aid Pharmacy** (263 Court St., 802/388-9573, 8am-8pm Mon.-Sat., 9am-5pm Sun., pharmacy 8am-8pm Mon.-Fri., 9am-6pm Sat., 9am-5pm Sun.).

Your best bet for a cash machine is at the intersection of Route 7 and Route 30, where there are a half dozen banks, including an ATM at **People's United Bank** (114 S. Village Green, 802/388-6316, 8am-5pm Mon.-Thurs., 8am-5:30pm Fri., 9am-noon Sat.) and **Citizens Bank** (36 Middle Rd., 802/388-6791, 9am-5pm Mon.-Fri., 9am-noon Sat.). Free Wi-Fi can be found at **Ilsley Public Library** (75 Main St., 802/388-4095, www.ilsleypubliclibrary.org, 10am-6pm Mon., Wed., and Fri., 10am-8pm Tues. and Thurs., 10am-4pm Sat., 1pm-4pm Sun.) and **Two Brothers Tavern** (86 Main St., 802/388-0002, www.twobrotherstavern.com). In an emergency, contact **Middlebury Police** (1 Lucius Shaw Ln., 802/388-3191).

GETTING THERE AND AROUND

There's no easy way to get to Middlebury from the highway—whatever route you take involves a long (though beautiful) drive across the Green Mountains. Probably the best option from I-89 is to take exit 3 south to Route 107, then head west on Route 125, and cross the mountains at Middlebury Gap (70 mi., 2 hrs. from White River Junction). To drive to Middlebury from Rutland, take Route 7 north (35 mi., 1 hr.).

Run by the Chittenden County Transportation Authority, the **Middlebury LINK** (802/864-2282, www.cctaride.org) provides several buses every day but Sunday between Middlebury (Exchange St. or Merchants Row) and Burlington ($4, 1.5 hrs.).

Addison County Transit Resources (802/388-2287, www.actr-vt.org) runs bus routes throughout the town of Middlebury.

Around Middlebury

Middlebury stands at the crossroads of several routes. To the east, Route 125 climbs into the mountains to the so-called Middlebury Gap, a dizzying pass through the mountains on roller-coaster slopes. Southward, Route 7 plays leapfrog with Otter Creek, Vermont's longest river, which tumbles down from the Green Mountain foothills into the southern end of Lake Champlain. To the west, meanwhile, the lake narrows at this point to a distance of only a few miles across. That made it prime defensive ground for generations of French, British, and American soldiers who protected the waterway from attack at **Fort Ticonderoga, Chimney Point,** and **Mount Independence,** just some of the many historical sites still present in the area.

MIDDLEBURY GAP

The only pass across the Green Mountains for 25 miles, Middlebury Gap was designated as a scenic byway by the state of Vermont as early as 1897. Route 125, which climbs steeply up from **Middlebury** to its peak at the village of **Ripton** before plunging just as precipitously down the other side, is lined with a dense forest of maple and birch mixed in with boreal spruce and fir. The road runs along a series of brooks, and there are plenty of opportunities in the area around Ripton to pull over and cool off in the water.

Robert Frost Interpretive Trail and Cabin

Robert Frost moved to Vermont in 1920 "to seek a better place to farm, and especially grow apples," and he did each of those things while writing a canon of poetry whose imagery now seems inextricable from the Green Mountain landscape. It is in keeping with his love of nature and "country things" that while his home and writing cabin have been preserved as a National Historic Landmark, they remain as simple as they were in the summers that he spent in Ripton from 1939 until his death in 1963. There's not much to see, in particular, but a slow walk through the property is a sublime way to channel the poet's affinity for wildness, and it's easy to imagine his writing taking shape in the cool shade of the surrounding forest.

The **Robert Frost Wayside Picnic Area** (Rte. 125, 1.9 miles east of Ripton) is a good place to start surrounded by pines the poet tended in his lifetime, and just east of there is the road to the Homer Noble Farm where you can see his farmhouse and writing cabin. They're only opened for special events (both are owned by Middlebury College), but you can take a seat on the porch and enjoy the peaceful setting that attracted Frost to this corner of the state. Just to the west of the farm on the way into Ripton is the **Robert Frost Interpretive Trail,** a 1.2-mile loop (0.3 mile accessible by wheelchair) that winds through fields and forests past plaques with excerpts from Frost's poems and passes a substantial patch of blueberry and huckleberry bushes that are a destination unto themselves in July and August when they're heavy with sweet fruit.

Events

When Frost summered in Middlebury,

he was here for the **Bread Loaf Writers' Conference** (1192 Rte. 125, Ripton, 802/443-5000, www.middlebury.edu, Aug.), one of the first retreats to bring working and aspiring writers together each summer for inspiration. The conference has grown in stature for more than 80 years; in addition to Frost, guests have included John Irving, Toni Morrison, and Norman Mailer. Now it lasts for 10 days in August, taking place in the little town of Ripton in the mountains 10 miles east of Middlebury; many of the readings by distinguished writers are open to the public.

LAKESHORE HISTORIC SITES

In the early days of the Revolutionary War, Lake Champlain was recognized as a prime strategic directive by both the colonial defenders and British attackers. If the Brits were able to sail down the lake from their home base in Canada, they could effectively cut the Americans' territory in half, isolating New England and forcing an early surrender of the troops there. To make sure that didn't happen, the Americans moved quickly to secure the lake's southern narrows on both the New York and Vermont side. Many of the fortifications they put in place still exist as some of the best-preserved Revolutionary War sites anywhere. History is still very much alive in the area, with tours and events that take advantage of their proximity.

Chimney Point State Historic Site

On the Vermont side of the lake are the remains of an earlier French settlement at the **Chimney Point State Historic Site** (8149 Rte. 17, Addison, 802/759-2412, 9:30am-5pm Wed.-Sun. late May-mid-Oct., $5 adults, children 14 and under free). In fact, the strategic area had seen waves of settlement by Native American tribes for more than 12,000 years. An 18th-century tavern on-site now has an exhibit of prehistoric Native American artifacts as well as interpretive maps that detail the history of the area.

Crown Point State Historic Site

At the time of the Revolutionary War, Lake Champlain was defended by two forts on the New York side of the lake, Crown Point and Fort Ticonderoga, both built several years before during the time of the French and Indian War. They were lightly defended in the early days of the war, allowing American troops under Benedict Arnold and Ethan Allen to capture them without bloodshed. Two years later, however, it was the Americans' turn to abandon Crown Point when they didn't have enough men to staff both forts in the face of a new British advance. The well-preserved ruins of the fort still stand at **Crown Point State Historic Site** (21 Grandview Dr., Crown Point, NY, 518/597-4666, www.nysparks.com, 9:30am-5pm Thurs.-Mon. May-Oct., $4 adults, $3 students and seniors, children under 12 free), accessible by a bridge across the lake. A visitors' site on the premises details the various chapters of French, British, and American occupation.

Mount Independence State Historic Site

Farther south down the lake, the Americans made their stand against the British at Fort Ticonderoga, also on the New York side of the lake. Because that fort faced south, however, the Americans also constructed a huge new fort on the Vermont side of the lake named Mount Independence. They survive today as the **Mount Independence State Historic Site** (497 Mount Independence Rd., Orwell, 802/759-2412 or 802/948-2000, 9:30am-5pm daily late May-mid-Oct., $5 adults, children 14 and under free), a virtual city where some 12,000 defenders once lived, making it the largest military city in the Western Hemisphere at the time. Today a visitors' center has exceptional exhibits of the life of the average colonial soldier during the Revolution, made up in part of artifacts found in archaeological digs on the site. Remains of some of the cannon batteries, blockhouses, barracks, and hospital have also survived

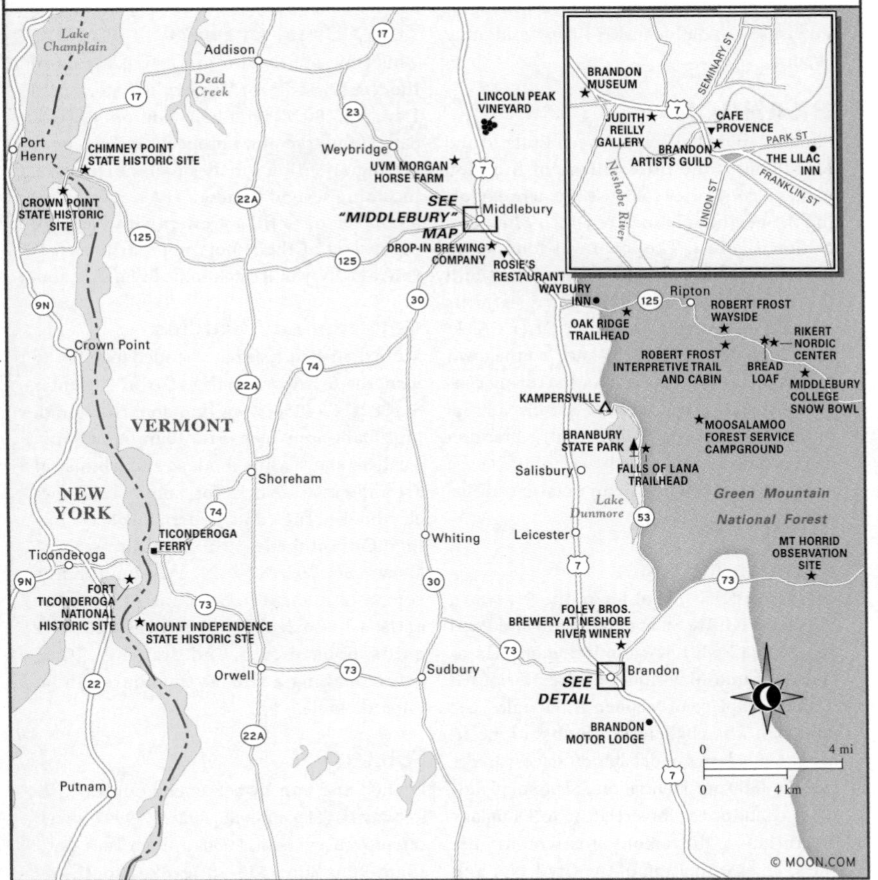

and can be viewed on several trails that run around the mountain. The longest route, the orange trail, takes about an hour round-trip.

In the end, all of the colonists' preparations were for naught, when they woke up on the morning of July 4, 1777, to find that the British had scaled the heights of Mount Defiance, which overlooked Fort Ticonderoga, and placed their cannons there. The Americans staged a daring midnight retreat across a floating bridge to Mount Independence, living to fight another day. Though that bridge is long gone, you can still take the nearby **Ticonderoga Ferry** (4831 Rte. 74 W., Shoreham, 802/897-7999, www.forttiferry.com, 7am-6pm early May-early July and Sept.-Oct.; 7am-7pm July-Aug., $12/18 cars one-way/round-trip, $1 pedestrians one-way) across to New York to view the **Fort Ticonderoga National Historic Site** (Ticonderoga, NY, 518/585-2821, www.fortticonderoga.org, 9:30am-5pm early May-late Oct., $17.50 adults, $16 seniors, $8 youth 5-12, children under 5 free), which has been meticulously reconstructed to its Revolutionary-era glory and populated with costumed historical reenactors who spice up visits with daily musket firings and other events.

BRANDON

Situated about halfway between Rutland and Middlebury, the little village of Brandon makes a good place to pause if you're exploring the northern branch of Green Mountain National Forest. The town was founded in 1761 and quickly became an important mill town, with both sawmills and gristmills situated at strategic points on Otter Creek. Supplies of iron ore nearby later led the town to become an important manufacturing center constructing iron stoves and railroad cars in the 19th century. More recently, Brandon has become a hub for artists who infuse the working-class town with an outsize creative culture.

Brandon Museum

On the western side of town, the **Brandon Museum** (Grove St. at Champlain and Pearl Sts., 802/247-6401, www.brandon.org, 11am-4pm daily mid-May-mid-Oct., free) is housed in the birthplace of Stephen A. Douglas, the politician who challenged Abraham Lincoln in a famous series of debates on slavery to decide the 1860 presidential race. The small museum contains exhibits relating to Douglas's life, including the famous cross-country debates, an examination of the Civil War and Vermont's active role in the abolitionist movement, and lots of historical photographs and other memorabilia.

Mount Horrid Observation Site

Don't mind the name; the view of the Mount Horrid cliffs is anything but. The trailhead to this observation site is just to the east of the Brandon Gap on Route 73. After a short but very steep hike, you can scan the forest below for moose and beaver, or look for the peregrine falcons that make their nest on the adjacent cliffs. Bring along your binoculars for prime bird-viewing.

Foley Bros. Brewery

This tiny, family-run brewery is a part of the **Neshobe River Winery** (79 Stone Mill Dam Rd., 802/247-8002, 11am-5pm Wed.-Sat., 11am-4pm Sun.) property and has been getting attention for its small-batch beers, including several standout IPAs. Stop by for a sampler, or to fill a growler with Pieces of Eight, one of their most popular brews. If you're lucky, you'll catch some live music, too.

Galleries and Studios

More than 40 artists have banded together to form the **Brandon Artists Guild** (7 Center St., 802/247-4956, www.brandonartistsguild.org, 10am-5pm Tues.-Sat., 10am-4pm Sun.), a gallery showcasing modern and whimsical art and crafts. Works for sale include jewelry, hooked rugs, and modern folk art paintings. Or visit the **Judith Reilly Gallery** (24 Conant Sq., 802/247-8421, www.judithreilly.com, afternoons Fri.-Sat. June-Oct.) in the artist's historical home, where she sells quilts, hooked rugs, and drawings. (Call before making a trip, as the hours can be unpredictable.)

Food

Owned and run by a French couple, **Cafe Provence** (11 Center St., 802/247-9997, www.cafeprovencevt.com, 11:30am-9pm Tues.-Sat., 10am-9pm Sun., $18-30) evokes south-of-France charm with yellow walls and sunny flavors. The bustling open kitchen adds to the energy of the handsome room at dinnertime.

Accommodations

Just south of town is the modest, affordable **Brandon Motor Lodge** (2095 Franklin St., Rte. 7, 800/675-7614, www.brandonmotorlodge.com, $75-149). Rooms have standard motel decor but are well kept, and all have access to a communal hot tub and pool. Well-behaved pets are welcome (with a $15 surcharge), and continental breakfast is included on weekends in the summer. If your muscles are travel-weary, you'll be delighted to know that the motel offers on-site massage from a local therapist.

A favorite for couples, **Lilac Inn** (53 Park St., 800/221-0720, www.lilacinn.com, $149-345) blends bed-and-breakfast comfort with more luxurious touches. Perks like in-room fireplaces and whirlpool tubs are available, and the convenient location makes for a leisurely stroll to town. The included breakfast is a multicourse treat. Dogs are allowed for $35 each.

Information and Services

Inside the Brandon Museum is a well-stocked information center, run by the **Brandon Area Chamber of Commerce** (4 Grove St., Rte. 7, 802/247-6401, www.brandon.org, open year-round), with gobs of brochures and a map for walking tours of town.

Brandon has a downtown **Rite-Aid Pharmacy** (1 Carver St., 802/247-8050, 8am-8pm Mon.-Sat., 8am-5pm Sun., pharmacy 8am-8pm Mon.-Fri., 9am-6pm Sat., 9am-5pm Sun.).

A 24-hour ATM is available at **First Brandon Bank** (2 Park St.) at the intersection of Route 7 and Route 73, as well as at the **National Bank of Middlebury** (5 Carver St., 877/508-8455, 8:30am-5pm Mon.-Thurs., 8:30am-5:30pm Fri., 9am-noon Sat.). In an emergency, contact the **Brandon Police** (1 W. Seminary St., 802/247-0222).

SPORTS AND RECREATION

Hiking and Biking

MIDDLEBURY

There's no better way to explore Middlebury than the **Trail Around Middlebury** (TAM), an 18-mile path that connects the town's various conservation areas, taking in bridges, cow pastures, and wooded trails. One of the best sections of trail passes through the **Otter Creek Gorge Preserve,** a 1.7-mile track that skirts the banks of Otter Creek, with views into the scenic gorge. The parking area is on Horse Farm Road, 0.2 mile north of the junction with Hamilton Road. This section and several others in the network are even accessible with strollers. Look for a map and guide produced by the **Middlebury Area Land Trust** (802/388-1007, www.maltvt.org), or print out a copy from the group's website.

MOOSALAMOO RECREATION AREA

This 20,000-acre wilderness reserve in the heart of the Green Mountain National Forest is as pristine as it is vast, with more than 70 miles of quiet hiking trails leading to waterfalls, lakes, and striking views of Lake Champlain and the Adirondacks. For those planning an overnight stay, the **Forest Service's Moosalamoo Campground** (802/747-6700, tent sites $10 pp) has 19 wooded sites, along with toilets, trash facilities, a grassy field, and a self-guided nature trail. It's accessible by car from Goshen-Ripton Road, off Route 125 a little south of Ripton center. A nearby trailhead marks the start of the popular **Moosalamoo Trail,** which climbs 2.9 miles to the summit of Mount Moosalamoo, a 4- to 5-hour round-trip.

A somewhat shorter but equally great hike begins at the roaring **Falls of Lana,** where you can hike 2.3 miles to the top of the Rattlesnake Cliffs for views of the mountains and Lake Dunmore below, a 3.5-hour round-trip. In the winter, many of the trails are groomed for snowshoeing and cross-country skiing. For more information, contact the nonprofit **Moosalamoo Association** (802/747-7900, www.moosalamoo.org).

Skiing

Middlebury has a long history of fielding champion ski teams in the Northeast College Athletic Conference. The team practices at the **Middlebury College Snow Bowl** (6886 Rte. 125, Middlebury, 802/388-4356, www.middleburysnowbowl.com, $35-55 adults, $35-45 students and seniors, $15 children under 6 and 70+), which dates back to

1934, making it the third-oldest ski area in Vermont. While the dozen or so trails won't win any awards for difficulty, they are no cakewalk either, with several expert trails careening down from the 2,650-foot main peak. More to the point, in an area full of ski resorts, the Snow Bowl is often deserted on weekdays, allowing skiers to take a half dozen runs in the time it takes to get up and down Killington once. Throw in cheap prices and an atmospheric base lodge, and the bowl is a good bet for an afternoon of fun.

A mile and a half away at the Bread Loaf campus, the **Rikert Nordic Center** (Rte. 125, 12 mi. west of Middlebury, Ripton, 802/443-2744, 8:30am-4:30pm daily, $19 adults, $12 Middlebury students, $6 children under 5, seniors free) has more than 25 miles of trails open to the public, skirting through the wilderness of the Green Mountain National Forest. The base lodge has rentals ($22 adults, $18 student/child) and a warm woodstove in winter.

GETTING THERE AND AROUND

From Middlebury, take Route 125 west to Chimney Point (20 mi., 30 min.) or Route 30 south and Route 73 west to Mount Independence (30 mi., 45 min.). Take Route 125 east to Bread Loaf and Middlebury Gap (10 mi., 20 min.). Take Route 7 south to Brandon (15 mi., 25 min.). You can also reach Brandon by taking Route 7 north from Rutland (15 mi., 25 min.).

Run by the Chittenden County Transportation Authority, the **Middlebury LINK** (802/864-2282, www.cctaride.org) provides regular bus service every day but Sunday between Middlebury (Exchange St. or Merchants Row) and Burlington ($4, 1.5 hrs.).

Addison County Transit Resources (802/388-2287, www.actr-vt.org) runs bus routes between Middlebury and Brandon on its Rutland Connector route, as well as a Snow Bowl Shuttle Bus to Bread Loaf and the Robert Frost trail.

Northern Green Mountains

The Green Mountains grow higher and wilder in the heart of the state, where alpine peaks tower over farms in verdant river valleys.

This region contains some of Vermont's best-loved destinations, from world-class ski resorts to the popular Ben & Jerry's factory, but even in glamorous Stowe, you're just a brief detour away from secluded dirt roads and shady swimming holes.

Easy access to outdoor adventures makes this a thrilling place to visit any time of year. In winter, the peaks are buried in snow—Mount Mansfield gets an average of 243 inches, drawing skiers and snowboarders to Stowe and Smugglers' Notch, the pair of resorts on the mountain's flanks. And if you want to escape the crowds and whirring

Highlights

Look for ★ to find recommended sights, activities, dining, and lodging.

★ **Vermont Historical Society Museum:** This museum is thoroughly modern in its unvarnished depiction of Vermont's historical contradictions (page 165).

★ **Morse Farm Maple Sugarworks:** Maple syrup season is as short as it's sweet, but you can sample Vermont's sweetest harvest year-round at this Montpelier sugaring mainstay (page 167).

★ **Rock of Ages:** Tour this granite quarrier and stare deep into the heart of Vermont's quarrying past from the vantage of a 600-foot-high viewing platform—then try for a strike at the granite bowling lane (page 171).

★ **Millstone Trails:** Experienced riders can explore some of Vermont's most technical mountain biking in a former quarry (page 173).

★ **Mountain Biking in Stowe:** A handful of great trail networks go from beginner-friendly to technical, making this a favorite place to ride in the state (page 187).

★ **Mad River Glen and Sugarbush Resort:** The Mad River Valley holds a pair of resorts with classic Vermont riding, from Mad River Glen's no-frills—and no snowboards—ethos to the long rides at Sugarbush (pages 196 and 199)!

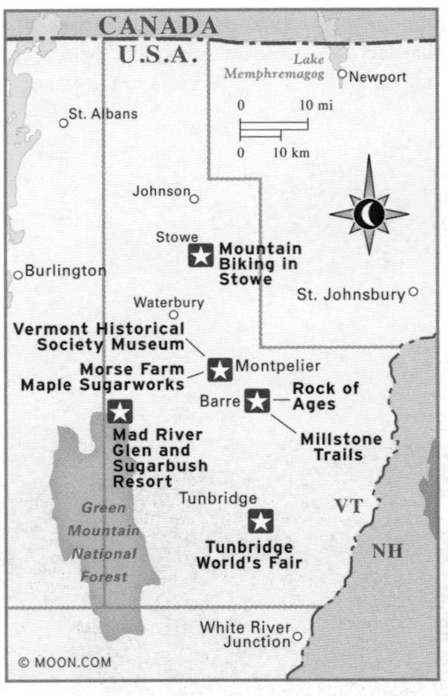

★ **Tunbridge World's Fair:** Tractor pulls, fried dough, and contra dancing are a taste of life in the White River Valley (page 209).

lifts, horse-drawn sleigh rides and snowshoeing let you take in the beauty and silence of the frozen landscape. There are even more ways into the mountains during the summer, as these mountain peaks are etched with hiking and biking trails and shot through with clean, cool rivers.

Most of the towns in this region are settled into deep river valleys, and farms still thrive on the rich soil here. And like a microcosm of the state, the Mad River Valley is an enchanting landscape of white steeples and red barns against a backdrop of dramatic peaks. The community here is a quirky mix of farmers, artists, and ex-urbanites that are fiercely protective of the valley's individuality. The White River Valley region, meanwhile, is a ridgeline—and a world—away. Parallel branches of the White River run through the area that defines Vermont's working landscape, a rural enclave filled with dairy cows and covered bridges.

Montpelier, the nation's smallest capital, has a thriving cultural life and a small-town soul, along with dozens of locally owned galleries and cafés in a historical downtown surrounded by forest and farmland. Nearby Barre is a grittier counterpoint to Montpelier's sweet center, but the town's granite quarries and monuments offer a compelling glimpse at Vermont's stonework past. In recent years, the entire region has become a foodie destination, and there's exquisite dining in tiny towns and bustling resorts and many opportunities to visit independent cheese makers, brewers, and farmers where they live and work.

PLANNING YOUR TIME

This area is small enough that any attractions can be reached by car in an hour, but you could easily spend a week visiting its resort towns and remote mountaintops. Many of the attractions are seasonal, from snow sports to maple syrup, but major sights are open year-round.

Most visitors ground their trip in one of a handful of small towns, like the alpine-chic village of **Stowe,** where world-class skiing and hiking are within easy reach, or neighboring **Waterbury,** one of Vermont's premier foodie destinations. Alternatively, stay in the **Mad River Valley** to enjoy its pair of ski areas—Sugarbush and Mad River Glen. The valley offers Vermont's mountain peaks, swimming holes, agricultural life, and culinary culture on a condensed scale, along with the state's most outlandish Fourth of July celebration.

Visiting the diminutive capital city of **Montpelier** is an afternoon well spent, and right next door, the city of **Barre** is a living monument to the granite industry.

The mostly agricultural **White River Valley** is a "Vermonter's Vermont," a working landscape of farms alongside a series of meandering rivers. It's a perfect place to wander, but if you'd like a taste of what life here is about, plan your trip to attend the ambitiously named Tunbridge World's Fair ... you can even try your hand at the tractor pull.

Previous: Lamoille Valley Rail Trail; Vermont Historical Society Museum in Montpelier; Rock of Ages near Barre.

Northern Green Mountains

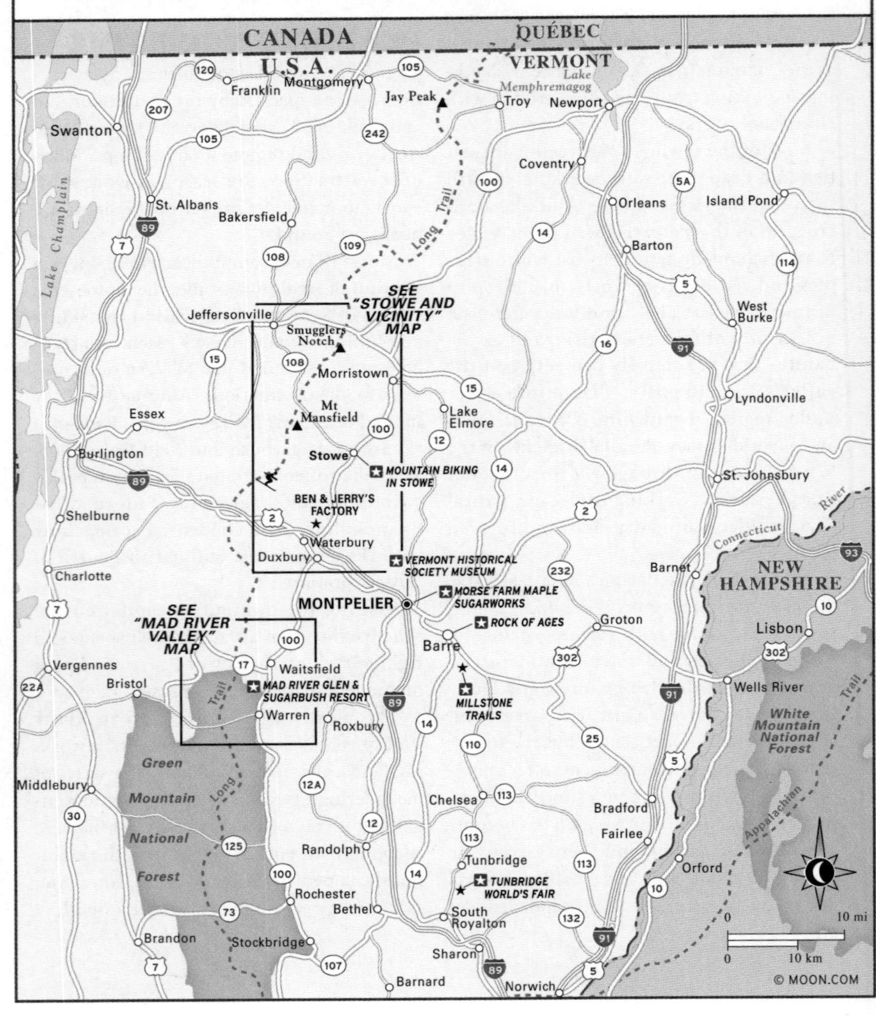

Montpelier and Barre

This pair of cities is at the precise heart of the state, but Montpelier and Barre can feel like a world unto themselves. The highway curves around Montpelier's city limits, but every other road winds away into farms and forests, and America's tiniest capital city has a small-town soul. Everyone seems to know each other in the downtown cafés and at the traditional contra dances held at the Capital City Grange. But during each year's legislative session, hotels and restaurants fill up with the farmers, professors, and professionals that make up Vermont's Citizen Legislature, a governing body that has always thought big.

Vermont was the first state to abolish slavery, recognize same-sex civil unions, ban oil extraction by "fracking," and require labeling of genetically modified foods, rulings that many Vermonters regard with pride. In 2018, Vermont racked up another first by becoming the first state to legalize marijuana by legislative vote, rather than with a ballot measure.

Just down the road, Barre's granite quarries and talented stoneworkers produced lofty monuments and simple headstones in a town that remains gritty and working-class. Like other quarrying towns in the state, Barre attracted a diverse group of immigrants and is sprinkled with statues and tributes to workers who arrived from Scotland, Spain, Scandinavia, Lebanon, Greece, and Italy. Most travelers don't make it a base, but a day trip to the town is a fascinating encounter with a time when Vermont's rock was on the world stage.

MONTPELIER

Wrapped by forested hills and bisected by the Winooski River, America's tiniest capital city has a small-town soul. Everyone seems to know each other in the downtown cafés, the natural food co-op, and at the traditional contra dances held at the Capital City Grange.

It's an easy place to explore on foot, and Federal-style brick buildings and Victorian mansions lend a bit of pomp to the capital's diminutive downtown. And at the center of it all is the gold-capped capitol, dramatic against a leafy backdrop that changes with the season. Just as the country's founders intended, most of Vermont's representatives undertake political life as a kind of community-serving side hustle, so if the politicians look more like farmers and retirees than the average DC politico, that's because they are.

State House

Montpelier's impressive **State House** (115 State St., 802/828-2228, www.leg.state.vt.us, 7:45am-4:15pm Mon.-Fri., 11:30am-3pm Sat., tours every half hour 10am-3:30pm Mon.-Fri., 11am-3:30pm Sat. July-mid-Oct.; 9am-3pm Mon.-Fri. mid-Oct.-June) dominates State Street with a 57-foot golden dome above a columned Renaissance Revival building that was built in 1859.

Fittingly for the state, the dome is topped by a wooden statue of Ceres, the goddess of agriculture. Look for a **statue of Ethan Allen,** the Revolutionary War figure, in the Greek Revival front portico, and a **cannon** that was seized at the Battle of Bennington (having completed Revolutionary service, it's now permanently trained on the Department of Motor Vehicles across the street). Tours of the building's interior take in statues and paintings of Vermont politicians who figured in state and national history, including Presidents Calvin Coolidge and Chester A. Arthur. You can also explore on your own, by accessing a cell phone audio guide that corresponds to numbered locations within the State House (vermontstatehouse.toursphere.com, 802/526-3221).

★ Vermont Historical Society Museum

From the beginning of Vermont's history

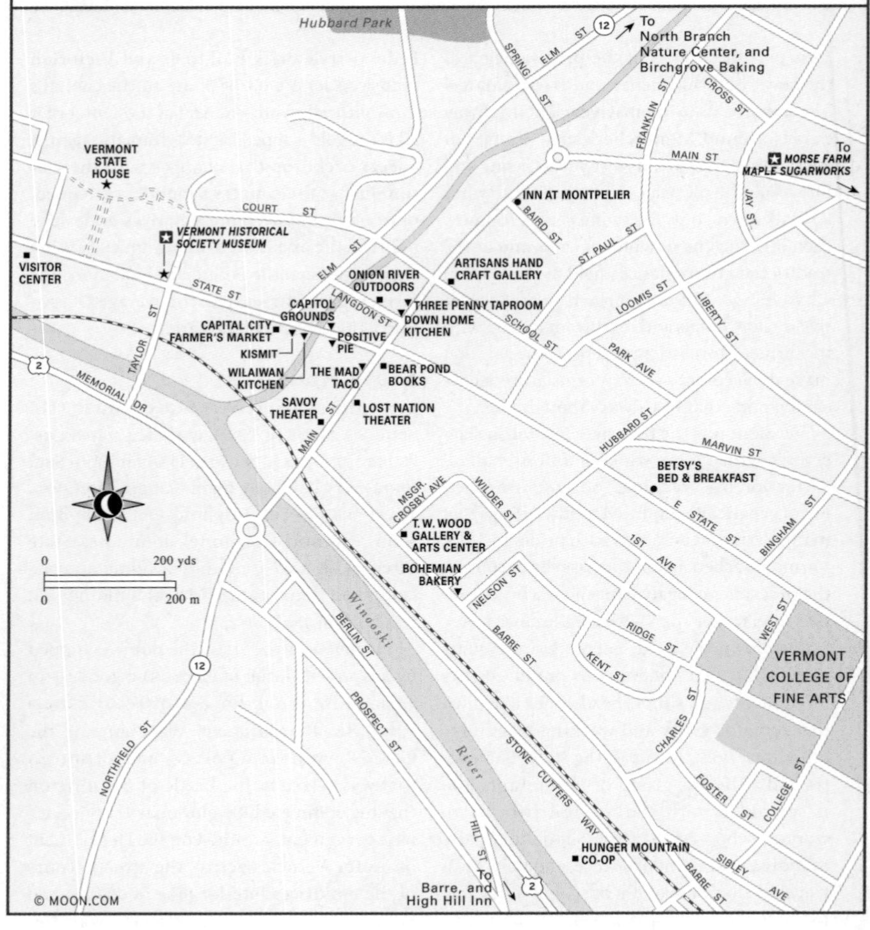

as an independent republic, its residents have struggled with the tension between "Freedom and Unity," the state's oxymoronic state motto. The state took that paradox as a starting point for a complete renovation of the **Vermont Historical Society Museum** (109 State St., 802/828-2291, www.vermonthistory.org, 10am-4pm Tues.-Sat., $7 adults, $5 students and seniors, children under 6 free, $20 families), a notably thoughtful journey back into the story of the state. Exhibits start with full-scale reconstructions of an Abenaki dwelling and the Revolutionary-era Catamount Tavern, and continue on to include Civil War artifacts, a room dedicated to Vermont-born president Calvin Coolidge, and even a collection on the early history of skiing. The museum continues to evolve and expand; a new building in Barre features its own collection of exhibits and artifacts. The gift shop has an extensive selection of books on Vermont history and culture.

★ Morse Farm Maple Sugarworks

In Vermont, you are never far from a sugarhouse. On the edge of the city, seventh-generation mapler Burr Morse has turned his farm into one of the premier maple syrup producers in the state. **Morse Farm Maple Sugarworks** (1168 County Rd., 800/242-2740, www.morsefarm.com, 9am-8pm daily Memorial Day to Labor day, 9am-6pm daily Labor day to Dec. 31, 9am-5pm Jan. 1 to Memorial Day, donations accepted) is a virtual museum of the industry, with old photographs and a "split-log" movie theater that shows a film of the sugaring process. A cavernous gift shop sells maple kettle corn and that most Vermonter of treats, maple creemees (soft-serve maple ice cream cones).

Galleries

One of the best of Montpelier's galleries is also the oldest. The **T.W. Wood Gallery & Arts Center** (46 Barre St., 802/262-6035, www.twwoodgallery.org, noon-4pm Tues.-Sat.) has been showcasing the work of Vermont artists for more than 100 years, with a permanent collection of modern art and rotating shows by local contemporary artists.

Mary Stone's hand-sculpted clay animal whistles are just one of the unique crafts on display at the **Artisans Hand Craft Gallery** (89 Main St., 802/229-9492, www.artisanshand.com, 10am-6pm Mon.-Sat., noon-4pm Sun.), a hub for jewelry, pottery, woodwork, and metalwork from Vermont artisans.

Entertainment and Events

With a destination-worthy beer list and a laid-back atmosphere, **Three Penny Taproom** (108 Main St., 802/223-8277, www.threepennytaproom.com) is Montpelier's best bar, and the adjoining restaurant serves appealing, dressed-up pub fare.

Montpelier's professional theater company, **Lost Nation Theater** (39 Main St., 802/229-0492, www.lostnationtheater.org) performs an eclectic mix of musicals, contemporary drama, and an annual fall Shakespeare production. The **Savoy Theater** (26 Main St., 802/229-0509, www.savoytheater.com) screens first-run and classic art films.

Shopping

Get the pick of the local crops (for a hiking picnic, an edible souvenir, or just as a snack) at **Hunger Mountain Co-op** (623 Stone Cutters Way, 802/223-8000, https://hungermountain.coop, 8am-8pm daily), a bounty of locally grown organic produce, gourmet cheeses, and other nourishing treats.

There are shelves full of classic tomes and local favorites at **Bear Pond Books** (77 Main St., 802/229-0774, www.bearpondbooks.com, 9am-6:30pm Mon.-Thurs., 9am-8pm Fri., 9am-5:30pm Sat., 10am-5pm Sun.), which sells a roster of Vermont's best fiction and nonfiction—plus sponsors regular readings.

For the most expansive stock of outdoor gear around, step into **Onion River Outdoors** (20 Langdon St., 802/229-9409, www.onionriver.com, 10am-6pm Mon., Wed.-Thurs., 10am-6:30pm Fri., 9am-5pm Sat., 10am-4pm Sun.). The selection of bicycles, cross-country skis, snowshoes, and camping and hiking gear (plus the footwear and clothing appropriate for all of it) is indeed impressive—as is the knowledgeable staff selling it.

Food

CASUAL

Rub shoulders with beer geeks, townies, and legislators at **Three Penny Taproom** (108 Main St., 802/223-8277, www.threepennytaproom.com, 11am-close Mon.-Fri., noon-close Sat., 11am-7pm Sun., $10-16), whose dressy pub food is above par, and whose brew list is beyond compare. Wait times for tables can be long on busy nights, but you can linger in the convivial bar, where patrons bond over pints that range from Vermont's mainstream (Hill Farmstead, Zero Gravity) to intriguingly fringe (Kombucha Hard Cider, Belgian Grisette).

LEADER
EVAPORATOR
CO INC

Bringing a welcome serving of Southern cuisine to Montpelier's restaurant scene, **Down Home Kitchen** (100 Main St., 802/225-6665, www.downhomekitchenvt.com, 8am-2pm daily, $10-15) serves hearty, comforting food in a cheery space downtown. Meat and three, griddle cakes, and fried chicken are based in fresh, often local ingredients, with excellent coffee and beer to go alongside.

Like its fraternal in Waitsfield, **The Mad Taco** (72 Main St., 802/225-6038, www.themadtaco.com, 11am-9pm daily, $10-14) serves Mexican fare with an anarchic Yankee streak. The menu is the same as at the Waitsfield location, but the Montpelier location has an appealingly utilitarian feel. The café is no frills, but tortillas come filled with classics like *carnitas* and pork *al pastor*, or culinary mashups: Try the smoked pork with kimchi and cilantro. The beer and the food are often local, and the hefty burritos are memorable.

Hearty pasta dishes and creative pizzas are on the menu at **Positive Pie** (22 State St., 802/229-0453, www.positivepie.com, 11am-9pm Sun.-Thurs., 11am-9:30pm Fri.-Sat., $11-23), which is also a mainstay of the Capital City music scene. The vegetarian pie "Moonshadow," is topped with crushed walnuts and artichoke hearts, and Italian classics like shrimp scampi and spaghetti Bolognese are prepared with care and fresh ingredients. The massive beer list includes many of the state's favorite brews.

A strong contender for Vermont's best Thai food, ★ **Wilaiwan Kitchen** (34 State St., 802/505-8111, 11am-2pm Mon.-Sat., $7-12) has a short menu of Thai-American classics and lesser-known dishes that changes weekly. Two pieces of local advice: The dining room is tiny, so it can be hard to score a table, and when a dish is labeled "spicy," the kitchen doesn't hold back.

UPSCALE

Moody decor and sophisticated food have made ★ **Kismet** (52 State St., 802/223-8646, www.kismetkitchens.com, 5pm-9pm Wed.-Fri., 9am-2pm and 5pm-9pm Sat., 9am-2pm Sun., $20-30, prix fixe $45) Montpelier's classic date-night restaurant; couples dine on tortellini with baked ricotta and pistachio butter, or crimini *en croute* bathed in garlic butter. Brunch is served on the weekends, and is sublime: Think savory bread pudding with bone marrow broth, and eggs *en cocotte*.

CAFÉS AND BAKERIES

For years, ★ **Bohemian Bakery** (78 Barre St., 802/461-8119, www.bohemianbakeryvt.com, 7:30am-1:30pm Wed.-Fri., 8am-2pm Sat.-Sun., $2-9) was based out of a tiny house in the northern woods, open to the public just one day a week, so sweets lovers rejoiced when they opened a Montpelier shop in 2017. Favorites include the wonderfully flaky croissants, caramel crispy kouign amann, and palm-size fruit tarts, and there are savory pastries and hearty quiche for lunch.

It's easy to miss **Birchgrove Baking** (279 Elm St., 802/223-0200, www.birchgrovebaking.com, 7am-11am Mon., 7am-3pm Tues.-Thurs., 7am-4pm Fri., 8am-4pm Sat., 8am-2pm Sun., $2-6), whose creative sweets are hidden away on a side street. But the cornmeal shortbread, lemon meringue tarts, and excellent espresso are the detour. There's very little seating inside the cheery bakery, which makes this a perfect place to pick up supplies for a hike up to the Hubbard Park Tower.

As much a local gathering spot as a place to find something to eat, **Capitol Grounds** (27 State St., 802/223-7800, www.capitolgrounds.com, 6:15am-5pm Mon.-Fri., 7am-5pm Sat., 8am-5pm Sun., $6-10) whips up made-to-order sandwiches, offers free wireless Internet service, and froths fair-trade cappuccinos all day long.

1: the golden-domed State House, presiding over the United States' smallest capital city; **2:** evaporator at Morse Farm Maple Sugarworks in Montpelier; **3:** Rock of Ages quarry near Barre

FARMERS MARKETS

Artisans and growers come out of the woodwork for the **Capital City Farmers Market** (State St. at Elm St., 9am-1pm Sat. May-Oct.), one of the best in the state. Vendors include the highly sought-after (and scarce) **Lawson's Finest Liquids** brewery, which isn't open to the public.

Accommodations

$100-150

In the heart of downtown, **Betsy's Bed & Breakfast** (74 East State St., 802/229-0466, www.central-vt.com/web/betsybb, $85-190), has 12 guest rooms spread between two Victorian mansions decorated with period antiques. The interiors are a bit timeworn and dark, but the friendly owners, Betsy and Jon, serve delightful breakfasts.

Drift off to the sounds of crickets and frogs (or falling snow) at ★ **High Hill Inn** (265 Green Rd., East Montpelier, 802/223/2727, www.highhillinn.com, $100-175). Comfortable rooms and a relaxed country setting make this hilltop inn feel like a getaway. The generous breakfast spread is a highlight.

$150-250

Two gracious Federal-style buildings (with no fewer than 10 fireplaces) comprise the **Inn at Montpelier** (147 Main St., 802/223-2727, www.innatmontpelier.com, $160-210). The antiques-filled common areas lead into 19 neat rooms, with canopy beds, colonial-style bureaus, and walls ranging from tomato-red to bold floral. A simple breakfast is served in the old-fashioned dining room, and in warm months, the gracious porch is the perfect place to watch the town drift by. Book well ahead during the legislative session (Jan.-Apr.).

Information and Services

Across from the State House, the **Capital Region Visitors Center** (134 State St., 802/828-5981, 6am-5pm Mon.-Fri., 9am-5pm Sat.-Sun.) has lots of brochures, maps, and advice on area attractions. Free Wi-Fi is available at many spots downtown, including **Capitol Grounds** (27 State St., 802/223-7800).

ATMs are available at many downtown locations, including at **Citizens Bank** (7 Main St., 802/223-9545, 9am-5pm Mon.-Fri., 9am-noon Sat.). Pharmacy needs can be taken care of at the **Rite-Aid Pharmacy** (29-31 Main St., 802/223-4787, 8am-9pm Mon.-Sat., 9am-9pm Sun., pharmacy 8am-8pm Mon.-Fri., 9am-6pm Sat., 9am-5pm Sun.). In an emergency, contact **Vermont State and Montpelier City Police** (1 Pitkin Ct., 802/223-3445). Urgent care is available at **CVMC Express Care** (1311 Barre-Montpelier Rd., Berlin, 802/371-4239, 9am-7pm daily).

BARRE

You may not have seen Barre, but you've definitely seen Barre Gray, granite that's left the Vermont ground to be shaped into government buildings and monuments. Local residents of Barre—rhymes with "cherry"—first discovered the stone in their hills shortly after the War of 1812, but the industry didn't take off until Montpelier erected a new State House in 1836 and ordered up a load of granite from its sister city for the task. The high quality of the stone's texture led to orders by other cities down the Eastern Seaboard, and almost overnight, the town mushroomed into a city.

Many of the workers who performed the arduous task of cutting the stone blocks out of the quarries were immigrants, first from Scotland, then after the turn of the 20th century, from Italy. While the granite trade is still a flourishing industry (mostly for cemetery headstones), the city has gone through hard times in the 20th and 21st centuries as other industries have dried up. For years, the monuments stood in stark contrast to the depressed-feeling downtown, but cafés and pubs have filled some vacant storefronts with shoots and starts of new life. And these days, some disused quarries are finding purpose as a part of Millstone Hill, a series of mountain bike trails that loops through the pitted landscape.

★ Rock of Ages

The granite industry isn't just a thing of Barre's past. The **Rock of Ages** (560 Graniteville Rd., Graniteville, 802/476-3119, www.rockofages.com) granite quarry is active, and quarriers still cut stone out of the deep holes that have been mined for more than 100 years. The company now gives narrated tours (10am-4pm Mon.-Sat. mid-May-late Oct., $5 adults, $4.50 seniors, $2.50 children 6-13) of its main quarry, where a platform looks out on massive machines cutting blocks of granite more than 600 feet below. Guides explain the meticulous methods for cutting the enormous blocks, which include boring dozens of small holes beneath the blocks and then blasting them free with dynamite. (Fun fact: The quarry was used in the opening shot of the 2009 *Star Trek* film, in which a young Captain Kirk drives a Corvette off the cliff.)

The site also features a visitors center (10am-4pm Mon.-Sat. May-late Oct., free), an outdoor granite bowling alley (free), and a "cut stone activity center" where you can try your hand at sandblasting and other activities. And if you are *really* thinking ahead, you can order your own headstone from a showroom on the premise.

Hope Cemetery

The immigrants who worked in the quarries were given one unusual perk—each of them received one block of granite for their very own. Many chose to work on their own tombstones, creating a lasting tribute to the handiwork of men who mostly toiled and died for monuments to others. The enormous **Hope Cemetery** (201 Maple Ave., 802/476-6245, dawn-dusk, tours available upon request, $5 adults, $3 seniors and children) is now a giant open-air sculpture gallery, with more than 10,000 gray granite headstones carved with art deco lettering and intricate representations of flowers, ships, and religious symbols. The town still administers burials here—with the only stipulation being that the headstones must be made of Barre Gray.

In modern times, residents have chosen fanciful markers such as a granite soccer ball and an actual-size granite race car. Some stones even contain life-size figures, such as the touching carving of a man and woman in adjoining beds reaching out to clasp hands for eternity. It's impossible to walk among them without contemplating a sculpture for your own plot.

Barre's Granite Monuments

Evidence of the granite trade remains all over town in the form of monuments erected by master carvers who worked in the quarries. At the turn of the 20th century, Scottish immigrant stonecutters banded together to produce a **statue of Robert Burns** on an enormous base on Washington Street. The memorial, considered one of the best granite sculptures in the world, was unveiled in 1899 on the occasion of the 100th anniversary of Burns's death. (As a point of national pride, the actual carving was done by Italian sculptors working on models by the Scots.)

The massive art deco warrior depicted in the 1924 **Soldiers and Sailors Memorial** on North Main Street is reminiscent of the figures at Rockefeller Center in New York. The statue, also known as *Young Triumphant*, was adopted as Barre's city seal.

A more recent memorial at last gives the generations of Italian stonecutters their due: Erected in 1985, the **Italian-American Monument** on North Main Street depicts a 23-foot-high apron-clad figure heroically grasping a hammer and chisel. The monument is dedicated to Italian sculptor Carlo Abate, who established the first school for stone carving in Barre in the early 20th century.

Entertainment and Events

The 1899 **Barre Opera House** (6 N. Main St., 802/476-8188, www.barreoperahouse.org) is a community theater space that hosts local and national musical performances.

You knew it was coming. The **Granite Festival of Barre** (7 Jones Bros. Way, 802/476-4605, www.granitemuseum.org, early Sept.) celebrates all things gray and stony, with stonecutting and etching demonstrations on the grounds of the granite museum, hands-on activities, and Irish music and a bocce tournament to pay homage to Barre's ethnic heritage.

Food

The ★ **Wayside Restaurant & Bakery** (1873 Rte. 302, Montpelier, 802/223-6611, www.waysiderestaurant.com, 6:30am-9:30pm daily, $7-19) has a Montpelier address, a Barre soul, and a roadside location that's smack between the two cities. This eatery has been in business for more than a century and is beloved by the locals and visitors that pack the comfy booths and lunch counter. There are homey soups, sandwiches, and salads along with hefty all-day breakfasts, but aficionados of old-time American food will appreciate rarely seen dishes like grilled beef liver and onions, or country-fried steak in beef gravy.

Barre locals Keith Paxman and Rich McSheffrey named **Cornerstone Pub & Kitchen** (47 North Main St., 802/476-2121, www.cornerstonepk.com, 11:30am-9pm Tues.-Sat., $11-23) for Barre's glory days, but the fare is strictly contemporary: Try the duck burger with red wine Dijon rémoulade, or the swordfish tacos with chipotle aioli. The food pairs perfectly with the extensive list of Vermont beers.

Get a cup of Barre's best coffee at **Espresso Bueno** (248 N. Main St., 802/479-0896, www.espressobueno.com, 6am-6pm Mon.-Thurs., 6am-close Fri., 7am-close Sat., 8am-2pm Sun., $2-7), which also serves simple breakfasts sandwiches and burritos. Caffeine lovers shouldn't miss their *caffè con panna*, a shot of the strong stuff topped with maple whipped cream.

Accommodations

You can walk downtown from **Maplecroft Bed & Breakfast** (70 Washington St., 802/622-0256, www.maplecroftvermont.com, $125-175), housed in a grand, old Victorian mansion with tastefully updated decor. A hot breakfast is included.

If you're visiting Barre to ride the exceptional Millstone Trails, you can sleep on-site at **Millstone Hill** (59 Little John Rd., East Barre, 802/479-1000, www.millstonehill.com, $105-225), an eclectic assortment of lodgings that includes a restored farmhouse, rustic lodge, loft, and cottage.

Set in a converted fire station, the **Firehouse Inn** (8 South Main St., 802/476-2167, www.ladder1grill.com, studios $165, one-bedrooms $189-229) has undeniable curb appeal, with brilliant red doors and a brick facade. Inside, two one-bedroom suites and two studio suites are updated and modern, with kitchenettes and small living areas. The downstairs restaurant and bar can get busy on weekend nights, but few guests complain of any noise—and it's a cozy spot to duck into for a drink.

CAMPING

There are primitive campsites available at **Millstone Hill** (59 Little John Rd., East Barre, 802/479-1000, www.millstonehill.com, $16/single occupancy, or $10 pp), with granite fire pits and picnic tables; bathroom facilities are at the adjacent lodge.

Information and Services

There is a string of banks along North Main Street, including **Key Bank** (315 N. Main St., 802/476-4135). You can fill prescriptions and fulfill other medical needs at **Rite-Aid Pharmacy** (335 N. Main St., 802/476-4311, 8am-9pm Mon.-Fri., 8am-8pm Sat., 8am-5pm Sun., pharmacy 8am-8pm Mon.-Fri., 9am-6pm Sat., 9am-5pm Sun.). For more serious medical care, the area's foremost hospital is **Central Vermont Medical Center** (130 Fisher Rd., 802/371-4100, www.cvmc.org). For nonmedical emergencies, contact **City of Barre Police Department** (15 4th St., 802/476-6613).

SPORTS AND RECREATION

★ Millstone Trails

Barre's landscape is honeycombed with quarries, and the high ground between the holes have been transformed into some of Vermont's most technical mountain biking. The 60 miles of single-track at **Millstone Hill** (park at 44 Brook St. or the end of Barclay Quarry Rd., Websterville, www.millstonetrails.com, $10) are some of the best in the state. You can bring skis and snowshoes to explore the trails in winter months (free), but they really shine on two wheels; the well-drained, technically challenging trails are well designed and never feel crowded. Tickets are available on the website, or at **Lawson's Store** (40 Churchill Rd., Websterville, 802/476-7661, 8:30am-6:30pm Mon.-Sat., 8:30am-1pm Sun., $10).

Hiking

The forested slope behind the capitol in Montpelier is part of **Hubbard Park,** a 185-acre stretch of forested land threaded with excellent walking trails. A trailhead directly behind the State House leads up to the **Hubbard Park Tower,** a squat stone structure that offers an excellent view over the town. Allow about 20 minutes to climb the **Statehouse Trail,** which is steep but has benches along the way; there are picnic tables and bathroom facilities adjacent to the tower. From there, seven miles of trails connect to various trailheads throughout the town. A trail map is available on **Montpelier's website** (www.montpelier-vt.org).

Skiing and Sledding

Downhillers can head straight to nearby Stowe, but cross-country skiers and snowshoers can find plenty to love in the Montpelier area. The best may be at **Millstone Hill** (park at 44 Brook St. or the end of Barclay Quarry Rd., Websterville, www.millstonetrails.com, free), with 25 miles of groomed trails that wrap around quarries and forest.

Or try **Morse Farm Ski Touring Center** (1168 County Rd., Montpelier, 802/223-0560, www.skimorsefarm.com, 9:30am-4:30pm Mon.-Fri., 9am-4:30pm Sat.-Sun., $14 adults, $6 youth 6-18, under 6 free; rentals $30 adults, $24 youth), with 15 miles of groomed trails for every skill level. After skiing the trails, you can warm up by the fire with a cup of cider or chill out with a maple syrup snow cone.

The best sledding hill around is at **Hubbard Park** (Parkway St., Montpelier) adjacent to the **Old Shelter Pavilion.** You can rent something to slide on at **Onion River Outdoors** (20 Langdon St., 802/225-6736, www.onionriver.com, 10am-6pm Mon., Wed.-Thurs., 10am-6:30pm Fri., 9am-5pm Sat., 10am-4pm Sun., $18/day).

GETTING THERE AND AROUND

Montpelier is directly off I-89 at exit 8, a 55-mile (1-hour) trip from White River Junction. To travel to Barre, from I-89 north take exit 6 and drive 10 miles east along Route 63, or from I-89 south take exit 7 and drive 10 miles east along Route 62.

Amtrak (800/872-7245, www.amtrak.com) runs trains to Junction Road in Montpelier. Buses from **Vermont Transit** (802/223-7112) stop at the Montpelier Bus Station (1 Taylor St.). The **Green Mountain Transit Agency** (802/223-7287, www.gmtaride.org) operates bus routes around Montpelier and Barre.

Stowe and Waterbury

The alpine-chic village of Stowe is shrine to adventure and relaxation, with world-class skiing, endless hiking, and nature-inspired spas around every curve of the river that runs through its heart. Rising right out of town is Mount Mansfield, Vermont's biggest peak, which dominates the skyline with 2,360 feet of vertical drop and 39 miles of rideable terrain. Intrepid visitors have been hiking up and skiing down the sides since 1913, and in 1933 the Civilian Conservation Corps cut trails through the thick forest—Mansfield got its first rope tow in 1936.

This continues to be one of New England's premier resorts, drawing flocks of alpine and backcountry skiers, as well as ice climbers and snowshoers. Summer and autumn are just as appealing, with endless hiking trails, golf courses, and bright foliage, all with a high-elevation climate that doesn't overheat on even the muggiest days. And if you arrive in Stowe from the south, you'll pass right through Waterbury, a small town that's got an outsize reputation for food and drink: It's the home of Ben & Jerry's, the renowned Heady Topper beer, and a population of devoted beer geeks brewing the next big thing in their basements.

STOWE

Upon arrival in Stowe's center, you might find that the curated cuteness of downtown—white church spire, alpine-style buildings, boutique shops—verges on cliché. But this particular New England town is an original, the real deal, and helped define the genre of adorable mountain resorts. Tourists have been coming here since the Civil War, drawn to the remarkable scenery and endless opportunities for outdoor adventure that continue to attract visitors from around the world. This is mountain living gone upscale, and if Stowe has acquired a commercial sheen since its founding in 1763, it's still got deep Vermont roots, with great dining and appealing accommodation that make it an excellent base for exploring the northern Green Mountains.

Gondola Skyride

The Abenaki called the highest peak in Vermont Moze-o-de-be-Wadso (Mountain with a Head Like a Moose). The 4,393-foot mountain has come down to us as the more prosaic Mount Mansfield. In the summer, Stowe Mountain Resort operates an eight-person high-speed **gondola skyride** (Mountain Rd./Rte. 108, 888/253-4849, www.stowe.com, 9:30am-4pm late June-mid-Oct., round-trip $29 adults, $20 youth 6-12, $87 families) up to the summit that takes in views of the village and surrounding mountains on the way up.

Stowe Mountain Toll Road and Smugglers' Notch

It's also possible to drive to the summit of Mount Mansfield on a winding, unpaved **toll road**, which takes off from Route 108 at the **Toll House Conference Center** (5781 Rte. 108/Mountain Rd., tolls $23 car and driver, $8 each passenger, free children 4 and under). The 4.5-mile long road is closed to motorcycles, RVs, and bicycles, and climbs steeply to the "nose" of Mount Mansfield, where it's possible to park, and continue to the "chin," the highest summit, on a 1.3-mile, one-way walking trail.

The views are spectacular, but for a scenic drive without the toll, just keep winding up **Route 108,** an incredibly twisty, curving road that's hemmed in by high cliffs, granite boulders, and trees that turn bright gold in the fall. Route 108 climbs through **Smugglers' Notch,** a mountain pass said to have been used to bring contraband from Canada during the years of Prohibition. Oversize vehicles should stay away, and all drivers should approach this road with great care, as hikers, rock climbers, and cyclists are often hidden behind the sharp corners.

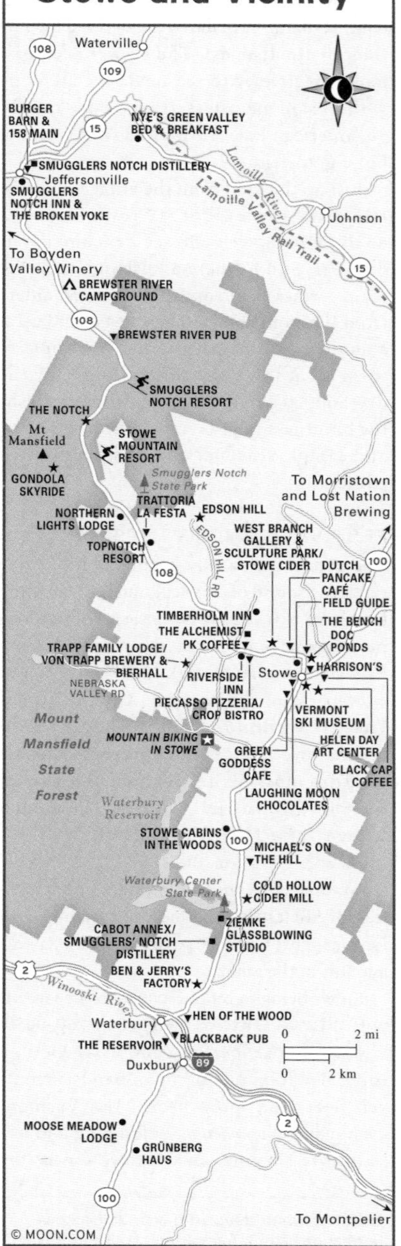

Trapp Family Lodge

What happens after "happily ever after?" Baron and Maria von Trapp, whose story is depicted in the musical *The Sound of Music*, moved to Vermont. After escaping the Nazis, the von Trapps came to Stowe and built the **Trapp Family Lodge** (700 Trapp Hill Rd., 802/253-8511 or 800/826-7000, www.trappfamily.com), which has grown over the years into a skiers' resort complex complete with lodge rooms, fitness center, and slope-side villas. The family is still actively involved with operations, and each generation, it seems, contributes its own unique stamp, like the recent addition of a brewery specializing in Austrian-influenced beer.

Visiting for a Linzer torte at the over-the-top DeliBakery and a family sing-along around the bonfire at night is a requirement for any serious Rodgers and Hammerstein fan. The lodge also shows a documentary about the family twice daily in St. George's Hall, along with the obligatory screening of *The Sound of Music* every Thursday night at 8pm.

Museums and Galleries

If you fantasize about laying the first ski tracks down the side of Mount Mansfield, the **Vermont Ski Museum** (1 S. Main St., 802/253-9911, www.vtssm.com, noon-5pm Wed.-Sun., $5) offers a dose of reality. The history exhibits give you an appreciation of just how gutsy it was to ski in the days before modern equipment, lifts, and clothing. Located in Stowe's former town hall, the museum has several rooms of exhibits, a plasma screen with ski videos, and a hall of fame of great names in Vermont skiing history.

The community-supported **Helen Day Art Center** (90 Pond St., 802/253-8358, www.helenday.com, 10am-5pm Tues.-Sat. year-round, donations accepted) has been dedicated to showcasing local art for more than 25 years. It inhabits the second floor of a Greek

Revival building in the center of town, with a sculpture garden out back.

A more extensive sculpture garden fills the grounds of the **West Branch Gallery and Sculpture Park** (17 Towne Farm Ln., 802/253-8943, www.westbranchgallery.com, 10am-5pm Tues.-Sun. year-round, free), a fantasia of random metal and stone objects strewn about a bucolic landscape a mile north of town.

Entertainment and Events

NIGHTLIFE

Mountain Road is lined with lively bars and restaurants for après-ski recovery, and most sport fireplaces, rustic decor, and the kind of comforting snacks that go well with beer. **Piecasso Pizzeria & Lounge** (1899 Mountain Rd., 802/253-4411, www.piecasso.com, 11am-9pm Sun.-Thurs., 11am-10pm Fri.-Sat.) is a local favorite, with lots of seats at the bar, creative pizza, and undeniably scrumptious chicken wings.

BREWERS AND DISTILLERS

Stowe is blessed with a wealth of locally made craft alcohols, starting with the Austrian lager beers at **Von Trapp Brewery & Bierhall** (1333 Luce Hill Rd., 802/253-5750, www.vontrappbrewing.com, 11:30am-9pm, Mon.-Sun.). Favorites include the malty Vienna Style Lager and the Helles Lager, and the Bierhall's menu of Austrian pub food—think cheddar and beer soup, hot soft pretzels, and many kinds of sausages—are perfect pairings for the entire lineup.

Famed for an aromatic IPA called **Heady Topper**—which has been called the "best beer on earth," **The Alchemist** (100 Cottage Club Rd., 802/882-8165, www.alchemistbeer.com, 11am-7pm Tues.-Sat.) has a short list of great beers that come in cans and lean hoppy. There are strict purchasing limits (that's four 4-packs of Heady Topper per person), but this is the best spot to pick up their beers in the state, including some that are rarely seen beyond the brewery.

In contrast, the beers at **Idletyme Brewing Company** (1859 Mountain Rd./Rte. 108, 802/253-4765, www.idletymebrewing.com, 11:30am-9pm daily) are defined only by their distinctiveness. The brewer is consistently creative, with seasonal specials along with a list of mainstays: try the Pink 'n' Pale, an American Pale Ale brewed with a hint of bitter grapefruit.

Just up the road from the village is the diminutive **Stowe Cider** (17 Town Farm Ln., 802/253-2065, www.stowecider.com, noon-6pm Fri.-Sun.), where a husband-and-wife team ferments European-style hard ciders from Vermont apples. Their kegs wind up at a number of local eateries, but you can taste them all at this cozy cidery shop. Try the dry-hopped Safety Meeting, whose refreshing bitterness might tempt craft beer lovers, and sample seasonal one-offs and limited editions.

FESTIVALS AND EVENTS

The von Trapp family keeps the hills alive (with the sound of classical music) by hosting **Music in our Meadow,** a series of outdoor performances in partnership with **Stowe Performing Arts** (802/253-7729, www.stoweperformingarts.com). And the **Stowe Theatre Guild** (67 Main St., 802/253-3961, www.stowetheatre.com) presents crowd-pleasing musicals throughout the year at the Stowe Town Hall Theatre. The annual **Stoweflake Hot Air Balloon Festival** (802/253-7355 or 800/253-2232, www.stoweflake.com, mid-July) offers opportunities for $10 tethered balloon rides, along with longer flights for those paying $500 for a package stay at the resort.

Stowe brings a bit of Bavaria to the Greens with **Stowe Oktoberfest** (802/760-9050, www.stoweoktoberfest.com, early Oct.), a three-day frenzy of oompah bands, schnitzel, beer, and more beer. Miss Vermont even makes a showing. Ski jumping and ice-sculpture carving shake Stowe out of the

1: Stowe's white-steepled church; **2:** the Stowe Recreation Path; **3:** Trapp Family Lodge in Stowe

1

2

3

Trapp Family Lodge
REGISTRATION & DINING
GUEST ROOMS
AVAILABLE TONIGHT

winter doldrums during the **Stowe Winter Carnival** (www.stowecarnival.com, late Jan.). A highlight is the Village Night Block Party, which fills the streets with bulky parkas and merriment.

Shopping

Sweets lovers can follow their noses to **Laughing Moon Chocolates** (78 S. Main St., 802/253-9591, www.laughingmoonchocolates.com, 9am-6pm daily) where confections are handmade on-site. True devotees can sign up for chocolate dipping workshops ($125/two people).

Artist Susan Bayer Fishman owns and runs **Stowe Craft Gallery** (55 Mountain Rd., 802/253-4693, www.stowecraft.com, 10am-6pm daily, 10am-7pm holiday season), an epic collection of many other artists' works—knickknacks like pewter measuring cups, glazed vases, and hand-carved backgammon sets.

Food

CASUAL

Run by the chefs behind the James Beard Award-winning Hen of the Wood, the more casual ★ **Doc Ponds** (294 Mountain Rd., 802/760-6066, www.docponds.com, 4pm-midnight Tues.-Thurs., 11:30am-midnight Fri.-Mon., $7-19) is a laid-back spot that takes Hen's farm-sourced cuisine into après ski territory, with a menu of hearty snacks and comfort food that include burgers, smoked meats, and ample pickled vegetables. Tunes come from a massive collection of vinyl records—the host spins, but takes requests—and nightly beer specials are great deals on some of the state's best pours.

With a fabulous beer list and lots of polished copper, **The Bench** (492 Mountain Rd., 802/253-5100, www.benchvt.com, 4pm-close Mon.-Fri., 11:30am-close Sat.-Sun., mains $16-24) serves pizzas, salads, and grown-up comfort food in a relaxed setting. There are 25 beers on tap, and in the snowy months it's hard to beat a seat at the bar, where you'll have a view of the wood-fired brick oven that's used for much of the menu (including the delightful roast duck).

For special occasions, family-run **Harrison's** (25 Main St., 802/253-7773, www.harrisonsstowe.com, 4:30pm-9:30pm Sun.-Thurs., 4:30pm-10pm Fri.-Sat., mains $16-34) is a longtime favorite. The classic American menu includes appealing vegetarian options and excellent desserts, and the Kneale family creates a welcoming atmosphere. It's always worth calling ahead for reservations, and in summer months, it's hard to beat a table on the patio.

The hearty, stick-to-your-ribs breakfasts at **Dutch Pancake Cafe** (Grey Fox Inn, 990 Mountain Rd., 802/253-8921, www.greyfoxinn.com, 8am-11am daily in winter; 8am-noon Mon. and Thurs.-Fri., 7:30am-12:30pm Sat.-Sun. in summer, $11-14) are just the (lift) ticket for carbo-loading before outdoor activities. Start with any of the 80 kinds of Dutch pancakes (which are thinner and more crepe-like than regular pancakes). The casual, noisy spot does an admirable job keeping big groups and kids happy.

If you're detoxing from all that comfort food, seek out the **Green Goddess Café** (618 S. Main St., 802/253-5255, www.greengoddessvt.com, 7:30am-3pm Mon.-Fri., 8am-3pm Sat.-Sun., mains $6-10) where breakfast and lunch include great salads, fresh juice, and plenty of vegetarian options alongside hearty sandwiches and egg dishes. Also, it's worth nothing that many of the listings in other sections of this chapter—notably the **Von Trapp Brewery & Bierhall, Piecasso,** and **Idletyme Brewing Company**—are also very worthwhile restaurants.

UPSCALE

The bustling low-ceilinged **Trattoria La Festa** (4080 Upper Mountain Rd., 802/253-8480, www.trattoriastowe.com, 5pm-close Tues.-Sat., $16-22) is owned by Italian brothers Antonio and Giancarlo DeVito, who greet everyone at the bar by the door. The place is a paragon of the trattoria genre: casual and family-style, but serving sophisticated dishes—solidly prepared pastas like spaghetti with tender baby shrimp in garlic white-wine sauce or yellowfin tuna with white puttanesca sauce. The tiramisu is to die for.

Ten minutes south of the village, ★ **Michael's on the Hill** (4182 Rte. 100, 802/244-7476, www.michaelsonthehill.com, 5:30pm-9pm Wed.-Mon., $28-43) is worth the trip for a special dinner. An elegant menu of European-influenced food prepared with local ingredients is served in a converted farmhouse, whose enclosed porch creates lots on intimate corners with tables for two.

CAFÉS

You'll see the whole town come and go in an afternoon at **Black Cap Coffee** (144 Main St., 802/253-2123, 7am-6pm Mon.-Fri., 7am-7pm Sat.-Sun., $2-8). Locals and visitors alike come for good espresso, simple sandwiches, and a cozy place to read the paper.

Excellent espresso, teas, and filling breakfast sandwiches make **PK Coffee** (1880 Mountain Rd., 802/760-6151, www.pkcoffee.com, 7am-5pm daily) a good stop on the way up to the mountain, and the counter is stocked with locally made pastries, granola, and other treats.

Accommodations

Stowe has a wide range of high-quality accommodations, and when rooms are empty, you can find great deals. Prices rise dramatically on the busiest weekends, so plan ahead for the best prices.

$100-150

For travelers on a budget, you can't beat a room at the **Riverside Inn** (1965 Mountain Rd., 802/253-4217, www.rivinn.com, $69-139), a homey, somewhat ramshackle farmhouse with charming owners and a great location. Motel-style rooms out back are newer and have coffeemakers and microwaves. It's a good choice for families and groups, as some rooms come equipped with several beds.

$150-250

Even closer to the slopes is **Northern Lights Lodge** (4441 Mountain Rd., 802/253-8541, www.stowelodge.com, $99-200), which offers hot breakfasts, a hot tub, and a sauna to help you prepare for (and recover from) your activities of choice.

The rustic and comfortable **Timberholm Inn** (452 Cottage Club Rd., 802/253-7603, www.timberholm.com, $110-240) is convenient to the mountain and village and includes an excellent homemade breakfast and warm cookies in the afternoon. A hot tub, shuffleboard, movie area make this a welcoming haven when the weather doesn't cooperate.

OVER $250

The local outpost of the quirky Lark Hotel chain, **Field Guide** (433 Mountain Rd., 802/253-8088, www.fieldguidestowe.com, $125-400) blends design-focused furnishings with local flourishes celebrating all things Vermonty. Stylish amenities set the hotel apart from the crowd here, and rooms are stocked with comfy robes, iPads, and luxurious toiletries. In common spaces, there are spots to lounge in the hot tub and pool or around the fire pit. Rates include a buffet breakfast of (very) small plates, and it's worth noting that Field Guide adjoins the excellent network of Cady Hill trails, so mountain bikers get backdoor access.

★ **Edson Hill** (1500 Edson Hill Rd., 802/253-7371, www.edsonhill.com, $225-450), which was redesigned in 2014, is drop-dead gorgeous from the picture-perfect interior to its setting on a hill with killer views. Rooms include breakfast in an enchanting dining room, and with a plush tavern, craft drinks, and menu of creatively wrought comfort food, you many never want to leave. The 38-acre property includes stables and hiking trails, as well as cross-country skiing (equipment is provided).

With loads of pampering and fantastic

recreation for adults and kids, **Topnotch Resort and Spa** (4000 Mountain Rd., 800/451-8686, www.topnotchresort.com, $229-690) wins the luxury-for-families award, hands down. Grown-ups can chill out on the slopes at either of the beautifully kept mountainside pools (one indoors, one outdoors) or in the glorious new spa's treatment rooms. Meanwhile, the children's activity program is extensive and well organized, so both they and mom and dad feel entertained by the day's end. Not for families only, the resort also manages to make couples feel catered to, with romantic dining at Norma's, sumptuously decorated suites with oversize tubs, and couples' massages.

Serious *Sound of Music* fans shouldn't miss a chance to stay at the **Trapp Family Lodge** (700 Trapp Hill Rd., 802/253-8511 or 800/826-7000, www.trappfamily.com, $225-430). The lodge definitely stresses the "family" part of the name, with comfortable accommodations and staff who are especially patient with children. Once a bit worse for wear, the lodge has slowly renovated over the past few years into a more modern style.

CAMPING

On the flanks of Mount Mansfield just before the Stowe Mountain Resort, the small **Smugglers' Notch State Park** (6443 Mountain Rd., 802/253-4014, https://vtstateparks.com/smugglers.html, tent sites $18-20, lean-tos $25-27) offers some 20 tent sites and 14 lean-tos for overnight camping. The sites are quite close together, though several "prime sites" offer more privacy and nice views from the cliffs flanking Mountain Road. The campsite has a restroom employing alternative energy, as well as hot showers and a trash station. Across the street, a moderately strenuous trail leads just under a mile downhill to the cascading Bingham Falls.

Information and Services

The **Stowe Area Association** (51 Main St., 877/467-8693, www.gostowe.com) runs a welcome center at the crossroads of Main Street and Mountain Road. Wireless Internet can be accessed around the corner at **Stowe Free Library** (90 Pond St., 802/253-6145). Also at Main and Mountain is a branch of **People's United Bank** (1069 Mountain Rd., 802/253-8525, 8:30am-4:30pm Mon.-Fri.).

Medical needs can be filled at **Kinney Drugs** (155 S. Main St., Cambridge, 802/644-8811, 8:30am-7pm Mon.-Sat., 9am-5pm Sun., pharmacy 8:30am-7pm Mon.-Fri., 8:30am-4pm Sat.). In an emergency, contact the **Stowe Police Department** (350 S. Main St., 802/253-7126).

WATERBURY

With a prime, highway-adjacent location between Stowe and the Mad River Valley, this riverside community makes a great base for exploring. It's an appealing first stop if you're set on checking out Vermont's thriving craft beer scene, too: Waterbury has a brewpub, a great beer shop, and a couple of bars with standout draft lists. This used to be the home of the award-winning Alchemist brewery, whose Heady Topper IPA was named the "best beer in the world" in 2014; the brewery has since opened a facility in Stowe that's a 25-minute drive from downtown Waterbury.

Beer aside, the Ben & Jerry's ice cream factory is still Waterbury's headliner, and though the tours are lackluster, it remains one of Vermont's most popular tourist attractions. Confusingly, Waterbury and Waterbury Center are separate towns, four miles apart on opposite sides of the highway—this section includes listings for both places.

Ben & Jerry's Factory

After a $5 correspondence course in ice cream making from Penn State, Ben Cohen and Jerry Greenfield opened their first shop in Burlington in 1978. From that small seed grew a company that revolutionized the American ice cream market, proving that Häagen-Dazs didn't have a lock on thick and creamy. Though most of it is made in a second factory in St. Albans, the company still produces ice cream in its flagship **Ben & Jerry's**

TOP EXPERIENCE

Hike the Long Trail's Iconic Peaks

The oldest long-distance hiking trail in the United States, the 272-mile **Long Trail** follows the spine of the Green Mountains from Massachusetts to Canada, rising over some of Vermont's most beloved summits along the way. Built by the Green Mountain Club between 1910 and 1930, the Long Trail was conceived as a "footpath in the wilderness" and is often cited as the inspiration for the 2,200-mile Appalachian Trail. In fact, the two trails overlap for 100 miles in the southern part of the state before going their separate ways—the Appalachian Trail continues through Vermont and New Hampshire as it heads to the northern terminus atop Maine's Mount Katahdin. Vermont's highest peak, Mount Mansfield, is on the Long Trail, and even if you're not planning an end-to-end trek, it's a great place to start exploring alpine Vermont. Here are some hiking high points of Vermont's Long Trail:

An exposed, rocky trail makes "Mount Abe" among Vermont's most scenic hikes.

- **Mount Mansfield:** At 4,393 feet, this is the tippy top of the Green Mountains, and on the Long Trail, it's just a 4.6-mile round-trip to the peak. Of course, there's more than one way to the top, and one favorite hike follows the lovely, bare Sunset Ridge. Not that it's limited to hikers only—you can drive the Toll Road, or hop a gondola from Stowe (page 186).
- **Mount Abraham:** The Long Trail climbs the 4,006-foot Mount Abraham on the 2.9-mile trail from Lincoln Gap, and the exposed rock that leads to the top is a favorite stretch of trail for many climbers (page 148). To tick off two of Vermont's "4,000 footers" on a single stretch of Long Trail, continue from Mount Abraham to Mount Ellen (page 203), an additional 3.7 miles from summit to summit. From the Mount Ellen summit, the Long Trail heads north to Appalachian Gap, a further 5 miles.
- **Camel's Hump:** While Mount Mansfield might tower over this 4,083-foot peak—formerly known as the even-more-evocative "Camel's Rump," the distinctive silhouette of Camel's Hump has become a symbol of the state. An 18.7-mile section of the Long Trail traverses the summit, and it's a stout day of hiking—there are plenty of shorter alternatives, including the 7-mile round-trip via the Monroe Trail (page 203).

If all those high peaks have you inspired to take on a **through-hike** of the Long Trail—that's an end-to-end walk—plan to start your hike somewhere between mid-June and early October. Most hikers finish the trail in about three weeks, and since the trail passes frequent small towns and road crossings, it's possible to make the trip without carrying more than several days of food at a time. While many hikers carry tents, which are lovely when clouds of mosquitoes and blackflies descend, a beloved part of the Long Trail experience is spending the night in "lean-tos," three-sided wooden shelters where hikers compare trail stories, make friends, and lay out their sleeping pads side by side.

The World's Best Beer?

In recent years, Vermont beer's been making headlines, and a brand-new style has been established as the state's characteristic brew: the **New England IPA** or **Vermont IPA** (imperial pale ale). In a 2013 piece in the *Boston Globe,* journalist Gary Dzen made a case for the designation, characterizing the beers as generally less bitter than their West Coast counterparts, with a focus on aromatics and a light, balanced flavor. They're usually less sweet and malty, too, and frequently dry hopped. (Hops are added during the fermenting process.)

A prime example is **Heady Topper,** a double IPA that was originally produced in Waterbury by **The Alchemist** (100 Cottage Club Rd., Stowe, 802/882-8165, www.alchemistbeer.com, 11am-7pm Tues.-Sat.) and is available only in 16-ounce cans. It's bracingly bitter but balanced and packs a wallop of hops that impart bright, fruity notes. It's inspired glowing accolades and huge lines at liquor stores, and Beer Advocate has dubbed it the "best beer in the world." The Alchemist brewery is now in Stowe, but visitors to Waterbury can pick up one of the distinctive four-packs without a special trip—stop by the **Waterbury Craft Beer Cellar** (3 Elm St., Waterbury, 802/882-8034, www.craftbeercellar.com, 11am-8pm Mon.-Thurs., 11am-9pm Fri.-Sat., noon-6pm Sun.).

But The Alchemist isn't the only Vermont brewery to have snagged the "best in the world" designation. Greensboro's **Hill Farmstead Brewery** (403 Hill Rd., Greensboro Bend, 802/533-7450, www.hillfarmstead.com, noon-5pm Wed.-Sat.) has been named "best brewery on earth" by influential beer website RateBeer.com for several years running, with a long list of styles named for brewer Shaun Hill's favorite relatives and philosophers. True beer lovers should make the trek to the Northeast Kingdom brewery, but there are two great Waterbury bars that consistently pour Hill Farmstead beers: settle into a seat at **The Reservoir** (1 S. Main St., Waterbury, 802/244-7827, www.waterburyreservoir.com, 3pm-11:30pm Mon.-Thurs., 3pm-midnight Fri., 11am-midnight Sat., 11am-11pm Sun.), or head down the street to the **Blackback Pub** (1 Stowe St., Waterbury, 802/244-0123, www.theblackbackpub.com, noon-midnight Tues.-Sun.), which is a strong contender for best beer list in the state.

factory (1401 Rte. 100, 802/882-2034, www.benjerrys.com, 10am-7pm daily May 20-June, 9am-9pm daily July-Aug. 18, 9am-7pm daily Aug. 19-Oct. 20, 10am-6pm Oct. 21-Dec., $4 adults, $3 seniors, children 12 and under free) in Waterbury.

Now that it's owned by the multinational corporation Unilever, the fact that the Ben & Jerry's factory is Vermont's most visited tourist attraction is a bit vexing to some locals, most of whom have done the lackluster tour more than once with visiting family. Groups sit through a 15-minute video then shuffle up to a viewing platform over the factory floor, but you do get a sample-size scoop of ice cream at the end. If you're not a die-hard fan, you might just spend your cash at the outdoor ice cream shop, where you can choose from the entire flavor collection. Ambitious eaters can tackle the Vermontster, a sundae made with 20 scoops of ice cream, four bananas, hot fudge, chocolate chip cookies, brownies, walnuts, and whipped cream, and which weighs in at 14,000 calories.

And you don't have to join a tour to visit the Ben & Jerry's **"Flavor Graveyard,"** which is a short walk uphill from the playground. Here, 30 tombstones are marked with flavors that didn't make it, including Honey, I'm Home, a honey-vanilla ice cream with chocolate-covered honeycomb pieces; Lemon Peppermint Carob Chip, which just speaks for itself; and the ill-fated Sugar Plum, a plum ice cream with caramel swirl that was the worst-selling flavor in B&J history. In three weeks on the market, it sold exactly one pint.

Cold Hollow Cider Mill

The cider—and cider doughnuts—at **Cold Hollow Cider Mill** (3600 Rte. 100, Waterbury Center, 800/327-7537, www.coldhollow.com, 8am-6pm daily) make it a mandatory stop for many skiers and hikers on their way to the hills. Cold Hollow is one of the leading producers of apple cider, which is still made on an old-fashioned hydraulic cider press from the 1920s, and if you head to the back during apple season, you can get free cups of cider as it dribbles out of the press.

Waterbury Reservoir

A sinuous body of water with great views of the Green Mountains, **Waterbury Reservoir** feels much remoter than it really is—which makes it a great place to get away without much fuss or driving. One way to access the reservoir is to camp at **Little River State Park** (3444 Little River Rd., 802/244-7103, https://vtstateparks.com/littleriver.html; see *Camping* in the *Accommodations* section for more information), or bring a boat and launch from the pullout next to the Waterbury Dam on Little River Road before the park entrance.

Alternately, you can head to the Waterbury Center side of the reservoir where **Waterbury Center State Park** (177 Reservoir Rd., Waterbury Center, 802/244-1226, https://vtstateparks.com/waterbury.html, day use 10am-sunset, $4 adults, $2 child) has a swimming beach, picnic areas, and a short nature trail.

The state park also maintains a wonderful network of 27 **remote campsites** that are free to use and accessible only by boat, which means that once you're settled in for the night, it's delightfully secluded. You'll have to bring a boat, rent one from the park, or grab one from **Umiak Outdoor Outfitters** (Waterbury Center State Park, 802/253-2317, www.umiak.com, stand-up paddleboards and kayaks from $24, canoes from $35), a Stowe-based company that maintains a summertime outpost in the park. As there's no system for reserving the campsites, it's worth starting early and figuring that you might need to visit a few before finding a place to settle. The park staff is a great resource for tips on the best campsites for your needs—they vary widely in size, but most have fire rings and pit toilets. Bring your own water.

Shopping

Beer lovers will find their tribe at the **Waterbury Craft Beer Cellar** (3 Elm St., 802/882-8034, www.craftbeercellar.com, 11am-8pm Mon.-Thurs., 11am-9pm Fri.-Sat., noon-6pm Sun.). It goes without saying that they've got all of Vermont's great brews, but they also stock shelves with bottles and cans from around the world. Bring a growler to fill up at the draft bar, or pick up some home-brewing equipment and just make it yourself.

If you're lucky enough to catch an artist at work, you can watch glassware take shape at **Ziemke Glassblowing Studio** (3033 Rte. 100, Waterbury Center, 802/244-6126, www.zglassblowing.com, 10am-6pm daily). The graceful swirled creations are for sale on-site.

Need proof that tea isn't just for drinking? Get it at **Vermont Liberty Tea Company** (29 Stowe St., 802/230-4686, vtlibertyteacompany.com, 9:30am-6pm Mon.-Sat., 11am-3pm Sun.), a panoply of exotic herbal infusions all under one roof. Find catnip toys, beauty products, accessories like tea strainers and caddies, plus teas you actually do drink—rare black tea blends and chamomiles, and fruit teas from apple to blackberry.

Nestled among patches of wildflowers, **Cabot Annex** (2657 Rte. 100, 802/244-6334, www.cabotcheese.coop/cabot-farmers-store, 9am-6pm daily) is as cute as roadside, strip-mall cheddar houses come. Stop in to sample Cabot cheeses and pick up a hunk of cheddar for the road. The shop also sells local crafts, microbrews, and wines. And right next door is the tasting room for **Smugglers' Notch Distillery** (11am-6pm daily) whose award-winning vodka and hopped gin are just the thing after grazing the cheese samples.

Food

Named for the rare mushroom that grows wild in the forests, ★ **Hen of the Wood** (92 Stowe St., 802/244-7300, www.henofthewood.com, 5pm-9pm Tues.-Sat., $22-35) is dedicated to seasonal cuisine fresh from local farms. Chef Eric Warnstedt, who's been nominated for a slew of James Beard Awards, is

Vermont with Kids

boiling maple sap fills the air with steam during sugar season at Morse Farm Maple Sugarworks

Vermont is ideal for families ready to get outside, sip maple syrup, and get some quality cuddle time with the local animals.

- **Ben & Jerry's Factory:** Stroll through a factory tour and visit the "Flavor Graveyard" (page 180).
- **ECHO Leahy Center for Lake Champlain:** On Burlington's waterfront, kids are guaranteed to get wet as they learn about frogs, snakes, and the resident lake monster, Champ (page 116).
- **Fairbanks Museum & Planetarium:** This treasure trove of mummies, dinosaur fossils, stuffed animals, and Civil War memorabilia also includes an interactive weather center for budding meteorologists (page 216).
- **Shelburne Orchards:** Once you've picked all the apples you can carry, there's fresh cider and doughnuts hot from the fryer (page 141).
- **UVM Morgan Horse Farm:** At the University of Vermont's farm, little ones can pet and ride the stallions and mares (page 151).
- **Morse Farm Maple Sugarworks:** Kids can learn how maple syrup is made and harvested, and then try maple ice cream and candy at the gift shop (page 167).
- **Shelburne Farms:** Cuddle baby sheep, learn how to make cheddar, and stroll the impressive grounds of this historical farm in the Champlain Valley (page 140).
- **Smugglers' Notch Resort:** Family-friendly policies and lots of gentle terrain make this resort among the best Vermont destinations for budding skiers and riders (page 195).
- **The Retreat Farm:** This working farm in Brattleboro also has a petting barn that encourages aspiring farmers to feed and groom the animals (page 33).

one of the best in Vermont, and while the menu changes constantly, there are always rich pâtés and a broad selection of artisan cheeses. The 19th-century mill building turned dining room features an ample North American wine list.

With a prime location downtown, **Prohibition Pig** (23 South Main St., 802-244-4120, prohibitionpig.com, 4pm-11pm Mon.-Thurs., 11:30am-11pm Fri.-Sun., $10-21), a brewery and restaurant that serves a filling menu of burgers, barbecue, and soul food. Start with pork rinds and pickled veggies; then dive straight into the beef brisket. Some of the beers on tap are their own. In the brewery out back, you can nurse a pint and nibble from a menu of tacos and bar snacks.

Just up the block is another choice beer restaurant. **The Reservoir** (1 S. Main St., 802/244-7827, www.waterburyreservoir.com, 3pm-11:30pm Mon.-Thurs., 3pm-midnight Fri., 11am-midnight Sat., 11am-11pm Sun., $11-20) cooks up comfort food for skiers, construction workers, and anyone who's heard about their legendary Truffle Fries. Many choice brews are on tap at this joint, which is the apex of Waterbury's "Beermuda Triangle" that also includes Prohibition Pig and the Waterbury Craft Beer Cellar.

Tucked into a downtown Waterbury basement, the unassuming **Blackback Pub** (1 Stowe St., Waterbury, www.theblackbackpub.com, bar noon-midnight Tues.-Sun., kitchen noon-3pm and 5pm-9pm Tues.-Sun., $7-23) has one of Vermont's best draft lists—the kind of place where local beer lovers visit to find the very freshest pours from Vermont breweries. While the beer is definitely the existential heart of this cozy joint, food options offer some appealingly fresh alternatives alongside hearty pub fare.

It's not easy to find ★ **Aztlan Foods** (44 Founder St., 802/244-5570, www.aztlanfoodsvt.com, 11:30am-3pm Mon.-Fri., $10-13), but determined burrito hunters will be rewarded with California-style Mexican food made by the inimitable Fred Dominguez. The super spicy El Bombero has a cult following. Aztlan is a genuine hole-in-the-wall, but the plain space is dressed up with bright tablecloths and paintings.

The Blue Stone (15 Stowe St., 802/882-8188, www.bluestonevermont.com, 11:30am-close Tues.-Sat., $12-17) proposes "serious pizza" and makes good with flatbreads topped with seasonal ingredients and pizza joint classics. Try the Stump Jumper, with oyster, shiitake and crimini mushrooms, goat cheese, fontina, and roasted garlic oil.

The sweetly artsy **Stowe Street Café** (29 Stowe St., 802/882-8229, www.stowestreetcafe.com, 7:30am-4pm Tues.-Sat., $3-11) is the place to go for excellent coffee and tea, and a morning selection of quiche, frittatas, and breakfast pastries. Lunchtime fare is light and spot-on, with a collection of sandwiches and soups, as well as hearty salads—try the protein bowl, with seeds, chickpeas, and hard-boiled eggs.

Accommodations

$100-150

Somewhere between hipster cabin and down-home Austrian chalet, the ★ **Grünberg House** (94 Pine St., 802/560-5004, www.grunberghaus.com, $110-175, breakfast is included) is relaxed and fun. Wall are decked with vintage ski gear, the inn is surrounded by 40 acres of forest that's webbed with walking trails, and the simple rooms are comfortable and quirky (some rooms have shared bathrooms). The highlight of the common space is the remarkable river stone fireplace, where you can toast marshmallows in the evenings, and there's even a DIY shop for tuning skis and fixing bikes. During the winter, you'll need a four-wheel-drive vehicle to reach the upper lot that's by the lodge—otherwise, there's a spot to park in the driveway, just off Route 100, and you can prearrange with the owners for a ride to the house. First-chair fanatics will probably miss the hot breakfast, which is served at 9am, but a continental version is available at 8am (coffee starts at 7am). The owners give discounts for all kinds of things—from working at a ski shop to membership in local organizations—so check before booking.

$150-250

With a collection of cozy, if somewhat dated, cabins set back from the road in Waterbury Center, **Stowe Cabins in the Woods** (513 Cabin Ln., Waterbury Center, 802/244-8533, www.stowecabins.com, $109-269) is a great option for travelers who'd like to prepare some of their own meals—all cabins have kitchens and coffeemakers, as well as cable television, air-conditioning, and Wi-Fi. The cabins allow pets for an additional $10 a night.

OVER $250

Tucked a half mile up a dirt road, the **Moose Meadow Lodge** (607 Crossett Hill Rd., 802/244-5378, www.moosemeadowlodge.com, $259-475) does cabin chic on a grand scale. The interior is all stripped logs and hunting trophies, with thoughtful finishes that give the place some glam appeal. The expansive 86-acre property has a stocked trout pond, and guests can stroll up to the Sky Loft, a glass-enclosed gazebo with wide views. Every room has a luxurious steam shower, and the main lodge has an indoor hot tub that's overarched with wooden boughs. A home-cooked breakfast is included.

For a truly unforgettable experience, though, book Moose Meadow Lodge's enchanting **Tree House,** a marvelous retreat perched in a pine tree that feels perfectly isolated from the world. The outdoor shower and bathroom are more romantic than rustic, and it even comes with a private pond. If you're caught up in the moment, note that the charismatic innkeeper performs weddings on-site.

CAMPING

Justly one of Vermont's most popular campgrounds, **Little River State Park** (3444 Little River Rd., 802/244-7103, https://vtstateparks.com/littleriver.html, campsites $18-25) has some 100 campsites nestled into state forest land on the Waterbury Reservoir. With 81 tent/trailer sites and 20 lean-tos tightly packed into two loops overlooking the water, the campground doesn't afford a lot of privacy—but it is centrally located amid some of Vermont's most popular tourist destinations (Waterbury, Stowe, Montpelier, and the Mad River Valley). The campground itself offers lots of amenities, including two beaches, several playgrounds, a nature center, and boat rentals. The campsites include several restrooms with hot showers and a dumping station, but no hookups. Trails leave the area to hike up to the river's massive flood-control dam. If you're willing to head to your campsite under paddle power, check out the remote (and free!) campsites maintained by **Waterbury Center State Park** (177 Reservoir Rd., Waterbury Center, 802/244-1226, https://vtstateparks.com/waterbury.html; see *Waterbury Reservoir* for more information).

Information and Services

The **Revitalizing Waterbury** (www.revitalizingwaterbury.org) runs a little information booth at the **Green Mountain Coffee Café and Visitor Center** (1 Rotarian Place, 802/882-2700, 7am-5pm Mon.-Fri., 8am-5pm Sat.-Sun.). Wireless Internet is available at the **Waterbury Public Library** (28 N. Main St., 802/244-7036, www.waterburypubliclibrary.com, 10am-8pm Mon.-Wed., 10am-5pm Thurs.-Fri., 9am-noon Sat.).

Pharmacy services are available at **Shaw's** (820 Waterbury-Stowe Rd., 802/241-4113, 6am-11pm Mon.-Sat., 7am-9pm Sun., pharmacy 8am-8pm Mon.-Fri., 9am-5pm Sat.-Sun.). Find an ATM at **People's United Bank** (80 S. Main St., 802/244-5108) or **Community Bank** (994 Waterbury-Stowe Rd., 802/244-1587, 9am-5pm Mon.-Thurs., 9am-5:30pm Fri.).

SPORTS AND RECREATION

Hiking

You'll earn your views on the hike up **Mount Mansfield.** The **Long Trail** heads straight up the east side of the peak and leaves from a trailhead on Route 108, 0.6 mile north of the Gondola Base Lodge parking lot in Stowe. It's 4.6 miles round-trip, with 2,800 feet of elevation gain, so you should budget at least four hours to complete the hike; when the trail goes almost vertical, you'll know you're almost there. When you see groups in flip-flops that took the gondola to the top, you've arrived.

A longer but slightly easier climb to the summit approaches from the west along the six-mile **Sunset Ridge Trail.** To get a bird's-eye view of Mount Mansfield itself, take the trail up **The Pinnacle,** the 2,740-foot peak on the east side of town. The trail rises gradually from Stowe Hollow for about a mile and a half, with a short rocky scramble at the top. For more information on these and other climbs, contact the **Green Mountain Club** (802/244-7037, www.greenmountainclub.org) or pick up a copy of the *Long Trail Guide*.

Just a half-mile walk from Route 108, **Bingham Falls** is lovely any time of year, but the spot really gets popular during the hottest days of summer—at the base of the 15-foot waterfall is a cool, deep pool that's ideal for swimming. To reach the trailhead from Stowe, drive toward Stowe Resort, and watch for a sign on the right shortly after you pass the toll house and Gondola Skyride.

Biking

Tracing lazy loops around Mountain Road and the West Branch River, the five-mile **Stowe Recreation Path** is perfect for a relaxed afternoon ride through the village. **AJ's Ski & Sports** (350 Mountain Rd., 802/253-4593 or 800/226-6257, www.stowesports.com) rents road and mountain bikes for kids and adults ($19-45 half day, $27-70 full day) at the foot of the path near the intersection with Main Street in Stowe.

★ MOUNTAIN BIKING

Stowe has mountain biking that's among the best in the state, with trails that range from challenging to beginner-friendly. It's worth downloading the app **TrailForks** for updated trail maps and conditions—to avoid ruining the trails, riders stay away when rain turns everything to mud.

At **Cady Hill Forest** (Mountain Rd., Stowe, parking lot just past the Golden Eagle Resort, no trail fee), a swooping network of single-track dips and climbs through a 258-acre property. Trail maps are posted at some intersections, or you can download the pdf map from **Stowe Land Trust** (www.stowelandtrust.org). Some trails lead to dead ends, and it is easy to get a little turned around while riding, but for the most part, you'll always end up back at a major, marked junction. These trails tend to be flowy and relatively smooth, and technical sections are short enough that less skilled mountain bikers can easily walk through them. Don't miss the wonderfully fun Bear's Trail.

The cross-country ski areas of **Trapp Family Lodge** (Trapp Hill Road, Stowe, 802/253-5719 or 800/826-7000, www.trappfamily.com, trail pass $10, under 12 $5) are given to mountain biking in the summer, with 20 miles of double-track, and six miles of single-track. These are Stowe's best mountain bike trails for beginning riders, and the property has gorgeous views of the Green Mountains—plus an on-site Austrian-style brewery that's perfect for post-ride recovery. Visit the outdoor center for trail passes, bike rentals, and gear.

From the trails at Trapp Family Lodge, you can also connect to a network called **Adam's Camp** (www.stowetrails.org, no trail fee), which has intermediate and advanced single-track that include some smooth-as-silk machine-built sections. The two networks are great for riding together, but keep in mind you'll need to purchase a trail pass to use the Trapp Family Lodge property. There are two primary access points to Adam's Camp: Stowe High School (413 Barrows Rd., Stowe), and a parking area on Ranch Brook Road, off Mountain Road. The trails are marked, but no maps are posted.

1
2

Skiing, Snowboarding, and Cross-Country

Stowe Mountain Resort (5781 Mountain Rd./Rte. 108, Stowe, 888/253-4849, www.stowe.com, $108 adults, $98 seniors, $88 children 6-12, children under 6 free) has an unmistakable "big mountain" feel, with 116 trails, high-speed quads and gondolas, and a vertical drop of 2,360 feet. From the top of the forerunner quad is unbeatable; look for Camel's Hump, Sugarbush, and Mount Abraham laid out below like a box of chocolate. It's a good fit for families, with plenty of trails for all skill levels, and for expert skiers the imposing "Front Four" are an East Coast proving ground. Child care is available, and you can order tickets online for discounted prices.

If Stowe's glitz and glamour don't appeal, you'll find a homier experience—and much cheaper lift tickets—at **Bolton Valley Resort** (Bolton Valley Access Rd., Bolton Valley, 802/434-3444, www.boltonvalley.com, $74 adults, $64 youth/student/senior, children under 7 free). This is mostly a locals' hill, but the 71 trails are a fun way to spend a day, and Bolton has night skiing through much of the winter. Bolton Valley Resort is a bit run-down these days—some habitués refer to it as "Broken Valley," but it has access to an extraordinary network of backcountry trails, and 15 kilometers of groomed Nordic trails (though these are not as well tended as those at other resorts).

Behind the Trapp Family Lodge, the **Trapp Family Lodge Touring Center** (700 Trapp Hill Rd., Stowe, 802/253-8511 or 800/826-7000, www.trappfamily.com, $25 adults, $20 seniors, $15 youth 12-18, $10 children 6-11, children 5 and under free) has some 60 miles of cross-country ski trails, through both groomed and ungroomed forest and meadowland. Plan your ski to pass by the **Slayton Cabin,** Trapp's hilltop warming hut, where you can cozy up with hot chocolate by the fire. Rentals are available on-site.

1: hiking Vermont's rocky summits; **2:** family-friendly skiing at Stowe Mountain Resort

Snowmobiles, Sleighs, and Sledding

Stowe Snowmobile Tours (802/253-6221, www.stowesnowmobiletours.com, tours $179-229) allow you to explore the woods in comfort, with fast-paced tours on top-of-the-line Polaris machines with heated handlebars.

Or you can dash through the woods to the sound of sleigh bells and draft horses at **Trapp Family Lodge** (700 Trapp Hill Rd., 802/253-8511 or 800/826-7000, www.trappfamily.com). Throughout the winter, open sleigh rides are given each weekend ($25/adult, $15/child 4-12, under 4 free), or you can book a private sleigh ride ($85/couple, $24/child).

For gravity-powered entertainment, rent a toboggan from **Shaw's General Store** (54 Main St., 802/253-4040, www.shawsgeneralstore.com, 9am-6pm Mon.-Thurs., 9am-7pm Fri.-Sat., 9am-5pm Sun., $15/day) or a more extreme sled from **Umiak Outdoor Outfitters** (849 S. Main St., 802/253-2317, www.umiak.com, 9am-6pm daily, $10-20/day), which features the latest from Mad River Rockets and Hammersmith and can point you to the vertiginous heights on which to test them. The best spot for sledding right in Stowe is **Marshall's Hill,** just behind the elementary school; to get there, turn onto School Street at **Black Cap Coffee** (144 Main St., Stowe).

Spas

The welcoming, expert staff at **Stoweflake Mountain Resort and Spa** (1746 Mountain Rd., Stowe, 800/253-2232, www.stoweflake.com, 9am-7pm Mon.-Thurs., 9am-8pm Fri., 8am-8pm Sat., 8am-7pm Sun.) doles out an enticing list of Vermont-themed treatments in its serene, plush rooms. Classes include yoga, Pilates, and spinning, and if you're making a day of it, you can grab lunch at the spa café with your bathrobe on ... or you can just while away your time in the steaming hot waterfall, in the sunlit co-ed portion of the spa. Stoweflake also has the most complete exercise facilities in town (along with a nine-hole golf course), which are available to all guests at the hotel.

Consistently voted one of the top-10 spas in the country, **Topnotch Resort and Spa** (4000 Mountain Rd., Stowe, 800/451-8686, www.topnotchresort.com, 8am-7pm daily) is tucked into a picturesque corner of Mount Mansfield. Glorious vistas result, best admired while undergoing one of the spa's quirky services—the likes of tarot reading, life coaching, and a slew of acupuncture. Of course, the requisite facials, massages, and herbal body treatments are also on offer.

GETTING THERE AND AROUND

From White River Junction, take I-89 north to exit 10, then Route 100 north to Stowe (75 mi., 1.3 hrs.). You'll pass through Waterbury Center along the way, but Waterbury is on the other side of I-89. The **Green Mountain Transit Agency** (802/223-7287, www.gmtaride.org) operates bus routes to Stowe, stopping at Town Hall and other locations downtown. In the winter, it also operates the free **Stowe Shuttle** (www.gostowe.com) between the town and the mountain.

Lamoille Valley

North of Stowe, small towns and big mountains line the sleepy Lamoille Valley, a verdant crease that cuts across the Greens, sloping south as it goes from west to east. It's as pretty a drive as any along Route 100, passing through villages full of clean, white church steeples, neat-as-a-pin farmhouses, main streets, and covered bridges.

SMUGGLERS' NOTCH AND JEFFERSONVILLE

On the other side of Mount Mansfield from Stowe, Smugglers' Notch was named for its reputation as a favorite passage for bootleggers smuggling whiskey from Canada during the 1920s. Now the mountain pass is home to a ski resort that's established itself as Vermont's most family-friendly big hill, though it's got plenty of great skiing and riding at all levels. Steep walls descend into the valley from Mount Mansfield to the west and the Sterling Mountain ridgeline to the east, making the drive along Route 108 especially scenic and the village of Jeffersonville seem especially snug.

The Road to Smugglers' Notch

The precipitous drive to this pass is the most dramatic in the state—traffic slows to a crawl as the narrow road winds between enormous cliffs and boulders. The **Notch Road** (Rte. 108) connects Stowe Mountain Resort with Smugglers' Notch Resort and is especially dramatic in autumn when brilliant trees tower over the route. The road is closed in the winter, but if you're equipped with cross-country skis or snowshoes, it's a wonderful outing. The cliffs are coated with jagged ice formations, and if you visit on an especially cold morning, you're likely to spot ice climbers scaling the frozen heights.

Sights

Sample award-winning vodkas along with gin, rum, and whiskey at **Smugglers' Notch Distillery** (276 Main St., Jeffersonville, 802/309-3077, www.smugglersnotchdistillery.com, 11am-5pm daily, free tastings). The father-son operation blends chemistry with creativity—they recently introduced an unusual gin that's infused with hops.

Jeffersonville is home to several fine galleries worth taking a peek at. The **Bryan Memorial Gallery** (180 Main St., Jeffersonville, 802/644-5100, www.bryangallery.org, 11am-4pm Thurs.-Sun. spring-fall; 11am-5pm daily in summer) is known as one of Vermont's premier showcases for local landscape artists, many of whom have drawn their inspiration from the countryside but a scant few miles away.

More local talent is on display at the aptly named **Visions of Vermont** (94 Main St., Jeffersonville, 802/644-8183, www.visionsofvermont.com, 11am-5pm Tues.-Sun.). The gallery started out featuring the artwork of impressionistic landscape painter Eric Tobin but has since grown to three buildings showcasing landscapes, still-life, and figure painting.

A few miles west in Cambridge, sample some of Vermont's best wines at **Boyden Valley Winery** (64 Rte. 104, Cambridge, 802/644-8151, www.boydenvalley.com, 10am-6pm daily). Cold-hardy Frontenac grapes make up the popular Big Barn Red, and Boyden also makes ice cider, fruit and dessert wines, and a variety of creative crème liqueurs. The $10 tastings include six wines, crème liqueur, truffle, and wineglass.

If you're driving over from Jeffersonville, you can't miss the awkwardly curved bridge as you cross the river into Cambridge—known locally as the **Wrong Way Bridge.** Some folks say they put it on backward, others contend that it was designed incorrectly, but it's undeniably odd.

Entertainment and Events

Relax with a pint of microbrew at the convivial **Village Tavern** (55 Church St., Jeffersonville, 802/644-6607, www.smuggsinn.com, 4pm-10pm daily) at Smugglers Notch Inn. The handsome-but-casual pub is a favorite for locals and visitors looking for a place to kick back and unwind at the end of a day.

Old-time pleasures abound at **Smugglers' Notch Heritage Winterfest** (Jeffersonville, 802/644-2239, www.smugnotch.com, late Jan.), which dials the clock back a century or two to fill downtown with sleigh rides, marionette shows, and a community bonfire. The highlight of the weekend is a traditional biathlon, where participants don wood-framed snowshoes and hoist muzzle-loaded muskets to test their endurance and shooting ability. Many participants get into the spirit with period dress as well.

Shopping

If you haven't sated your sweet tooth by now, stop in at the **Vermont Maple Outlet** (3929 Rte. 15, Jeffersonville, 800/858-3121, www.vermontmapleoutlet.com, 9am-5pm daily), which produces maple candy and maple cream in addition to all grades of syrup. They also serve towering cones of maple creemee.

Food

Reasonably priced barbecue and burgers keep a crowd of regulars coming back to **Brewster River Pub** (4087 Rte. 108, Jeffersonville, 800/644-6366, www.brewsterriverpubnbrewery.com, 2pm-2am Mon.-Fri., noon-2am Sat.-Sun., $8-20), which is particularly popular as an après-ski hangout. The menu features a large list of salads and locally grown veggies served by an affable staff, and ski equipment bolted to the walls and ceilings reminds you not to linger too late and miss the first chair.

The Broken Yolk (55 Church St., Jeffersonville, 800/644-6371, 7am-2pm daily, $7-13) is a diminutive café attached to the Smugglers Notch Inn, where the specialty is huevos rancheros made with local farm eggs. Pancakes (blueberry, chocolate chip, or banana) are also a hit.

A local favorite for a leisurely Sunday brunch, **158 Main Restaurant & Bakery** (158 Main St., Jeffersonville, 802/644-8100, www.158main.com, 7:30am-3pm and 4pm-9pm Tues.-Sat., 8am-2pm Sun., breakfast and lunch $7-14, dinner $9-25) serves all three meals in a convivial downtown space. All the menus—breakfast, lunch, dinner, and brunch—are extensive and centered around classic American fare. The hearty salads are a highlight.

The summer-only ★ **Burger Barn** (Rte. 15 and Rte. 108, by the Mobil station, Jeffersonville, 802/730-3441, hours vary, $4-8) serves burgers, hot dogs, and "fried stuff," out of a brightly painted trailer on a patch of grass.

Try the Alamo Burger, with onion rings and barbecue sauce, or the Samuel de Champlain, a burger piled with brie, apples, prosciutto, and maple mustard.

Accommodations

A working farm converted to a B&B, **Nye's Green Valley Bed & Breakfast** (8976 Rte. 15 W., Jeffersonville, 802/644-1984, www.nyesgreenvalleyfarm.com, $75-125) has extensive gardens and fields full of sheep, goats, and horses that overlook stunning mountain views. The rooms are furnished with homey antiques that you can get cozy with.

The renovated rooms at **Smugglers Notch Inn** (55 Church St., Jeffersonville, 802/644-6607, www.smuggsinn.com, $89-149) include Jacuzzi tubs, fireplaces, and comfortable beds, plus they are completely kid-friendly. The common spaces are somewhat bare-bones and dated, but scrupulously clean, and stocked with games and books.

CAMPING

A shallow stream runs through the forested **Brewster River Campground** (289 Campground Dr., Jeffersonville, 802/644-6582, www.brewsterrivercampground.com, sites without/with electric $25/30, lean-to $43, cabin $54, apartment $80), which is just off Route 108 on the way toward Smugglers' Notch. There are 20 sites here, including three spots that have water and electric for RVs, and the property also has a lean-to, cabin, and a very pleasant one-bedroom apartment that's a great deal for the area. The bathhouse is clean and tidy, and the generous sites offer a bit of welcome privacy. No pets allowed.

Information and Services

The **Smugglers' Notch Area Chamber of Commerce** (802/644-8232, www.smugnotch.com) stocks an unstaffed information booth at the corner of Routes 15 and 108 in Jeffersonville. You can find an ATM at **Union Bank** (44 Main St., 802/644-6600, 8am-4pm Mon.-Thurs., 8am-6pm Fri.) and a pharmacy at **Kinney Drugs** (155 S. Main St., Cambridge, 802/644-8811, 8:30am-7pm Mon.-Sat., 9am-5pm Sun., pharmacy 8:30am-7pm Mon.-Fri., 8:30am-4pm Sat.).

MORRISTOWN

Funky little Morristown is quintessential Vermont—sleepy and fiercely rural, yet with a distinct counterculture edge in the many independent businesses and eateries in the town center, which belies its sleepy veneer. You'll notice that just about everybody calls this place Morrisville, which is technically a village in Morristown, but whatever you call it, the town serves as a perfect lunch stop or quiet getaway from the bustle of Stowe and Smugglers' Notch.

Sights

Stop by **Rock Art Brewery** (632 Laporte Rd., 802/888-9400, www.rockartbrewery.com, 10am-6pm Mon.-Sat.), one of Vermont's highest-quality craft brewers. (Its symbol is the flute-playing rascal Kokopelli, who shows up in Native American petroglyphs in the American Southwest.) There's a viewing area that's accessible at any time, but at 2pm and 4pm, an employee is available to talk you through Rock Art's brewing process. Tastings are $4 and include samples of four beers. Try the Ridge Runner, an English barleywine style beer with a slightly bitter flavor that's rich with black and chocolate malts.

On the east side of Morristown is a rare covered railroad bridge. The 109-foot **Fisher Bridge** (Rte. 15, 11 miles south of Rte. 100) once served to carry the St. Johnsbury and Lamoille Country Railroad trains over the Lamoille River. It was built double high to let the trains through, with a vented cupola (which now serves as a giant birdhouse for local tweeters) to allow the steam to escape.

Entertainment and Events

DISTILLERS

Just south of town on Route 100, **Green Mountain Distillers** (171 Whiskey

Run, Morristown, 802/253-0064, www.greendistillers.com, noon-5pm Thurs.-Sat.) makes small batch, organic vodka, gin, and maple liqueur, and in 2017, they released an aged whiskey from their handmade pot still. The owners, Tim and Howie, are passionate about their work and amazing sources of distilling facts and alcohol lore.

FESTIVALS AND EVENTS

Genuine country fun for one and all can be found at **Lamoille County Field Days** (Johnson, 802/635-7113, www.lamoillefielddays.com, July), a weekend fair featuring events like arm wrestling, antique tractor pulls, and a women-only underhanded skillet toss.

Shopping

Midway between Jefferson and Morristown sits **Johnson Woolen Mills Outlet Store** (Box 612, Johnson, 802/635-9665, www.johnsonwoolenmills.com, 9am-5pm Mon.-Sat., 10am-4pm Sun.), which has been weaving clothing for hardy Vermonters since the mid-19th century. Nowadays the company produces and peddles quality jackets, overalls, shirts, nighties, and kids' clothing.

Food

Some of Vermont's best barbecue is out in the country at ★ **Black Diamond Barbecue** (639 Morristown Corners Rd., 802/888-2275, www.blackdiamondbarbecue.com, 3pm-9pm Thurs.-Fri., 11:30am-9pm Sat., $11-29). The wood-fired barbecue pits turn out succulent pulled pork, smoked chicken, and other meats, complemented with a great list of cocktails and craft beers.

Lost Nation Brewing (87B Old Creamery Rd., 802/851-8041, www.lostnationbrewing.com, 11:30am-9pm Wed.-Sun., $10-17) has a taproom and restaurant on the edge of town. Sandwiches, salads, and hearty entrées go well with their excellent brews, like the refreshing Gose, made with coriander and sea salt.

Pick up hiking snacks at **Thompson's Flour Shop** (7 Main St., 802/888-2106, 7am-5pm Mon.-Fri., 8am-5pm Sat., $3-9), a homey bakery that also does brisk trade in hearty sandwiches and soups. The bakery makes their own oversize English muffins, which they use in a truly delightful breakfast sandwich that oozes Vermont cheddar.

Accommodations

A few miles down the road from Morristown, the four guest rooms and two one-room suites at **Fitch Hill Inn** (258 Fitch Hill Rd., Hyde Park, 802/888-3834, www.fitchhillinn.com, $119-219) all have prime views of the inn's surrounding gardens and mountains. Inside they sport simple but well-kept antiques, beds laid with handmade quilts, and private baths (some with whirlpool tubs); the suites have miniature kitchens and fireplaces.

An indoor movie theater, Jacuzzi, and pool come in handy on extra chilly days at the **Maple House Inn Bed & Breakfast** (103 Maple St., 802/888-6565, www.maplehouseinnofvt.com, $139-199), whose lovely suites have deep soaking tubs and easygoing country decor. If you do make it out of the inn, however, it's just a short walk to the center of town.

CAMPING

One of the most unique state parks in Vermont, **Green River Reservoir** (Green River Reservoir Dam Rd., Hyde Park, 802/888-1349, https://vtstateparks.com/htm/grriver.htm, $15-18) is a strictly "paddle-in" campground, with 28 campsites scattered along the undeveloped shoreline of the reservoir, accessible only by canoe, kayak, or other boat. Boats powered by motors exceeding five miles per hour are prohibited on the lake, which makes for a blissfully serene experience. Each of the sites has a maximum number of people allowed—from 3 to 12—and some are so remote that at night you won't see another light, unless you count the millions of stars above you. The reservoir is surrounded by a hardwood forest of beech, birch, and maple, which is home to animal species including white-tailed deer, moose, black bears, bobcats, and coyote. The waterway itself is home to a loon nesting site as well as other avian species including mergansers, great blue heron, and occasionally, bald eagles.

Equally beloved (if somewhat less wild) is **Elmore State Park** (856 Rte. 12, Elmore Lake, 802/888-2982, https://vtstateparks.com/htm/elmore.htm, $18-29), with tent and RV sites, and historical buildings constructed by the Civilian Conservation Corps during the Great Depression. There's also a sandy swimming beach, small concession stand, and boat rentals on-site.

Information and Services

The **Lamoille Valley Chamber of Commerce** (34 Pleasant St., 802/888-7607, www.lamoillevalleychamber.com) has information on Morristown and the surrounding area. Regional hospital services are available at **Copley Hospital** (Washington Hwy., 802/888-8888). Fill prescriptions at **Rite-Aid Pharmacy** (48 Congress St., 802/888-2226, 8am-8pm Mon.-Sat., 9am-5pm Sun., pharmacy 8am-7pm Mon.-Fri., 9am-6pm Sat., 9am-5pm Sun.). Take out cash at **Union Bank** (20 Lower Main St., 802/888-6600, 8am-4pm Mon.-Thurs., 8am-6pm Fri.).

SPORTS AND RECREATION

Hiking and Biking

Good for families, the moderate hike up to **Prospect Rock** is a 90-minute round-trip jaunt that affords a good view of the notch's dramatic cliff face. The trailhead is in Johnson, seven miles east of Jeffersonville, on Hogback Road.

Leaving from the top of Smugglers' Notch Road, a steep 1.1-mile hike leads to scenic **Sterling Pond,** a lovely body of water stocked with trout; the path around the lake is level and easy, a 1.4-mile loop. The trail follows blue blazes from the east side of the Smugglers' Notch information booth.

The impossibly quaint scenery of the Lamoille Valley makes it a favorite for cyclists, especially since the **Lamoille Valley Rail Trail** (www.lvrt.org) opened between Cambridge and Hyde Park. The off-road bike path follows Route 15 and the Lamoille River for 17 miles, passing farms with beautiful views of the mountains. Another great ride is Upper Pleasant Valley Road, which wends south from Jeffersonville, with little traffic, rolling terrain, and perfect views.

To rent a pair of wheels, stop by Jeffersonville's **Bootlegger Bikes** (60 S.

Elmore State Park

Rte. 108, Jeffersonville, 802/644-8370, www.bootleggerbikes.com, rentals from $9/hour, $30/day), which also has child trailers and "trail-a-bikes" that can attach to the back of an adult-size frame.

Boating and Fishing

It doesn't get much better than a paddle down the **Lamoille River,** which meanders gracefully through a country landscape of mountain-framed farms. **Umiak Outdoor Outfitters** (849 S. Main St., Stowe, 802/253-2317, www.umiak.com) rents kayaks and canoes by the hour or the day ($45-55/day). The outfitter also leads guided trips down the Lamoille and Winooski Rivers.

Skiing

On the other side of the mountain pass from Stowe, **Smugglers' Notch Resort** (4323 Rte. 108, Smugglers' Notch, 800/419-4615, www.smuggs.com, $79 adults, $59 seniors and youth 6-18, children under 6 free) has positioned itself as the ideal family resort. In addition to three peaks (roughly broken down into beginner, intermediate, and expert), the resort has a half-pipe for snowboarders and an indoor FunZone complete with inflatable slides and minigolf.

Zip-Lining

Fly through the treetops on 4,500 feet of ziplines at **ArborTrek Canopy Adventures** (1239 Edwards Rd., Smugglers' Notch, 802/644-9300, www.arbortrek.com, from $99). Accompanied by naturalist guides, you'll whiz by sugar maples, birch trees, and hemlocks.

GETTING THERE AND AROUND

From Stowe, head north on Route 100 for 8 miles (15 min.) to Morristown. For Jeffersonville and Smugglers' Notch, take Route 108 north from Stowe up and down the precipitous sides of Mount Mansfield for 10 miles (20 min.). Note, however, that the road is often closed because of snow from November to April. During those months, you'll need to take the long way around to Jeffersonville from Morristown along Routes 100 and 15 West (16 mi., 30 min.).

The **Green Mountain Transit Agency** (802/864-2282, www.gmtaride.org) operates routes to Morristown from Waterbury and Stowe, with transfers from Montpelier. There is no public transportation to Smugglers' Notch; however, the resort offers van service from Burlington's airport and train station (802/644-8851 or 800/419-4615, ext. 1389) for a $45 charge each way (one child free per paying adult, additional children are $35 each).

Mad River Valley

The peaks that flank the Mad River Valley seem to protect it from passing time. A blend of pastoral beauty and culture have made it a haven for artists, farmers, and eccentrics, while the valley's two ski resorts have grown into serious skiing destinations.

It's a compact place—just 30 minutes from one end to the other—but nowhere else in Vermont can you find such iconic, varied scenery and activities so close together. Incredible skiing, vibrant agriculture, and forested hikes to waterfalls make this spirited region a perfect distillation of the state.

WAITSFIELD

Of this village's original settlers, 11 of 13 were veterans of the Battle of Lexington, the kick-off to the Revolutionary War. Bits of the original colonial architecture remain sprinkled throughout the town, which is the cultural center of the valley. Beyond the picture-perfect historical facades are start-up technology companies, artisans, and artists. It's a

Mad River Valley

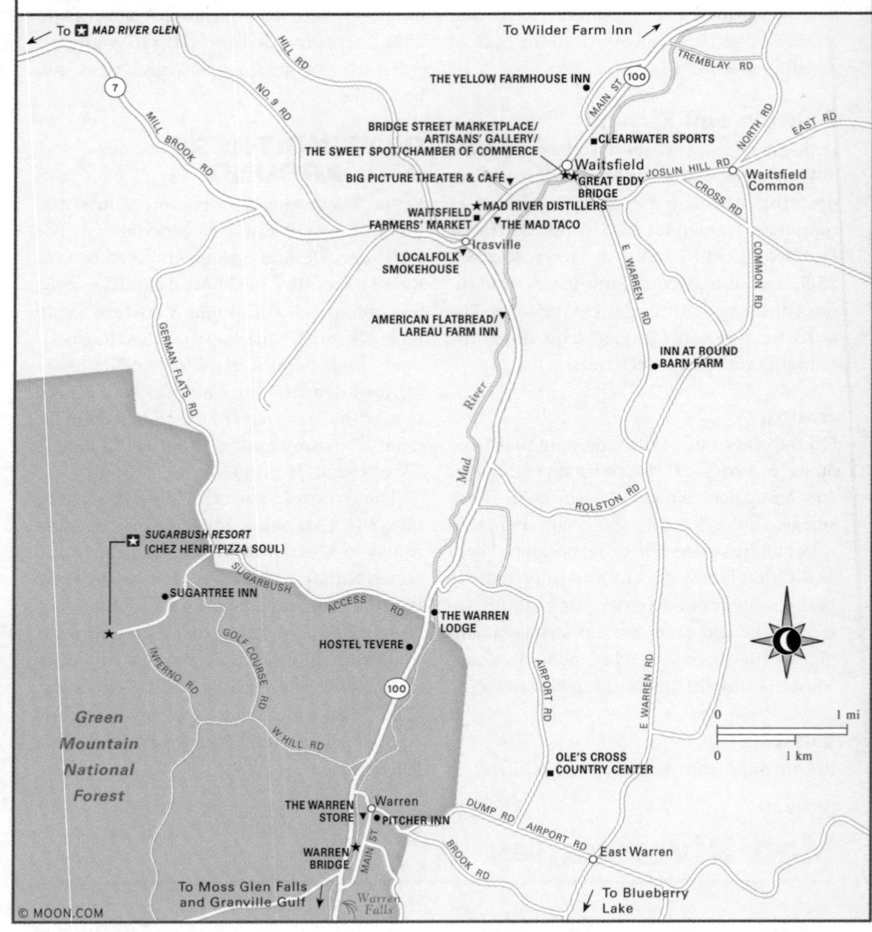

sophisticated community that enjoys an extraordinary quality of life.

Waitsfield's restaurants and accommodations make it a logical base for exploring the valley, and even if you're passing through, it's a compelling place to pass an afternoon visiting little shops and enjoying the sunny beach by the town's covered bridge.

★ Mad River Glen

In an era of ski resort consolidation, rising lift ticket prices, and runaway base lodge development, **Mad River Glen** (Rte. 17, 5 mi. west of Waitsfield, 802/496-3551, www.madriverglen.com, $89 adults, $72 seniors and youth ages 6-18) has its own agenda. MRG is the only cooperatively owned ski resort in the United States and the only one on the National Register of Historic Places. The 1,800 skier-owners still staunchly ban snowboards and limit grooming to about half the trails, mostly novice and intermediate pistes.

It's an enjoyably unfashionable outlook that has earned passionate supporters, including a devoted set of lift-serve telemark skiers, whom you can spot dropping their knees all over the hill. Mad River Glen's (mildly annoying) motto is "Ski It If You Can," and the mountain's steep, narrow, and notoriously hairy advanced trails, which comprise about half of the runs, are truly challenging. Experts should take a run at Paradise, a precipitous tumble down exposed ledges, rocky moguls, and a frozen waterfall to get to the bottom. In practice, though, the resort is a friendly, community-oriented place where families and skiers of all abilities are welcomed. Just don't try to sneak in a snowboard.

Mad River Distillers

Sample maple rum, bourbon whiskey, and other spirits at the Waitsfield tasting room of **Mad River Distillers** (89 Mad River Green, www.madriverdistillers.com, 10am-6pm Mon.-Sat., 9am-3pm Sun.). This Warren-based distillery sources many of its ingredients from within the state, and the bottles have been racking up awards. Don't miss the Calvados-inspired apple brandy made with fruit from Shoreham's Champlain Orchards. To visit the distillery itself, you'll need to head to nearby Warren, where daily tours take place at 1pm ($10).

Covered Bridge

Waitsfield's historical downtown is anchored by the 1833 **Great Eddy Bridge,** the second-oldest operating covered bridge in the state, which crosses the Mad River at the intersection of Route 100 and Bridge Street. (Only the Pulp Mill Bridge in Middlebury is older.) During the flooding following Hurricane Irene in 2011, the water line came up all the way to the base of the bridge, but the span stood, a testament to the nearly 200-year-old construction. There's also a little beach and swimming hole right under the bridge.

Entertainment and Events

The sophisticated, artsy vibe at **Big Picture Theater and Cafe** (48 Carroll Rd., off Rte. 100, 802/496-8994, www.bigpicturetheater.info, 8am-9pm daily) makes for one-stop evening fun—cutting-edge movies, film series, even an on-site restaurant where you can dine before the show ($9-18, reservations recommended on movie nights).

During August, the whole valley comes alive for the monthlong **Festival of the Arts** (802/496-6682, valleyartsvt.com/art), in which the area's many artisans hold art shows and classes, and local restaurants and lodging offer special rates and events.

Shopping

Step into the **Artisans' Gallery** (20 Bridge St., 802/496-6256, www.vtartisansgallery.com, 11am-6pm daily) in the Old Village area of Waitsfield, and prepare to feel bewildered by the enormous selection. Upward of 175 local craftspeople sell their goods here, which means you'll have no problem finding jewelry, woodblock prints, hand-painted wooden bowls, and stoneware.

The most comprehensive outdoors outfitter in the area, **Clearwater Sports** (4147 Main St., 802/496-2708, www.clearwatersports.com, 10am-6pm Mon.-Fri., 9am-6pm Sat., 10am-5pm Sun.), offers scads of gear and all the equipment rentals and guided tours you need to put it to proper use.

On the corner of Route 100 and Bridge Street (the same intersection as the Great Eddy Bridge), the **Bridge Street Marketplace** was once an inn and tavern for wayfarers. Damaged in a devastating flood in 1998, it was restored into a country version of Covent Garden, with craft shops and eateries spread out among five different buildings.

Food

★ **American Flatbread** (48 Lareau Rd., 802/496-8856, www.americanflatbread.com, 5pm-9:30pm Thurs.-Sat., $12-22) has a devoted following, and deservedly so. Thursday through Saturday nights, the unassuming farmhouse setting turns into a party, swarmed by lovers of the organic menu of wholesome and gourmet pies, salads, and desserts made entirely from sustainable, farm-fresh Vermont ingredients. Reservations aren't accepted, but do as the locals do and show up at 5pm to put your name on the wait list. You can request a specific time to come back, or just wait by the bonfire with a pint until your name is called.

There's usually a crowd at **Localfolk Smokehouse** (Rte. 17 and Rte. 100, 802/496-5623, 4pm-close Tues.-Sun., $10-18), a ramshackle-looking barbecue joint in an old Waitsfield barn. The menu has barbecue classics, tacos, and pub snacks, but regulars head straight for the meats: pulled pork, ribs, and chicken smoked on-site and served with Southern-style sides. There's often music on weekends, and the late-night local scene can be boisterous.

Tucked into an unpromising-looking cluster of shops on Route 100, ★ **The Mad Taco** (5101 Main St., 802/496-3832, www.themadtaco.com, 11am-9pm daily, $9-13) serves Mexican favorites with rebellious flair. Snag a burrito or taco loaded up with *carnitas* or yams, and head straight for the assortment of house-made salsas and hot sauces. They come in squeeze bottles marked with a heat rating of 1-10—the spicy stuff is no joke. The Mad Taco also has a bar stocked with favorite local brews on draft and a few Mexican options in bottles.

In an adorable riverside shop, **The Sweet Spot** (40 Bridge St., 802/496-9199, www.thesweetspotvermont.com 8am-4pm Mon.-Sat., 8am-2pm Sun., $2-12) is exactly that. Creative homemade tarts and cookies and quality espresso drinks, as well as a dreamy assortment of house-made ice creams, make this a perfect place to fortify yourself for an afternoon's adventures. If you're looking for something a bit more bracing to go with your brownie, The Sweet Spot also serves a nicely chosen list of cocktails, including some classic ice cream drinks.

FARMERS MARKETS

Like in many of Vermont's small towns, the **Waitsfield Farmers' Market** (Mad River Green, 802/472-8027, www.waitsfieldfarmersmarket.com, 9am-1pm Sat. May-Oct.) is one of the week's most important social events, where residents come down from the hills and stock up on community (and gossip) along with fresh produce and prepared foods. There is perhaps no better way to clue into the spirit of the valley than the boisterous event full of craft booths, organic produce from local farms, and stages full of folk, Latin, and Celtic musical performers.

Accommodations

$100-150

Bright, creative touches make the vibrant rooms at ★ **The Wilder Farm Inn** (1460 Rte. 100, 800/496-8878, www.wilderfarminn.com, $137-177) as appealing as the homey common areas and rambling grounds. The owners, Linda and Luke, have decorated each one in a different style—from shabby chic to contemporary—so check out the options before choosing where to lay your head. The inn lends guests snowshoes for winter outings and inner tubes for trips down the Mad River, just across the street.

On a quiet property just outside of town, **The Yellow Farmhouse Inn** (550 Old Country Rd., 802/496-4623, yellowfarmhouseinn.com, $139-179) is as comfortable as it is lovely: With woodstoves in the guest rooms, it is especially cozy in the winter. Home-baked cookies, lavish breakfasts, and friendly hosts make this a spot that many travelers come to year after year.

Under the same ownership—and on the same property—as the lovably bohemian American Flatbread, **Lareau Farm Inn** (48 Lareau Rd., 802/496-4949, www.lareaufarminn.com, $100-150) names its rooms after principles its management holds dear—love, patience, and respect among them. The inn has the rambling feel of a family farmhouse and is enjoyably relaxed. With delicious breakfasts and free wireless Internet included—not to mention the attention of a genuinely warm staff—Lareau couldn't offer better value.

OVER $250

The ultraromantic ★ **Inn at the Round Barn Farm** (1661 E. Warren Rd., 802/496-2276, www.theroundbarn.com, $179-359) is a harmonious blend of old-fashioned style and thoughtful modern luxuries. Most rooms in the 19th-century farmhouse have skylights, king-size beds, whirlpool tubs, gas fireplaces, and jaw-dropping mountain views. Executive chef Charlie Menard prepares a multicourse breakfast that is both generous and refined, a memorable experience.

Information and Services

The **Mad River Valley Chamber of Commerce** (802/496-4309, www.madrivervalley.com) runs a visitors center in the historical General Wait House on Route 100 in Waitsfield. Get on the Internet through Wi-Fi hotspots at **Three Mountain Café** (107 Mad River Green, 802/496-5470) or **Big Picture Theater and Cafe** (48 Carroll Rd., 802/496-8994, www.bigpicturetheater.info).

An ATM is located at **Northfield Savings Bank** (Mad River Shopping Center, 802/496-9700, 8:30am-5pm Mon.-Thurs., 8:30am-5:30pm Fri.), right on the Mad River Green. Pharmacy goods can be found at **Kinney Drugs** (5091 Main St., Waitsfield, 802/496-2345, 9am-6pm Mon.-Fri., 9am-1pm Sat.) and as well as at **Northfield Pharmacy** (14 Depot Square Northfield, 802/485-4771, 9am-6pm Mon.-Fri., 9am-2pm Sat., 8am-noon Sun.).

WARREN

Not a shingle is out of place in Warren's cute center, whose general store, artists' studios, and single elegant inn look more like a movie set than a real town. But this rural community is also home to Sugarbush Resort, a sprawling cluster of six peaks with 53 miles of trails, not to mention the vast backcountry that abuts the mountain.

And while Warren might seem a bit prim at first glance, there's serious verve behind the colonial facade. Soak up the weird during Warren's justifiably famous Fourth of July parade, an unrestrained celebration that is among the most independent of Vermont's Independence Day events. Locals spend the year constructing complicated floats with themes that range from politics to all-purpose Vermont pride and accompany them through town in sundry dress (and undress).

★ Sugarbush Resort

Once known as "Mascara Mountain" for its tendency to draw the jet-setting crowd, **Sugarbush** (1840 Sugarbush Access Rd., 802/583-6300 or 800/537-8427, www.sugarbush.com, $84-91 adults, $65-71 seniors and youth 7-18, children 6 and under free) has come a long way to rightly earn its place as Vermont's Second Slope, often favorably described as a more welcoming "alternative" to Killington. It's second to Killington in the number and difficulty of the slopes it offers. Sugarbush boasts 111 trails descending from two summits, Lincoln Peak and Mount Ellen. But it may have the most difficult trail in the East: the rock-and-glade ride known as the Rumble. Sugarbush is also prized for the high amount of natural snow it gets each year, as storms from Lake Champlain unload their cargo after passing over the mountains. Not that it needs it—the Bush has one of the most sophisticated snowmaking systems around. As a bonus, Sugarbush and Mad River Glen have worked out lift packages that include both mountains—so you can experience big-mountain skiing on Sugarbush then head up-valley to ride Mad River Glen's gnarly glades.

Warren Bridge

Warren has its own covered bridge, the 55-foot-long **Warren Bridge,** which sports an unusual asymmetrical design. (The angles on the eastern and western sides are slightly different.) The bridge is off Route 100, just below downtown.

Warren Falls and Moss Glen Falls

With crystal clear pools and a natural rock slide, **Warren Falls** is one of the best swimming holes in the state. To get there, travel

1

2

TOP EXPERIENCE

Cool Off in a Swimming Hole

While it's nothing compared with the sweltering heat of southern New England states, summer in Vermont can bring some hot, sticky days. When that happens, skip the air-conditioning and head for one of the state's many rivers, which stay blissfully cool no matter the weather. Searching out swimming holes is a passion for many locals, and there are endless "secret" places to swim that don't appear on any maps. These are some of the most beloved places to swim in the state, but wherever you are, it's worth asking where to go—you might just find your own favorite spot.

- **Warren Falls, Warren:** A series of cascades drop into pools deep enough for a (cautious) dive—this is among the most beautiful swimming holes in Vermont. It's no surprise that Warren Falls can get crowded on hot summer days, and it's hard to begrudge the crowd as you slip and slide around the rocks (page 199).
- **Dorset Quarry, Dorset:** This one's not a river, but earns a spot on the list because it's just that great. A flooded, disused marble quarry, there's plenty of room here to stretch out in the sun or find a cozy patch of shade, and the daring line up to jump from the quarry's highest point (page 61).
- **Bristol Falls, Bristol:** A mix of shallow and deep pools is interspersed with sections of fast-flowing river, but the star attraction of this spot is the 15-foot waterfall that drops into a churning pothole. Think twice before following anyone's lead when jumping here, since the underwater landscape changes each year as rocks shift around on the bottom of the river (page 147).
- **Bingham Falls, Stowe:** With cool, deep water at the base of a beautiful waterfall, this swimming spot's easily worth the half-mile hike in from the trailhead. The river flows straight from the high mountains, so jumping into the Bingham Falls swimming hole can be a shock to the system—hop in straight after the hike for maximum effect (page 187).
- **Clarendon Gorge, Clarendon:** It's worth making a trip to this series of swimming holes just to watch sweaty Long Trail hikers bliss out in the water—the footpath crosses the river here. It's a 15-minute drive south of Rutland, and there's a lot to explore, starting with the 30-foot suspension bridge that stretches across the river (page 106).

south on Route 100 from Warren; the parking area is 0.75 mile south of the intersection of Warren's Main Street and Route 100. A short path leads to the falls. A few miles farther south in Granville (population 309), **Moss Glen Falls** is another scenic spot (without swimming, however). A multi-pitched cataract that drops 125 feet through a narrow gorge, the waterfall is just as beautiful frozen in winter as it is gushing in summer. A viewing platform is accessible from the highway. The falls themselves are part of the **Granville Gulf State Reservation,** a seven-mile stretch of pathless wilderness that is among the most scenic drives in the Green Mountains. Keep an eye out for the moose that frequent the area's streams and beaver ponds.

1: farm in Mad River Valley; **2:** cascading pools at Warren Falls

Events

Warren's **Fourth of July parade** (www.madrivervalley.com/4th) is an unorthodox event that celebrates the independence of both America and small-town Vermont. Eye-catching floats and costumes often have a political theme that set this parade apart from simple flag waving, but it's also a welcoming and thoroughly entertaining glimpse of life in the Mad River Valley. The parade starts at

10am on Main Street, and festivities wrap up by 8:30pm. Fireworks are held at Sugarbush Resort in the evening. The parade is free to attend, but a $1 donation is requested at the entrance to the town; in return, you'll receive a numbered "buddy badge." There's two of every number, and the badges are given out randomly. If you find your matching pair, the two of you can head to the village gazebo to collect a prize. Parking can be a challenge, but a free shuttle bus is available.

Shopping

For food, provisions, and local gossip, everyone heads to **The Warren Store** (284 Main St., 802/496-3864, www.warrenstore.com, 7:45am-6pm daily). Spend a few days here, and you'll be on a first-name basis with the friendly staff at this eclectic provisions shop, full of Vermont-made odds and ends (from pillows to salad bowls). They have a nice selection of unusual wines for sale and churn out excellent creative sandwiches from the deli—all with bread baked on-site.

A definite do-not-miss is the **Granville Bowl Mill** (45 Mill Rd., Granville, 800/767-4711, www.bowlmill.com, 8am-4pm Mon.-Fri.), a venerable factory and showroom originally founded in 1857 that makes wooden bowls and cutting boards from Vermont wood the old-fashioned way—on 19th-century equipment, then perfected with 20th-century sanding techniques. While not cheap, the one-of-a-kind bowls come in a multiplicity of shapes, sizes, and woods, including cherry, yellow birch, and sugar maple (some with the hole from the sugar tap still in the wood).

Food

Warren has appealing—but limited—dining options. Breakfast means a trip into Waitsfield or pastries at The Warren Store, which is also a convenient stop for simple lunches if you don't want to drive up the mountain access road.

The elegant and refined **275 Main at The Pitcher Inn** (275 Main St., 802/496-6350, www.pitcherinn.com, 5:30pm-10pm Wed.-Mon., $25-42) boasts a superlative and hefty international wine list and a menu to match. Global in its influences but local in most of its ingredients, the kitchen emphasizes organic seasonal produce and fresh game such as grilled Vermont-raised lamb. For a particularly memorable experience, reserve a private dinner for two in the restaurant's wine cellar.

An unlikely whiff of Paris in a mountain setting, **Chez Henri** (80 Sugarbush Village Dr., 802/583-2600, www.chezhenrisugarbush.com, 4:30pm-close Mon.-Thurs., 11:30am-close Fri.-Sun. Nov-Apr., $19-43) makes dining a transporting experience. Classic bistro meals like *canard aux fruits* and onion soup *gratinée* are served in an intimate setting warmed by an open fire.

Snag thin-crust pizzas with all fixin's at **Pizza Soul** (Sugarbush Village, 802/496-6202, www.pizzasoul.com, pizzas $14-26), a quirky joint right at the base of the mountain. It's open daily from 11:30am during busy periods; hours and days vary, so call first.

Accommodations

UNDER $100

If the valley's ubiquitous antiques and romance aren't for you, try the stylish ★ **Hostel Tevere** (203 Powderhound Rd., 802/496-9222, www.hosteltevere.com, dorm beds $35 summer, $40 winter). It's a convivial place to land after a day on the slopes or floating the Mad River, and the hostel's bar keeps some of the best local brews on tap. There's also a winter dart league on Thursday nights that's open to visitors, and the bar regularly hosts live music on Friday (early-to-bed types should request a dormitory that's farther from the stage). All dorms are mixed gender, with 4-8 beds; linens are provided, and towels are available for rent ($2).

$150-250

Right at the base of the Sugarbush access road, **The Warren Lodge** (731 Rte. 100, 802/496-3084, www.thewarrenlodge.com, $99-215) was entirely renovated in 2016 with a blend of rustic design and modern comfort. Motel-style standard rooms have refrigerators and flat-screen televisions, and there are a range of suites, a cottage, and an efficiency that can be good deals for groups. It's the outdoor spaces, though, that make this such a nice spot—there's a nearby swimming hole, and the lodge property connects to a network of hiking trails.

Just half a mile from the Sugarbush lifts, the **Sugartree Inn** (2440 Sugarbush Access Rd., 802/583-3211, www.sugartree.com, $150-195) offers plush beds and generous breakfasts to help you prepare for (and recover from) your day on the slopes. There's also a spa for soaking sore muscles, and though the inn has no televisions, you won't miss them once you're settled in by the fire with a book from the well-stocked library.

OVER $250

Exquisitely decorated, the Relais & Chateaux-designated ★ **Pitcher Inn** (275 Main St., 802/496-6350, www.pitcherinn.com, $375-550) houses 11 rooms and suites—each individually decorated in a Vermont theme and with Wi-Fi, CD players, TVs, whirlpool tubs, and radiant floor heating; a few have wood-burning fireplaces. There's also a stand-alone spa on the property, which is right in the center of town.

SPORTS AND RECREATION

The Mad River Valley abounds with recreational activities. In addition to the suggestions below, the Mad River Glen ski area runs the **Mad River Glen Naturalist Program** (802/496-3551, www.madriverglen.com/naturalist-prorgrams) with guided tours that range from moonlit snowshoeing expeditions to wildlife-tracking trips to rock climbing.

Hiking and Biking

Three out of five of the peaks in Vermont above 4,000 feet rise from the Mad River Valley. While not the highest mountain in Vermont, the distinctly shaped **Camel's Hump** is one of the best loved. Originally named "Camel's Rump," its shape is identifiable for miles around, and its summit is a great chance to see the unique (and uniquely fragile) eastern alpine ecosystem.

The most popular ascent of Camel's Hump is up the **Monroe Trail** (7 miles round-trip), a rock-hopping ascent from a birch-and-beech forest up to the unique alpine vegetation zone of its undeveloped summit. The parking area for the trail is at the end of Camel's Hump Road in Duxbury. There is a trail map available on the website for **Camel's Hump State Park** (https://vtstateparks.com/camelshump.html). The state park itself doesn't have a visitors center or services, but ample information on access is available on the website.

Two more peaks, **Mount Abraham** and **Mount Ellen,** can be hiked singly or together, following the Long Trail along the 4,000-foot ridge between them. Mount Abraham used to be known as Potato Hill, but the (admittedly lumpish-looking) mountain was eventually rebranded with a grander name befitting Vermont's fifth-highest summit. The Long Trail climbs 2.9 miles to Mount Abraham from Lincoln Gap, and then continues an additional 3.7 miles to Mount Ellen. From there, continue north another 5 miles to reach Appalachian Gap.

For information on all of these hikes, contact the **Green Mountain Club** (802/244-7037, www.greenmountainclub.org), or pick up a copy of the club's indispensable *Long Trail Guide,* available at most bookstores and outdoors stores in Vermont.

This is an idyllic area for cycling, and you can take your pick of the Mad River Valley's beautiful back roads. If you're feeling ambitious, you can tackle the "gaps," the steep mountain passes that lead to the neighboring Champlain Valley. Lincoln Gap and Appalachian Gap, two of the steepest in the state, can be connected in a leg-punishing loop that does a staggering amount of climbing in 35 miles. Stop by Waitsfield's **Clearwater Sports** (4147 Main St., Rte. 100, Waitsfield, 802/496-2708, www.clearwatersports.com) for biking maps of the area, as well as tips on organizing a "gap ride."

If the mountains seem too daunting, the **Mad River Path Association** (802/496-7284, www.madriverpath.com) manages several walking and biking trails that weave in and out of the villages of the valley, taking in farms, woodlands, and bridges along the way. Bicycles can be rented from Clearwater Sports in Waitsfield.

Boating and Tubing

With a steady flow and the occasional patch of white water, the Mad River is ideal for anything that floats. **Clearwater Sports** (4147 Main St., Rte. 100, Waitsfield, 802/496-2708, www.clearwatersports.com) leads affordable all-day tours on the Mad and Winooski Rivers ($85 pp), as well as moonlight paddles. They also offer canoe and kayak rentals ($40-90) and inner tubes ($18), with an optional shuttle service. Book ahead when possible.

Swimming

There's endless swimming in the Mad River Valley. **Warren Falls,** with a natural rock slide, is a perennial favorite. To get there, travel south on Route 100 from Warren; the parking area is 0.75 mile south of the intersection of Warren's Main Street and Route 100. A short path leads to the falls.

The family-friendly swimming hole at **Warren Riverside Park,** on Route 100 across from the Sugarbush Access Road is another favorite. You can cool off right in Waitsfield at the **Great Eddy Swimming Hole,** just south of Bridge Street in the heart of downtown.

You'll find warmer, calm water at **Blueberry Lake,** on Plunkton Road in Warren. It's a quiet haven: perfect in a kayak or canoe and a pleasant place to swim with kids. To reach the lake from Brook Road in Warren, turn right on Plunkton Road, and take the first left after Lois Lane. There's a short walk to the lake. For a quick dip, there's also swimming beneath the **Great Eddy Bridge** in downtown Waitsfield.

Skiing

In the shadow of Sugarbush and the surrounding mountains, **Ole's Cross Country Center** (Airport Rd., Warren, 802/496-3430, www.olesxc.com, $18 adults, $15 youth and seniors) has 30 miles of trails through deep woods and farm country. Another great spot for forested skiing is **Blueberry Lake Cross Country and Snowshoeing Center** (Plunkton Rd., Warren, 802/496-6687, www.blueberrylakeskivt.com, $14), with 19 miles of trails. Both ski areas have rentals and lessons and are groomed for both Nordic and skate skiing.

Ice-Skating

Waitsfield's outdoor skating rink, the **Skatium** (Village Sq., Waitsfield, 802/496-8845) is a community gathering place in winter. The rink has skate rentals during public skating hours, generally all day on Saturday and Sunday from early December as long as the ice lasts, as well as other hours during the week that vary by season. During the winter, call the rink directly for a full schedule.

Horseback Riding

Ride in Viking style on an Icelandic horse. In addition to the usual walk, trot, canter, and gallop, they've got a fifth gait, the *tölt,* a fluid, running walk. The **Vermont Icelandic Horse Farm** (3061 N. Fayston Rd., Waitsfield, 802/496-7141, www.icelandichorses.com, rides $60-220) breeds well-mannered purebreds for rides that last an hour or all day.

GETTING THERE AND AROUND

For the Mad River Valley, take exit 9 from I-89 to Route 100B and then Route 100 south to Waitsfield. The distance from Montpelier is 20 miles (30 min.). The winter-only **Mad Bus** (802/496-7433, www.madrivervalley.com) shuttle stops at various locations in Waitsfield and Warren, along with routes to Sugarbush, Mad River Glen, and Montpelier.

White River Valley

The interstate—along with most tourists—bypasses the winding roads through this sleepy stretch of the Vermont Piedmont, which is etched with parallel river valleys, each one a branch of the White River. But if it's a backwater, it's a beautiful one, speckled with tiny towns and covered bridges and home to folks that don't seem to mind the isolation. There's no better way to mingle with the locals than a trip to the **Tunbridge World's Fair,** an eclectic celebration of country life that happens each September, complete with funnel cakes and prize heifers. Just down the road in South Royalton, you can visit the enormous granite pillar that marks **Joseph Smith's Birthplace,** which may be the only picnic spot in the state with piped-in tunes from the Mormon Tabernacle Choir. And tiny Rochester is home to **Liberty Hill Farm,** one of the most beloved farm stays in Vermont, where you can get a hands-on taste of the agricultural life. The valley roads—100, 12, 14, and 110—run north-south, so sights, accommodations, and dining along each one are included with the town that is the most significant destination along the way. The roads are listed from west to east.

ROCHESTER: ROUTE 100

Once declared the "model town of the United States," the tiny village of Rochester has a wide green surrounded by stately 19th-century homes and an eclectic collection of shops and galleries. They combine to make the village a quiet home base for exploring the mountains or a convenient stopover on your way across the peaks. Route 100 continues north into the Mad River Valley, one of Vermont's most scenic destinations, and the vertiginous Brandon Gap Road connects it to Route 7, to the west.

Shopping

Stroll through exhibits by local artists (and pick up a few of their pieces while you're at it) at **Bigtown Gallery** (99 N. Main St., 802/767-9670, www.bigtowngallery.com, 10am-5pm Wed.-Sat. and by appt.). Thought-provoking collages, watercolors, sculpture, and paintings abound, mostly of a contemporary ilk.

Read up on a little bit of everything at **Sandy's Books and Bakery** (30 N. Main St., 802/767-4258, www.seasonedbooks.com, 7:30am-6pm Mon.-Sat., 7:30am-2pm Sun.), a hodgepodge of new, used, and rare collectible titles. Throughout, the focus is on environmental topics, from building homes with renewable resources to animal husbandry. There's also a scratch-bakery on-site, with whole grain bread, pastries of all kinds, and coffee and tea.

Food

With a casual pub and a more formal dining room, **The Huntington House Inn** (19 Huntington Pl., 802/767-9140, www.huntingtonhouseinn.com, dining room 5pm-9pm Fri.-Sun., pub 4pm-10pm Sun.-Mon. and Wed.-Thurs., 5pm-late Fri.-Sat., $15-22) is a locals hangout with a hearty menu. Steak, seafood, and pasta dishes come with a seasonal vegetable and potatoes, on the dining room menu, and the pub menu is a casual mix of burgers, flatbreads, salads, and other comfort food. The beer list features favorite pours from around the state.

Also the home of the beloved Country Store, the **Rochester Café** (Rte. 100, 802/767-4302, www.rochestercafe.com, 7am-5pm daily, $7-10) serves belly-filling treats like pie à la mode, maple milk shakes, towering stacks of pancakes, and hefty sandwiches. A spot in the old-fashioned booths is a perfect vantage point for watching the locals come and go.

Accommodations

The rooms at **The Huntington House Inn** (19 Huntington Pl., 802/767-9140, www.huntingtonhouseinn.com, $129-169) are simple and comfortable, right at home with Rochester's old-fashioned, small-town charm. A country breakfast is included, and suites with kitchens and living rooms are also available in an adjacent building for $225/night.

There's no better way to experience the muck and miracles of country life than by staying at ★ **Liberty Hill Farm** (511 Liberty Hill, 802/767-3926, www.libertyhillfarm.com, $139 adults, $75 youth, $65 children under 12) where you can spend the day gathering eggs, milking cows, and baling hay. The friendly and hardworking Kennett family has been welcoming guests at the farm, which was Vermont's first Green Agritourism enterprise, since 1984. The per-person rate gets you a comfortable country room, plus a hearty breakfast and dinner served at the family table.

Information and Services

Info on the area, along with a wireless hotspot, can be found at **Rochester Public Library** (22 S. Main St., 802/767-3927, www.rochestervtpubliclibrary.com, 12:30pm-7pm Tues. and Thurs., 9am-1pm Sat.).

RANDOLPH AND BETHEL: ROUTES 12/12A

Randolph is a collection of brick storefronts and mill buildings that span the White River, with a thriving downtown whose architecture reflects a railroading past. Many locals live up on the dirt roads that twist away from the valley floor; when they go "into town," this is what they mean. Randolph's appealing restaurants and cafés are the social hubs of the immediate region. A wealth of farmers and artisans are in this stretch of verdant country, and many of the sights involve visiting them where they live and work.

Eight miles down the road, the little town of Bethel has a similarly charming center, built with the profits from river-powered mills and an endemic strain of "white granite," which was used to build many Washington landmarks, including Union Station and the Smithsonian's Museum of Natural History. Bethel is named for the Levant town of Beth El, which makes several appearances in the Bible, most notably as the site where Jacob dreamed of a ladder that stretched to heaven; until the Civil War, however, it had the more prosaic name of Marsh's Mills.

Sights

Randolph is heaven to covered-bridge hunters, with three that were built in the same year, 1904. No fewer than five more **covered bridges** span the river in the nearby town of Northfield. Three of them are lined up on **Cox Brook Road,** including two that can be seen at once (the only place that's true in the whole state). The pick of the bunch is the **Braley Bridge,** with an unusual truss design, on self-referential Braley Covered Bridge Road in East Randolph.

The **Randolph Historical Museum** (9 Pleasant St., Randolph, 802/728-6677, 1pm-4pm third Sun. of the month May-Oct., admission by donation) is an excellent, if small, historical museum, if you manage to show up on the one day it opens each month. It managed to procure the tombstone of Justin Morgan, owner of the colt that started the bloodline of the famous Morgan horse, one of the first breeds developed in America. (The tombstone for the horse, meanwhile, is in a graveyard in nearby Tunbridge.) Other exhibits include a reconstructed early barbershop and drugstore.

Most dairy farmers are too busy milking and feeding the cows to have much time for entertaining guests. The family farmers at the all-organic **Neighborly Farms of Vermont** (1362 Curtis Rd., Randolph, 802/728-4700, www.neighborlyfarms.com, 8:30am-2pm Mon.-Thurs. year-round) are an exception, happy to show off their 50 Holsteins and demonstrate milking and cheese making (10 different varieties) to visitors. Be sure to try the farm's clothbound cheddar, which took the gold medal in the Eastern States Exhibition—in Vermont that's worth bragging rights for life. In the spring, the farm runs a maple sugar operation as well.

You won't find many breweries smaller than the two-man brew shack at **Bent Hill Brewery** (1972 Bent Hill Rd., Braintree, 802/249-1125, 2pm-6pm Thurs.-Fri., noon-6pm Sat.-Sun., free samples) where Mike Czok and Cody Montgomery grow hops on-site and turn out an impressive quantity of beer from their 50-gallon system. Their brews tend to be malty, flavorful, and not too hoppy. The Blood Orange Imperial IPA is a standout, as is the Maple Red Ale. There's also a sugar shack on-site, and maple syrup is available for sale.

A little bit farther down the road is another great farm worth a visit. **Fat Toad Farm** (787 Kibbee Rd., Brookfield, 802/279-0098, www.fattoadfarm.com, farm store 9am-5pm Mon.-Fri., 10am-4pm Sat.-Sun., tours by reservation, $12 adults, $5 children 6-12, under 6 free) turns their goats' milk into caramels of all kinds, most notably a variation on the Mexican version of *dulce de leche* called *cajeta*. Inspiration for the concoction was brought back by one of the farmer's daughters after a study abroad in Mexico, and the combination of tangy sweetness has fast become a local favorite. The farm runs a small self-serve store with varieties including vanilla, cinnamon, and coffee. The farm can be tricky to find; it's just 10 minutes from the interstate, but roads are poorly signed. It's much easier to use the hand-drawn map on the farm website, which includes step-by-step instructions, or you can pick up a free copy at **Floyd's Store** (2964 Rte. 66, Randolph, 802/728-5333).

Entertainment and Events

The pride of Randolph is the **Chandler Center for the Arts** (71-73 Main St., Randolph, 802/728-6464, www.chandler-arts.org), a turn-of-the-20th-century music hall restored to its former glory in the 1970s. The hall plays host during the year to a schedule of plays and musicals, as well as annual events: The **Central Vermont Chamber Music Festival** (www.centralvtchambermusicfest.org) offers string quartet performances by some of the state's best music performers on two Saturdays in August, and the hotly anticipated **Mud Season Variety Show** each March showcases the talents of local community members, who perform everything from Broadway numbers to clogging.

Dancers and musicians fill five stages with performances that celebrate Vermont's Celtic and French Canadian heritage at the **New World Festival** (Randolph, 802/728-9878, www.newworldfestival.com, $35-40), which takes place at the end of August.

Shopping

Around since 1845 (the original hitching rail for horses is still in front), **Floyd's General Store** (3 Main St., Randolph Center, 802/728-5333, 7:30am-6pm Mon.-Fri., 7:30am-5pm Sat., 9am-noon Sun.) is both grocery store to locals and tourist shop for visitors. Step inside and grab a few pieces of penny candy or locally made cheddar for the road.

Food

Sandwiches are named for local landmarks at the **Bethel Village Sandwich Shop** (269 Main St., Bethel, 802/234-9910, 7am-4pm Tues.-Wed., 7am-6pm Thurs.-Fri., 8am-3pm Sat.-Sun., $6-9), like the Lilliesville, which comes piled with smoked turkey and homemade cranberry mayo. The little café has a cheerful demeanor and sunny decor, but has just a few tables inside; consider bringing a picnic lunch to **Preserve Peavine** (375 Peavine Blvd., Bethel, 7am-7pm), a riverside park a short distance away.

Tucked on a downtown side street, the ★ **Black Krim Tavern** (21 Merchants Row, Randolph, 802/728-6776, www.theblackkrimtavern.com, 4:30pm-10pm Tues.-Sat., $16-21) prepares thoughtful and refined food in a pleasingly moody space with dark walls and a cozy atmosphere. The chef's husband grows much of the produce the restaurant uses in dishes like seared sea bass with whipped buttercup squash and barbecued *unagi* with radishes. The menu changes frequently.

On warm summer evenings, a table at **One Main Tap & Grill** (2 Merchants Row,

Randolph, 802/565-8117, 4pm-10:30pm daily, $11-30) is an ideal place to watch the comings and goings of downtown Randolph. Outdoor tables spread across the sidewalk, and burgers, flatbread, and wings complement the extensive tap list.

Accommodations

A bed-and-breakfast that's now just available through Airbnb, **Energy Rising B & B** (143 Fish Hill Rd., Randolph, 802/728-9382, $85, two bedrooms $150, three bedrooms $225) is homey and comfortable. It's just a mile from the highway, but feels a bit like a fairytale cottage, and the owner, Dede, provides a continental breakfast. You'll likely meet the owner's friendly cat in the eclectic common spaces, and there's an outdoor deck that's ideal for summer evenings.

Camping

The state parks in this area are mostly day-use only, but one exception is **Silver Lake State Park** (20 State Park Rd., Barnard, 802/234-9451, https://vtstateparks.com/silver.html, campsites $18-25), a small campground on the shores of a lake popular for swimming, boating, and fishing in summer. The 39 tent sites and 7 lean-tos are well spread out, and the camping area is equipped with restrooms, running water, hot showers, and a sanitary station (but no hookups). During the day, however, the campground can get quite crowded with families and tourists up from Woodstock and Quechee. The grassy beach has canoe and rowboat rentals, as well as a shaded picnic shelter.

Information and Services

For more information about Randolph and the entire White River Valley, contact the **Randolph Area Chamber of Commerce** (31 VT Rte. 66, Ste. 1, 802/728-9027, www.randolphvt.com), which stocks the usual assortment of maps and brochures in its downtown office. The state also runs a welcome center along I-89 in Randolph.

Randolph is the area's regional hub, with routine and emergency medical services available at **Gifford Medical Center** (44 S. Main St., 802/728-7000, www.giffordmed.org). Pharmacy needs can be taken care of at **Rite-Aid Pharmacy** (12 N. Main St., 802/728-3722, 8am-8pm Mon.-Fri., 8am-6pm Sat., 8am-5pm Sun., pharmacy 8am-8pm Mon.-Fri., 9am-6pm Sat., 9am-5pm Sun.). Get cash at any of a cluster of banks downtown, including **Bar Harbor Bank and Trust** (21 Main St., 802/728-9611, 8am-5pm Mon.-Thurs., 8am-5:30pm Fri.). The local arm of the law is the **Randolph Police Department** (6 S. Bay St., 802/728-3737).

SOUTH ROYALTON: ROUTE 110

The railroad runs straight through the center of picturesque South Royalton, which is home to 694 people and Vermont's only law school. Locals walk the tracks as the quickest way to the town green, which is at the heart of village life. In summertime it fills with outdoor concerts, and it hosts a beloved skating rink during winter months. Much of the architecture remains sweetly old-fashioned, from the white-steepled church to the decorative brick buildings lining the tiny downtown.

There's one other thing to note as you explore South Royalton—there are likely more Utah license plates here than in the rest of Vermont combined. This unassuming town is the birthplace of Joseph Smith, the founder of the Church of Latter-day Saints and has become an important pilgrimage for church members.

Sights

One of the most singular characters in U.S. history, Joseph Smith started a movement that grew into a religion. It all started with his discovery and description of golden plates that the angel Moroni had left in the woods of upstate New York thousands of years earlier. The revelations he transcribed from them became the basis of the Church of Jesus Christ of Latter-day Saints, or Mormonism,

The Royalton Raid

After the early years of the Revolutionary War, most of the fighting moved south out of New England. One exception was the infamous Royalton Raid, which occurred in 1780 toward the end of the war. Some 300 Mohawk fighters under British command descended upon Royalton as well as several other towns along the White River, burning homes, destroying livestock, and killing four men. The raid seems to have been an attempt to terrorize the frontier settlements and burn anything of value that might have aided the Americans in another attempt at attacking Montréal or Québec. It's still remembered in Royalton as a cruel act of terrorism on a mostly civilian population. An arch on the town green is dedicated to a woman who lost her child in the attack, then successfully negotiated for the release of several other children who were taken captive as the raiders retreated back to Canada.

an incredibly successful denomination that now counts millions of adherents around the world.

Smith's saga started in South Royalton, where his birth is memorialized by a 40-foot-tall granite shaft known as the **Joseph Smith Birthplace Memorial** (357 LDS Ln., South Royalton, 802/763-7742, www.lds.org/placestovisit, 9am-5pm Mon.-Sat., 1:30pm-5pm Sun. Nov.-Apr., 9am-7pm Mon.-Sat., 1:30pm-7pm Sun. May-Oct., free). The site has become an important pilgrimage for members of the Church of Jesus Christ of Latter-day Saints, with historical exhibits that fall somewhere between informative and evangelical.

South Royalton's other white granite monument, an arch on the town green, memorializes the **Royalton Raid,** an incident during the Revolutionary War in which 300 Mohawks, commanded by the British, raided several settlements in the area, killing 4 people and taking another 25 captive.

The scenic Route 110 leads to pretty **Tunbridge,** which has five **covered bridges** that are listed on the National Register of Historic Places. From south to north, you'll pass the **Cilley Bridge** just south of town, then the **Mill Bridge,** reconstructed after ice destroyed it in 1999. The **Larkin Bridge** is just east of 110 on Larkin Road, and a few miles farther on are **Flint Bridge** and **Moxley Bridge** in quick succession.

With just a one-and-a-half-barrel brewing system, **Brocklebank Craft Brewing** (357 Dickerman Hill Rd., Tunbridge, 802/685-4838, www.brocklebankvt.com, 3pm-7pm Fri., noon-6pm Sat.) proudly calls itself a nanobrewery, but their sessionable (read: low alcohol) beers can pack a big, hoppy flavor. The brewery keeps four beers on tap at any given time, chosen from a long list of IPAs, pilsners, ESBs, and a supersmooth porter. As the brewery's set back on a country road with spotty cell reception, it's worth copying directions from the website before making the trip.

★ Tunbridge World's Fair

If you've never seen a six-year-old farm girl strain her muscles at a kiddie tractor pull, you've missed some of the grit and gumption that power Vermont's working landscape. It's all on display—along with pig races, prize heifers, and contra dancing—at the **Tunbridge World's Fair** (802/889-5555, www.tunbridgeworldsfair.com, mid-Sept., $10-15, children under 12 free). The fair has run almost continuously since 1867, pausing only for World War II and the 1914 influenza epidemic, and remains a classic example of Vermont's rural fairs. Greasy food, carnival rides, and proud 4-H members fill the small community of Tunbridge, 10 minutes up Route 110 from South Royalton.

Shopping

When residents of "SoRo" need picnic supplies, locally make beauty products, and home-brewing equipment, they head to the

1
2
3
10-8

South Royalton Market (222 Chelsea St., South Royalton, 802/763-2400, www.soromarket.com, 7:30am-7pm Mon.-Fri., 8am-6pm Sat., 9am-6pm Sun.), a laid-back cooperative right on the town green. Hot meals are available at lunchtime.

Food

With a prime spot on the tracks and a rough-hewn, relaxed interior, the ★ **Worthy Burger** (56 Rainbow St., South Royalton, 802/763-2575, www.worthyvermont.com, 4pm-9pm Mon.-Thurs., 11:30am-10pm Fri.-Sat., 11:30am-9pm Sun., $8-15) has made South Royalton a dining destination. Keep it simple with a grass-fed beef burger, or add toppings like local cheese, habanero-pickled pineapple, and sautéed kale. Like at the Worthy Kitchen, a sister restaurant in Manchester, the beer list is noteworthy, and some of Vermont's best brews flow out of the Worthy Burger's 18 taps.

Gaze out to the picturesque town green as you munch inexpensive sandwiches and burgers at **Chelsea Station** (108 Chelsea St., South Royalton, 802/763-8685, 6am-3pm Mon.-Sat., 8am-noon Sun., $6-8), where both booth and counter service are swift and friendly.

Locals get nostalgic about the down-home breakfasts at **Eaton's Sugar House** (5894 Rte. 14, South Royalton, 802/763-8809, 7am-2pm Mon.-Fri., 7am-3pm Sat.-Sun., $6-12). The ramshackle exterior isn't promising, but inside, pumpkin pancakes come drenched with maple syrup, and the home fries are always crispy.

Accommodations

The simple, country-style rooms at **Antiqued Inn Time Bed & Breakfast** (1217 Back River Rd., South Royalton, 802/763-7370, www.antiquedinntime.com, $100-150) make this a welcoming place to land. There is a backyard pond and woods to explore. The hearty breakfasts are a highlight, as are the Rikerts, the friendly owners.

Equally hospitable is the **South Royalton B&B** (1408 Back River Rd., South Royalton, 305/491-7083, $100), which offers three bedrooms in an old farmhouse with shared baths. The proprietor, Evelyn, is a professional baker. Her pies and quiche make the homemade breakfast a treat. At the time of writing, bookings were exclusively available through Airbnb.

The two eponymous cabins at **Vermont Twin Cabins** (195 Deerhaven Rd., South Royalton, 802/369-0532, www.vermonttwincabins.com, $190-220, 2-night minimum) are both rustic and well cared for, with nicely stocked kitchens and fireplaces that are ideal for chilly autumn nights. The cabins are set next to a lovely pond, and the property include trails that can be skied and snowshoed in the winter. Bookings are through Airbnb.

Information and Services

For info on the area, pop into the **Royalton Memorial Library** (23 Alexander Pl., South Royalton, 802/763-7094, www.royaltonlibrary.org, noon-6pm Tues.-Fri., 10am-1pm Sat.), which also offers wireless Internet.

There are branches of **Bar Harbor Bank and Trust** in Bethel (1583 Rte. 107, 802/234-5549, 8am-5pm Mon.-Thurs., 8am-5:30pm Fri., 9am-noon Sat., 24-hour ATM) and South Royalton (52 Railroad St., 802/763-7771, 7:30am-4pm Mon.-Thurs., 7:30am-5:30pm Fri., 9am-noon Sat.). Fill prescriptions at the **Ride-Aid Pharmacy** (12 N. Main St., Randolph, 802/728-3722, 8am-8pm Mon.-Fri., 8am-6pm Sat., 8am-5pm Sun.). In an emergency, contact the regional **State Police** (2011 Rte. 107, Bethel, 802/234-9933).

SPORTS AND RECREATION

Hiking and Biking

Rochester is the jumping-off point for numerous hikes into a wild portion of the **Green**

1: demonstrating the use of an old-fashioned wood splitter at the Tunbridge World's Fair; **2:** Ferris wheel at the Tunbridge World's Fair; **3:** covered bridge in the White River Valley

Mountain National Forest (Rochester Ranger Station, 99 Ranger Rd., Rochester, 802/767-4261, www.fs.usda.gov/gmfl), which has been proposed as a national wilderness area. This part of the forest features a cluster of tall mountains with evocative names, including Romance Mountain, Monastery Mountain, and Mount Horrid (the last of which features a steep 0.75-mile hike up to the Great Cliff, a 600-foot vertical overlook of Brandon Gap). A trail map for the area is available at the ranger station.

If you'd rather tackle the forest on two wheels, you can rent a suitable steed at **Green Mountain Bikes** (105 N. Main St., Rochester, 802/767-4464, www.greenmountainbikes.com, 10am-6pm daily, $35/day), which also specializes in arranging personalized mountain biking tours that circumvent the sometimes draconian policies of the National Forest Service.

Boating, Tubing, and Fishing

The White River is especially idyllic from the vantage point of an inner tube, though it's worth waiting for a scorcher, as the water stays cool through the summer. **Vermont River Tubing** (Rte. 100, Stockbridge, 802/746-8106, $15) offers something to float on, a car shuttle, and advice on where to put in.

The river also has some of the best fly-fishing in the Northeast. Contact **Stream and Brook Fly Fishing** (802/989-0398, www.streamandbrook.com) for guided trips along the river, or just stake out a spot downstream of the **Roxbury State Fish Hatchery** (Rte. 12A, Roxbury).

Swimming

The clear, cold branches of the White River contain dozens of exemplary swimming holes, though it's important to be cautious, as the river bed changes every season. Ask a local, or check out www.swimmingholes.org/vt. If you prefer still water, it's hard to beat jumping off the floating bridge into **Sunset Lake** in Brookfield.

GETTING THERE AND AROUND

The White River Valley area is located in the "V" formed by the intersection of I-89 and I-91. To drive to South Royalton from White River Junction, take I-89 north to exit 2, then Route 14 east (20 mi., 25 min.). For Bethel, take exit 3 to Route 107 west (25 mi., 30 min.). For Rochester, continue along Route 107 west to Route 100 north (12 mi., 20 min.). For Randolph, take I-89 north from White River Junction to exit 4, then Route 66 west (32 mi., 40 min.).

Amtrak's Vermonter service stops in Randolph at Depot Square (800/872-7245, www.amtrak.com). Elsewhere in the area, public transportation is by shuttle bus offered through **Stagecoach Transportation Services** (802/728-3773, www.stagecoach-rides.org), which runs regular service to Randolph (Depot Sq.), Bethel (Mascoma Bank parking lot, 264 Main St.), and Rochester (Village Green).

Northeast Kingdom

First-time visitors to Vermont may come for the postcard-ready landscapes in the southern Green Mountains, but the Northeast Kingdom defines the way that many locals see the state: beautiful and a bit unruly, with a rural culture all its own.

Sweeping along the international border, the Kingdom stretches from Lake Champlain to the tiny outpost of Island Pond. The grandiose title appeared in 1949, when U.S. Senator George Aiken said that it's "such beautiful country up here, it ought to be called the Northeast Kingdom." The name stuck—perhaps because it resonated with Vermonters who'd long viewed their home as a place apart. The quirky population includes everyone from fourth-generation farmers to hippie academics who love this region for its isolation and

Highlights

Look for ★ to find recommended sights, activities, dining, and lodging.

★ **St. Johnsbury Athenaeum:** This gorgeous library and museum is a true shrine to literature, filled to the brim with books and art (page 217).

★ **Craftsbury Outdoor Center:** Cross-country skiers come from all over the East to kick and glide the perfectly groomed trails here; head to the lodge and you might be sipping hot chocolate next to elite college skiers or Olympians (page 225).

★ **Kingdom Trails Network:** Bike the Kingdom on more than 100 miles of trails that swoop and flow through the northern forest, comprising the best riding in Vermont (page 229).

★ **Lake Willoughby:** A deep, clear lake flanked by high cliffs, Willoughby is among Vermont's most beautiful places, and a year-round place to ski, hike, paddle, and swim (page 236).

★ **Bread & Puppet Theater:** A former dairy barn houses rabble-rousing political theater and thought-provoking "cheap art" (page 236).

★ **Jay Peak Resort:** The legendary "Jay Cloud" dumps great piles of snow on this resort, which tempts French-speaking skiers and riders across the border from the mountains in Québec. It's the wet and warm après-ski that really sets Jay apart, since the fully-enclosed on-site water park is always heated to balmy summer temps (page 241).

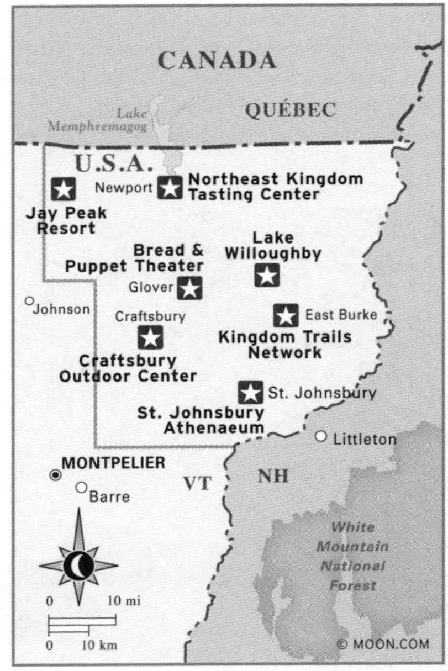

★ **Northeast Kingdom Tasting Center:** Sample tasting menus of cheese and cured meats alongside distinctive ice ciders and distilled spirits (page 245).

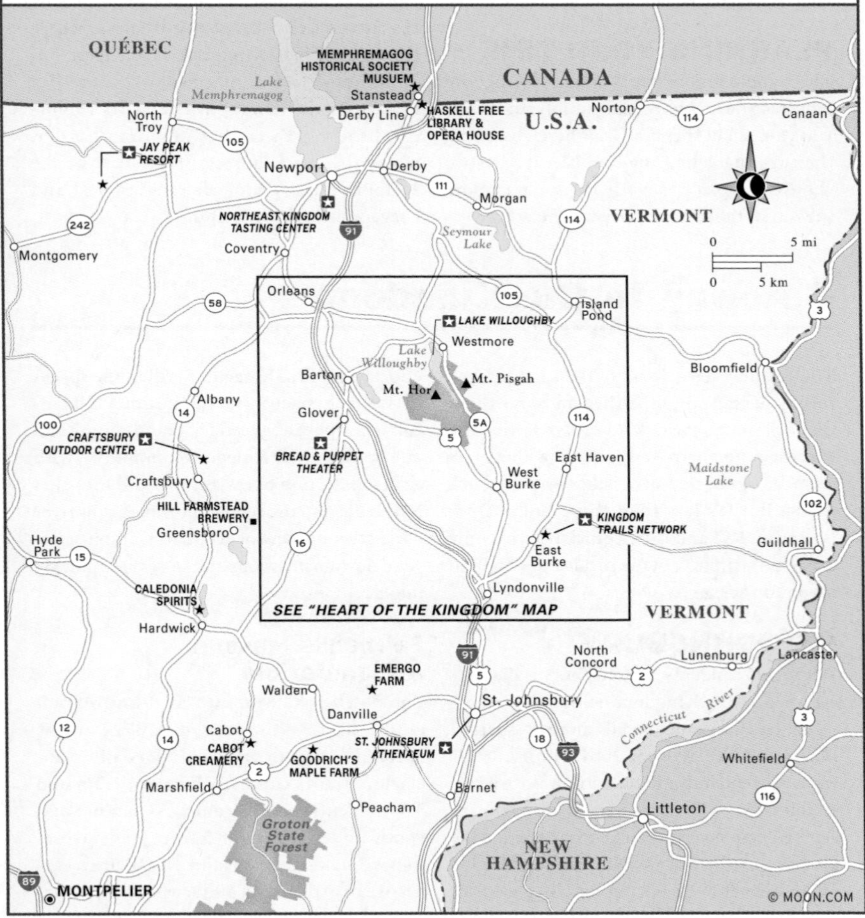

independent spirit. Indeed, while Vermont as a whole has drawn its fair share of writers, the Northeast Kingdom (or NEK for short) is legendary for its creative set—including Wallace Stegner and Howard Frank Mosher, a beloved Vermont author who wove the Kingdom's landscape and characters into a kind of country-bred magical realism.

For visitors, the Kingdom offers year-round outdoor adventures: Paddle glacier-carved lakes that reflect fall foliage, bike the spine of the Green Mountains, and ski Jay Peak, an isolated mountain that harvests heavy snowfall from passing clouds. As in much of Vermont, the places in between the towns define this rural region, whether you're hiking above stunning

Previous: Lake Willoughby in winter; handmade puppets at Bread & Puppet Theater; biking the Kingdom Trails Network.

Lake Willoughby, watching political theater at Bread & Puppet, or just finding—then losing—your way on the Kingdom's endless back roads.

PLANNING YOUR TIME

The remoteness of the Northeast Kingdom requires your own transportation, and while you can easily spend a week here absorbing the rural pace of Kingdom life, it's best to choose one place to settle in as you explore the rest of the area with leisurely day trips.

On the way into the Kingdom, stop in **St. Johnsbury,** or "St. J," which makes a good home base, as does the neighboring **East Burke-Lyndonville** area, where the world-class Kingdom Trails gaze out at some of Vermont's best scenery. But for a taste of Kingdom life at its remotest, head north to the Canadian border, where the quiet shores of **Newport**'s Lake Memphremagog hide a swinging past and a legendary lake monster.

Gateway to the Kingdom

This southwestern swath of the Kingdom is a rolling passage into the rhythm of northern life, full of contrasts (and cows). Seen from the rest of northern Vermont, it's a long drive from nowhere and accessible only by back roads. But it's less than three hours from Boston on I-91 and I-93, a quick trip that only deepens the impact of the rural landscape and mountain scenery.

ST. JOHNSBURY

With 7,500 residents, St. Johnsbury is the largest town in the Kingdom, with a downtown whose faded elegance recalls more prosperous times. At the turn of the 20th century, "St. J" was a railroad hub and industry was thriving. St. Johnsbury's fortunes were made by the inventor Thaddeus Fairbanks, who invented the modern platform scale, with sliding weights on an arm above a spring-loaded platform. Construction of the scales instantly made Fairbanks—and the town—rich. His brother Erastus was later responsible for bringing the railroad to town in 1850, and later he twice became the governor of Vermont.

The Fairbanks family never forgot where they came from, and generations invested heavily in the town, building an academy, natural history museum, and art gallery, infusing their hometown with a love of learning. Their legacy has kept St. Johnsbury alive through hard times, but recent revitalization efforts have finally begun to fill in the spaces between these cultural institutions. The result is an appealing blend of grand county seat and hardscrabble Kingdom community, with a small selection of restaurants and inns that infuse life into the center of town. A slow river winds through the heart of St. J, and just beyond downtown, shops and stores fade quickly into deep country.

Fairbanks Museum & Planetarium

The **Fairbanks Museum & Planetarium** (1302 Main St., 802/748-2372, www.fairbanksmuseum.org, 9am-5pm daily, planetarium shows run daily between 11am and 3:30pm, entrance $9 adults, $7 seniors and youth under 17, under 5 free; planetarium shows $5) is a delicious throwback to an earlier age of exploration and science, with a menagerie of colorful stuffed parrots, menacing polar bears, Egyptian mummies, and Japanese fans displayed in crowded glass cases in a turreted Victorian exhibition hall.

The museum was founded in 1891 by Franklin Fairbanks, a philanthropist who himself made careful daily observations of weather and atmospheric conditions. That work is carried on in the museum's weather gallery, home to the public radio program "Eye on the Sky," which broadcasts remarkably detailed weather information and star

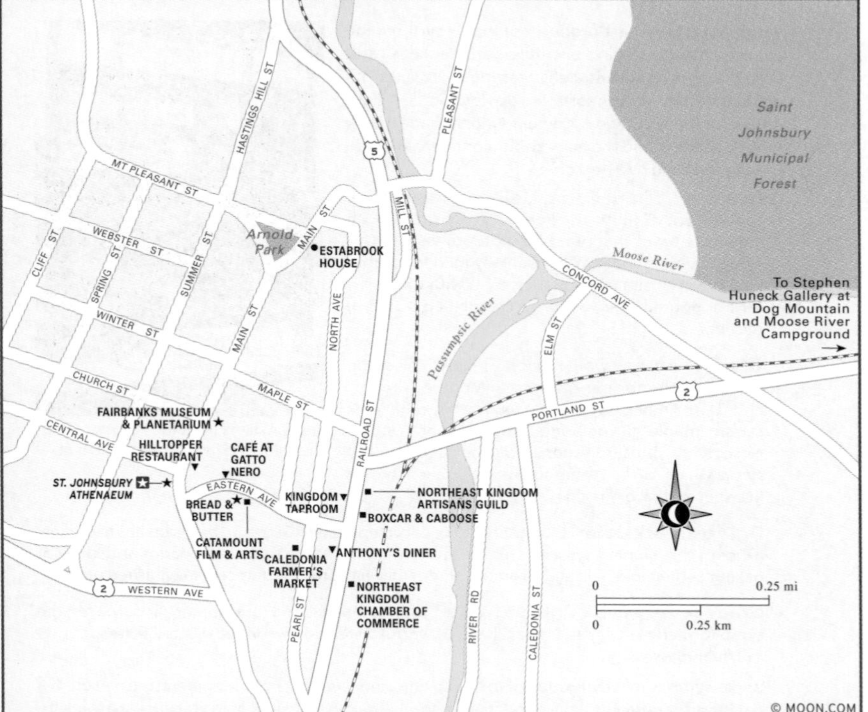

reports across the state. The planetarium is one of only a few in New England, and the shows explore the universe with the same spirit of earnest discovery as the rest of the museum.

★ St. Johnsbury Athenaeum

The **St. Johnsbury Athenaeum** (1171 Main St., 802/748-8291, www.stjathenaeum.org, 10am-5:30pm Mon., Wed., Fri., 2pm-7pm Tues., Thurs., 10am-3pm Sat.) is an extraordinary library, with towering shelves and winding staircases that are the stuff of bookworms' dreams. The institution doubles as an art museum, with dozens of fine canvases by American landscape and portrait painters. Highlights include the powerful *Domes of the Yosemite,* by Albert Bierstadt, and the enigmatic *Raspberry Girl,* by Victorian-era realist Adolphe William Bouguereau. Don't miss the children's library, which is wrapped with murals that illustrate children's stories that were popular in the 1930s, when they were commissioned. Margary Eva Lang Hamilton's "Heidi" and "The Song of Hiawatha" are sweetly nostalgic—and remarkably, the artwork was financed by the Civil Works Association as a part of Franklin D. Roosevelt's New Deal. The museum has been restored to a high gloss, and black-walnut gleams from the floors and walls.

Stephen Huneck Gallery at Dog Mountain

Dog lovers, this is your temple. After emerging from a life-threatening coma, artist Stephen

A Jug by Any Other Name...

Vermont is the largest producer of maple syrup in the country, but these days even die-hard Yankees can't keep the syrup grades straight. Starting in 2014, the old grading system—which sorted syrups into Grade A Light Amber (or Fancy), Grade A Medium Amber, Grade A Dark Amber, Grade B, and the hair-raising, commercial Grade C—was replaced by a new one:

Sugar makers track the variations in the color and taste of each batch of syrup.

- **Grade A Golden Color, Delicate Taste:** Once called "Fancy," this is the lightest syrup grade, with a delicate flavor that often has notes of vanilla. This syrup is best enjoyed with relatively mild foods that won't overwhelm its subtleties; try it with Greek yogurt or poured over vanilla ice cream (Ben & Jerry's, of course).
- **Grade A Amber Color, Rich Flavor:** This grade combines the former grades of "Medium Amber" and "Dark Amber," syrups that tend to have the most classic "maple" flavor. Some tasters will notice butterscotch or buttery notes in this perfect pancake syrup, which can be swapped for cane sugar or honey in sweet and savory recipes.
- **Grade A Dark Color, Robust Flavor:** Formerly called Grade B, this syrup has the fullest flavor of the "sipping syrups." This is a favorite among many syrup aficionados and ideal for baking as the more delicately flavored grades may be harder to detect in the finished product.
- **Grade A Very Dark Color, Strong Flavor:** Mostly used for commercial purposes, the syrup formerly known as Grade C has a powerful taste and can be substituted in recipes that call for molasses.

Maple syrup is mostly produced in March and April, and changing temperatures result in a fluctuating spectrum of colors and flavors. While the overall trend is to start the season with pale syrup and end with the darker stuff, a cold snap in April can easily produce a batch of straw-colored syrup with that "delicate taste." The new names may be unwieldy, but the previous system seemed to imply that "Fancy" was superior to "Grade B," which is simply a question of personal preference. The best way to explore Vermont's sweetest product is to find a sugar maker at a shop or farmers market, and just sample the sweet stuff until you find your favorite.

Huneck was inspired to create a church celebrating the spiritual bonds we have with man's best friend. The resulting **Dog Chapel** (143 Parks Rd., 800/449-2580, www.dogmt.com, 11am-4pm Mon., Fri., 10am-5pm Sat.-Sun.) resembles a diminutive New England church, but instead of saints, the stained-glass windows depict canines. The walls are covered with images and handwritten notes to beloved pets that have died, and visitors are encouraged to add their own tributes. A three-mile hiking trail loops through the woods behind the chapel, with some lovely views of the valley below; it goes without saying that there are no leash laws on Dog Mountain. A gift shop sells the artist's trademark woodblock prints of retrievers. Sadly, Huneck ended his own life in 2010; the chapel is as much a memorial to the man as it is a testament to his lifelong work.

Entertainment and Events

You can catch anything from jazz performances to movie revivals and gallery shows at **Catamount Film & Arts** (115 Eastern Ave., 802/748-2600, www.catamountarts.org). The community center's diverse roster attracts an energetic, enthusiastic segment of the town.

If you've ever wondered how soap was made, rugs braided, or tools forged, your questions will be answered at the **Fairbanks Festival of Traditional Crafts** (Fairbanks Museum, Sept.), a 30-year tradition that honors those keeping alive the ingenuity we now take for granted. Displays are very much hands on, with modern artisans encouraging participation by visitors.

Shopping

Its claim to be the "maple center of the world" is a bit overblown, but if you're in the market for maple swag, you can find it all at **Maple Grove Farms** (1052 Portland St., 800/525-2540, ext. 5547, www.maplegrove.com, 9am-5pm Mon.-Fri. Apr.-Dec. and 9am-5pm Sat.-Sun. June-Dec.). While you're there, peek inside the demonstration sugarhouse.

A must-stop for families (not to mention bookworms) is **Boxcar & Caboose Bookstore** (394 Railroad St., 802/748-3551, www.boxcarandcaboose.com, 9am-5:30pm Mon.-Fri., 10am-4pm Sun.), a combination bookstore, café, and kids' playroom complete with comfy leather chairs, espresso drinks, and a train table.

Score heirloom-quality carved wooden chairs, luminous glass bowls, and handwoven scarves at **Northeast Kingdom Artisans Guild** (430 Railroad St., 802/748-0158, www.nekartisansguild.com, 10:30am-5:30pm Mon.-Sat.), a collective of more than 100 craftspeople.

When the summer harvest starts rolling in, **Caledonia Farmers' Market** (Municipal Plaza behind Anthony's Diner, 802/592-3088, 9am-1pm Sat. May-Oct.) is a sight to behold, bursting with riotous floral bouquets and perfect vegetables. The whole town comes out to fill their baskets.

Food

Aside from excellent espresso and locally baked pastries, the real draw of the **Café at Gatto Nero Press** (190 Eastern Ave., 802/748-2900, 7am-5pm Mon.-Fri., 9am-5pm Sat.-Sun., $2-7) is its charmingly quirky location inside an intaglio printmaking art studio and gallery. They're "squid ink" is an eye-opening take on the red eye that blends strong-brewed coffee and a shot of espresso, and if you're lucky, you'll see the handmade images roll off the press while you sip.

Set in a historic brick building, ★ **Bread and Butter** (139 Eastern Ave., 802/424-1590, 7am-4pm Mon. and Wed.-Fri., 7am-1pm Sat., $5-13) serves breakfast and lunch in a pleasingly hip and spare space. Breakfast includes fancy toast topped with maple butter or local jam, and the lunch menu of hearty sandwiches includes great vegetarian options. Premade meals are great for snagging pre-hike picnic fare, and there's a rotating list of desserts that are made in-house.

High school students from the St. Johnsbury Academy serve and prepare the meals at the **Hilltopper Restaurant** (1216 Main St., 802/748-8965, www.stjacademy.org, 11:15am-12:45pm Tues.-Thurs., $6-13), and the menu includes "signature dishes" developed by the culinary studies class, as well as sweets from the baking and pastry classes. The quality of the meals and experience far exceed the prices, and the cheerful, brightly lit dining room is an appealing place to dine. The students create the menu, so it ranges from classic French to Asian fusion but always includes simple and well-prepared soups and salads.

A constantly rotating tap list of excellent beers is the mainstay of **Kingdom Taproom** (397 Railroad St., 802/424-1355, www.kingdomtaproom.com, noon-10pm Wed.-Thurs., noon-midnight Fri.-Sat., noon-8pm Sun., $6-9), a stylish and dimly lit basement pub that is a cozy retreat in winter months. A creative "beer color chart" above the taps guides drinkers to their beer of choice. The menu is limited but appealing. Pub snacks, flatbreads, sandwiches, and salads predominate, but the taproom also offers entrées like chicken potpie or bangers and mash.

For hearty breakfasts and American fare, **Anthony's Diner** (50 Railroad St., 802/748-3613, 7am-4pm Sun.-Wed., 7am-8pm Thurs.-Fri., $6-18) is a cozy locals' joint that's reliable and friendly. Inside the homey exterior, you'll find classic paper place mats on the tables, two-person booths, and a counter lined with stools. Burgers are hefty and house-made pies are a treat.

Sitting on the deck at **Bailiwicks on Mill** (98 Mill St., 802/424-1215, www.bailiwicksfinerestaurant.com, 5pm-close Mon.-Thurs., 11:30am-3pm, 5pm-close Fri.-Sun., $9-30) is a sublime way to end a summer day. The inside is charming too: The atmospheric restaurant is lined with exposed brick walls and twinkly lights and fills up most nights with families and couples eating from an eclectic assortment of seafood, steaks, and salads. The menu always includes a handful of appealing vegetarian options, like Bombay pakoras or ratatouille.

A 15-minute drive from downtown St. J, the superb restaurant at ★ **Rabbit Hill Inn** (48 Lower Waterford Rd., Lower Waterford, 802/748-5168, www.rabbithillinn.com, 6pm-close Thurs.-Tues. Nov.-Aug., 6pm-close daily Sept.-Oct., reservations required, $22-38) draws diners from around the region. Spanish octopus comes with a Calabrian pepper puree, and pork ragu is paired with house-made pappardelle pasta. Save room for dessert, which is creative and finely wrought: A rhubarb custard tart blends buckwheat ice cream and birch syrup. There are just 14 tables at the restaurant, and a single seating each night; pine plank floors, white walls, and simple decor are elegant and right at home in the country.

Accommodations

A stay at the centrally located **Estabrook House** (1596 Main St., 802/751-8261, www.estabrookhouse.com, $95-150) offers a glimpse into the town's grand past. The 1896 Victorian home has been beautifully renovated and features four individually decorated rooms filled with antiques. One of the rooms has a private bathroom; the others share a bath that's outfitted with a gorgeous claw-foot tub. Coffee and tea are available all day in the dining room, and the leisurely breakfasts are filling and delicious.

Travelers who've brought furry friends on a pilgrimage to Dog Mountain can bed down at the **Fairbanks Inn** (401 Western Ave., 802/748-5666, www.stjay.com, $99-199). The motel-style operation offers a heated pool, rooms and minisuites with private balconies or poolside patios, and microwaves and refrigerators. The inn could use a bit of sprucing up, but it's a decent option for a night with your pup.

Lavishly decorated and tranquil to its core, ★ **Rabbit Hill Inn** (48 Lower Waterford Rd., Lower Waterford, 802/748-5168, www.rabbithillinn.com, $180-355) fills rooms with luxuries like fluffy robes, private porches, and fireplaces. But you may be tempted to leave your room once you hear about the perks in the rest of the property—afternoon tea and pastries, apple cheddar crepes at breakfast, and candlelight dinners prepared by Matthew Secich.

CAMPING

Just east of town, near Dog Mountain, the **Moose River Campground** (2870 Portland St., 802/748-4334, www.mooserivercampground.com, tent sites $35-39, RV sites $40-63, RV rental from $105) has a grassy spread of campsites that are clean and set back from the road. All sites, which are priced for up to four people, have wireless Internet, picnic tables, and fire rings, and the more expensive RV sites have cable television access. Weekend activities, which are more geared to older adults than families with children, include bingo, luaus, and ice cream socials.

Information and Services

The **Northeast Kingdom Chamber** (2000 Memorial Dr., 802/748-3678 or 800/639-6379, www.nekchamber.com) runs a well-staffed

Water-Witching

Called dowsing or "water-witching," the practice of using a brass rod or Y-shaped twig to find metals, gems, or water buried in the ground goes back to the Middle Ages. Those who still swear by the ancient art come together at the **American Society of Dowsers Bookstore** (184 Brainerd St., Danville, 802/684-3417, www.dowsers.org, 8am-4pm Mon.-Fri.), which has a full selection of books and divining rods for purchase. While you are there, walk the labyrinth, a magical maze purported to bring wholeness and healing to those who walk it; a hundred-some dowsers come together each June to share dowsing stories and techniques at the **American Society of Dowsers Conference** (802/684-3417, www.dowsers.org).

welcome center inside the Green Mountain Mall.

State authorities in the area can be found at the **Vermont State Police** (1068 U.S. Rte. 5, Ste. #1., 802/748-3111). Two full-service hospitals serve the area: **Northeastern Vermont Regional Hospital** (1315 Hospital Dr., 802/748-8141) and **North Country Hospital** (189 Prouty Dr., Newport, 802/334-7331). Get prescriptions filled at **Rite-Aid Pharmacy** (502 Railroad St., 802/748-5210, 8am-9pm Mon.-Fri., 8am-8pm Sat., 9am-6pm Sun., pharmacy 8am-8pm Mon.-Fri., 9am-6pm Sat., 9am-5pm Sun.). Free public Wi-Fi is available at the **St. Johnsbury Athenaeum** (1171 Main St., 802/748-8291) and **Boxcar & Caboose Bookstore** (394 Railroad St., 802/748-3551).

WEST OF ST. JOHNSBURY

An air of quietude blankets the landscape south and west of St. Johnsbury, where tranquil back roads lead to small towns and family farms. **Danville** is situated around two ponds, Joe's Pond and Molly's Pond, supposedly named after an Abenaki man and his wife who befriended early settlers. The serene downtown belies the fact that it is home to some of the area's stranger attractions, including a giant corn maze, a widely attended "ice-out," and a center for the medieval practice of water-witching.

The little town of **Peacham** is a small community with an enchantingly old-fashioned setting—Peacham starred in the movies *Ethan Frome* and *The Spitfire Grill* as the quintessential New England village. One glance at its town green and white church spire, and you'll see why. And while it would be easy to blaze through the map-dot down of **Marshfield,** locals make a habit of stopping by while driving across the state, as the town's long-running bakery is among the most beloved in Vermont.

Set in the countryside north of the main road, there's not much to see in **Cabot**—just a collection of modest white clapboard houses arranged around a general store, library, and a couple of gas pumps—but it's home to a famous local cheese maker whose visitors center is well stocked with samples, and it's a great destination for tasting maple syrup in the early spring.

Great Vermont Corn Maze

If you've ever wondered what it's like to be a lab rat, venture into the rows at the **Great Vermont Corn Maze** (1404 Wheelock Rd., Danville, 802/748-1399, www.vermontcornmaze.com, 10am-2pm Mon.-Fri., 10am-3pm Sat.-Sun. Aug.-mid-Oct., $15 ages 16-59, $10 ages 5-15 and 60 and up, children under 4 free), more than three miles of twisting confusion carved each year amidst 12-foot-tall cornstalks. Owners Mike and Dayna Boudreau have been constructing the maze for better than 15 years, getting progressively trickier with each course. Participants quest for the elusive "bell of success" in the center of the maze, which can take anywhere from one to four hours. The complex

Ice Out at Joe's Pond

Weather is a serious topic of conversation in Vermont. As winter temperatures begin to ease in early spring, neighbors gather in country stores and sugar shacks and ask, "When's the ice going out?" The small community that surrounds Joe's Pond had long been placing bets on when the ice would break; in 1988 they made it official, recording bets in a spiral-bound notebook—$1 each, winner take all. For a couple of decades, the system was simple: An electric clock on shore was attached to a cinderblock that was wired to a pallet out on the ice. When the cinderblock went down, the clock was disconnected. These days, Ice Out's gone (relatively) high-tech. The electric alarm clock was replaced by a weatherproof model, a spreadsheet replaced the notebook, and 24-hour webcams are trained on the cinderblock so you can watch the ice melt from around the globe at www.joespond.com.

Join in the fun by placing your own bets at **Hastings Store** (2748 Rte. 2, West Danville, 802/684-3398, 6:30am-6pm Mon.-Sat., 8am-1pm Sun.), where a dollar will get you a stake. If you need some help gauging the exact date and time that the ice is going to break, the shopkeeper is generally happy to share the list of previous years' ice outs, but as any Vermonter can tell you, there are no guarantees when it comes to weather.

also has a smaller corn maze for kids, along with a barnyard minigolf course among the animal paddocks. To relive the '80s horror film *Children of the Corn*, come in October when the farm is transformed into "Dead North: Farmland of Terror" just in time for Halloween.

Goodrich's Maple Farm

Nestled among the hills, **Goodrich's Maple Farm** (2427 Rte. 2, Cabot, 800/639-1854, www.goodrichmaplefarm.com, 9am-5pm Mon.-Sat.) is one of Vermont's largest sugarhouses that's open to the public and has been a family business since 1793. Proprietors Glenn and Ruth Goodrich are always happy to take time to explain the syrup-making process. But they really shine during the farm's semiannual maple seminars, where they explain how to install and repair the plastic tubes for the sap, as well as how to boil it down efficiently.

Cabot Creamery

Enormous white silos loom over the factory campus of **Cabot Creamery** (2878 Main St./Rte. 15, Cabot Village, 800/837-4261, www.cabotcheese.coop, 9am-5pm daily May 21-Oct., 10am-4pm daily Nov.-Dec., 10am-4pm Mon.-Sat., Jan.-May 20). From a simple farmer's cooperative started in a farmhouse 100 years ago, Cabot Cheese has grown to become Vermont's best-known (if not best) producer of cheddar cheese. Though the company now makes 15 million pounds of cheese annually, it is still run as a farmers' cooperative (with now more than 2,000 farm families) and still operates on the same land where it began. There are no longer tours of the cheese-making facilities, but it's still fun to stop by and graze the samples if you're passing through.

Food

A welcome addition to the snack bar that's available in West Danville is **Three Ponds** (12 Rte. 15, West Danville, 802/227-3200, 7am-3pm Thurs.-Mon., $8-13), which serves "local comfort food" in a cozy café space. Breakfast features eggs, pancakes, breakfast burritos, and homemade hash, while the appealingly old-fashioned lunch menu ranges from burgers to soups and shepherd's pie.

In heated discussions of which Vermont establishment has the best maple creemees, Vermont-speak for soft-serve ice cream, a frequent contender is **Abbi's Ice Cream** (611 Rte. 2 E., Danville, 802/684-2265, $2-5). It has

1: Fairbanks Museum & Planetarium in St. Johnsbury; **2:** St. Johnsbury Athenaeum, a small-town library; **3:** skiing on the impeccably groomed trails at Craftsbury Outdoor Center

MUSEUM OF NATURAL SCIENC
1

1871
ST. JOHNSBURY ATHENAEUM
ART GALLERY
AND
FREE PUBLIC LIBRARY
2

3

no fixed hours and a boatload of quirk—you can even browse piles of antiques/junk while you eat your ice cream—but it's a great place to join the crowd of locals who make quick turns off Route 2 when they see that Abbi's is open for business.

With more than four decades in business, ★ **Rainbow Sweets** (1689 Rte. 2, Marshfield, 802/426-3531, 9am-6pm Wed.-Thurs., 9am-9pm Fri., 9am-6pm Sat., 9am-5pm Sun., $3-8) is an oddball gem with remarkably good sweets. The owners, Katherine Clark and Steven Wallach, have created a menu that draws heavily on the flavors of the Austro-Hungarian empire: Think creamy cakes and slender tortes. As for the rest, well, they do what they want, with spinach turnovers, cookies, confections, and Moroccan b'stilla, a sweet-savory pastry that's aromatic with cinnamon. According to local legend, Marshfield locals with new babies come to Rainbow Sweets to weigh—and take photos of—the kids in Steven's giant, old-fashioned flour scale.

When Peacham's only store closed in 2002, residents were left with nowhere to gather, so in true Vermont style, they formed an LLC and opened the **Peacham Café** (643 Bayley Hazen Rd., Peacham, 802/357-4040, www.peachamcafe.org, 7am-2pm Wed.-Fri., 8am-2pm Sat.-Sun., $3-9) in August 2014. The cheerful space was built in the former firehouse, and the chef serves breakfast and brunch classics like pancakes and omelets. Try the Vermonti-Cristo, French toast stuffed with cheddar, ham, and fruit preserves, topped with (of course!) Vermont maple syrup.

Accommodations

Set in the rolling hills of Groton State Forest, ★ **Seyon Lodge** (2967 Seyon Pond Rd., Groton, 802/584-3829, https://vtstateparks.com/seyon.html, $85-95) is a year-round lodge run by the state parks. The simple rooms are a great deal and appointed with country-style quilts and furnishings, and you can rent rowboats to get out on nearby Noyes Pond, a favorite for fly fishers. If arranged in advance, the lodge prepares breakfast, lunch, and dinners for guests (breakfast $6-10, lunch $8-12, dinner $20-25) using ingredients from local farms. During the winter months, there's often a blazing fire in the living room, making it a cozy place to meet other guests.

Once a 1970s back-to-the-land commune named for a rabble-rousing Joe Hill tune, **Pie-in-the-Sky Farm Bed & Breakfast** (93 Dwinell Rd., Marshfield, 802/426-3777, www.pieinsky.com, single occupancy $95-105, double occupancy $120-135, suites $190-230 for up to 5 people, rates include breakfast) kept the name and a bit of the hippie spirit. There's a hot tub and sunroom for lounging around the property, ducks and sheep wandering around, and room to walk, snowshoe, or cross-country ski on the 100-acre property. Breakfasts a generous affair, and the innkeepers pride themselves on catering to a wide range of special diets.

A stay at the **Emergo Farm B&B** (261 Webster Hill, Danville, 888/383-1185, www.emergofarm.com, $120-160) gives a taste of daily life on a working dairy that stretches over 230 acres of countryside. The Websters have farmed this land for six generations, and they're generous with their knowledge and stories. The bright rooms are decorated with unfussy antiques, and one includes a private kitchen and sitting room. A hearty farm breakfast is served at the communal dining table.

CAMPING

There are no motors allowed on **Ricker Pond** (18 Ricker Pond Campground Rd., Groton, 802/584-3821, https://vtstateparks.com/ricker.html, camping $18-25) in **Groton State Forest**, which makes it a blissfully calm place to spend the night, and there's also a swimming beach that's ideal for cooling off on hot summer days.

For an even more secluded experience, **Kettle Pond** (6993 State Forest Rd., Groton, 802/426-3042, https://vtstateparks.com/kettlepond.html, camping $18-25) has remote campsites that are accessible only on foot and by boat. It's worth noting that Groton State Forest can have staggering mosquitoes and blackflies—it all depends on when you arrive in the life cycle, but it's worth packing bug juice.

Information and Services

For more info on the area, contact the **Danville Chamber of Commerce** (802/684-2247, www.danvillevtchamber.org) or the **Hardwick Area Chamber of Commerce** (802/472-5906, www.heartofvt.com/hardwick). You can find ATMs in downtown Hardwick at **Union Bank** (103 Rte. 15, 802/472-8100). Fill prescriptions at **Rite-Aid Pharmacy** (82 Rte. 15 W., Hardwick, 802/472-6961, 8am-8pm Mon.-Fri., 8am-6pm Sat., 9am-5pm Sun., pharmacy 8am-8pm Mon.-Fri., 9am-6pm Sat., 9am-5pm Sun.). In an emergency, contact the local **police department** (20 Church St., Hardwick, 802/472-5475).

CRAFTSBURY, GREENSBORO, AND HARDWICK

Immaculate white buildings surround **Craftsbury**'s common, a grassy expanse that's the quiet heart of this town. The common is just the beginning of its charms, for the village sits in the middle of the miles of cross-country skiing and biking trails that traverse the surrounding countryside.

Fifteen minutes down the road, **Greensboro** is a speck of a town, without much more than a tiny general store. It has two other things to entice visitors from neighboring Craftsbury, though: Hill Farmstead Brewery—whose rare, sought-after beers have made the town into a sort of pilgrimage spot—and forested hills surrounding a gem-like lake. In his classic novel *Crossing to Safety*, Wallace Stegner described the view from Greensboro's Barr Hill as a blend of "wild and cultivated, rough woods ending with scribed edges against smooth hayfields—this and the accent dots of white houses, red barns, and clustered cattle tiny as aphids on a leaf … green woods and greener meadows meet blue water." A short hike up Barr Hill is just as enchanting as it was when Stegner spent summers in the rural community, and the view is little changed.

After lean decades of being down-and-out, **Hardwick** found a kind of renewal with Vermont's growing local food scene, and the town is home to Caledonia Spirits, an award-winning distillery that's among the finest in the state.

★ Craftsbury Outdoor Center

The expansive **Craftsbury Outdoor Center** (535 Lost Nation Rd., Craftsbury Common, 802/586-7767, www.craftsbury.com) is an extraordinary resource at any time of year. Sixty miles of **cross-country skiing** trails wind through fields and forests, looping Big Hosmer and Little Hosmer lakes ($10/adults, $5 students and seniors). The circuit is tracked for classic Nordic skiing, but the outdoor center is best known as a skate-skiing destination, and you might find you're sharing the trails and lodge with some of New England's most elite skate skiers. Rental equipment is available, and there's a small café in the lodge, which also welcomes skiers to bring their own food to the simple space.

In summer months, the property opens to hikers, runners, and mountain bikers with paths that seem to go on forever (free entry in summer). The Outdoor Center runs many programs and classes focusing on Nordic skiing, running, and **sculling;** sculls are available to rent once you've taken a lesson or proved your skills during a flip test.

Bonnieview Farm

Right on Craftsbury Common, **Bonnieview Farm** (2228 S. Albany Rd., Craftsbury Common, 802/755-6878, www.bonnieview.org, open anytime, call before visiting) makes beautiful cheeses from unpasteurized sheep's milk. Varieties include Ewe's Feta, a creamy raw sheep's milk cheese, Mossend Blue, a natural rind blue cheese, and Coomersdale, a semi-hard cheese with a natural rind and nutty flavor. It's a treat when farmers Neil and Kristen have a chance to show you a bit of the 470-acre plot, which is covered in fluffy sheep, and lambing season on the farm is as cute at the Kingdom gets.

Eden Ethical Dogsledding

Learn to mush with the teams at **Eden Ethical Dogsledding** (1390 Square Rd., Eden, 802/635-9070, www.edendogsledding.com, dogsledding for Vermonters/out-of-state from $350/425, dog carting from $295), and you'll be flying through forested trails with a champion dogsledder. The owner, Jim Blair, places the focus on education, and the tours are a great chance to pick his brain about everything from pack dynamics to sledding techniques.

Hill Farmstead Brewery

Supplicants wait in line from one to four hours to pick up a jug from **Hill Farmstead Brewery** (403 Hill Rd., Greensboro Bend, 802/533-7450, www.hillfarmstead.com, noon-5pm Wed.-Sat.), a testament to great beer, scarcity, and hype, not necessarily in that order. Brewer Shaun Hill works on his grandfather's farm, and beers like Abner, Anna, and Arthur are named for his ancestors; he also has a "philosophical series," which includes Beyond Good and Evil, and Birth of Tragedy, named for works by the nihilist writer Nietzsche. Fancy names aside, the beer is delicious, and Hill Farmstead has been named Best Brewery in the World several times. The retail store is open to the rest of the brewery, so you can glimpse the gleaming tanks where the magic happens.

Miller's Thumb

A small gallery set in a converted gristmill building, **Miller's Thumb** (14 Breezy Ave., Greensboro, 802/433-2045, www.millersthumbgallery.com, 10am-6pm daily mid-May-Oct.) is a lovely spot for browsing work by local artists that ranges from fine art to clothes and crafts.

Caledonia Spirits

The Romans called Scotland Caledonia, and Scottish settlers brought the musical name to the rolling county that stretches from Lake Willoughby to Lake Groton. A few of the transplants brought stills, too, and Hardwick's **Caledonia Spirits** (46 Log Yard Dr., Hardwick, 802/472-8000, www.caledoniaspirits.com, noon-5pm daily, free tastings) was founded by Todd Hardie, a beekeeper and descendant of Scottish distillers. The distillery is now run by distiller Ryan Christian, and the award-winning distillery produces some of the state's best spirits, including an unusual barrel-aged gin called Tom Cat. Sample a bit of everything at the small tasting room; if things are quiet, someone is usually happy to show you around the working distillery, where vats of honey ferment into mead and a column still towers to the ceiling.

Shopping

With a motto like, "If you can't find it here, you probably don't need it," **Willey's Store** (7 Breezy Ave., Greensboro, 802/533-2554, 7am-6pm Mon.-Fri., 8am-6pm Sat.-Sun.) had better deliver the goods—and it does, with vast shelf space holding everything from cast-iron bakeware and nifty tools to flypaper and organic produce. Willey's also happens to be among the best places in the state to shop for the locally produced Jasper Hill cheese, which racks up awards around the country, and there is an incredible selection of beers, including some from nearby Hill Farmstead Brewery.

In Craftsbury, gossip and groceries are always available at the **Craftsbury General Store** (118 S. Craftsbury Rd., Craftsbury, 802/586-2440, www.craftsburygeneralstore.com, 7am-8pm daily), which has country tables to linger with a cup of coffee, and just about everything else. Baby food, oil paintings, and DVDs fill the shelves, and the deli has plenty of appealing options for picnics. Wednesday nights, the store hosts **Globe Trotting Dinners,** with meals from around the world.

Food

There are no restaurants in Craftsbury or Greensboro, but there's prepared food available at the **Craftsbury General Store** (118 S. Craftsbury Rd., Craftsbury, 802/586-2440, www.craftsburygeneralstore.com, 7am-8pm daily) and **Willey's Store** (7 Breezy Ave., Greensboro, 802/533-2554, 7am-6pm Mon.-Fri., 8am-6pm Sat.-Sun.). Nearby Hardwick and Glover have appealing eateries.

Homey decor matches home-style food at **Connie's Kitchen** (4 S. Main St., Hardwick, 802/472-6607, 6:30am-2pm Mon.-Fri., 7am-2pm Sat., $2-8). Whoopie pies, doughnuts, and homemade bread are a nostalgic treat, and breakfast sandwiches, burritos, daily soup specials, and other simple fare are reliable and tasty.

The cozy booths at **The Village Restaurant** (74 South Main St., Hardwick, 802/472-5701, 6am-8pm daily, $5-18) give the light-filled diner an old-fashioned feel. Most tables have views of the Lamoille River. Great home fries, corned beef hash, and egg breakfasts are the morning mainstays, with plenty of sandwiches and salads at lunch. Weekend nights are a bit fancier, and onion rings give way to prime rib and chicken marsala.

An outpost of the Montpelier-based flatbread business, **Positive Pie** (87 S. Main St., Hardwick, 802/472-7126, www.positivepie.com, 11:30am-9pm Sun.-Thurs., 11:30pm-9:30pm Fri.-Sat., $10-20) has hand-tossed, thin crust pizza along with a menu of pasta, salads, and burgers. The pizza is usually great, and there's an excellent beer list, but service can be shaky on busy nights, making for long waits.

British-style cream tea is served in a flower-filled haven at **Perennial Pleasures Nursery and Tea Garden** (63 Brickhouse Rd., East Hardwick, 802/472-5104, www.perennialpleasures.net, noon-4pm Tues.-Sun. late May-early Sept., $10-25). Homemade scones and other dainties—both sweet and savory—are served on china, with preserves and whipped cream. Reservations are required.

Accommodations

The **Craftsbury Outdoor Center** (535 Lost Nation Rd., Craftsbury Common, 802/586-7767, www.craftsbury.com, $195-310, extra person $80, extra child 7-12 $40) offers very simple lodging on their expansive property, which includes three wholesome, well-prepared meals in their on-site dining room; apartment-style accommodations and private cabins are also available ($250-380). There is no cell service at the Craftsbury Outdoor Center, but landlines are available for guest use.

With a sandy beach on Caspian Lake, **The Highland Lodge** (1608 Craftsbury Rd., Greensboro, www.highlandlodge.com, $120-230) is a great bet for families, as their kitchen-equipped cottages sleep up to eight people ($25 extra pp above five). Facilities are basic and rooms are plain, but the crystal clear lake is sublime on a hot summer day. The lodge has kayaks, canoes, and paddleboats for rent.

In a gorgeously restored Victorian, **The Kimball House** (173 Glenside Ave., Hardwick, 802/472-6228, www.kimballhouse.com, $99-119) has the feel of a haven. Rooms are old-fashioned and comfortable, and the owners, Sue and Todd, are gracious hosts. The home-cooked breakfast is a highlight, and a perch on the wide porch is a glorious spot to watch the sun rise and set.

SPORTS AND RECREATION

Biking

The **Lamoille Valley Rail Trail** (www.lvrt.org) will eventually stretch 93 miles from the Connecticut River Valley to Lake Champlain, but the existing 17-mile section between West Danville and St. Johnsbury is great for a day of riding. The crushed stone surface is suitable for everything from road bikes with slightly wider tires to mountain bikes, and it winds over a series of country roads and through thick forest. It's worth bringing the trail map that's downloadable on the website, as it's possible to lose your bearings while making road crossings. To ride from West Danville, park across from the general store by Joe's Pond, where a number of sites are adjacent to the path. The ride is very pleasant as an out-and-back, or you can make a longer day of it by looping back through the small roads north of Danville and St. Johnsbury.

Groton is a great place to access the partially completed **Cross Vermont Trail** (www.crossvermont.org), which will create an east-west link between Burlington and Newbury, a rural community on the eastern edge of the state. The trail will use old rail beds, new trails, and sections of Class 4 roads—that's the local designation for old dirt roads that are no longer maintained by the state. In Groton, the Cross Vermont Trail follows the old Montpelier & Wells River Railroad, once a narrow-gauge steam train that ran from 1867 to 1956. Best suited to mountain bikes, a 12.74-mile section passes through Groton State Forest between the towns of Groton and Marshfield, passing a series of campgrounds along the way. From the Groton end, the trail begins at the junction of Highways 302 and 232, heads north past Ricker Pond and Kettle Pond, then emerges at the Marshfield Town Office (122 School St.), where daytime parking is available. For complete trail maps, visit the Cross Vermont Trail website.

Hiking

BARR HILL

The **Barr Hill Natural Area** (1521 Barr Hill Rd., Greensboro, www.nature.org) is a 256-acre preserve owned by the Nature Conservancy and a fine place for a stroll. The gentle trail can be walked as a 0.3- or a 0.8-mile loop through red spruce and hardwood forests that have very fine views of the northern Green Mountains. From Willey's Store in downtown Greensboro, drive north on Wilson Street for 0.1 mile; then bear right onto Lauredon Avenue; at 0.6 miles, bear left onto Barr Hill Road. The road dead-ends in a parking area and trailhead and a sign points to the beginning of the trail.

GROTON STATE FOREST

The expansive Groton State Forest covers 26,000 acres and contains seven state parks that are thick with trees, broken only by secluded lakes and granite outcroppings. There are hikes throughout the forest, but one of the most popular is the easy walk to **Owl's Head,** a three-mile round-trip that takes about 1.5 hours. The granite-topped summit offers views of Kettle Pond to the west and Lake Groton to the southeast, and if you arrive in August, you may find a ripe crop of wild blueberries on top. The trailhead is signposted from Campground B at **New Discovery State Park** (4239 Rte. 232, Marshfield, 802/426-3042, https://vtstateparks.com/newdiscovery.html).

An excellent kid-friendly hike skirts **Kettle Pond,** a gentle, three-mile walk with very little elevation gain. The trailhead is at the Kettle Pond Group Camping Area (6993 State Forest Rd., Groton, 802/426-3042, https://vtstateparks.com/kettlepond.html). Get information on hiking and other recreation at the **Groton Nature Center** (1595 Boulder Beach Rd., Groton, 802/584-3827, https://vtstateparks.com/groton-nature.html, 2pm-6pm Wed.-Thurs., 10am-4pm Fri., 10am-6pm Sat., 9am-2pm Sun., Memorial Day-Columbus Day).

Skiing and Snowshoeing

The area's premier cross-country skiing is at the **Craftsbury Outdoor Center** (535 Lost Nation Rd., Craftsbury Common, 802/586-7767, www.craftsbury.com), but there are about four miles of maintained Nordic trails at **Seyon Ranch State Park** (2967 Seyon Pond Rd., Groton, 802/584-3829, https://vtstateparks.com/seyon.html, $4) as well as a snowshoe-only trail that wind through thick forest to Noyes Pond.

In the winter months when maple production is slow, Ruth and Glenn Goodrich lead guided snowshoeing tours on their 900 acres of property at **Goodrich's Maple Farm** (2427 Rte. 2, Cabot, 800/639-1854, www.goodrichmaplefarm.com). Trips include bird-watching and a warm fireside lunch beneath the trees.

Boating and Swimming

This region is speckled with lakes and ponds, many with public swimming areas, and river swimming spots abound. The best way to find a swimming hole is always to ask a local, but you can't go wrong at **Joe's Pond** in Danville (Rte. 15 and Rte. 2), **Kettle Pond** (6993 State Forest Rd., Groton, 802/426-3042, https://vtstateparks.com/kettlepond.html) in Groton State Forest, or **Boulder Beach State Park** (2278 Boulder Beach Rd., Groton, 802/584-3823, https://vtstateparks.com/boulder.html). Boats are available to rent at all the parks in Groton State Forest.

GETTING THERE AND AROUND

To drive to St. Johnsbury from the south, take I-91 north (60 mi., 1 hr.) from White River Junction. From Montpelier, you are better off leaving the interstate and cutting across the Kingdom on U.S. 2 east to Cabot (20 mi., 40 min.) or St. Johnsbury (40 mi., 1 hr.). From St. J, drive west on U.S. 2 to Danville (8 mi., 15 min.) and Cabot (20 mi., 25 min.). From Cabot, drive north on Routes 215 and 15 to Hardwick (12 mi., 25 min.). From Hardwick, it's another 10 miles (20 min.) up Route 14 to Craftsbury. To get to Greensboro from Craftsbury, take Creek Road to Ketchum Hill Road, which turns into Town Highway 23. Turn left (east) onto Town Highway 5 to Greensboro (8 mi., 20 min.). Peacham is south of Danville, which is on Route 2 (8 mi. west of St. Johnsbury). From Danville, turn south onto Peacham Road (7 mi., 14 min.).

Heart of the Kingdom

Rolling farmland and pure lakes enchant in the central part of the Northeast Kingdom, where you can escape modern life and cell service on a maze of rural roads. The landscape is broken only by the tiny towns that are the heart of Kingdom culture and make the ideal jumping-off places for outdoor adventures. Pack hiking boots, skis, a bike, and canoe paddles to explore every nook and cranny of this scenic and rugged region—but if you're planning a trip to Lake Willoughby's nude South Beach, all you really need is sunscreen. This region also includes the extraordinary Kingdom Trails, a sprawling network of mountain bike trails that has put tiny East Burke on New England's adventure map.

EAST BURKE AND LYNDONVILLE

The tiny town of **East Burke** is a mountain bike mecca. A hundred miles of trails swoop through rolling fields and forests with splendid views of the northern mountains, and on busy weekends, bicycles outnumber cars on the back roads of this farm community. The Kingdom Trails are remarkable, and not just because of flowy, bermed descents and technical single-track. The trail system is run by a nonprofit and supported by an unusual alliance of local landowners who've agreed to open their property to cyclists. The organization is committed to keeping the trails affordable and have created routes for all skill levels, and just across the road at Burke Mountain Resort, lift-served mountain bike trails offer serious downhilling.

Lyndonville is Burke's laid-back, country-mouse cousin, as well as the self-dubbed "Covered Bridge Capital of the Northeast Kingdom." While the town is imbued with student energy from Lyndon State College, this is quiet living at its most content, with backcountry roads that just cry out for a long, relaxed road trip to the middle of nowhere, summer concerts on the common, and an annual county fair that is one of the oldest in the state.

★ Kingdom Trails Network

This is the best riding in Vermont. Carriage

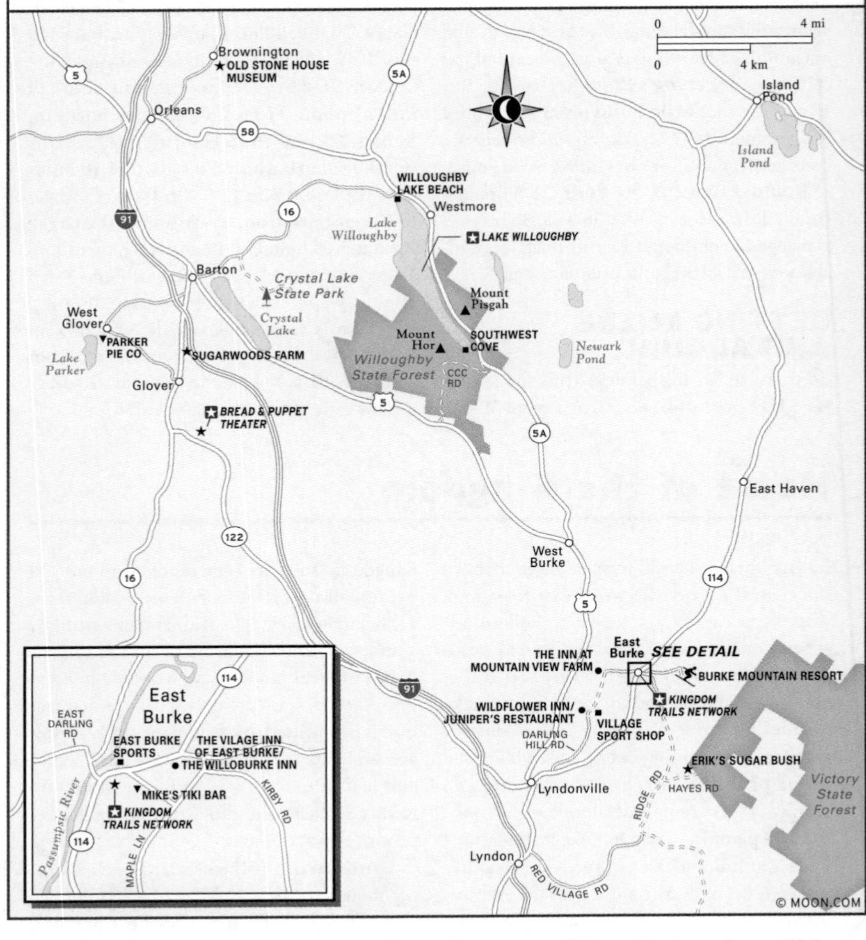

paths, railroad rights-of-way, and forest trails have been stitched together into the **Kingdom Trails Network** (Kingdom Trails Association, 478 Rte. 114, East Burke, 802/626-0737, www.kingdomtrails.org, $15), a cyclist's wonderland. The **Tap and Die** trail is a rolling hoot as riders whip over quick ascents and swerve through curves lined with high berms. **Sidewinder** is a flowy classic, and one of the Northeast's most exhilarating rides. There are trails for every ability, and the mountain bike enthusiasts that staff the visitors center can tell you where to start and what to avoid. The trails leave from the village area in East Burke, just behind Burke General Store; in the winter they're accessible on cross-country skis.

Mountain bikes of all kinds are available to rent in East Burke's two bike shops. Both stock a variety of clipless pedals for cyclists who've brought their own shoes; each of the shops has a stash of fat bikes with cushy, cartoonish tires. **East Burke Sports** (439 Rte. 114, 802/626-3215, www.eastburkesports.com, 8:30am-5:30pm daily, $50-90/day) carries a variety of bikes from Trek, Salsa, and Santa Cruz. The trailside **Village Sport Shop** (2075 Darling Hill Rd., Lyndonville, 802/626-8444, www.villagesportshop.com, 9am-6pm Mon.-Fri., 8:15am-5:30pm Sat., 8:15am-5pm Sun., $40-90/day) stocks Surly, Giant, Pivot, and Scott.

Burke Mountain Resort

If all that climbing seems like too much work, the lifts at **Burke Mountain Resort** (223 Sherburne Lodge Rd., East Burke, 802/626-7300, www.skiburke.com) will whisk you—and your mountain bike, skis, or snowboard—to the top of Burke Mountain, which dominates the skyline. The Burke Mountain Resort trails used to be connected with the Kingdom Trails, but they've since split, and you need a separate ticket to access these with a bicycle ($40/$30 Fri.-Sun., adult/child).

In the winter, Burke Mountain Resort is home to the Burke Mountain Academy, where young ski racers have been training since 1970; the school's alumni include more than 30 Olympians. You'll spot the students streaking past you on the 50 trails and glades that sprawl over 2,011 feet of vertical rise ($69 adults, $49 juniors 6-18, $59 college students, under 5 free). The on-site Nordic center is free to access.

Erik's Sugar Bush

Erik's Sugar Bush (273 Back of the Moon Rd., Kirby, 802/535-5865, www.erikssugarbush.com, hours vary, call for availability) produces maple syrup the natural way from 2,000 trees on Kirby Mountain. Tours of the process and meet-and-greets with the farm's oxen are offered during sugaring season, when the whole family helps tap trees, collect sap with the team of oxen, and feed the fire in the evaporator. Make like a local and stand around the sugarhouse, tasting the day's syrup. The Waring family also makes a range of products with their syrup, like maple candy and jelly, as well as maple cream, which may be the most addictive maple of all.

Entertainment and Events

Tractor pulls, pig races, and alpaca shearing are on the schedule at the **Caledonia County Fair** (802/626-8104, www.vtfair.com, late Aug.), which has taken place in Lyndonville for more than 150 years. Just in time for Christmas, the **Burklyn Arts Festival** (early Dec.) brings out the creativity of the Kingdom for a juried craft competition and gift sale in Lyndonville.

Shopping

Need to gear up before hitting the slopes? Do it at **East Burke Sports** (439 Rte. 114, East Burke, 802/626-3215, www.eastburkesports.com, 8:30am-5:30pm daily). The shop sells whatever you need for cycling, skiing, hiking, camping, or snowboarding and has a well-trained staff happy to help with the selection process.

Invented in 1899 for use on cow udders, the now-famous **Bag Balm** (91 Williams St., Lyndonville, 844/424-2256, www.bagbalm.com, by appt.) product is used on humans and creatures alike to soothe cuts, skin irritations, and abrasions. Admiral Byrd packed some on a 1937 trip to the North Pole, and it protected the paws of search and rescue dogs in the aftermath of September 11, 2001. It's made right in Lyndonville at the Dairy Association Co., where you can swing by for a visit and pick up one of the distinctive green cans.

Browsing is encouraged at **Green Mountain Books & Prints** (1055 Broad St., Lyndonville, 802/626-5051, 10am-6pm Mon.-Fri., 9am-5pm Sat.), a quiet shop stocked to its gills with used and rare books and old maps and prints.

Food

EAST BURKE

Come early to snag a bag of macaroons or lemon squares from ★ **Aunt Dee Dee's Homemade VT Baked Goods** (185 Mountain Rd., East Burke, 802/535-1206,

The Bridges of Lyndonville

Randall Bridge

Known as the covered bridge capital of the Northeast Kingdom, Lyndonville is home to five beautiful specimens, two of which are still working. And while modern-day admirers may view the structures as quaint relics, they were an absolute necessity when most of them were constructed in the 19th century; uncovered wooden bridges deteriorate quickly from the elements, and a covering protects them—and extends their lifetime. Lyndonville's bridges are well kept, and even those that aren't operational are still excellent examples of their kind.

- **Chamberlain Mill Bridge** (South Wheelock Rd.) is a Queenpost bridge with unusual gables.
- **Miller's Run Bridge** (Center St.) is a reconstruction from the mid-1990s.
- **Randall Bridge** (off Rte. 114), built in 1867, is a 68-foot-long bridge that sports very open construction, so taking a gander at the internal structure is easy.
- **Sanborn Bridge** (at the junction of Rtes. 5, 122, and 114) dates back to 1867.
- **Schoolhouse Bridge** (S. Wheelock Rd.), built in 1879, is a 42-foot-long structure that replaced another bridge original to the spot.

8am-2pm Fri.-Sun., $2-7), based in a home on the mountain access road. The pastries are a special treat, but the bakery also turns out racks of fresh bread, and hearty sandwiches that are perfect for a day on the trail.

Right in the center of town, the **Northeast Kingdom Country Store** (466 Rte. 114, East Burke, 802/626-4611, www.nekcountrystore.com, 7am-7pm Mon.-Thurs., 7am-8pm Fri., 8am-8pm Sat., 8am-6pm Sun., $3-9) has a café menu of salads, soups, and sandwiches and makes a convenient lunch spot if you're riding the trails. Hearty breakfast sandwiches and burritos and house-baked desserts are also available.

Excellent coffee and breakfast sandwiches are the draw at **Café Lotti** (603 Rte. 114, East Burke, 802/437-3633, www.cafelottivt.com, 7am-4pm Mon.-Thurs., 7am-5pm Fri.-Sun., $3-9), which is right in the Burke village. While most swing by for a quick shot of espresso before hitting Kingdom Trails, comfy seating and a sunny, inviting space make this a nice place to linger.

A great sit-down alternative to Burke's slew of casual cafés, the **Foggy Goggle Osteria** (66 Belden Hill Rd., East Burke, 802/427-3500, 4pm-9pm Mon. and Thurs.-Sat., Sun. brunch 10am-1pm, dinner $10-30, brunch $8-15) is a mostly Italian dinner spot in a homey converted farmhouse. Italian American classics like chicken marsala and eggplant parmesan share a menu with burgers, house-smoked meats, and even some pad thai. Sunday brunch is a hearty affair, with generous omelets, stacks of pancakes, and steak and eggs.

Fake palms and steel drums give ★ **Mike's Tiki Bar** (44 Belden Hill Rd., East Burke, www.mikestikibar.com, 3pm-close Mon.-Fri., noon-close Sat.-Sun. May-Oct., $3-8) a bit of island spirit. It's the life of the riding scene and even has an on-site shower to wash off the trail dust before sidling up to the thatch-covered bar. Cheap beer and a volleyball net complete the "spring break in the backwoods" vibe, and in the parking lot, the **Vermont Food Truck Company** (802/626-1177, 11am-9pm daily May-Oct., $4-9) serves burgers and burritos to the hungry crowd.

LYNDONVILLE

Lyndonville's eclectic-international **Café Sweet Basil** (32 Depot St., Lyndonville, 802/626-9713, www.cafesweetbasil.com, lunch 11:30am-2pm Wed.-Fri., dinner 5:30pm-8:30pm Wed.-Sat., $9-13) is crowded and cozy, with a sweetly small-town feel. Much of the dinner menu is Mexican-inspired, with quesadillas and flautas of all kinds. Salads and sandwiches are on offer at lunchtime, when the tables fill with locals. Reservations are recommended at dinner.

Slide onto a stool at the **Miss Lyndonville Diner** (686 Broad St., Lyndonville, 802/626-9890, 6am-8pm Mon.-Thurs., 6am-9pm Fri.-Sat., 7am-8pm Sun., $7-12) for great, true-to-style versions of classic American dishes. Breakfast—which is served all day—comes with fat slices of toasted, homemade bread, the corned beef hash is crisp and savory, and the juicy hamburgers have serious heft. It's worth saving room for a fluffy piece of old-fashioned diner pie: chocolate cream pie and maple cream pie are especial favorites.

Accommodations

Lyndonville is a small town with limited lodging options. The Kingdom Trails system passes right by **The Wildflower Inn** (2059 Darling Hill Rd., Lyndonville, 802/626-8310, www.wildflowerinn.com, $229-259), which is perched on a ridgeline with sweeping views. Rooms are simple and some bathrooms are dated, but it's still a lovely place to watch the day begin and end. Breakfast is included, and guests can take their pick from the menu at the on-site Juniper's Restaurant. Check the website for discounts, including a mountain bike rate that includes trail passes. The inn has a two-night minimum in the summer and on weekends year-round. (It's worth noting that the Wildflower Inn made headlines in 2011 when they refused to host the wedding reception of a same-sex couple. The owners lost a lawsuit, paid a settlement, and no longer host weddings or wedding receptions, but insist that their inn welcomes guests of all sexual orientations.)

Just up the road in East Burke, the ★ **Inn at Mountain View Farm** (3383 Darling Hill Rd., East Burke, 800/572-4509, www.innmtnview.com, mid-May-Oct., $215-375) has equally stunning views. The inn is on a 440-acre property that was once a creamery: The historical farm buildings are in mint condition and offer a glimpse of 19th-century agricultural life. The rooms are decorated with sweet country style, and the buildings are full of unusual antiques. Farm-style breakfasts and afternoon tea are included. This is also the home of the Mountain View Farm Animal Sanctuary, and guests can visit the rescued horses, goats, pigs, cows, and sheep that live out their years in the scenic spot.

Casual and convivial, ★ **The Village Inn at East Burke** (606 Rte. 114, East Burke, 802/626-3161, www.villageinnofeastburke.com, rooms $100-110, studio $125,

3-bedroom apartment from $150) has seven welcoming rooms and a three-bedroom apartment in the heart of the town. A full kitchen is available for guest use, and rooms include a home-style hot breakfast. The river wraps around the back of the property, so you can cool off in the inn's own swimming hole, or opt for the Jacuzzi in the well-kept garden. There are also fire pits and picnic areas provided, and pets are welcome with the innkeeper's permission.

Also centrally located, **The Willoburke Inn** (638 Rte. 114, East Burke, 802/427-3333, www.willoburke.com, $165-195) has elegant, laid-back style and a charming garden beside Dishmill Brook. A continental breakfast is included, and the inn's common spaces are a relaxing place to unwind after a day on the trails.

CAMPING

A forested network 25 sites and five lean-tos, **Burke Mountain Campground** (Burke Mountain Rd., East Burke, 802/626-7400, www.skiburke.com, May-mid-Oct., tent sites $35-40, lean-tos $45-50) has easy bike access to the Kingdom Trails and the Burke Mountain Resort trails. The sites themselves are somewhat no-frills—and there's just one shower area for the entire campground—but reservations at the campground do get you access to the pool and hot tub at the Burke Hotel, just up the access road. Dogs are allowed on leash, and there's Wi-Fi in the campground office.

With just two sites, you need to plan ahead if you want to snag a spot at ★ **Camp Kent** (201 East Darling Hill Rd., East Burke, 802/777-7123, www.campkentvermont.wixsite.com/info, Mon.-Wed. $35, Thurs.-Sun. $50). Once a family camp spot, Camp Kent has been upgraded with wood-framed tent platforms, picnic tables, fire rings, portable toilets, and room for several tents (the sites can be booked for up to six people). The "camperside" site has room for a trailer or pop-up, while "trailside" is right at the bottom of Kitchell Trail for a ride-in, ride-out place to sleep. Camp Kent has no running water, but the sites are stocked with five gallon jugs.

Information and Services

The **Burke Area Chamber of Commerce** (802/626-4124, www.burkevermont.com) runs an information kiosk at the corner of Route 5 and Route 5A. Wi-Fi is available at **Bailey's and Burke Country Store** (466 Rte. 114, 802/626-4611). The **Kingdom Trails Welcome Center** (478 Rte. 114, East Burke, 802/626-0737, www.kingdomtrails.org, 8am-4pm Mon.-Fri.) is the nerve center of the Kingdom Trails and the place to go for passes, maps, and advice. In the winter, head to **The Nordic Adventure Center** (2072 Darling Hill Rd., Lyndonville, 802/626-0737, www.kingdomtrails.org, 8am-4pm daily Dec.-Apr.).

On I-91 South, the state of Vermont's **Lyndonville Information Center** (I-91 S. between exits 24 and 25, 802/626-9669) has information on the entire Northeast Kingdom. The **Lyndon Area Chamber of Commerce** (802/626-9696, www.lyndonvermont.com) runs an information booth on Memorial Drive right off exit 24 in downtown Lyndonville.

Several banks are located in Lyndonville town center, including **Union Bank** (183 Depot St., 802/626-3100, 8am-5pm Mon.-Thurs., 8am-6pm Fri., 8:30am-noon Sat.) and **Community National Bank** (1033 Broad St., 802/626-1200). Pharmacy needs can be taken care of at **Lyndonville Pharmacy** (101 Depot St., 802/626-6966) as well as **Rite-Aid Pharmacy** (412 Broad St., 802/626-4366, 8am-8:30pm Mon.-Sat., 9am-6pm Sun., pharmacy 8am-8pm Mon.-Fri., 9am-6pm Sat., 9am-5pm Sun.).

LAKE WILLOUGHBY AND GLOVER

Flanked by high cliffs and dense forest, glacier-carved **Lake Willoughby** is among the most dramatic places in Vermont. The twin

1: the Inn at Mountain View Farm in East Burke; **2:** sheer cliffs framing the deep water of Lake Willoughby

1912
the INN at MOUNTAIN VIEW FARM
1
2

peaks of Mount Pisgah and Mount Hor cast dramatic shadows on the water, peregrine falcons nest high on the mountains, and the steep, forested hills turn brilliant in the fall. Winter brings ice climbers to the Lake Willoughby cliffs, while the surrounding countryside holds almost endless cross-country and backcountry skiing. Nearby is the tiny farming community of **Glover,** which is also home to the one-of-a-kind Bread & Puppet Theater, whose revolutionary plays, protests, and papier-mâché have influenced generations of leftist activists. Fifteen minutes west of Lake Willoughby, the former mill town of **Barton** once produced everything from doors to bowling pins. The community has gone quiet over the years, but you're likely to pass through on your way to some of the Kingdom's most memorable sights; for a look at a thoroughly untouristy town, stop for a stroll as you're driving by.

★ Lake Willoughby

The clear, chilly waters of this spectacular lake plunge to a depth of 320 feet, and the beauty of the spot has drawn nature lovers for many years. Adorably compact steamboats shuttled tourists across the lake in the late 1800s, and in the early 1900s, the poet Robert Frost and his family camped out the lake's northern shore, writing: "a fair, pretty sheet of water, Our Willoughby! How did you hear of it? I expect, though, everyone's heard of it." Despite its famous landscape, Lake Willoughby never seems to be overcrowded, and the area's sheer remoteness makes it feel like a revelation when you arrive from the hills to the lakeshore.

On the lake's northern extreme, **Willoughby Lake Beach** has a short, exposed stretch of sand right next to the road, a parking area with portable toilets, and great views along the water. Even more scenic, though, is **Southwest Cove,** the little beach on the south end of the lake. A short walking path leads to a series of rocks that are perfect for picnics and sunbathing, then descends a short stone staircase to a little nude beach. (The existence of the nude beach is perpetually being debated, so be sure to pay attention to any posted rules.)

The lake's eastern shore is dominated by **Mount Pisgah,** the western by **Mount Hor,** dramatic peaks that are both named for mountains in the Torah, Bible, and Qur'an—some scholars think that Pisgah referred to modern-day Jordan's Mount Nebo, where Moses is believed to have first sighted the Promised Land, and the tomb of Moses's brother Aaron is thought to be located on one of the region's two historic Mount Hors. Both peaks make delightful, if vigorous, **hikes.**

Much of the southern end of the lake, including the two main peaks, is surrounded by **Willoughby State Forest,** an area that used to be farmland, and was reforested by the Civilian Conservation Corps in the 1930s. A dirt road winds up into the forest from the lake, which becomes a fabulous network of maintained **cross-country ski trails** in the winter.

TOP EXPERIENCE

★ Bread & Puppet Theater

"Art is for kitchens!" proudly trumpets one poster for sale at **Bread & Puppet Theater** (753 Heights Rd., Glover, 802/525-3031, www.breadandpuppet.org, 10am-6pm daily June-Oct., free), a barn-cum-museum, and the home of a performing puppet troupe. With its mission that art should be accessible to the masses, B&P began more than 50 years ago with counterculture hand- and rod-puppet performances on New York's Lower East Side. Founder Peter Schumann moved back to the land in the 1970s, taking over an old farm in the middle of the Kingdom and presenting bigger and more elaborate political puppet festivals every summer. Along the way, the troupe virtually invented a new art form, pioneering the construction of larger-than-life papier-mâché puppets of gods and goddesses and other figures that now regularly spice up the atmosphere at left-of-center political protests around the world. On the grounds, the old barn has been transformed into a museum filled with 10-foot-tall characters from past plays, along with photographs and descriptions of the political context of the times. Downstairs is a "cheap art" store, where you can buy original works for $5 or less—and even hang them in your kitchen.

The troupe still performs on its original farm stage in Glover throughout the summer, and the rollicking shows are a classic Vermont experience that's truly not to be missed. Since the audience sits on the grassy hill that wraps around the outdoor stage, it's very worth bringing a blanket or low chairs, as well as a hat to keep off the sun.

Old Stone House Museum

Constructed of heavy stone granite blocks, the **Old Stone House Museum** (109 Old Stone House Rd., Brownington, 802/754-2022, www.oldstonehousemuseum.org, 11am-5pm Wed.-Sun. mid-May-mid-Oct., $10 adults, $5 students, free for active military and their families) once served as a boys' dormitory and school. Now a local history museum, it houses the collection of the Orleans Historical Society, including Victorian-era furniture and cooking implements and some of the original schoolbooks from the academy library. Behind the museum is a wooden observation platform on Prospect Hill that commands the surrounding farm country.

Events

A "grand cavalcade" of livestock and farm machinery kicks off the annual **Orleans County Fair** (Barton, 802/525-3555, www.orleanscountyfair.net, mid-Aug.), which features a demolition derby and country music performances among its attractions.

One of the most active Native American tribes in the Northeast, the Clan of the Hawk, Northeast Wind Council of the Abenaki Nation of Vermont, holds its **Clan of the Hawk Pow Wow** (123 Evansville Rd., Rte. 58, Brownington, 802/754-2817, www.theclanofthehawk.org) the first weekend in August, an open-to-the-public event with drumming, dancing, and sales of traditional crafts.

Food

★ **The Parker Pie Co.** (161 Country Rd., West Glover, 802/525-3366, www.parkerpie.com, 11am-9pm Tues.-Thurs. and Sun., 11am-10pm Fri.-Sat., $8-16) is a legend. It's known for great pizzas, but it's the vibe that counts—Parker Pie is a timeworn local hangout and a destination in one, and the best place to take in Glover's eclectic, backwoods scene. It's an intriguing mix of people: Homesteading academics, dyed-in-the-wool Vermonters, and unreconstructed hippies share tables on Saturday nights. Salads, sandwiches, and calzones round out the pizza menu, and the chef keeps it fresh with burger nights and tacos. The bar's got some of the Kingdom's best selection of Hill Farmstead beers on tap and hosts regular evenings of trivia and music.

The adorable **Busy Bee Diner** (2985 Glover St., Glover, 802/525-4800, 7am-2pm daily, $3-9) only has 20 seats, but it's worth the wait for hefty plates of breakfast classics and sandwiches. Sidle up to the counter for a cup of coffee and a homemade doughnut, stack of strawberry-topped pancakes, or a slice of strawberry-rhubarb pie mounded high with whipped cream. The Formica counter is more "grandma's kitchen" than "classic diner," which only adds to its charm.

With a sweet location in a Barton village house, **Parson's Corner** (14 Glover Rd., Barton, 802/525-4500, 5am-2pm Wed.-Mon., $4-10) has tall windows to let in the sunshine, painted booths, and a stool-lined counter. The menu is "Diner Fare with Culinary Enthusiasm," which translates to simple food prepared with care. Breakfasts and lunch are served throughout the day; eggs all ways, home fries, and pancakes line up beside green tomato BLTs, soups, and salads. They make their own ice cream, which is outrageous atop the sweet bread pudding.

There's not much to be found on the shores of Lake Willoughby, which makes the otherwise unremarkable **Willoughby Lake**

Store (2003 Rte. 5A, Orleans, 802/525-3300, 7am-6pm Mon.-Thurs., 7am-7pm Fri.-Sat., 7am-5pm Sun.) a total bonus. There's coffee, breakfast sandwiches, beer, and basic supplies, as well as a summertime ice cream window.

Serving dinner just in the busy summer and fall months, the dining room at the WilloughVale Inn, **Gil's Bar and Grill** (793 Rte. 5A S., Westmore, 802/525-4123, www.willoughvale.com, 5pm-8pm Wed.-Sun., $13-23), has solid pub fare that includes chili, burgers, and grilled meats. The cozy dining room has views of the lake, and there's often a crowd of locals and tourists at the big wooden bar—even aside from the fact that it's the only game in town, it's welcome place to spend an evening by the lake.

Accommodations

Simple, rustic, and inexpensive, **Pine Crest Motel & Cabins** (1288 Barton-Orleans Rd., Barton, 802/525-3472, www.pinecrestmotelandcabins.com, $82-120) is Barton's sole lodging, and the most convenient to Bread & Puppet Theater. Motel rooms and cabins have names like Porcupine Palace or Raccoon Retreat, and there's a pleasantly old-fashioned feel to the place, which sprawls out beside the Barton River on the outskirts of town.

Rodgers Country Inn & Cabins (582 Rodgers Rd., West Glover, 800/729-1704, www.rodgerscountryinn.com, B&B $80, cabins $200, discounts for single-occupancy and weekly stays) is perched amidst farm fields, with two secluded cabins tucked into the nearby woods. The property is vast and has views that stretch over the countryside. The innkeepers, Jim and Nancy, prepare a home-style cooked breakfast each morning, and dinner is available for $15/adults, $7.50/children.

WilloughVale Inn & Cottages (793 Rte. 5A S., Westmore, 802/525-4123, www.willoughvale.com, rooms $119-259, cottages $329-369), perched on the shores of Lake Willoughby, is a lovely spot to watch the sun illuminate Mount Pisgah and Mount Hor. All the rooms are clean and comfortable, with tasteful decor and all the amenities. Renovations to the "luxury suites" place those rooms—which have breathtaking views, enormous fireside tubs, and cushy king beds—in a category of their own. The cottages have fully appointed kitchens and are a good value for families. The WilloughVale has an on-site restaurant, and a continental breakfast is included with all stays in the main inn.

CAMPING

On the shores of Crystal Lake, **Bel-view Campground** (620 Eastern Ave., Barton, 802/525-3242, www.belviewcampgroundvt.com, mid-May-mid-Oct., $30 tent, $40 motorhome) is familiar and simple, and a pretty brook runs by the property. By Lake Willoughby, **White Caps Campground** (5659 Rte. 5A, Westmore, 802/467-3345, www.whitecapscampground.com, $25 tent, $40 RV with water and electric, $50 RV with full hookups) also has a no-frills "dry cabin," with access to the campground facilities. Spaces are tightly packed, but you can't beat the location. Just up the road, **Will-O-Wood Campground** (227 Will-O-Wood Ln., Brownington, 802/525-3575, www.will-o-woodcampground.com, $28 tent, $30 RV with hookups) is a friendly and convivial option and a short drive from the lakeshore.

Free, primitive camping is also available in the **Willoughby State Forest**, where the dirt CCC road off Route 5A leads to a series of pullouts. To comply with the state regulations on camping, sites must be 1,000 feet from traveled roads, 100 feet from water, and 200 feet from trails, and camping is only allowed below 2,500 feet of elevation, so the high parts of Mount Pisgah, Mount Hor, and Bald Mountain are off limits.

Information and Services

The local **Barton Chamber of Commerce** (802/239-4147, www.centerofthekingdom.com) runs three information kiosks in Barton: across from the post office, at the gas station, and at Lake Willoughby's North Beach.

Find medicines and other goods at **Kinney**

Drugs Store (16 Church St., 802/525-4098, 8am-6pm Mon.-Fri., 8am-3pm Sat., 8am-1pm Sun.), along with an authentic old-time soda fountain in back. There's also a branch of **Community National Bank** (103 Church St., 802/525-3524, 8am-5pm Mon.-Fri., 9am-noon Sat.) in town.

SPORTS AND RECREATION

The marvelous **Kingdom Trails** mountain biking area and **Burke Mountain Resort** are amazing places to get outdoors, but they're just the beginning of this area's recreation options.

Hiking

WILLOUGHBY STATE FOREST

Views of Lake Willoughby's fjord-like cliffs sustain hikers as they climb the steep trail to the top of the 2,751-foot **Mount Pisgah,** on the lake's eastern shore. The 3.9-mile round-trip **South Trail** leaves from Route 5A, just south of Willoughby's Southwest Cove, and passes peregrine falcon nesting areas on the Pulpit Rock formation on the way up. At the top, hikers must continue along a short descent to reach a panoramic vista.

Across the lake, 2,648-foot **Mount Hor** is a somewhat easier ascent, with great views that stretch to Québec's Mount Orford. To reach the trailhead from Lake Willoughby, turn right into the parking lot that's just opposite the South Trail. From there, follow the CCC road 1.8 miles (the road can be quite rough at times). Pull into a parking lot on the right, where there's a sign for the **Herbert Hawkes Trailhead.** The trail follows the ridge for 0.7 miles, then branches: Follow the left branch 0.2 miles to the summit or the right branch 0.6 miles to a pair of overlooks. (It sometimes seems that Robert Frost wrote a poem about every single thing in New England, and Mount Hor is no exception: "Great granite terraces in sun and shadow, Shelves one could rest a knee on getting up—With depths behind him sheer a hundred feet," from *The Mountain,* 1915.)

Just to the west of Willoughby, 3,315-foot **Bald Mountain** is the highest peak in the area and can be ascended in a pleasant, three-hour round-trip. To reach the trailhead from Westmore, take Long Pond Road to a parking area across from Long Pond. Four miles round-trip, the trail is mostly enclosed by forest, but hikers can climb the fire tower on the summit for 360-degree views.

Swimming

EAST BURKE AND LYNDONVILLE

The rivers that flank East Burke are full of swimming holes that are perfect for cooling off after a day on the trail—some of the village inns have their own "secret" spots, or you can just keep an eye out as you ride through the forest. Easiest and most popular, though, is the swim spot behind Ruby Lee's Ice Cream, just north of the bridge where East Darling Hill Road crosses the Passumpsic River in East Burke. It's fairly shallow, but well worth a dip.

LAKE WILLOUGHBY AND GLOVER

The two beaches on **Lake Willoughby** are the main spots for swimming here, but the water is warmer at **Crystal Lake State Park** (96 Bellwater Ave., Barton, 802/525-6205, https://vtstateparks.com/crystal.html, late May-early Sept.), which has nearly a mile of sandy beach, marked by a granite bathhouse built by the CCC, a concession area, and several dozen charcoal grills and picnic tables. Rowboats and canoes are also available for rent.

Skiing, Riding, Snowshoeing, and Fat Biking

For downhill skiing and riding, **Burke Mountain Resort** is the main destination here, but the rolling terrain of this area is filled with great cross-country access, too. In wintertime, the **Kingdom Trails** are transformed into a 9.3-mile (15-km) network of ski trails that start in the yurt at **The Nordic Adventure Center** (2059 Darling Hill Rd., Lyndonville, 802/626-0737, www.

kingdomtrails.org, 8am-4pm daily, Dec.-Apr. or when conditions allow, trail passes $15 adults, $7 youth 8-15). **Fat bikes** are not allowed on the cross-country ski trails, but 25 miles of mountain bike trails are groomed for winter fat biking—trails are closed when the snow softens too much, so call the Nordic Adventure Center before making the trek to East Burke.

A true gem for cross-country skiers is the network of trails in **Willoughby State Forest** (www.fpr.vermont.gov), which is maintained by the **Memphremagog Ski Touring Foundation** (www.mstf.net). The access point for the trails is the CCC Parking lot off Route 5A, just south of the southern edge of Lake Willoughby, and it's worth printing out a map before coming. The MSTF updates their website—albeit somewhat inconsistently—with trail conditions, but there's no office or services near the ski trails, which wind up the CCC access road into the state forest and wrap around Bartlett Mountain, with side loops that can easily fill a day of exploring. The cross-country ski trails pass the trailhead for the **Herbert Hawkes Trail** up Mount Hor, which can be followed on **snowshoes,** and just across the road from the CCC road parking lot is the **Mount Pisgah South Trail,** also popular for snowshoeing.

GETTING THERE AND AROUND

From St. Johnsbury, much of the heart of the Kingdom is accessible from I-91. For Lyndonville, take exit 23 (8 mi., 10 min.); for Glover and Barton, exit 25 (30 mi., 30 min.); and for Brownington, exit. 26 (38 mi., 43 min.). From Lyndonville, take Route 114 north to East Burke (12 mi., 20 min.).

If you must rely on public transportation, **Rural Community Transportation** (802/748-8170, www.riderct.org) runs limited shuttle bus service between St. Johnsbury (leaving from the Vermont Welcome Center) and Lyndonville.

Border Country

This northern edge of Vermont is wild and remote. Quebecois French and English mingle in diners and bars here, and Vermont's only boreal forests throw dark shade over winding roads. Before security tightened in the early 21st century, the towns in this region enjoyed a binational fluidity, with residents strolling across the international border to visit a friend or grab dinner—it was a sign of changed times when a Derby Line man was arrested in 2010 after he walked down the street into Canada to pick up a pizza.

Grand old Victorians in Derby and Newport testify to this area's affluent past, but recent decades were lean ones for much of the border region. With new lodges, lifts, and a fully enclosed water park, Jay Peak is the biggest draw in the area, but the tiny towns of Newport, Derby, and Island Pond make charming side trips, and there are ample ways to while away your time by the shores of Lake Memphremagog, whose long history includes bootleggers and a legendary lake monster. Above all, however, this wooded territory is a place to get a glimpse of Vermont as it was a generation ago, filled with wilderness, farms, and a fiercely proud rural population.

JAY PEAK AND MONTGOMERY

The town of Jay was once just a crossroads in the woods, overshadowed by the mountain that now dominates both the area's landscape and economy. **Jay Peak** is Vermont's 12th-highest mountain, but seems to scrape every bit of snow out of passing clouds; in the memorable snow year of 2014, the resort got buried under more powder than anywhere in the continental United States.

For years, it was just a classic, local hill,

but that all changed in 2008, when the resort broke ground on a $250-million renovation. These days, Jay Peak Resort's got upscale accommodations, on-site restaurants, and the Pump House, a 50,000-square-foot indoor water park with a retractable roof. At the time, the economic benefits were hard to argue with, but the whole affair turned out to be a classic Ponzi scheme—money moved from one place to another, contractors weren't paid, and in 2017, a fraud lawsuit ended in a $150-million settlement.

Despite the controversy, and local laments that Jay has lost a bit of soul, even the crustiest old-timers find it hard to complain while whipping up the mountainside in a high-speed quad. If you'd prefer to avoid the glare from those shiny new buildings, nearby **Montgomery** is a respite from Jay's frenetic pace. It's a sweet town in a green valley, with six covered bridges and a few stylish, appealing B&Bs. Winding through backyards and fields, the quiet Trout River is pocked with idyllic swimming holes where you could while away a week of summer afternoons.

★ Jay Peak Resort

The main attraction here is the skiing and riding at **Jay Peak Resort** (830 Jay Peak Rd., Jay, 802/988-2611, www.jaypeakresort.com, $84 adults, $59 seniors, $66 youth 6-18, $22 children 5 and under). Its 385 acres of terrain see an average of 377 inches of snow a year, accessible on a whopping 50 miles of trails. The glades are legendary, as is the backcountry terrain, but 40 percent of the trails are rated intermediate and 20 percent are easy, making it a relatively easy place to ski with a mixed group. Even for the Northeast Kingdom, though, Jay gets bitingly cold, so come prepared with plenty of layers.

PUMP HOUSE

Sun-starved locals—from both sides of the border—flock to the enormous **Pump House** (Hotel Jay, Slopeside Rd., 800/451-4449, www.jaypeakresort.com, $39 adults, $29 youth 4-15, under 3 free), an indoor water park within Jay Peak Resort where it's always 85 degrees. Looping waterslides, a perpetual surfing wave called the Flowrider, hot tubs, and a meandering river are all under a glass roof that lets in the sun on even the chilliest days. Towering above them is La Chute, the biggest, scariest slide of all. Riders climb into a glass-topped chamber, listen to an ominous countdown—3 ... 2 ... 1 ...—then a trapdoor opens and they plummet earthward at 45 miles per hour. The slide goes through a 360-degree rotation and ends in a water-filled trough after a *very* long six seconds.

Covered Bridges

The little town of Montgomery has no fewer than six **covered bridges,** all built between 1863 and 1890 by brothers Sheldon and Savanard Jewett. You can spot several of the bridges from the main road, or hunt them all down with a map or GPS coordinates from the **Montgomery Historical Society** (www.montgomeryhistoricalsociety.org).

Shopping

There's not much in the town of Jay, but for memorabilia, snacks, and beer, you can stop by **Jay Country Store** (1077 Rte. 242, 802/988-4040, 6am-8pm Mon.-Thurs., 6am-9pm Fri.-Sat., 7am-8pm Sun., deli $4-9). Their on-site deli has somewhat lackluster sandwiches, salads, and pizza.

Food

Housed in a former one-room schoolhouse, **The Belfry Restaurant and Pub** (Rte. 242 at Amidon Rd., Montgomery, 802/326-4400, 4pm-9pm Sun.-Thurs., 4pm-10pm Fri.-Sat., $8-20) is more like a town meeting hall. The joint teems with a blend of locals and tourists tucking into pasta dishes, Friday fish fries, and a menu of pub food. The food, in a way, is beside the point. This piece of Jay predates the new resort and is a convivial place to spend a winter evening in a wooden booth or a summer night on the patio, which has stunning views of the mountains.

In an old Montgomery house, ★ **Bernie's**

The Jay Cloud

At the wild, northern extreme of the Green Mountains, Jay Peak has a mythic pull for many East Coast skiers. The mountain seems to get more than its fair share of powder—it got buried in a record amount in the 2014-2015 season—and aficionados claim that it's light and fluffy as the stuff that lands on the Rockies. Locals swear that it's the effect of the Jay Cloud, a fluffy haze that supposedly stalls on the peak and dumps its frozen contents on happy skiers.

Even in summer months, a thick cloud can settle over Jay Peak.

Mark Breen is a meteorologist at St. Johnsbury's Fairbanks Museum whose public radio broadcasts keep locals apprised of Vermont's highs and lows, and he's a Jay Cloud believer. "There's little doubt that it is a real thing," he said, but pointed out that cloud caps are common on most mountain ranges. "The cloud is created because moist air is directed by the winds to go up the slopes of Jay Peak—this actually happens on lots of mountains. As the air goes up, it gets colder, and as it gets colder, it creates condensation, just like you have condensation on windows or a cold glass of ice water. With enough moisture, that starts coming out of the clouds, so you get additional amounts of snow."

What's unusual at Jay Peak, said Breen, is its position at the northern extreme of the Green Mountains. "It's the first clump of mountains that air out of Québec will run into, so when there's cold, moist air coming out of Québec, it reaches Jay Peak first. It hasn't lost any of its moisture and has its full complement of snow, so it does give Jay Peak a lot more snow than any other place around it."

All that snow is a blessing for great riding, but Jay Peak's exposure to the broad, flat Canadian shield also means there's little protection from howling winds off the Québec plains. The bitter payoff for all those fat, white flakes is a seriously chilly breeze, so savvy skiers will get good and bundled up before hitting the slopes.

Restaurant (72 Main St., Montgomery, 802/326-4682, www.berniesvtfood.com, 6:30am-11pm daily, $5-19) doesn't look like much from the outside, but the interior is bright and cozy, with orange walls, a gleaming bar, and a bustling crowd at any time of day. This is a good place to see a bit of local life drift by, as townspeople stop by for lunch or coffee and pie. The menu is a grab bag of dishes that range from chicken wings to chicken marsala, but the food is well prepared, and this is an affordable, homey alternative to the resort's restaurants.

The **Jay Village Inn** (1078 Rte. 242, Jay, 802/988-2306, www.thejayvillageinn.com, 6:30am-9pm Sun.-Thurs., 6:30am-10pm Fri.-Sat., $4-35) is pleasantly dark, with a broad stone fireplace and wood on every surface. Painful-looking photos document the restaurant's "Ghost Wing Challenge," but the menu is full of milder options like sandwiches, soups, barbecue, and salads. Breakfasts are hearty, with house-made country hash, steak and eggs, and piles of blueberry pancakes.

With the snow comes ★ **Miso Hungry** (location and hours vary, 518/605-4474, www.misohungryramen.com, 11am-5pm Sun.-Thurs., 11am-6pm Fri.-Sat., during the

1: Jay Peak, in a prime location that catches all kinds of weather and gets piles of snow each winter; **2:** Jay Peak's enclosed trams, a godsend for chilly riders

1
2
JAY PEAK
VERMONT
JAY PEAK
TRAM HAUS LODGE

ski season, $7-12), a food truck that serves ramen bowls stacked high with all the fixin's and other Japanese treats that may be the best après-ski snack in the border country. Call or check the website for each season's parking spot.

There are a range of dining options on-site at Jay Peak Resort: **Alice's Table** (802/327-2323, hours vary widely with season, $12-30) is the upscale option, with locally inspired dishes, while **The Foundry** (802/988-2715, 7:30am-9:30pm Sun.-Thurs., 7:30am-10pm Fri.-Sat., $13-40) is a gleaming, industrial pub with flatbreads, bar food, and a view of the slopes. **Mountain Dick's Pizza** (802/988-2740, 11am-9pm Sun.-Thurs., 11am-10pm Fri.-Sat., $8-16) has the feel of a cafeteria and pizzas to match. The resort dining isn't particularly memorable, but is convenient. With a bit of time, however, it's worth going farther afield.

Accommodations

Rustic and comfortable, **The Woodshed Lodge** (113 Woodshed Rd., Jay, 802/988-4444, www.woodshedlodge.com, rooms with shared bath $95, private bath $115) offers home-cooked breakfasts and country style under 10 minutes from Jay Peak Resort. A dartboard, board games, and hot tub are great after an evening of exploring, and there are plenty of indoor spots to curl up and relax.

Among the more unique options in the Northeast Kingdom, ★ **Shéady Acres** (2956 Mountain Rd., Montgomery Center, 802/326-3130, www.sheadyacres.com, $145-250) has five themed cottages surrounded by 25 acres of forest and fields. Choose between themes that include a Japanese teahouse, Irish farmhouse, Vermont sugarhouse, a Caribbean cottage, and an adobe "Santa Fe" cottage, all of which are very well appointed and comfortable, with compact kitchenettes. There's an outdoor fire pit and hot tub, and some cottages are pet-friendly. When visiting in winter, it's much easier to access the cottages with four-wheel drive and snow tires.

In the heart of Montgomery, **The Inn** (241 Main St., Montgomery, 802/326-4391, www.theinn.us, $170-210) is an ode to "timber chic," an eclectic and appealing blend of taxidermy, antiques, and arty stencils with northwoods flair. Each of the 12 rooms are distinct and range from the romantic honeymoon suite to an economy bunk room that feels like a grown-up take on summer camp. The common area is delightful in winter, when a blazing fire and radiant floors make the inn a cozy haven. A hot breakfast is included in the on-site restaurant, which also serves meals to the public and has a bar stocked with fun, seasonal cocktails made with local spirits. The Trout River runs behind this property, with excellent swimming nearby. On busy weekends, there's a $25 surcharge for a single night's stay.

Right next door is the **Phineas Swann Bed & Breakfast** (195 Main St., Montgomery, 802/326-4306, $177-234). Vintage posters and cheerful decor are as welcoming as the friendly owners, who have made their B&B the most dog-friendly in the state. Pooches are welcome in many of the rooms for a one-time $25 fee, or upgrade and treat your pet to a Deluxe Dog Spa Package. Fido can indulge in regular walks, a cushy dog bed, fancy dog treats, and a subscription to an animal-only television channel to watch while you're away, and you get special "cuddle privileges," so your pet can climb in bed with you. Humans get a hearty full breakfast in the sunlit dining room, and there's an outdoor spa on-site.

With a variety of lodging options, **Jay Peak Resort** (830 Jay Peak Rd., Jay, 802/988-2611, www.jaypeakresort.com) tempts visitors to sleep where you ride with package deals that include water park access and lift tickets. The first option is **Hotel Jay** ($100-500) where the 176 suites cater to conference travelers. Rooms include duvet comforters and flat-screen HD TVs; suites with kitchens and sitting areas are especially welcome for families. Even in the winter, you can walk from your room to the water park in your bathing suit. The second spot is the homier **Tram Haus Lodge** ($265-456). Designed as studios and multi-bedroom suites, guest chambers sport kitchenettes, locally made wool blankets, and spot-on views of the mountain's aerial trams.

CAMPING

Thirty wooded campsites are scattered along at pretty stream at **Millbrook Campground** (1184 Rte. 100, Westfield, 802/744-8085, www.millbrookcampground.com, May-Sept., tent sites $23, RV sites $33, no credit cards), which has a play area, showers, Wi-Fi, and a friendly, family-oriented atmosphere. There's a general store within walking distance where you can pick up supplies.

Information

The **Jay Peak Area Chamber of Commerce** (802/255-3023, https://topofvt.com) staffs an information center at the intersection of Routes 100 and 242 in Jay.

NEWPORT AND DERBY LINE

The remote town of **Newport** straddles the southernmost end of Lake Memphremagog, a stunning body of water ringed by mountains and inhabited (supposedly) by a lake monster named Memphre. It retains the feeling of a frontier; the town's charm is somewhat rough hewn, and the wildness of the forested shore is a constant reminder of how far this is from southern Vermont's gentle landscape.

In the late 1800s, Newport was a resort center. Guests arrived on the glamorous *Lady of the Lake* steamship and stayed at the luxurious, 400-room Memphremagog House hotel. Through the middle of the 20th century, the opera house in nearby Derby Line hosted vaudeville and speaking tours, while big band-era greats like Tommy Dorsey, Glenn Miller, and Louis Prima presided over the dance floor at Newport's International Club, said to be the largest in New England. In those days, however, Newport was not so remote. The Boston-Montréal rail line passed right through town, but when the last passenger train departed in 1965, it left the community stranded in the broad expanse of the Northeast Kingdom.

In recent years Newport has seen a revival, partly driven by the renaissance of artisanal food and drink production based in the surrounding country. In the heart of downtown, the Northeast Kingdom Tasting Center gathers the best of the region under one roof. The waterfront is lively in summer, frequented by small sailboats from Québec that pass through the dock-side customs. Accommodations, while limited, are appealing.

Eight miles to the north, **Derby Line** was mistakenly extended into Canadian territory by poor surveying. Rather than causing an international incident, however, the present-day borders were created in a treaty between the United States and Canada. Since then, Derby Line has always had a spirit of international cooperation, signified by the town library and opera house that was intentionally built athwart the line.

★ Northeast Kingdom Tasting Center

Sample the best of the Kingdom in the **Northeast Kingdom Tasting Center** (150 Main St., Newport, 802/334-1790, 11am-6pm Mon.-Thurs., 8am-8pm Fri.-Sat., 9am-3pm Sun.), a space shared by cheese makers, brewers, bakers, and cider makers. Shelves are filled with seemingly every edible product from the region, including some that are hard to come by elsewhere. Most items come from outside of Newport, but the basement of the Tasting Center serves as an aging facility for **Eden Ice Cider,** whose owners led the collaborative effort to start the tasting center. Rows of pristine oak barrels smell intensely of sweet apples, and you can learn about the extraordinary process of making the cider. (The apples are frozen before use, which concentrates their flavor.) Sample some at the **Tasting Bar** (noon-6pm Mon.-Thurs., 10am-8pm Fri.-Sat., 9am-3pm Sun., $3-9), where you can also try a variety of local ciders, wines, and spirits paired with things to nibble on, like cheese from Jasper Hill in Greensboro, cured sausage, and treats from the on-site bakery.

Haskell Free Library & Opera House

You can find a book in Vermont and check it out in Québec at this Victorian library and performance center. The **Haskell Free Library & Opera House** (93 Caswell Ave., Derby Line, 802/873-3022, www.haskellopera.com, 9am-5pm Tues., Wed., Fri., 9am-6pm Thurs., 9am-2pm Sat., $5 suggested donation) is the only cultural institution in the world that sits astride an international border. (Look for the thin black line that runs down the middle of the reading room, separating the United States from Canada.) It also happens to be the answer to the trivia question: "What's the only theater without a state in the United States?" since the opera house's stage is actually in Canada, while the audience sits in Vermont.

The building was constructed in 1901 by a local lumber mill owner who had married a Canadian woman—the couple intentionally built it for the use and enjoyment of citizens of both countries. The striking turreted neoclassical building is unique in having a first floor of granite capped with a second story of yellow brick. More than 100 years later, the building was recently gutted and rehabbed to revive musical performances in the opera house upstairs. In addition to the novelty of standing astride the border, staff are often available to give tours of the renovated theater. Call ahead to check availability.

Memphremagog Historical Society Museum

On the second floor of a state office building is the quaint **Memphremagog Historical Society Museum** (100 Main St., Newport, 802/334-6195, 11am-4pm Wed.-Sun., free), with exhibits on the history of the Abenaki, who used the lake as a major trade route, as well as photographs of the early resort history of the area. Along the lake, the society has created a self-guided walking tour with 10 markers in French and English pointing out natural features and historical buildings.

Food

Tucked into the NEK Tasting Center, the **Newport Ciderhouse Bar & Grill** (150 Main St., Newport, 802/334-1791, www.newportciderhouse.com, 11:30am-close daily, $8-16) has a convivial feel and pleasingly industrial decor. A seat at the polished bar is the best place in town to strike up a conversation or sample hard-to-find ciders and beers. The menu is a casual collection of sandwiches, soups, salads, and snacks, but the food is consistently very good and locally sourced. The daily soups are a highlight (especially when served with crispy grilled cheese triangles), but small plates are a temptation: chicken liver pâté with apple chutney, soft pretzels with beer cheese, or shrimp fritters are made to stand up to the notable beer list.

Newport might be the last place you'd anticipate the scent of lemongrass and galangal, but **Dusit Thai** (158 Main St., Newport, 802/487-9305, 11am-2:30pm and 4:30pm-9pm Tues.-Sun., $11-22) defies expectations. During a wintertime trip to Vermont, the Thai owners fell in love with the snowy mountain scenery and moved here from Bangkok to start a restaurant. Familiar Thai classics like pad thai and drunken noodles share a menu with less common dishes; try the *laab gai,* a spicy minced chicken salad with herbs, or deep-fried shrimp in tamarind sauce. The interior is as warming as the food: Exposed brick and richly embroidered cloth from Thailand predominate.

The best view in town may be from the **Eastside Restaurant & Pub** (47 Landing St., Newport, 802/334-2340, 11am-close Mon.-Fri., 7:30am-close Sat.-Sun., $9-24), where you can watch the sunset from a table on the lakeside deck. Some customers arrive by boat, and watching them maneuver is part of the fun. The extensive lunch and dinner menus feature fried appetizers, seafood, burgers, and steaks; hearty breakfasts include every possible twist on eggs. The cocktail list of brightly colored tropical drinks is a charmingly incongruous touch in the northwoods setting.

It's officially spring in the kingdom when the signs go up at **Tim & Doug's Ice Cream** (54 Coventry St., Newport, 802/334-8370, 10am-8pm daily Apr.-Oct., $2-8) ... even if that means lining up for cones in a down coat. Portions are enormous at this beloved spot, which is attached to the eclectic Pick & Shovel Hardware Store.

The Austrian chef-owner at the ★ **Derby Line Village Inn** (440 Main St., Derby Line, 802/873-5071, www.derbylinevillageinn.com, 4:30pm-close Wed.-Sat., 11am-3pm Sun., $18-29) serves exceptional versions of classic German and Austrian dishes like schnitzel and sauerbraten in a grandly furnished historical building. Some items give a nod to regional favorites—like the chicken schnitzel poutine—but the spirit is distinctly old-world. Visiting at Christmastime is a particular treat, as the inn is gorgeously decorated. From time to time, the chef trades his whisk for an accordion, and lucky visitors may be treated to renditions of holiday tunes.

Hearty breakfasts draw a steady crowd of locals at the **Brown Cow Restaurant** (350 E. Main St., Newport, 802/334-7887, 5am-1pm Mon.-Sat., 8am-2pm Sun., $4-12). Belgian waffles come piled with fruit and whipped cream, and eggs come mounded high with home fries and toast. Take a seat at the counter or grab a table with a gingham-checked tablecloth. The Brown Cow serves lunch too—classic sandwiches and salads—but you can get breakfast until closing time.

Accommodations

The Swedish-inspired ★ **Little Gnesta B&B** (115 Prospect St., Newport, 802/334-3438, www.littlegnesta.com, $90-140) is decorated with elegant minimalism, while oversize windows and white walls fill the downtown Victorian with plenty of light. Ruth, the gracious owner, sets out a European breakfast of granola, yogurt, breads, and cheeses, and her Malti-poo, Philip, serves as an enthusiastic welcoming committee. On weekends, there's a $35 surcharge for booking a single night. Ruth also maintains extended-stay apartments across the road.

On a sprawling property with lake views, **Cliff Haven Farm Bed and Breakfast** (5463 Lake Rd., Newport, 802/334-2401, www.cliffhaven.net, $80-175) is comfortable and convivial. The decor in rooms and common spaces combines country-style antiques with modern conveniences, and the home-cooked farm breakfast is a highlight. Jacques and Mim LeBlanc have given up farming to be innkeepers, but their son taps the maple trees on the 300-acre spread and makes syrup in the family sugarhouse. During sugar season you can join in the fun, learn about the process, and sip the sweet stuff straight from the pan. There is a 20 percent discount if you book three nights or more.

On the cusp of the international border, the ★ **Derby Line Village Inn** (440 Main St., Derby Line, 802/873-5071, www.derbylinevillageinn.com, $135-145, two-night minimum) is a richly furnished bed-and-breakfast in a gorgeous mansion that evokes this region's prosperous past. In winter, the inn feels delightfully isolated and cozy, with an electric fireplace in each of the five rooms.

CAMPING

With a prime location right on Lake Memphremagog, the town-owned **Prouty Beach Campground** (386 Veterans Ave., Newport, 802/334-7951, off-season 802/334-6345, www.newportrecreation.org, tent sites $35, RV sites $43-46) is a great place to hang out by the water. There's horseshoe pits, shuffleboard, a disc golf course, and a campground store selling firewood and basic supplies. Each site has a little fire ring and a picnic table, and if you want to take a spin around the lake, canoes, kayaks, and rowboats are available for rent from $10/hour.

Services

Several branches of **Community National Bank** are in the area, including one in

Newport (100 Main St., 802/334-7915) and one in Troy (4245 Rte. 101, 802/744-2287), at the intersections of Routes 100 and 101 on the way to Jay. There is also a **Chittenden Bank** (15 Main St., 802/334-6511, 9am-5pm Mon.-Fri., 9am-noon Sat.). There's a **Rite-Aid Pharmacy** (95 Waterfront Plaza, 802/334-6785, 8am-9pm Mon.-Fri., 8am-8pm Sat., 9am-6pm Sun., pharmacy 8am-8pm Mon.-Fri., 9am-6pm Sat., 9am-5pm Sun.) in downtown Newport.

ISLAND POND

This town was chartered as "Random" in 1731, and the name stuck for 100 years. These days it's technically Brighton, but everyone calls it Island Pond, which is the largest of the eight ponds in the area. The scenic body of water surrounds a 22-acre island, which is just the beginning of the surfeit of outdoor offerings of the area, including the seven-*million*-acre **Silvio O. Conte National Wildlife Refuge.** The refuge is open to the public, but only for those prepared to navigate it by car or bicycle, with map or GPS in hand; there are few trails and resources for visitors.

Island Pond is filled with rusting railroad infrastructure and was the junction of the international Grand Trunk railway, which was completed between Montréal and Maine in the mid-1800s. It gave the area a brief industrial boom, which was tragically cut short when railway entrepreneur Charles M. Hayes died in the sinking of the *Titanic* in 1912, starting the slow decline of the area's economic might. More recently, it has become a stronghold of the Twelve Tribes, a Christian commune that has come into sustained conflict with law enforcement and the anticult movement.

In truth, there's not much to do in the town formerly known as Random. It's quiet and far-flung, with a charming pond and rotting railway infrastructure. Its appeal lies mainly in isolation and natural beauty, for Island Pond is the last town in the Northeast Kingdom's northeastern corner. For those looking to find the seemingly uncharted edges of this wild region, it is a compelling outlier on a map of the state.

Sights

Island Pond (or IP as it's known) is prime territory for spotting **moose,** which regularly feed among the streams and meadows along the Nulhegan Basin (better known as Route 105). The local chamber of commerce produces a "moose map" with locales of back roads and nature refuges where the big quadrupeds are known to lurk. Your best bets for a sighting are early morning and late evening. It goes without saying that drivers should use caution at night.

Though IP's railroad days are long behind it, the **Island Pond Historical Society** (Canadian National Railway Station, 2nd Fl., Main St., 907/750-9563, by appt., free) displays photos, tools, old newspapers, and other train-related memorabilia on the second floor of the old international rail station.

Events

Every Friday night in summer, residents gather to dance the night away under the stars at the **Friday Night Live** (www.islandpondchamber.org, 6pm-10pm). The weekly event features live music and sometimes karaoke at the bandstand on the town green overlooking the lake.

Food

Takeout from **Jesse's Little Kitchen** (30 Elm St., 802/723-6276, 11:30am-9pm Wed.-Mon., $4-12) is one of the best of the few dining options in town; pizzas, calzones, and sandwiches make excellent picnic fare on outings to the pond, and the friendly owners are full of local lore and knowledge. If you're coming from afar, call first, as the chef takes occasional days off to recuperate from the busy kitchen schedule.

The food at the **KT Rays on the Pond** (69 Cross St., 802/723-4590, 7am-8pm Tues.-Sun., $6-18) might not be memorable, but cold beer, fried American fare and seafood, and a spot by the water keep it bustling. On sunny days, snag a spot on the patio, where you can watch the entire town come and go.

The third (and final) option in town is **Friendly Pizza** (31 Derby St., 802/723-4616, 11am-9pm Tues.-Sun., $5-15), which serves basic pizzas and grinders in a utilitarian space.

Accommodations

The only game in town is the **Lakefront Inn & Motel** (127 Cross St., Island Pond, 802/723-6507, www.thelakefrontislandpondinn.com, $94-129, suites $125-325), a somewhat run-down option that has the advantage of being right on the water. Guest rooms have Wi-Fi and small seating areas, and the adjacent dock is a great place to catch an Island Pond sunset.

CAMPING

Lovely and remote, **Brighton State Park** (102 State Park Rd., 802/723-4360, https://vtstateparks.com, campsites $18-25, cabins $48) has 5 cabins, 23 lean-tos, and some 60 tent sites tucked into a stand of white birch on the pristine shores of Spectacle Pond. It's not uncommon to see moose on the park's nature trails. Just a short walk from the campground, campers have use of a sandy beach with boat rentals, play area, and a small nature museum. The beach has a bathhouse with restrooms, while the campground has three restrooms, hot showers, and dumping station (but no hookups).

Information and Services

For info on Island Pond and around, stop by the downtown **Island Pond Welcome Center** (11 Birch, 802/723-9889, hours vary), or check out the website of the **Island Pond Chamber of Commerce** (www.islandpondchamber.org). For info on the recreational offerings of this corner of Vermont, check the website of the **Northeast Kingdom Travel and Tourism Association** (802/626-8511, www.travelthekingdom.com). Wi-Fi is available at **Island Pond Public Library** (49 Mill St., 802/723-6134, 10am-7pm Tues. and Thurs., 2pm-6pm Wed., 10am-5pm Fri., 10am-2pm Sat.).

SPORTS AND RECREATION

Hiking

The **Hazen's Notch Association** (1423 Rte. 58, Montgomery, 802/326-4799, www.hazensnotch.org) maintains 15 miles of hiking trails in forested conservation land. High Ponds Farm is a restored organic farm at the base of Burnt Mountain with walking trails among the orchards and woodland speckled with beaver ponds. More rigorous trails lead up to the summit of Burnt Mountain, a 3,100-foot peak with views of the notch below. All of these trails leave from the High Ponds Farm parking area, some two miles east of Montgomery Center. Directions and a trail map are available on the association's website. Trails are open during daylight hours, from mid-May to mid-December. During the winter months, some are groomed for cross-country skiing, when a trail access fee is charged ($12 adults, $5 children).

The **Long Trail** comes north right over the top of Jay Peak, and is easily accessible from a parking area on Route 242. Park 1.4 miles west of the Jay Peak ski area, and follow signs to the Long Trail North. It's a 3.2-mile round-trip to the summit, a steady climb through fir and deciduous forest that transitions into evergreens stunted by the altitude and harsh weather. The "Jay Cloud" likes to linger in any season, and even when it's sunny at the road, views from the peak may be elusive. The round-trip takes 2-2.5 hours.

Biking

Gentle and easy-to-ride, the **Newport-Beebe Bike Path** runs along the lakeshore from Newport, six miles on crushed limestone to the Canadian border. Pack your passport, and you can continue into Canada, where the **Tomifobia Nature Trail** extends from the border town of Beebe to Ayer's Cliff, an additional 12 miles of former rail bed. Bicycle rentals are available at **The Great Outdoors**

(59 Waterfront Plaza, Newport, 802/334-2831, www.greatoutdoorsvermont.com, 9am-6pm Mon.-Fri., 9am-5pm Sat.,10am-3pm Sun., $13/day).

Another excellent, off-road option is the **Missisquoi Valley Rail Trail** (www.mvrailtrail.org), which runs 26.4 miles along the scenic river from St. Albans to Richford, Vermont. The trail surface is a mixture of pavement and crushed limestone, that's easy to ride on a hybrid bike, and maps can be downloaded from the MVRT website, which also has great suggestions for loop rides if you want to avoid an out-and-back.

Boating

If you've got your own boat and are planning a trip, you could try a portion of the remarkable **Northern Forest Canoe Trail** (802/496-2285, www.northernforestcanoetrail.org), which stretches 740 miles across New York, Vermont, Québec, New Hampshire, and Maine. An extraordinary section connects Island Pond to Lake Memphremagog, a trip that can be completed in 4-5 days of paddling.

Skiing

This area's main attraction may be the lifts at Jay Peak, but there's plenty more snow to play in! Try **Jay's Nordic Center** (830 Jay Peak Rd., Jay, 802/988-4653, www.jaypeakresort.com, $15 adults, $10 youth 6-18), or head to the trails at the **Hazen's Notch Association** (1423 Rte. 58, Montgomery, 802/326-4799, www.hazensnotch.org, $12 adults, $5 children).

Swimming

Aside from **Prouty Beach** in Newport and the ample swimming in **Island Pond**—Brighton State Park is a great spot for a dip—there are endless swimming holes scattered through border country. Just outside of Montgomery Center is the popular **Three Holes,** which is fed by a series of pretty waterfalls. To reach the swim spot, head east on Route 242 from the intersection of Routes 58, 118, and 242, then watch for a disused school on the right that has a few parking spots. From there, follow train tracks on the left—it's a five-minute walk to the swimming hole.

The swimming at **Jay Branch Gorge,** aka **Four Corners,** is also wonderful; to reach the falls, start at the intersection of Routes 105 and 101, just south of North Troy. Go south on Route 101 for 0.2 miles, cross the Jay Branch Bridge, and park across from Four Corners Store. An easy-to-follow path goes 400 feet to the waterfall and swimming hole, which fills with locals on hot days.

GETTING THERE AND AROUND

From St. Johnsbury, head north on I-91 and take exit 27 for Newport (45 mi., 40 min.) or exit 29 for Derby Line (50 mi., 1 hr.). To travel to Jay, take I-89 to exit 26, then north along U.S. 5, and Routes 14, 100, 101, and 242 (55 mi., 1.2 hrs.). From central Vermont, Jay is also accessible along Route 100 north (40 mi., 1 hr. 15 min.) from Stowe. To get from Jay to Montgomery, head southwest on Route 242, and then turn north onto Route 118 (15 mi., 30 min.).

From Lyndonville, take Route 114 north past Burke (12 mi., 20 min.) to Island Pond (25 mi., 35 min.).

Rural Community Transportation (802/748-8170, www.riderct.org) runs shuttle buses between Derby Line and Newport.

Background

The Landscape

The Green Mountains are the backbone of the Vermont, a rolling series of peaks and fertile river valleys that create a landscape of contrasts. Forested mountaintops overlook dreamy pastures dotted with Holstein cows, and farm fields abut wild places accessible only on foot. The patchwork views from mountain peaks are rarely of wilderness only, but of a shifting equilibrium between human and natural spaces.

Those peaks—whether in the Green Mountains themselves, or the more southerly Taconic Range—are a part of the Appalachian Mountains, which many geologists believe are the oldest mountain

range on earth. Indeed, when compared with the jagged peaks of the Rocky Mountains, the Vermont's summits look comfortably worn in, eroded by millennia of weather.

At the southern end of the state, mountains occupy nearly the entire border, flinging up peaks alongside the Battenkill and Connecticut River Valleys. As the Green Mountains head toward Canada, they shelter a series of rivers that run north-south, and one major Vermont river valley that fractures the range from east to west, funneling water into the verdant Champlain Valley.

The Champlain is Vermont's most heavily populated area, with sediment-enriched soil that now supports thriving agriculture. A longer growing season and milder temperatures makes this a kinder place to cultivate the soil than elsewhere in the state. Here, find orchard trees lining the lakeshore and woolly sheep gazing out at the Adirondack Mountains on the opposite shore.

It's startling that even in the state's largest city—Burlington has some 42,000 residents—asphalt streets run into dirt farm roads in a handful of miles. Vermont is one of the most rural of the United States, and even now, more than half of the roadways are unpaved tracks that are frozen in winter, dusty in summer, and churning mud during the spring thaw.

GEOLOGY

A billion years ago, Vermont's eastern border was waterfront property, leading the edge of a proto-continent known as Laurentia. As the tectonic plate that held Laurentia moved slowly eastward, it folded under its neighbor and melted, causing an upwelling of magma beneath the surface of the ocean. That upwelling—about 500 million years ago—formed a chain of island peaks off the coast of the continent. Eventually, the landmass of Laurentia crashed into these islands during the Ordovician period around 440 million years ago, pushing them up into what is now the Taconic Mountains of southwestern Vermont.

About a hundred million years later, in the Devonian period, Laurentia rammed into another subcontinent to the south called Avalonia, rolling over the smaller landmass to create more upwelling of magma. At the same time, geologically speaking, the continent collided with its neighboring continent, Baltica—the precursor to Europe—causing the ocean floor between them to buckle and fold back over the continent. The combination created the Green Mountains, which at that point were the size of the present-day Himalayas, and must have been an awe-inspiring sight for any passing placoderms. A bit later, during the Triassic period, a great fault opened up in the middle of the region, creating a 100-mile-long rift valley that would later become the Connecticut River.

At this time, all of the world's continents briefly joined together in a giant landmass called Pangaea, but the commingling didn't last long. By the Jurassic period, 200 million years ago, the continents were again on the move, and North America and Europe split up to create the Atlantic Ocean. (Concurrently, a field of volcanoes opened up in the area of New Hampshire, creating the massive granite peaks of the White Mountains, younger than the Greens by several hundred million years.) New England's fiery birth was followed by a long period of erosion and settling before fire handed off its job to ice—and the last great ice age began.

Temperatures began to cool gradually about a million years ago. By the Pleistocene epoch, some 80,000 years ago (a mere hiccup in geologic time), a massive ice sheet began to build up over Canada, more than a mile thick in places. As it did, the sheer weight of the ice caused it to flow southward in a huge glacier, leveling the earth, gouging out valleys, and breaking off mountaintops as it flowed. Rolling and ebbing across the mountains for

Previous: Even with a changing economy, Vermont remains a fundamentally agricultural state.

several thousand years, the glaciers acted like a giant steamroller, grinding the Greens down to their current more modest heights and carving out long, deep trenches that would eventually fill with water to create the Northeast Kingdom's glacial lakes and Lake Champlain.

When the last of the glaciers retreated 15,000 years ago, it had depressed the rock beneath it to below sea level, and in its wake came the Champlain Sea, which stretched as far south as the present-day lake, and west across Ottawa. Fossilized whalebones and shells are a lingering testament to Vermont's seaside past, and a mountain view into the Champlain Valley shows a landscape shaped by water. The ice dams finally broke 10,000 year ago and all of the accumulated water drained down the Connecticut and St. Lawrence Rivers, creating the Vermont we know today.

CLIMATE

Mark Twain once said that "if you don't like the weather in New England, just wait a few minutes." It's got a nice ring, but leaves one wondering if the aphorism-spouting author ever spent an entire winter—or summer—up here. The transitions between seasons in Vermont are dramatic as they come, but in the buzzing peak of summer, or winter's deep, silent heart, it can seem like the weather may hold indefinitely. And while complaining about the climate is one of the state's leading pastimes, it's easy to love a heat wave from the shady cool of a swimming hole and hard to hate the snow when you're whipping down a ski slope.

Vermont's weather comes courtesy of its location on the dividing line between the cold polar air mass to the north and warm tropical air currents from the south. Sometimes one wins out, sometimes the other, but neither goes without a fight. Add a constant supply of moisture from the ocean on one side and a great lake on the other, and you are guaranteed an exciting mix.

Despite the regular precipitation, however, Vermont sees more than its fair share of clear days, when the sky is blue and you can see for hundreds of miles from the peak of Mount Mansfield. Moreover, the moderating effect of the warm Gulf Stream ocean currents ensures that for the most part the region doesn't see the same extremes of temperature that affect Midwestern states.

Winter

Winter temperatures are in the mid-20s, but can be much colder with wind chill. The most reliable skiing comes in the middle of winter, in chilly January and February (though the "January thaw" may melt out the base in low-lying areas). Later in the year, the snow can be more unpredictable, but March also means longer days and more light on the slopes. There are sometimes periods of cold weather with little snow; resorts address this issue by making the white stuff themselves, but those conditions are perfect for skating on lakes and ponds, where the ice turns thick and strong as cement.

Spring

In early spring, long-frozen roads melt into sloppy mud, and the weather can turn downright nasty. But while the blend of snow and rain that forecasters call a "wintry mix" might not be very pleasant, those conditions—low pressure, daytime temperatures above freezing—are ideal for getting maple sap to flow, usually from late February to early April. Intrepid visitors who time the season right will be rewarded with a glimpse of a remarkable season, when clouds of steam pour out of sugarhouse chimneys, and the woods are alive with activity.

Shortly after the trees dry up in April, the lilacs begin to bloom and everything turns green. It's an exhilarating time after the long winter, and it's not uncommon to see locals sporting T-shirts and shorts as soon as temperatures hit the low 40s. Warm days and cool nights can be ideal, but springtime sometimes brings drenching rains that lead straight into summertime heat. This is the time to spot a riot of wildflowers in the forest, from jack-in-the-pulpit to multihued trillium.

Summer

Summer in Vermont is glorious. From June through September, the weather is generally warm, with highs in the 70s or 80s, and in July and August temperatures can remain balmy even at night. The fields are alive with insects' creaking and chirping, and the deciduous forests take on an electric green reminiscent of jungle canopies. Though high humidity can mean sticky nights, there are rarely more than a few weeks of truly hot weather, and those are the perfect time to seek out cool hollows and swimming holes.

Fall

In September, a chilly tinge in the evening and morning air means that autumn is arriving. This is the season that gets all the press, and it's hard to deny the appeal of Vermont's crisp weather and brilliant foliage. Cold nights turn apples and root vegetables sweet, and in later fall, the air is scented with a pleasant smell of fermentation, as wild fruit piles up below trees deep in the forest.

The trees' color changes when green chlorophyll is reabsorbed by the plant, leaving behind spectacular reds, oranges, and yellows. A cottage industry of New England websites is dedicated to pinpointing each year's "peak foliage," a moment when all the trees shine and shimmer, illuminating the hillsides. But there are many "peaks": Colors start to change in the north and at high elevations, then move downslope—and down the state—as the cool weather progresses. Unless you arrive after a big windstorm knocks down the leaves, you can travel accordingly and find your own perfect peak.

ENVIRONMENTAL ISSUES

When arriving in Vermont from neighboring states, it's easy to see the bucolic landscape as perfectly preserved, free from the environmental problems that plague less pastoral places. And indeed, significant efforts have been made to clean up the pollution of the mills and factories that boosted the economy in the 20th century.

But the state has its environmental problems, notably fertilizer- and pesticide-tainted rainwater runoff that drains from farm fields into rivers and lakes. As a result, Lake Champlain has periodically high nitrogen levels that results in algal blooms—these can be harmful to swimmers, and warning notices are posted at beaches during blooms.

Another challenge for Vermont is how to sustainably distribute services to rural areas; when a dirt road contains just several households, extending the power grid to each one uses a disproportionate amount of resources. Many homes are "off the grid," and heat with wood and mount solar panels on their roofs, but usually supplement those cleaner sources of energy with a generator that keeps the lights on when it's cloudy—a noisy, relatively dirty way to produce household energy.

And many of these rural dwellers must travel relatively long distances to jobs in town, which means that even tiny back roads can fill with traffic during commute hours. This leads some to question the sustainability of country life—an ironic twist for those who have come to Vermont fleeing cities.

Plants and Animals

TREES

The view from most Green Mountain peaks is a mix of forest, cultivated farm, and pastureland, a patchwork of greens dotted with farmhouses and lakes. The thick foliage looks primeval and wild—untouched nature bordered by the pastoral. But two hundred years ago, the "green" in the Green Mountains was almost entirely pasture. Vermont has been an agricultural state since it was settled by Europeans, and in the late 18th and early 19th centuries, most of the trees were razed to create grazing land for sheep. Even the towering oak trees and sugar maples are often second-growth, and as it entered the 21st century, Vermont had more trees than it did a century and a half ago. (In 2017, a study found that for the first time, Vermont is losing forest—not to sheep this time, but to residential sprawl in suburban and urban areas.)

The majority of the state is covered by a mix of broadleaf trees and evergreens. The forest is dominated by oak and maples—including the famous sugar maple that yields the region's annual crop of maple syrup every spring. Arguably, this is the best mix of trees for leaf peeping, since maples produce some of the brightest colors, while oaks are slower to turn, extending the season and providing a range of colors at any one time.

Leaves begin to change from bright green to red, orange, and yellow as winter approaches, when there is not enough light or water for photosynthesis. Trees use winter as a time to rest, living off the food they have stored up during summertime rather than on the energy created by their leaves. As the chlorophyll disappears from their leaves, the green fades into yellow, red, purple, brown, and orange hues—many of which are amplified by the leftover glucose trapped in the leaves after the tree has stopped photosynthesizing.

White pine becomes more common as you travel north, where it can frequently be found growing on reclaimed agricultural land. That tree has smoother bark than its cousin, the red pine; to tell them apart, count the needles: White pine needles grow in clusters of five (W-H-I-T-E), while red needles grow in clusters of three (R-E-D). Other trees growing in this region include hemlock and ash.

As you climb up into the mountains and Northeastern Highlands, the deciduous trees eventually give way to a boreal forest of spruce and fir. Unlike pines, whose needles grow in clusters, on spruces and firs the needles are directly attached to the stem. These coniferous trees are better suited to the harsh climates of higher altitudes. Mixed in with the evergreens is an understory of hardy broadleaf trees, including aspen, beech, and birch. Few New England scenes are more iconic than a stand of white-and-black-striped paper birch trees in winter or festooned with canary-yellow leaves in fall.

FLOWERS

In spring, the forest fills up with a startling array of wildflowers, some arresting and flamboyant, and some that are only visible to the most observant, or slow-moving, hikers. Look for the delicate lady's slipper, a member of the orchid family that grows in wetland areas and gets its name from down-curving flowers that resemble women's shoes. The translucent flower, found in pink, white, and yellow varieties, relies on companionable fungi in the soil for its nutrients.

Other favorites include Dutchman's-breeches and trout lily; trillium also grows in many colors throughout the Vermont woods. One of the first flowers to bloom in April is the bloodroot, which carpets the ground with clusters of white flowers. As the season progresses, other wildflowers visible in the fields and meadows include the fuchsia-colored, anemone-like New England aster; orange clusters of wood poppy; wild bleeding heart;

bright-red wild columbine with its distinctive tubelike flowers; and the ghostly sharp-lobed hepatica, which grows in deep woods and swamps and features eight blue-purple petals arranged around an explosion of fine white stamens.

WILD EDIBLES

In recent years, an interest in local food has drawn attention to long-standing traditions of harvesting—also known as foraging and wild crafting—edibles from the forest. In early spring, the first woodland treats to ripen are called fiddleheads, the tightly spiraled tips of the ostrich fern, which grows in damp soil, especially along riverbanks. Great care must be taken in harvesting and preparing these, as they're easily mistaken for nonedible ferns, can be overharvested, and must be blanched before cooking. For sustainable harvesting of fiddleheads, never take more than two fronds from a cluster of ferns.

Next come ramps, a slender wild onion that grows in clumps; these especially must be judiciously picked, or whole stands can be destroyed. Wild mushrooms grow throughout the season, exploding in cool, damp weather and disappearing entirely during heat waves. Chanterelles, hen of the woods, and black trumpet are favorite varieties, but harvesting is for experts only. As they say, all mushrooms are edible...some only once.

In midsummer, blackberries, black raspberries, and thimbleberries proliferate, giving way to apples as the weather begins to cool. Most apples that you find in the forest aren't truly wild; look carefully and you may find traces of old stone walls between the trees, signs that the apple trees have been planted by a farmer who once tried to cultivate a challenging stretch of land that's since been abandoned.

In winter, foragers on skis harvest *chaga*, a parasitic mushroom that grows on trees—mostly birches—and is valued for its medicinal uses and deliciously roasty flavor, which recalls chicory coffee. There are many other edibles in the Vermont woods—notably nettles, garlic mustard, and cattail tubers—and don't forget maple syrup, which beats them all hands down.

Vermont's Green Report Card

When *National Geographic Traveler* magazine rated the world's destinations (via a survey of 200 specialists in sustainable tourism in 2009) on how they have dealt with development pressures, environmental problems, and mass tourism, Vermont came out at the top of the heap. Specific criteria for the rankings included environmental and ecological quality, social and cultural integrity, conditions of historical buildings and archaeological sites, aesthetic appeal, quality of tourism management, and outlook for the future. In all of these, Vermont came in at number five—on the entire planet. Moreover, the report calls out the state's dedication to conservation and environmental concerns, as well as its outlawing of billboards. Apparently they don't call it the Green Mountain State for nothing.

ANIMALS

Get up early and head to the water for great odds of spotting some of Vermont's wild creatures. While all animals must be treated with caution, even more intimidating creatures—like black bear and moose—are unlikely to be a threat if you don't act like one yourself. Unfortunately, one place that people often encounter animals is on roadways, so drive cautiously, especially at dawn and dusk, or you risk spotting your first moose as it traverses the hood of your car.

Land Mammals

Coming face-to-face with a moose is a humbling experience. Up to six feet tall, nine feet long, and with an antler span of five-and-a-half feet, a bull moose often startles those unprepared for just how *big* it is. Because of that, the herbivore has few enemies—natural or otherwise. In recent years, the moose population in Vermont has declined, due to increased hunting permits to address overpopulation, as well as the effects of winter ticks. The best places for spotting them are in the Northeast Kingdom, especially in the Island Pond area, and in Granville Gulf in the Mad River Valley. In the autumn, moose retreat to the deep forest, where they are much harder to encounter.

It's worth noting that moose only *look* like gentle giants. The enormous creatures can be dangerous, but if they attack, it generally happens in two seasons, and for two reasons: Female moose are especially tetchy in early summer, when accompanied by calves, and bull moose get rowdy in fall mating season. Regardless of the time of year, keep your distance.

Rather less imposing are the white-tailed deer that are common in the backwoods. At one point in Vermont's history, deer were hunted almost to extinction; thanks to more stringent hunting and forest protection laws since the 1930s, the population has made a comeback and now numbers more than 150,000 animals, which most naturalists regard as too many for optimal forest health.

The last documented specimen of mountain lion—also called catamount—was taken in Maine in 1938, and the giant cat is generally accepted to be extinct from the region. But reports of catamount sightings have persisted, and some naturalists think that like other cats, the iconic creature may be making a comeback.

Not to be confused with the more aggressive grizzlies of western states, the black bear is generally quite shy, often seen exploring garbage dumps at night. In recent years, its numbers have been increasing (to as many as 6,000 at last count), which has caused run-ins with campers as the bears search for food. If you encounter one, stay at a safe distance and bellow loudly—that is usually enough to scare one away. Red foxes inhabit both open fields and mixed forest, while the larger gray fox prefers the deep woods.

The most common mammals, by far, are rodents, which exist in multitudes. Gray and red squirrels, chipmunks, and raccoons are familiar sights in both suburban and rural areas. Wilderness locales are home to skunks, martens, minks, ermines, opossums, six types of shrew, two types of mole, mice, rabbits (including cottontail, jackrabbit, and snowshoe hare), flying squirrels, beavers, voles, otters, and porcupines. One of the lesser-known critters is the fisher, a large weasel known for its agile climbing and lush pelt. In addition to rodents, the fisher has been known to prey on raccoons and porcupines (not an easy feat). Finally, Vermont is home to nine species of bats; tragically, a fungal disease called white-nose syndrome has severely impacted the population in the region, so it's a special treat to see the tiny creatures flitting through the dusk, catching insects and calling to each other.

Reptiles and Amphibians

The streams and ponds of Vermont teem with frogs, toads, turtles, and other amphibians. Anyone who has camped near standing water in New England is familiar with the deep-throated sounds of bullfrogs, which can seem like competing bullhorns at night as the eight-inch-long males puff up their resonant throat sacks in competition for mates. An even more cherished sound in spring is the high-pitched chirping of the spring peepers, frogs that herald the beginning of warm weather. A half-dozen different types of turtle inhabit the area, mostly concentrated around Lake Champlain; most common is the painted turtle, which sports colorful mosaics of yellow stripes on its neck and shell. Rarer is the common snapping turtle, which can live up to its name if provoked. Wetland areas and swamps are also home to many species of salamander, which outdo each other with arresting shades of red, blue, and yellow spots and stripes. The most striking of all is the Day-Glo orange body of the eastern newt.

The most commonly encountered snake is the common garter snake, a black-and-green-striped snake that is ubiquitous throughout

Wildlife Photography Tips

You know the feeling—you finally get that moose, black bear, or loon in your viewfinder and snap what you think is the perfect shot, only to get a picture back later of a far-off indistinct blob. Wildlife can be notoriously difficult to photograph well. Here are a few tips for your jaunts in the woods of Vermont.

- **Use a good zoom lens.** You'll need at least 300 millimeters, if not 400 millimeters. Alternatively, get a digital camera with at least 4.0 or 5.0 megapixels (6.0 or 7.0 would be better). That way, you can "zoom" in on the computer later and the image will hold its resolution.
- **Pay attention to the background.** Animals with dark bodies will look better against a light background, such as an overcast sky. Those with light bodies will look better against a dark background like water or a blue sky. Avoid backgrounds that are too busy, like a tree-filled forest or green field.
- **Shoot in the early morning or late afternoon.** The soft, indirect light at these times will flatter your subjects. (Bright light isn't always the best for photography, since direct sun can wash out details or create too harsh a contrast.) Luckily, early morning and late afternoon are when animals are most active anyway.
- **Find a hidden spot upwind from a water source, assume a comfortable position, and wait.** Once the animals feel the coast is clear, they will come out of hiding to give you a good shot. (Good hunters know to let their prey come to them, and photography is no different.)

the state. Aquatic habitats around Lake Champlain are inhabited by the large northern water snake, which is harmless despite its aggressive demeanor. Woodland habitats are home to the ringneck, red-bellied, and milk snakes, among other species. Only one type of snake in Vermont is venomous: the timber rattler, which is identifiable by its dark W-shaped crossbands on a tan body. Many nature lovers would count themselves lucky to spot the reclusive snake, but if you do hear the distinctive dry rattle, keep your distance.

In springtime, many amphibians migrate across roadways to reach vernal pools for reproduction. If you see signs posted, drive cautiously to avoid squishing red efts, salamanders, and frogs.

Insects and Arachnids

You don't have to be a naturalist to notice the blackflies and mosquitoes that are the vanguard of Vermont's insect population. They're most annoying in spring and early summer and can generally be kept at bay with insect repellent.

Vermont is also rich breeding ground for spiders, most of which are absolutely harmless. The only poisonous variety, however, is the black widow, which is recognizable by its jet-black body with a broken red hourglass on its abdomen. These spiders are extremely rare; while their venom is a neurotoxin, only about 1 percent of bites end in death.

Birds

New England's location on the Atlantic Flyway from Canada makes the region prime bird-watching country. The region is home to some 200 species of birds, including great horned owls and snowy owls, that breed, winter, or live year-round in the region. Some common species like the black-and-white chickadee, blue jay, and cardinal are spotted in both rural and urban areas. Others, like the elusive wood thrush, inhabit only the deep forest, where its liquid warblings reward hikers with a mellifluous serenade. Likewise, the ghostly "laughing" of the common loon is a common sound on northern lakes.

History

EARLY HISTORY

Native Inhabitants

Hard on the heels of the last glaciers retreating northward, humans began to move into the area now known as Vermont about 11,000 years ago. The first to arrive were a people historians call Paleoindians, who lived mainly in the area of Lake Champlain. For a time when water levels were higher, the lake backed up the St. Lawrence waterway to become an arm of the ocean, and the Paleoindians lived off its rich marinelife. When the ocean disappeared so did the people, who dispersed into other regions or became assimilated into new cultures. For the next few thousand years, Vermont was home to two distinct cultures, the Archaic culture from 7000 BC to 1500 BC, a hunting and fishing people, and the Woodland culture from 1500 BC to 700 BC, a more sedentary people who cultivated vegetables and hunted with bow and arrow. Finally, around AD 700, the latter people had developed into a distinct Native American tribe—the Abenaki, an Algonquin-speaking people whose name is derived from the word *Wabanaki,* meaning "People of the Dawn."

Unlike the famous Iroquois Confederacy, the Abenaki did not have centralized leadership, and the Abenaki consisted of relatively small bands that spent spring and summer in large villages along river floodplains including the Connecticut, Winooski, and Missisquoi, planting corn, beans, and squash. In the fall, they migrated to inland hunting grounds in search of moose, deer, and beaver for food and pelts.

Early Settlement

The first recorded entry of European settlers into Vermont came years before the Pilgrims touched down at Plymouth Rock. In 1609, French explorer Samuel de Champlain sailed with an Algonquin war band down the St. Lawrence River in a raiding party against their enemies, the Iroquois. He discovered the lake that now bears his name, sailing for several months around its rivers before leaving, never to return again. (He also left record of a mythical sea creature that is still said to live in the lake, whom later generations would call "Champ.") As New France continued to expand in Canada and New England began to be populated in Massachusetts Bay and Virginia Colonies, the region that would become Vermont was largely ignored by Europeans except for occasional forays by the French to trade furs with the Abenaki. In 1666, Fort St. Anne was briefly established on the Isle La Motte by New France's governor, Sieur de Courcelles, for protection against the incursions of the Dutch and their Mohawk allies from New Netherland to the west, but it was abandoned after only a few years.

As population increased, however, it was inevitable that Vermont would become attractive to those on all three sides of its borders. Between 1680 and 1763, the waterways of Vermont saw increasingly bloody clashes between the French and British, along with their Native American allies, who were seeking to control the fur trade and later the farmland along the Champlain and Connecticut River Valleys. The first permanent settlement in Vermont, Fort Dummer, was built in 1724 in modern-day Brattleboro as a defense against increasingly hostile Native American raids in that area. In the decades that followed, the British expanded their hold rapidly up the Connecticut River, at the same time that the French established settlements down along the shores of Lake Champlain.

It was the British who eventually won out. The French and Indian War, which broke out in the Western Hemisphere in 1754, was but a small theater in the larger Seven Years' War that was fought between European nations from India to the Caribbean. It had the result, however, of permanently wiping the

French—as well as the Abenaki—out in the territory. By this time, the French had fortified Lake Champlain with two forts, one named Carillon (which would later be renamed Fort Ticonderoga) and the other Crown Point. Neither was any match for Lord Jeffrey Amherst, the British general who brought his troops up the valley in 1759 and sacked both of them. At the same time, the British raided villages of the Abenaki, who had allied with the French. The next year, the British under General James Wolfe pushed on all the way to Montréal, taking the city and forcing the French to sue for peace. The Treaty of Paris in 1763 ended French occupation of the American colonies and set the boundary between Vermont and Canada at the 45th parallel. No sooner did hostilities between France and England end, however, than a new conflict began.

Flatlanders and Mountain Boys

Once Vermont was in the hands of the British colonists, the question immediately arose—which colonists? The land between the Connecticut River and Lake Champlain was immediately claimed by two competing interests: the newly formed colony of New Hampshire to the east and the lands of New York, which had succeeded New Netherland to the west. Starting in the 1750s, the ambitious governor of New Hampshire, Benning Wentworth, began selling grants to the land across the Connecticut in what would become known as the New Hampshire Grants. More than 100 townships were established, including his namesake town of Bennington, hard up against the border of what is now New York.

The governor of that territory, De Witt Clinton, retaliated by demanding that Wentworth revoke his claims, taking the dispute all the way to England's King George III. The king decided in favor of New York, setting the boundary at the Connecticut River and demanding that the owners of the New Hampshire Grants pay taxes anew to New York. The settlers of these territories, some 20,000 to 30,000 strong, were loath to serve their new master, which employed a manorial land system that was foreign to the freemen who had come out of the town meeting system in Massachusetts and Connecticut. The first stirrings of Vermont identity began with meetings of the leaders of these territories at a tavern in Bennington. "The gods of the valleys are not the gods of the hills," defiantly stated one of their leaders, the towering giant Ethan Allen. Losing their fight in court, Allen and the other rabble-rousers took up arms to form a militia called the Green Mountain Boys, ridiculing the flatlanders from New York and stirring up riots against New York sheriffs that were known as the Anti-Rent Wars. By 1773, the Green Mountain Boys were burning houses, beating rent collectors, and publicly humiliating New York sympathizers. The skirmishes culminated in a courthouse riot in the town of Westminster in 1775 that left two Vermonters dead—the so-called "Westminster riot." The incident helped galvanize public support on the side of the Green Mountain Boys, solidifying resistance to the New York overlords. By this time, however, world events had been set in motion that would have a much greater effect on the course of history in Vermont—eventually making it independent of any master.

WAR AND REVOLUTION

The Road to Revolution

Even a decade before the outbreak of the Revolutionary War, few American colonists even considered independence from the Crown. Relations with England, while sometimes tense, were mutually beneficial, giving the colonies protection and a ready market for their goods and providing England a source of raw materials and income. The French and Indian War directly benefited not only the burgeoning territory of Vermont, but also the larger colonies of Massachusetts, New York, and New Hampshire, which could now trade without competition from the French or fear of raids from the Algonquin or Mohawk

The Naming of Vermont

Despite their longtime presence around Lake Champlain, the French don't seem to have used any variation on the words "green mountains"—or *les montagnes vertes*—to describe the region. Rather, evidence suggests that the name of the state was a French twist on the English, and not the other way around. In fact, the term Green Mountains was not in widespread use until 1772, when the Green Mountain Boys were starting their rampage against the New Yorkers. When, several years later, the men of the New Hampshire Grants decided to form their own republic, they first took the name New Connecticut, because leaders such as Ethan Allen had originally hailed from that state.

It was Allen's boyhood friend, Philadelphia doctor and self-taught scholar Thomas Young, who originally suggested the change to "Vermont." Young sent a copy of the Pennsylvania constitution as a model for the new republic and at the same time recommended the name. It's anyone's guess why he suggested a translation into French.

tribes. Millions of words have been spilled over what caused the quick snowball to war, but it essentially comes down to one: taxes.

Saddled with debt from its mammoth military undertakings, England decided to levy taxes on the colonies to pay for the war. After all, the Crown reasoned, hadn't the colonies been the ones who benefited the most from the defeat of the French and Indian tribes? Unfortunately for England, the colonists saw things differently. When the British Crown levied a series of taxes directly on the colonies starting in 1765, the American colonists reacted with violent protests, including the famous Boston Tea Party of December 1773, when colonists dumped 90,000 pounds of tea into Boston Harbor. From there it was only a matter of time until overt hostilities broke out, starting with the Battles of Concord and Lexington in April 1775 and followed by the much larger Battle of Bunker Hill in Boston two months later. The British lost more than 1,000 men at Bunker Hill, while the colonists only lost half that, showing the world that the American Revolution was definitely *on*.

As for Vermont, well, from the beginning the Green Mountain Boys threw in their lot with the Revolutionaries—making a short rhetorical leap from resistance to the tyranny of New York to resistance to the tyranny of England. Just a month after the Battles of Lexington and Concord, Ethan Allen and his men were planning an attack on Fort Ticonderoga. Only at the last minute were they joined by a Connecticut colonel named Benedict Arnold, who had been charged with an identical task by the militia of that state. While accounts differ, it seems Arnold and Allen agreed to a hasty joint command, taking the fort with a scant 80 men and not a shot fired. A consummate boaster, however, Allen made sure he got most of the credit for the raid. The incident made him an instant hero, bolstering his image throughout the colonies and granting new legitimacy to the Boys' fight for independence.

Shortly thereafter, a second group of Green Mountain Boys, under Allen's able second Seth Warner, captured Crown Point. Soon, however, Allen got his comeuppance after a botched raid on the British town of St. John—and then an even more harebrained scheme to take Montréal with 100 men in September 1775. Captured by the British in the engagement, Allen was held as a prisoner of war in England for the next two and a half years. Control of the Boys passed to Warner, while larger preparations for the defense of Lake Champlain were overseen by Arnold. Whatever ignominious deeds Arnold would perpetrate later in the war, he is still remembered as a hero in the Champlain region for his noble defense of the lake.

Throughout the summer of 1776, he

worked his men feverishly to build a ragtag flotilla of some 15 gunboats to defend the lake against an imminent attack down the lake from British general Richard Montgomery. The fateful battle took place in October off the shore of Valcour Island, where Arnold had set an ambush for the much larger British fleet. After a daring nighttime escape through the British line, all but four of Arnold's ships were destroyed. He was able to escape, however, and the British retreated back up the lake to repair and resupply, delaying their conquest of the lake for another year. That year would give the Americans precious time to raise troops and prepare their defenses, ensuring that the Revolution wasn't over before it began. As far as turning points of history go, Arnold's defense of Champlain may just have saved the United States.

Despite the war, however, Vermonters hadn't forgotten their own struggle for independence from the hated New Yorkers to the west. With Ethan Allen's capture, leadership of the struggle went to his younger brother Ira, who was both shorter in stature and shrewder in politics than his brother. With Ira's urging, delegates from the New Hampshire Grants met several times in the town of Dorset, where they agreed to form a political entity removed from jurisdiction of both New Hampshire and New York. In January 1777, the assembly officially declared itself an independent state they called New Connecticut—changed to "Vermont" that June upon the recommendation of a Philadelphia doctor.

Even as the delegates were ratifying their new constitution in Windsor, however, the hounds of war began barking again across the state. A new British army under General John "Gentleman Johnnie" Burgoyne was moving down the valley with some 10,000 troops—and this time, he wouldn't be turning back.

Mount Independence and Hubbardton

When colonial militias took over Fort Ticonderoga on the New York side of Lake Champlain early in the Revolutionary War, they immediately encountered a problem. The fort had been built to fend off invasions from the south during the French and Indian War, but would be of little use in countering the anticipated British thrust down Lake Champlain from Canada. General Philip Schuyler, who took command of the northern theater for the Americans, attempted to solve the problem by building a massive fortification on the high ground of the Vermont side of the lake to protect Ticonderoga and defend against a northern attack. Begun right after the signing of the Declaration of Independence on July 4, 1776, the breastworks were jubilantly named after the new document as Mount Independence.

In the summer of 1776, more than 12,000 defenders lived there, making it the largest military city in the Western Hemisphere at the time. By the time of the British attack the following summer, however, many troops had been pulled away to defend New York, and those at the forts numbered less than 3,000, too few to adequately protect against outflanking by the British. General Arthur St. Clair, who was commanding the forts after Arnold's departure, woke up in Fort Ticonderoga on the morning of July 4, 1777, to find that the British were scaling the heights of Mount Defiance on the New York side of the lake with cannons and would soon command an invincible position over his troops. In the dead of night, he ordered retreat of the entire garrison across a floating bridge between "Fort Ti" and Mount Independence.

As St. Clair fled south, he was pursued by British troops under General Simon Fraser. The Redcoats eventually caught up with the Americans on a hilltop outside the little town of Hubbardton. There, St. Clair had placed his most experienced men, a regiment of Green Mountain Boys under Colonel Seth Warner, who executed a brilliant set of maneuvers to temporarily delay the British in the short but bloody Battle of Hubbardton. Despite the heavy death toll—354 American casualties to 183 British—the brave rearguard action allowed St. Clair to escape with the bulk of his troops. Many of them would return a few months later to best Burgoyne at the Battle of Saratoga in upstate New York, the eventual turning point of the war.

Before that crucial victory would take place, however, there were still Gentleman Johnnie's men to reckon with. That showdown would occur a scant few weeks after Hubbardton during the Battle of Bennington. The battle would prove to be the first in which the Americans beat the British in combat, a fact that more than any other, perhaps, gave Vermont the legitimacy it needed to finally become its own independent republic.

The Battle of Bennington

Fresh from victory at Fort Ticonderoga, Burgoyne was marching down the Hudson River Valley to meet up with British troops from New York. The plan was to cut off New England from supplies and reinforcements from the rest of the colonies, thereby setting it up for easy capture. Feeling the pinch of a lack of supplies himself, however, the general made a fatal mistake when he decided along the way to capture a large storehouse of food and munitions in the small town of Bennington, Vermont.

Under command of the German colonel Friedrich Baum, Burgoyne sent some 500 troops—including several hundred dreaded Hessian mercenaries—to raid the town. Unbeknownst to him, however, the American colonel John Stark had previously set off from New Hampshire with 1,500 troops of his own. On August 16, Stark took the battle to the enemy, swarming up a ridge along the Wolloomsac River to attack Baum's position. In a short but vicious battle, his militiamen killed Baum and captured many of his men. Certain of victory, the excited Americans began pursuing the enemy, but they were surprised by a relief column of another 600 Hessian soldiers under Lieutenant Colonel Von Breymann. Stark was pushed to retreat back toward Bennington. The tide of the battle turned once more, however, with the arrival of Warner and 300 of his Green Mountain Boys, who had marched from Manchester, Vermont. In the second engagement, the Germans were routed and fled back to the Hudson, while the Americans claimed victory.

The battle was an embarrassing defeat for Burgoyne, whose army suffered some 900 casualties to Stark's 70. At a time in the war when American morale was low, the battle also proved once again that backcountry farmers and militiamen could defeat the most disciplined troops of Europe. Just two months later, with his forces depleted and short on provisions, Gentleman Johnnie was forced to surrender at Saratoga, and the continued existence of a new United States was all but assured.

The Vermont Republic

As any history book will tell you, the Revolutionary War was won not by the Americans, but by the French and Spanish, who entered the war after the victory at Saratoga and blockaded American ports against the British, swinging the tide of battle in favor of the newly independent republic. In 1783, a full decade after the Boston Tea Party, British general Charles Cornwallis surrendered at Yorktown, leaving 13 newly independent states.

Vermont was not among them. Despite the bravery of its militiamen in the early years of the war, Vermont was simply too much of a hot potato for the shaky new Continental Congress to touch. New York still refused to release its claim on the land, and later, southern slave-owning states objected to the admission of another free state into the Union. That left Vermont in the unique position of being an independent republic from 1777 to 1791, when it was finally admitted as the 14th state in a compromise that also admitted Kentucky a year later.

In the intervening years, Vermont conducted all of the affairs of a sovereign state, electing its first governor, Thomas Chittenden, in 1778, printing its own money, and even asserting its right to enter into a separate peace treaty with England. In fact, Ethan and Ira Allen went so far as to make overtures

The Will to Secede

Vermont started out as an independent republic, and some want it to end up that way. Led by citizens angered by what they consider the country's post-9/11 tightening of freedoms, the state's secessionist movement is getting plenty of attention—and followers. "Vermont did not join the Union to become part of an empire," argues the group, known as the Second Vermont Republic. Attracting everyone from descendants of old Vermonter stock to New York transplants, the plucky group explains it this way:

> Vermont seceded from the British Empire in 1777 and stood free for 14 years, until 1791. Its constitution—which preceded the U.S. Constitution by more than a decade—was the first to prohibit slavery in the New World and to guarantee universal suffrage. Vermont issued its own currency, ran its own postal service, developed its own foreign relations, grew its own food, made its own roads, and paid for its own militia. No other state, not even Texas, governed itself more thoroughly or longer before giving up its nationhood and joining the Union. Over the past 50 years, the U.S. government has grown too big, too corrupt, and too aggressive toward the world, toward its own citizens, and toward local democratic institutions. It has abandoned the democratic vision of its founders and eroded Americans' fundamental freedoms.

The group held a convention at the Vermont State House in September 2012 and is aiming to gain enough support to hold a statewide vote on independence.

to England to bring the republic back under control of the Crown—though to this day it remains unclear how much it was an honest tender and how much a ruse to force the United States to act to bring Vermont into the fold. The Allen brothers continued to throw a long shadow over the state from their new home base near Burlington, where they became rich as land speculators through their new Onion River Trading Company. Whatever was going on politically in the state, residents were now freed of control of both England and New York, and many were elated about their new ability to control their own destiny.

19TH AND 20TH CENTURIES

Boom Times

After Vermont finally became a state in 1791, speculators descended on the state. In 20 years, its population more than doubled to 217,000 in 1810. Pasture was cleared for sheep and cattle, and as the trees came down, business boomed in lumber and potash. While the economy was primarily agricultural, new technologies also spurred the production of woolen and cotton mills on the state's fast-flowing rivers. As the industrialists began amassing wealth, they turned toward educational and cultural pursuits. Two universities, the University of Vermont and Middlebury College, were founded in 1791 and 1800, respectively.

From the beginning of Vermont's statehood, the state was split politically between the Federalists, who aligned themselves with business interests and strong federal government and held sway on the east side of the Green Mountains, and the Democratic-Republicans, who favored a more agrarian economy with a strong interest in states' rights and dominated in the Allens' strongholds west of the mountains. Gradually, the latter group lost support as the state assembly joined the rest of New England in supporting the Federalists, and the Allen brothers and their Green Mountain Boys eventually saw their political sway slip away.

Nationally, the Federalists reached their apogee when John Adams was elected president in 1796. A backlash, however, soon found the southern agrarians in power under

Virginian Thomas Jefferson, and the influence of the Federalists waned. Vermont joined with the other New England states in opposing the War of 1812 (thankfully, a push to secede and form the New England Confederacy around this time failed). In spite of that, Vermont wasn't spared the fighting. In a case of déjà vu all over again, 10,000 British troops, this time under General George Prevost, set out to march down the Champlain corridor against only a few thousand American militiamen. Vermont was saved from battle by the heroics of naval commander Thomas MacDonough, whose flagship—felicitously named *Saratoga*—outdueled the British fleet and pounded the land positions, forcing them to retreat.

Social Ferment

The War of 1812 signaled the end of Vermont's big boom, even though industry continued to expand steadily through the next several decades. Renewed competition with British goods caused Vermont industry to suffer. At the same time, favorable tariffs for wool led to a rush of sheep grazing, changing the character of many farms from crop to livestock production. More than anything else, however, the times between the War of 1812 and the Civil War were ones of intense social change, as old ideas gave way to new ones.

For several decades, Vermont saw a wave of religious revivalism brought on by missionaries from Massachusetts and Connecticut who were determined to "civilize" their bumpkin cousins up north. As in the rest of the country, thousands of people gathered to see holy-rollers who toured the state as part of the Second Great Awakening.

As religious fervor waned in the 1830s, a new cause shook the state—abolitionism. Vermont, in fact, was one of the first states to write antislavery laws into its constitution, even before it was a state. One of the first articles in its constitution of 1786 expressly forbade ownership of slaves. Now, spurred on by the fiery speeches of Massachusetts abolitionist leader William Lloyd Garrison and escaped slave Frederick Douglass, the cause was taken up again all over the state. By 1850, the state was nearly universally in support of abolitionism, and its leaders in national politics were increasingly outspoken in their condemnation of slavery.

No amount of speechifying, however, could prevent the inevitable political clash of the Civil War. While none of the actual fighting of the war took place in Vermont, the state answered the call for troops, fielding 17 regiments by war's end and participating in all of the major battles in Virginia, Maryland, and Pennsylvania. In fact, the Second Vermont Brigade played a decisive role in the Battle of Gettysburg, when it came to the aid of the Army of the Potomac after the devastating Pickett's Charge threatened to break the back of the army. At that crucial moment, the Vermonters executed a series of military maneuvers to outflank the Confederate line and cause the rebels to rout, thus saving the day for the Union and ensuring a victory in the battle that spelled the beginning of the end for the Confederacy—another turning point for which the country has Vermont to thank.

Civil War to World War II

The time after the Civil War was a period of flux for the state. The railroad had arrived in Vermont in 1850, transforming patterns of settlement and trade. Urban centers grew as rural areas remained static, and new industries emerged that changed the character of the state. The development of granite quarrying in Barre brought immigrants from Scotland, Italy, and French Canada to the state to cut stone, creating a highly skilled and prosperous workforce. At the same time, the discovery of marble in the Valley of Vermont enriched the town of Rutland and created the fortune of Redfield Proctor, who would become governor and U.S. secretary of war. But friction with workers over wages led to labor strife and strikes into the first part of the 20th century.

By the early 20th century, Vermonters were already idealizing their agrarian past. Poet Robert Frost captured the public's yearning for a simpler era in verse—even if his poems held deeper, darker meanings below the surface. Frost lived in Shaftsbury from 1920 and brought many writers to the state with the Bread Loaf Conference in Ripton. What he did in verse, artist Norman Rockwell would do with images, painting many of his neighbors into illustrations of idealized country life for decades from his home in Arlington.

Vermont's misty optimism came to a crashing halt after World War I in the Great Flood of 1927, a natural disaster that destroyed thousands of homes and decimated herds of livestock throughout the state. As the Great Depression hit, Vermont struggled with an economy that lagged behind the rest of the nation and was increasingly dependent on federal programs such as the Civilian Conservation Corps, which created 30 camps employing some 10,000 Vermonters to help build the state's park infrastructure.

At the same time, the Olympic Games at Lake Placid in nearby New York in 1932 spurred a winter sports craze throughout the state—starting with a rope tow on a small hill in Woodstock and spurred on by forestry chief Perry Merrill, who encouraged the development of ski resorts all over Vermont over the coming decades. As World War II came and went, that development more than any other would point the way to Vermont's economic rebirth.

Modern Times

By the mid-20th century, Vermont was undeniably struggling. Factory farms in the Midwest were making it difficult for Vermont's smaller farms and dairies to compete, and many went out of business or fell victim to consolidation. At the same time, cheaper textiles from the South spelled the end of Vermont's industrial mainstay. As the state entered the 1960s and 1970s, however, it found that its lack of commerce and industry added to its appeal as a tourist destination. With the development of the federal interstate system, more and more travelers flocked to Vermont to drive its mountain roads and explore its unspoiled villages. While the state first focused on summer tourism, it would actually be winter tourism in the form of ski resorts that would spell the biggest boon for the state. Not everyone welcomed the influx of visitors, of course, with longtime residents grousing about the "summer people" and "resortification" that threatened to upset the very balance that made Vermont such a popular destination to begin with. On the whole, however, Vermont has entered the 21st century gracefully, with a steady influx of visitors bringing cash into the state and a well-educated workforce able to succeed in the new knowledge-based economy.

Government and Economy

GOVERNMENT AND POLITICS

When the Puritan settlers came to Vermont from Massachusetts and Connecticut, they brought with them the tradition of participatory democracy, wherein every free man was required to attend meetings that had legal standing to determine all the important matters in the town. While most Vermont towns are now run by an elected board of selectmen, the tradition of the town meeting still continues in the annual Town Meeting Day, which occurs each year on the first Tuesday in March. Then residents in each town gather to debate issues ranging from snowplowing to war in Iraq and to vote directly on binding resolutions by hand vote or secret ballot.

Vermont is reliably to the left of the aisle politically—its recent status as the first state in the nation to approve civil unions for gays and lesbians (and later the first state to approve gay marriage by an act of the legislature rather than a decision of the courts) is a good indication of that. Its politics are more complicated, however, than such easy stereotyping might suggest. From the first days of the Green Mountain Boys, Vermonters have held independence up as their watchword. On social matters, they've always evinced a live-and-let-live philosophy that has survived to the present day despite periodic revivals and temperance movements.

On economic issues, however, the beliefs and practices of voters are much more conservative—part of the reason that Republicans dominated politics here well into the 1970s. Vermont's traditional independence has led at times to strong antitax sentiment and a resistance to "big government" handouts. That changed somewhat in 20th century, partly through the vision and leadership of Senator George Aiken, who defined the progressive wing of the Republican Party for more than 30 years, charting a moderate course toward land use and regulation that selectively supported elements of Franklin D. Roosevelt's New Deal. That tradition continued into modern times with Senator Jim Jeffords, a Vermont Republican who switched parties to become a Democrat in protest against the conservative excesses of President George W. Bush.

In the past 30 years, however, the state has swung toward the more liberal end of the Democratic Party. Former governor Howard Dean launched a fiery presidential campaign in 2004 that galvanized grassroots Democrats with a fervent opposition to the Iraq War. But Vermont's most cherished politician might be Bernie Sanders, who was the Burlington mayor then a senator before campaigning against Hillary Clinton in the 2016 election. Far from the polarizing figure he sometimes appeared to be on the national campaign trail, Bernie is seen by many Vermonters as a pragmatic, well-respected politician who's worked with colleagues of all political stripes.

ECONOMY

Since its founding as a state, the Vermont economy has been underpinned by agriculture—especially beef, sheep, and dairy farms. Over the years, farming and logging enterprises have gone through times of boom and bust, with only dairy farming surviving as a major source of income for the state. Even that industry has seen its share of decline over the years—decreasing from more than 10,000 farms 60 years ago to fewer than 2,000 today. At the same time, however, milk production has actually increased due to technological innovations. Today, only 3 percent of the state's working population is engaged in agriculture, many of them involved in production of artisan and organic foods, specialty cheeses, and of course maple syrup. Vermont supplies more than one million gallons of the sweet stuff annually and is the top producer in the country, with more than a third of national production. In the record year of 2016, the state's maple syrup harvest skyrocketed to 1.9 million gallons.

Over the decades, Vermont has also developed a healthy manufacturing sector, starting with the textile mills and gristmills of the 19th century and continuing with marble and granite quarrying and machine tool manufacturing into the 20th century. While manufacturing has declined in Vermont, as it has across the country, granite quarrying is still big business in Barre. Starting in the 1980s, Vermont also developed an active technology center, with computer company IBM setting up shop in Essex Junction outside of Burlington. The company now accounts for more than a quarter of manufacturing in the state and is a major employer, despite layoffs in 2002. With technology creating more freedom than ever, the state has seen a new influx of independent knowledge workers and start-up technology companies in the past two decades. Vermont's gross state product was still only $31 billion in 2017.

Driven by the big-name winter ski resorts, as well as busloads of visitors who come every fall to view foliage, tourism is also a major contender. Tourists spent roughly $3 billion dollars in 2017.

People and Culture

When famously taciturn Vermonter (and president) Calvin Coolidge was once approached by a socialite, the story goes that she said to him: "Someone bet me that I couldn't get you to say three words in a row." To which, it is said, he replied: "You lose."

Silent Cal is a good stand-in for the classic Vermonter that features in Yankee jokes and stories, and like most New Englanders, Vermonters like to think of themselves as more stoic than your average American. And while there are plenty of friendly locals, Vermonters tend to err on the side of giving others space to breathe, without a lot of chipper friendliness.

Vermonters often describe independence and self-sufficiency as important values, and many have a fierce pride in their home state. And while that pride helps cement communities and keeps traditional life alive, there's a somewhat darker, nativist edge to it. As they say, "just because a cat crawls in an oven to have kittens, don't make 'em biscuits." In other words, "just because you moved here from New York, doesn't make you—or your kids—local."

But Vermont has always been an immigrant state (even aside from the obvious fact that Europeans are recent arrivals), from the waves of Polish, Italian, and German workers that came to work the granite to the intellectual homesteaders that left big Eastern cities to find the good life in the 1930s, and back-to-the-land hippies that continued that movement in the '60s and '70s. More recently, the Burlington area has been a refugee resettlement area, and Serbians, Sudanese, Bhutanese, Nepalese, and Syrian Vermonters are keeping the immigrant tradition alive.

In present day Vermont—as it was a century ago—there is some cultural tension about new arrivals. But it may be that the constant influx of new ideas has helped maintain the state's characteristic culture, which will likely continue to attract immigrants and idealists for generations to come.

STATISTICS

Vermont is home to 623,000 people. That's roughly the same number of residents who live in Boston, New England's largest city. The state's largest city, by far, is Burlington, with just 42,000 residents, bolstered by three of its surrounding suburbs, Essex (19,000), South Burlington (19,000), and Colchester (17,000). Outside the Burlington area, the only substantial population centers are Rutland and Bennington, each with about 16,000 people, and Brattleboro with 12,000. The state capital, Montpelier, has a scant 7,500 souls.

Annual median household income is $51,841, about equal the U.S. average. Vermonters are an educated group, with 90.6 percent of the population having received at least a high school diploma, and 33.3 percent have at least a bachelor's degree. In terms of marital status, 55 percent of Vermonters are married, 27 percent remain unmarried, and 10 percent are divorced.

ETHNICITY

According to census figures, Vermont averages far higher than the rest of the country in its number of Caucasian residents—96.7 percent compared to the nation's 62 percent. The next-largest ethnic groups in the state are Hispanic residents (1.7 percent), Asian residents (1.4 percent), and African-American residents (1.2 percent). Persons of American Indian descent number only 0.4 percent.

RELIGION

According to the Pew Research Center, 41% of Vermonters are "absolutely certain" there's a God, with only Massachusetts coming in lower—at 40%. When it comes to saying that religion is "very important," the Green Mountain State is at the bottom of the

Vermont on Film

The kaleidoscopic foliage and picturesque church spires of New England have proven irresistible to filmmakers over the years. Since the 1920s, more than 100 movies have been filmed in Vermont. Here are 10 favorites.

- ***The Trouble with Harry*** (1954): One of Alfred Hitchcock's stranger films is a black comedy about a dead body that shows up in a small New England town, much of it filmed in Craftsbury Common in the Northeast Kingdom. Shirley MacLaine has her first film role.
- ***Terror Train*** (1979): A campy horror film with Jamie Lee Curtis and David Copperfield—playing a magician—makes a stop at the station in Bellows Falls.
- ***The Four Seasons*** (1980): Alan Alda directed a story about three couples going through various midlife crises against the backdrop of foliage and ski slopes in Vermont. It was partly filmed at Edson Hill Manor in Stowe.
- ***Baby Boom*** (1986): For everyone who ever wanted to leave the rat race, there's this film, in which Diane Keaton has a baby and leaves a yuppie existence in Manhattan for the laid-back Vermont farmhouse. The movie was filmed in the village of Peru, outside Manchester.
- ***Beetlejuice*** (1987): Though it takes place in Connecticut, all of the exterior shots for this paranormal black comedy were shot in East Corinth. Michael Keaton and Winona Ryder star in the movie.
- ***Ethan Frome*** (1993): The stark Northeast Kingdom landscape of Peacham lends a dramatic backdrop to this adaptation of Edith Wharton's masterpiece about an unfortunate farmer, played by Liam Neeson.
- ***The Spitfire Grill*** (1996): Peacham takes another star turn in this film, a dark sleeper hit about a woman out of prison who finds work at a restaurant in a small New England town.
- ***A Stranger in the Kingdom*** (1997): Though set in the Northeast Kingdom, this adaptation of Howard Frank Mosher's tale of small-town race and retribution with Martin Sheen was filmed in the central Vermont towns of Chelsea and Vershire.
- ***Me, Myself & Irene*** (2000): The Farrelly brothers' dark comedy about multiple personality disorder starring Jim Carrey features shots in Burlington, Middlebury, and Waterbury, including a cameo of Ben & Jerry's ice cream factory.
- ***The Cider House Rules*** (2003): Even though John Irving's novel is set in Maine, the adaptation starring Tobey Maguire, Charlize Theron, and Michael Caine was filmed just about everywhere else in New England, including the Scott Farm apple orchard in Brattleboro and the train station in Bellows Falls.

list. Of the religious types, the majority are Christians: Vermonters identify as Catholics, Mainline Protestants, and Evangelical Protestants, in that order.

LANGUAGE

English is by far the most widely spoken language in the state, but 29% of Vermonters speak a language other than English at home. In some communities with strong French Canadian ties, older people still speak French at home, and French words trickle into daily use: Some English-speaking Vermonters call their grandparents "mamey" and "papey," terms derived from the French.

And Vermont English has a few of its own distinctions: Native speakers tend to replace *t* with a glottal stop (the sound that separates the words in "uh-oh"), use yowling diphthongs where other Americans might use a simple vowel, and drop the *r* in words ending with that letter. The regional dialect is lessening with each generation, and it's a treat to talk to folks that retain the distinctive sound.

THE ARTS

Music and the arts are an important part of New England's cultural scene, and there are plenty of places to catch a show—from Brattleboro's independent art galleries to the many festivals on Burlington's waterfront.

But much of the culture found in this area of the country is just as easily seen in its streets, pubs, and colleges. A thriving rock and folk music scene dominates the nightclubs and bars around the University of Vermont (which spawned the band Phish). And no matter how far afield you go, it seems there's always an independent artisan practicing a craft in a welcoming studio—be it glassblowing, painting, or sculpture.

One thriving Yankee tradition is contra dancing, a folk dance similar to square dancing. At a contra dance, however, couples line up facing each other in long rows; they progress up the line, dancing with each successive pair. The organized chaos is guided by a "caller," who walks the dancers through the steps before each song starts and keeps things running smoothly throughout the number. Contra dances are usually held with live music, almost always with a fiddle, but sometimes with mandolins, banjos and guitars.

Contra dances remain popular with a fascinating blend of old-timers, young hippies and various countercultural types. Attire ranges from barefoot dancers in flowing skirts to farmers dressed up in boots and their nicest overalls.

SHOPPING

What Vermont lacks in designer boutiques and department stores, it more than makes up for in unique, artistic, independent shops and galleries. The proliferation of crafts here is impressive—from blown glass and pottery to hand-stitched sweaters and handcrafted specialty foods. (Can anyone ever have enough maple syrup in their pantry?) Find all of it in the many country stores that anchor the centers of many Vermont towns, or visit the artists' studios directly; they can be found everywhere, from centrally located town greens to the mountain roads.

Essentials

Transportation

Vermont is easily accessible by road, rail, and air (and even water if you are coming by ferry from New York). While Burlington International Airport is the most obvious destination, in some cases it can be cheaper to fly into airports in neighboring states. Amtrak's rail network isn't very extensive, but it does connect to several major cities. Those that aren't on the train routes are accessible by bus or car.

AIR

Without so much as a stoplight to mark the entrance, the tiny **Burlington International Airport** (1200 Airport Dr., South Burlington, 802/863-1889, www.btv.aero) is the main air portal to Vermont. Flights in and out of the airport tend to be more expensive than those to larger airports in the United States, but there are nonstop routes connecting Burlington with Atlanta, Charlotte, Chicago, Detroit, New York City, Philadelphia, and Washington, D.C.

It may be worth checking, however, to see if you can get a cheaper or more direct flight to the much larger **Boston-Logan International Airport** (1 Harborside Dr., East Boston, MA, 800/235-6426, www.massport.com/logan). The largest transportation hub in the region, it is only a two-hour drive from Brattleboro, so it can provide an even quicker trip to southern Vermont. The airport serves nearly 30 airlines, of which a dozen are international.

Several of New England's smaller regional airports may be an option as well. **Bradley International Airport** (Schoephoester Rd., Windsor Locks, CT, 860/292-2000, www.bradleyairport.com) halfway between Springfield, Massachusetts, and Hartford, Connecticut, is only an hour-or-so drive from Brattleboro along I-91. In addition to a half dozen major domestic carriers, Bradley is also served by Air Canada. In New Hampshire, **Manchester Airport** (1 Airport Rd., Manchester, NH, 603/624-6556, www.flymanchester.com) is an hour and a half from Brattleboro and two hours from Killington. Manchester is served by Delta, Southwest, United, and US Airways.

Another good option is the **Montréal Pierre-Elliot Trudeau International Airport** (Rue Hervé St. Martin, Montréal, QC, 514/394-7377, www.admtl.com), which has direct flights to five continents. You can also fly into the **Albany International Airport** (737 Albany Shaker Rd., Albany, NY, 518/242-2200, www.albanyairport.com), which sits just over 60 miles away from Brattleboro and has car rentals and several convenient bus routes out of its terminal. It is served by most major domestic airlines as well as Air Canada.

TRAIN

Train service in Vermont tends to be the slowest and most expensive way of getting around, but taking a train through the rolling countryside has undeniable charm. **Amtrak** (800/872-7245, www.amtrak.com) runs frequent trains along the aptly named **Vermonter** route, which connects to St. Albans from New York (10 hrs.) and Washington, D.C. (14 hrs.). Along the way, it passes through Brattleboro, White River Junction, Montpelier, Waterbury, Essex Junction (close to Burlington), and other locations, and the Vermonter now allows bikes on board with advance reservations. Also, Amtrak's **Ethan Allen** route offers once-a-day service to Rutland from New York City (10 hrs.). Connecting to that route at Albany, New York, Amtrak's **Adirondack** route offers service to Rutland from Montréal, Québec (15 hrs.).

BUS

Many parts of this predominantly rural state aren't served by buses, but if you stick to major towns, the bus can be an attractive alternative for those who lack their own wheels. For more information on service in a particular region, check out the website of the **Vermont Public Transportation Association** (www.vpta.net).

Vermont is accessible from many domestic and Canadian locations via **Greyhound Bus Lines** (800/231-2222, www.greyhound.com). Buses stop in several major cities, including Burlington, Brattleboro, Montpelier, Rutland, and White River Junction. Hours to Brattleboro from major cities are as follows: New York (5.5), Philadelphia (9), Montréal (6.5), Washington (13), Buffalo (14), Toronto

Previous: lighthouse in Lake Champlain.

Car Rental Companies

The following companies all have branches at Burlington Airport, as well as at the other locations listed.

- **Alamo** (877/222-9075, www.alamo.com)
- **Avis** (800/230-4898, www.avis.com): Brattleboro (1380 Putney Rd.), South Burlington (1890 Williston Rd.)
- **Budget** (800/527-0700, www.budget.com): South Burlington (1890 Williston Rd.)
- **Enterprise** (800/261-7331, www.enterprise.com): Barre (1246 Rte. 302), Bennington (96 Northside Dr.), Brattleboro (801 Putney Rd.), Middlebury (1410 Rte. 7S), Rutland (131 S. Main St.), South Burlington (1116 Shelburne Rd. and 1891 Williston Rd.), St. Albans (16 Swanton Rd.), St. Johnsbury (26 Memorial Dr.), and White River Junction (60 Jasmin Ln.)
- **Hertz** (800/654-3131, www.hertz.com): Barre (697 South Barre Rd.), Rutland (1004 Airport Rd.), and South Burlington (1335 Shelburne Rd.)
- **National** (800/227-7368, www.nationalcar.com)
- **Thrifty** (877/283-0898, www.thrifty.com): White River Junction (93 Beswick Dr.)

(15), and Cleveland (16). Plan on an additional 3-4 hours for Burlington—except from Canadian locations, from which you should subtract the same amount.

With more limited destinations—but quicker service—**Megabus** (www.us.megabus.com) offers routes from Burlington and Montpelier to Boston (4 hrs.). Booking well in advance can mean very cheap fares, and there's (spotty) Wi-Fi available on the buses.

CAR

The major auto route into Vermont is **I-91,** which enters the southeast corner of the state at Brattleboro, 3.5 hours from New York or 7.5 hours from Washington, D.C. From the west, the main route into New England is **I-90,** also known as the Massachusetts Turnpike (or Mass Pike for short). From there, you can connect to I-91 at Springfield to drive to Brattleboro (1.5 hrs.) or take the more scenic path up Route 7 in western Massachusetts to Bennington (1 hr.). From Boston, drive up I-93 to I-89 to enter the state at White River Junction, or drive west on Route 2 to connect with I-91 to Brattleboro; either route takes about 2 hours. From Montréal, take Autoroutes 10 and 35 to Route 133, which connects to I-89 at the border—2 hours total to Burlington.

The state has also designated a network of **Vermont Byways** (www.vermont-byways.us), highways or other public roads with special scenic, historical, or cultural import. These can be meandering and slower, but are often the quickest route to the Vermont's loveliest spots.

Driving Conditions

Road travel can be treacherous and slow in the winter, and it's essential to plan for extra time when driving in snowy or icy conditions. Some mountain passes are only open seasonally; travelers can get roadway information ahead of time by contacting the Vermont Agency of Transportation and State Police; they have teamed up to offer travel information at the telephone number 511, which can be accessed anywhere in the state.

And while it's not easy to negotiate frozen roads, it's even worse when they thaw. Spring is "Mud Season," when long-icy dirt roads melt into churned quagmires. Over half the roads in the state are unpaved, so take their condition into account while planning your route. Locals have become accustomed to negotiating the mucky tracks; spring driving is a delicate equilibrium between slow-moving caution, and a more aggressive technique summed up by the saying: "When in doubt, throttle out."

FERRY

Three ferries make the trip across Lake Champlain from New York: Plattsburgh to Grand Isle (12 min., 24 hours/day, year-round service), Port Kent to Burlington (1 hr., mid-June-late Sept.), and Essex to Charlotte (20 min., year-round service). For more information, contact **Lake Champlain Transportation** (King St. Dock, 802/864-9804, www.ferries.com).

VISAS AND OFFICIALDOM

All visitors entering from Canada need a valid passport or enhanced license, and some may require a visa. In checking through customs, they may be asked to provide tickets and documents for their return to Canada or onward destination if traveling by air, rail, boat, or bus. If you are driving a rental car, be sure to bring a copy of the rental agreement, as officials are often on the lookout for stolen vehicles.

Crossing the border requires going through immigration customs both ways, and the process is usually pretty routine, though vehicles are occasionally searched. Visitors who are 21 years or older may bring the following into the United States: 200 cigarettes or 50 cigars or 4.4 pounds of tobacco; one liter of alcohol; gifts worth up to $100. The Department of Homeland Security is changing the rules on crossing borders fairly frequently these days, so it's wise to check with the **Foreign Affairs and International Trade Canada office** (www.canada.gc.ca) before your trip.

Recreation

There is a heady abundance of mountains, lakes, parks, and rivers in Vermont, and what some call "recreation" is just everyday life for outdoorsy locals. Of course, what you do depends on season and geography—in winter, skiers flock to the snowy peaks of the Green Mountains; fall and summer bring hunters, anglers, hikers, and mountain bikers to trails and streams. (Spring, on the other hand, is often far too muddy for any of the latter. April is when Vermonters get their reading done.) Meanwhile, the widely varied parks and preservation lands throughout the state are excellent grounds for bird-watching, year-round.

BIKING

The gentle landscape in Vermont means that there are many ways to get where you're going, a boon for cyclists. The state makes a convenient **bicycle map of the state** (www.vermontvacations.com). The most notable rail trail runs through the **Missisquoi Valley** (www.mvrairtrail.com) from St. Albans to Richford, on the Canadian border.

Mountain bikers shouldn't miss the extraordinary **Kingdom Trails Network** (www.kingdomtrails.org) in East Burke, but the state's richest cycling resource may be its quiet dirt roads. Many of these are passable on a road bike, but may be a more comfortable ride with somewhat cushier tires. Most bigger towns have shops for renting bicycles, and whether you're renting or not, shop employees usually know their regions' best rides—and are happy to share their knowledge. Fat biking (on snow) is gaining popularity in some resort areas (notably Stowe), but each has their own regulations about using fat bikes on Nordic trails—ask first.

HUNTING, FISHING, AND BIRD-WATCHING

Every season, without fail, droves of dedicated sports enthusiasts descend upon the backwoods of Vermont, seeking to watch, catch, or take home some of its bounty. Local regulations and licensing requirements can be strict; certain animals (specific rules apply to most species for trapping, baiting, shooting, and catching) are protected in certain districts. So be certain to check with the local Fish and Game offices of your area of interest before planning your trip.

Hunting areas are well regulated and plentiful, particularly farther north, where animals from woodcock and deer to turkey and moose roam. Moving-water fishing takes place mostly in summer and early fall. Serious trout and bass anglers gravitate toward the Missisquoi, Battenkill, and Connecticut Rivers. In winter, ice fishing is popular in many small northern towns—particularly in the area around Lake Champlain. The sport requires hardy enthusiasts to cut holes in the ice above ponds and lakes and then catch fish as they cruise beneath the hole.

At any time of year, bird-watchers can feast their eyes in any number of wildlife refuges. Some of the best include the Missisquoi and Silvio O. Conte National Wildlife Refuges.

KAYAKING AND CANOEING

Wherever there's water in Vermont, there are usually plenty of places to put in a kayak and head out for a paddle. The most spectacular destination is the **Northern Forest Canoe Trail** (www.northernforestcanoetrail.org), which 740 miles from Old Forge, New York, to Fort Kent Maine, crossing Vermont's Northeast Kingdom along the way. Another great resource is the **Lake Champlain Paddlers' Trail** (www.lakechamplaincommittee.org), a network of camping sites on Lake Champlain that's only accessible by boat; you can get a short guidebook to the trail by donating to the Lake Champlain Committee, which works to ensure clean waterways.

Meanwhile, there are river-rafting opportunities for nearly every skill level. Highlights include the Class II Battenkill, which is the best run in the summer and flows under four picturesque covered bridges; Otter Creek, a Class II, north-running river into Lake Champlain; Class II sections of the Winooski River, which runs past stunning natural scenery and small waterfalls; and the Lamoille River, which ranges from flatwater to Class III.

ROCK CLIMBING

Vermont's rock climbing might not be as extensive, or famous, as that in neighboring New Hampshire and New York, but the state has a dedicated climbing community. The best guide to Vermont rock is ***Tough Schist***, by Travis Peckham, which is usually available at the state's outdoor gear stores, with updates posted on **Vermont Rock** (www.vermontrock.com). Popular climbs are found in Bolton's Upper West and Lower West climbing areas, Groton State Forest, Smugglers' Notch, and Marshfield Ledge, among many others.

SAILING

Vermont may be landlocked, but residents take full advantage of its lakes by getting out on them in as many ways as possible. On the larger lakes, that includes sailing—particularly on Lake Champlain, where several chartering companies can be found and schooners can be rented for day cruises, and Lake Memphremagog, where a marina serves sailors who make their way to and from Canada.

SKIING AND WINTER SPORTS

Snow lovers rejoice: Vermont's got plenty of it, and during the cold weather months, mountain towns fill with riders from around the world. Killington, Sugarbush, Stowe, and Mount Snow dominate the scene, with glamorous lodges, high-speed lifts, and snowmaking equipment that keep visitors sliding from November through April, even through the dreaded January thaw. The smaller resorts are worth exploring, as well, and make up for their lack of expensive infrastructure with affordable lift tickets, low-key local scenes, and

Backcountry Skiing

There's a lifetime of resort skiing in the state, but for many Green Mountain skiers, the real thrills are far off the beaten track. For those equipped with touring or backcountry equipment, there's endless powder on remote peaks.

Two classic point-to-point tours start at **Bolton Valley Resort** (Bolton Valley Access Rd., Bolton, 802/434-3444, www.boltonvalley.com): The **Woodard Trail** descends a long ridge from the top of Bolton to the Waterbury Reservoir and the **Bolton-Trapps tour** follows the **Catamount trail** to end near Stowe's Trapp Family Lodge.

But backcountry skiing in Vermont has its controversies, as some have heedlessly cleared trails on public and private lands, downing trees to make clean lines down mountainsides. In 2009, two skiers cut more than 1,000 trees on Big Jay to "improve" a backcountry area known as The Cut; defacing the public land earned them suspended prison sentences and near-universal criticism. The crisis did have a bright side: It raised awareness about sustainable trail development and use, and most backcountry riders find lines with their skis—not saws.

Backcountry areas in Vermont are unpatrolled, and many don't have access to cell service for contacting rescuers, so it's vital that all off-piste adventures start with some serious precautions. Several resorts offer classes in avalanche safety, winter ski travel, and survival. For more information, seek out David Goodman's excellent *Backcountry Skiing Adventures: Vermont and New York* (Appalachian Mountain Club Books, 2001).

room to breathe; ski-only Mad River Glen keeps it real with judicious grooming and down-home lodges, Bolton Valley Resort is adjacent to endless backcountry exploration, and Suicide Six is historical, family-friendly, and fun.

If downhilling isn't your thing, many resorts have groomed trails for cross-country skiing (both Nordic and skate skiing), as well as dedicated snowshoe trails—some even welcome fat bikes onto their snowy paths. Up in the Northeast Kingdom, the Craftsbury Outdoor Center is the finest cross-country in the state, though Stowe's Trapp Family Lodge is another favorite. And no matter the town, there's probably a sledding hill and ice-skating rink nearby; the best way to find one is to ask a local.

Throughout the coldest part of the winter, bays and ponds around the state are dotted with tiny houses, "shacks" for ice fishing. They range from bare-bones lean-tos to posh shelters where anglers kick back and wait for the fish to bite. When the ice is thick, people drive over it to reach their shacks; the frozen surface can support a startling amount of weight, but it's always worth looking for yourself and asking around—at least one truck ends up submerged each spring.

Accommodations and Food

Throughout the book, accommodation listings include the range of rates for a standard double room in high season (roughly May-Oct.). Depending on location, prices can be much higher during peak times (e.g., foliage or ski season) and steeply discounted in late fall and spring. Food listings include the range of prices for dinner entrées, including sandwiches but not salads. Lunch is often significantly cheaper.

Peak travel here is in the fall, particularly in late September and October when the foliage is at its most dramatic, and many hotels jack up their prices by a factor of two during this brief crowded season. If leaf peeping isn't your thing, you can save a lot of money by traveling in late August or early September when the summer humidity has dissipated but hotel prices are lower.

BED-AND-BREAKFASTS

In rural areas, bed-and-breakfasts may be the only accommodations available, and they vary from plushly romantic getaways to homey, timeworn farmhouses. The prices are equally varied, but tend to start around $80 for the very cheapest rooms, with average prices closer to $120. All prices include breakfasts, which tend to be hearty.

CAMPING

New Englanders love camping, and most state parks have a place to lay your bedroll (or plug in your RV). Some of the most popular sites may fill up on holiday weekends, so it's worth calling ahead. While most state parks provide hot showers and dumping stations for RVs, few provide hookups.

Rates for camping vary by park, but generally run from $18-29 per person for tent and trailer sites, and $21-25 per person for lean-tos. Some parks also have cabins or cottages, available for $50 per day and $560-610 per week. Reservations can be made more than two weeks in advance online at https://vtstateparks.com, or through the central reservation line, 888/409-7578 (9am-4pm Mon.-Fri.). Less than two weeks in advance, it's necessary to call the park directly. A credit card is needed to secure a reservation; payment is refundable, less a $10 cancellation fee, up until the day before the reservation.

LOCAL CUISINE

Vermonters are passionate about food, and recent years have seen an explosion of interest in farm-to-table dining, farmers markets, and everything local and sustainably produced. Restaurants trumpet the provenance of their produce, and farmers who spend most of their time in muck boots have undeniable star appeal. So what does that mean for diners?

With ingredients front and center, restaurant meals can be of a very high quality. The cooking is often updated and creative takes on all-American food: well-prepared meat with vegetable sides, pizzas and burgers, or "gastropub" fare, a sort of grown-up bar food that's heavy on salt and grease and goes great with beer. There's almost always a vegetarian option, but they tend not to be the highlights of the menu.

Almost all good restaurants in Vermont change their menus seasonally; don't miss a chance to try springtime fiddleheads—the edible tip of the ostrich fern, foraged in the woods, with a delicate taste that resembles asparagus—or ramps, slender wild leeks. Summer brings wave after wave of heirloom tomatoes, fresh berries, and piles of veggies, and apple trees are heavy with fruit in the autumn.

Cheese is a highlight: Aficionados can follow the Vermont Cheese Trail, a collection of small, often out-of-the-way dairy farms and artisanal cheese makers that have made waves with their extraordinary products. And of course, maple syrup is a regional obsession;

the amber liquid is made across the state, from family-owned sugarhouses to industrial-scale production.

These days, you can't talk about Vermont's culinary culture without mentioning beer, cider, wine, and spirits. Green Mountain brewers consistently top world beer rankings, and the local abundance of apples means that cider is a favorite locavore alternative. There's a "trail" for each of these, so if you'd like to explore the Vermont's best drinks (and you've got someone to drive you around), it's easy to shape a trip around your favorite local liquids.

Travel Tips

ACCESS FOR TRAVELERS WITH DISABILITIES

Public transportation in the majority of Vermont is wheelchair-accessible, as are most newly built hotels, museums, and public buildings. Many campgrounds are not accessible, and the same is true of many historic accommodations; in general, the remoter the destination, the greater the possibility that it will not be. The state website includes a page with info on accessible travel in Vermont that profiles a few activities, but there are not a great deal of resources listed (https://www.vermontvacation.com/inclusive-vermont). The Department of Forests, Parks, and Recreation has a more useful listing (http://fpr.vermont.gov/accessibility), including links to adaptive skiing programs and an ADA map of state parks.

TRAVELING WITH CHILDREN

Travel all over Vermont is extremely family-friendly, most hotels offer cribs in rooms upon request, and public transportation and attractions offer discounted fares for children. The majority of restaurants are happy to offer high chairs, and many have kids' menus, though options are often limited to things like chicken fingers and macaroni and cheese. The state also goes further than most in welcoming public breast-feeding for mothers and infants. Many upscale bed-and-breakfasts, however, do not accommodate children under the age of 12 or 13; it's worth calling ahead.

LGBT TRAVELERS

Few states in the country are friendlier to gay and lesbian visitors than Vermont. The state has significant and thriving gay and lesbian communities and was the first in the nation to legalize civil unions of same-sex couples in 2000. In 2009, it crossed a new milestone by authorizing same-sex marriages, identical in every way to opposite-sex unions, by state statute. Up until that landmark law, only three other states had approved gay marriage (Massachusetts, Iowa, and Connecticut), all of them by judicial ruling. The Vermont law was quickly copied by other states, including New Hampshire and New York, soon after its passage.

The **Vermont Gay Tourism Association** (www.vermontgaytourism.com) compiles lists of lodging and services that are explicitly gay-friendly, and some establishments post VGTA's sticker—a rainbow maple leaf. The state also has a brief page about LGBT tourism in Vermont (https://www.vermontvacation.com/LGBT).

HEALTH AND SAFETY

In general, there are few safer states to be in than Vermont; the state's rate of crime (both violent and nonviolent property crimes) is low compared to the national average—both in its towns and its rural areas. Travel misadventures are more likely to be the result of accidents and poor planning in the state's natural areas. Always carry emergency supplies like extra clothing, water, and food, and don't depend on calling for help if you get lost, as cell phone coverage can be scant in remote areas.

Ticks and Lyme Disease

Snakes, bears, and moose are thrilling to spot, but ask what Vermonters are scared of and they'll say ticks. The eight-legged creatures are tiny—from the size of a poppy seed to just under 3 millimeters—and are easy to miss. Some deer ticks are carriers of Lyme disease, a bacterial infection named for Lyme, Connecticut. Taking the following precautions will help protect against Lyme:

- When walking through high grass and bushy areas, wear long pants and tuck them into your socks.
- Regular DEET-containing insect repellent has some deterrent effect, but it's far more helpful to treat your clothing with permethrin, which actually kills the critters.
- Shower within a few hours of coming inside, and check carefully for ticks. If you find a tick, use tweezers to grasp it near your skin, and firmly remove without twisting. Don't worry if the mouth parts remain in the skin; once they are separated from the body, they can no longer transmit the bacteria that cause Lyme.

Don't panic if you find a tick, as it takes around 36 hours for the bacteria to spread. Carefully checking for ticks once a day is a good practice. Should you contract Lyme disease, the first symptoms are often flu-like, and occur 3-30 days after infection. They're often, but not always, accompanied by a rash or bull's-eye redness around the bite, and prompt treatment is generally effective.

In case of an emergency on the slopes, almost all ski resorts do offer basic medical attention by staff instructors trained in emergency care. Some also have an emergency medical technician and rescue services available on their ski patrols 24 hours a day. But in general, the smaller the resort, the fewer the medical offerings. When serious injuries occur, visitors are brought to one of the state's regional hospitals or medical centers—of which there are roughly 25.

Throughout the state, 911 remains the telephone number for emergencies. The Vermont State Police Department number is 802/244-8727, and the Vermont Department of Health can be reached at 800/464-4343.

LEGALIZED MARIJUANA

In January 2018, Vermont became the first of the United States to legalize possession of marijuana by legislative vote, rather than a ballot initiative. Not that marijuana dispensaries will be setting up shop anytime soon; as of the time of writing, buying and selling marijuana remained illegal under Vermont law. Here's what you can and can't do with weed in the state.

- **Possession:** Anyone over the age of 21 can possess up to one ounce of marijuana or five grams of hashish for personal use.
- **Cultivation:** Vermonters can grow up to two mature plants and six immature plants per "dwelling unit." The plants must be grown in a locked space that's out of view and only accessible to people over the age of 21, and landlords can prohibit growing marijuana on leases.
- **Consumption:** You *can* get arrested for smoking marijuana, which will be still illegal in any public space, including hotel rooms and parks. That means that marijuana can only legally be consumed in a private dwelling. While conclusive tests for marijuana intoxication are elusive, operating a vehicle under the influence of marijuana will definitely remain illegal.
- **Federal law:** Marijuana is considered illegal by the federal government, which means that by possessing marijuana in Vermont, you still run the risk, however slim, of being arrested by federal authorities.

Information and Services

MONEY

Vermont imposes a sales tax rate of 6 percent on most purchases, including goods, entertainment, and telephone calling cards. Certain items are exempt, including clothing items of $110 or less, food, and medicine. Taxes on meals and lodging are 9 percent; on alcoholic beverages, 10 percent.

A 15-20 percent tip is customary in restaurants, bars, and hair salons and spas. At hotels in cities, $1 per bag for porters is the norm, doormen usually receive $1 for hailing a taxi, maids usually receive $1-2 per night, and concierges are given anywhere from a few dollars to $20, depending on the services they have provided. For taxi rides, 10 to 15 percent is customary.

COMMUNICATIONS AND MEDIA

Cell Phones and Internet Access

Vermont is a perfect place to disconnect from cell phones—and in the remoter parts, you might not have a choice, as coverage can be spotty. Even in the towns, norms are a bit different than in other parts of the country, and some establishments post signs asking that customers refrain from talking on the phone in line, cafés, and restaurants. Just about everywhere has wireless Internet coverage, from cafés to bars. In the tiniest towns, local libraries are a good place to find easy Internet access, as many (if not all) offer free terminal use in varying time increments.

Magazines and Newspapers

Several regional magazines provide useful information for travelers, including ***Vermont Life,*** the state-run periodical dedicated to all things Vermont. Newspapers of the larger communities include ***Burlington Free Press, Seven Days, Rutland Herald, Bennington Banner, Brattleboro Reformer, Barre Times-Argus,*** and ***Manchester Journal.***

MAPS AND TOURIST INFORMATION

Maps

If you are going to be spending a lot of time in the state or driving to remoter areas, you'll want to pick up DeLorme's ***Vermont Atlas and Gazetteer***—the granddaddy of state atlases, with detailed maps of every town in the state. (Purchase one online at http://mapstore.delorme.com.)

For help in locating hard-to-find spans on remote country creeks, authors Robert Hartnett and Ed Barna have produced ***Vermont Covered Bridges Map & Guide,*** with locations and information on more than 100 covered bridges.

For biking, look for the ***Lake Champlain Region Bikeways Map and Guide*** at tourist centers and bike shops (and through www.champlainbikeways.org). Covering more than 1,300 miles of territory, this biking map to the Burlington area is produced by local nonprofit Champlain Bikeways.

For canoeing, the map series ***Northern Forest Canoe Trail Maps*** (802/496-2285, www.northernforestcanoetrail.org), by a Waitsfield-based nonprofit, covers 13 sections of a 700-mile network of canoeing trips through the northeastern United States and Québec. Maps for sections 4, 5, and 6 include paddles through Vermont starting in Lake Champlain and passing through the Missisquoi River, Lake Memphremagog, and the Clyde and Nulhegan Rivers to the Connecticut River.

Hikers can purchase ***Vermont's Long Trail Waterproof Hiking Map*** from the **Green Mountain Club** (802/244-7037, www.greenmountainclub.org), which covers the entire length of the state's most famous hiking trail.

Business Hours

Business hours vary widely between cities and

towns, but many stores and offices in larger towns follow a schedule of 9am to 5pm or 6pm on weekdays; 10am to 6pm on Saturdays; and noon to 5pm on Sundays. In smaller cities and towns, particularly those in rural areas, expect more erratic weekend hours—or the possibility that they may simply stay closed until Monday. If in doubt, call an establishment in advance to verify hours. Most bars and clubs close their doors by 2am at the latest (and oftentimes by 1am).

Resources

Suggested Reading

FICTION AND MEMOIR

Bohjalian, Chris. *Midwives.* New York: Harmony Books, 1998. A meditation on life and death told through the decisions and trial of a Vermont country midwife, this book was an Oprah's Book Club selection and won the New England Book Award for its mesmerizing prose.

Elder, John. *Reading the Mountains of Home.* Harvard University Press, 1998. Middlebury professor John Elder offers thoughtful meditations on wildness and civilization in a book that unfolds over a year's explorations of the natural world.

Heekin, Deirdre. *An Unlikely Vineyard.* Chelsea Green Publishing, 2014. The multitalented owner and wine director of Woodstock's beloved Osteria Pane e Salute tells the story of establishing a biodynamic vineyard in Vermont.

Irving, John. Many of the most popular books of this cult Vermont-based novelist are set in New England, including *The World According to Garp,* which takes place in part at a New England boarding school, and *A Prayer for Owen Meaney,* which concerns several generations of a troubled New England family.

Lindbergh, Reeve. The youngest daughter of Charles A. and Anne Morrow Lindbergh moved to Vermont after college and now lives in St. Johnsbury. She's written two novels about country life in Vermont: *Moving to the Country* and *The Names of the Mountains,* as well as a book of thoughtful essays about her adopted home, *View from the Kingdom,* and several Vermont-themed children's books, including *There's a Cow in the Road!* Her latest memoir, *Forward From Here,* comes to grips with the legacy of her often angry and unhappy aviator father, whom, she discovers, secretly fathered seven other children in Europe.

Mayer, Archer. One of the most prolific of all of Vermont's writers, Mayer has been turning out Lt. Joe Gunther mystery novels at the rate of about one a year for more than a decade (26 books at last count). The Brattleboro-based author draws on his own experience as a county medical examiner and investigator for the state's attorney's office to inject a dose of realism into his gritty tales, which are set in villages and towns all across the state.

McKibben, Bill. *Wandering Home.* Crown: 2005. Now an iconic climate change activist, McKibben has long been beloved for his eloquent take on the New England landscape. In *Wandering Home,* he blends an account of a walk from Vermont to New York with conversations and musings on the environment.

McMahon, Jennifer. *The Winter People.* Doubleday: 2014. A haunting thriller set in rural Vermont, this paranormal thriller weaves the landscape into a tale that alternates between past and present horrors.

Miller, Peter. *Nothing Hardly Ever Happens in Colbyville, Vermont.* Colbyville, VT: Silver Print Press, 2009. One of the foremost black and white photographers in Vermont, Miller opens this book of engaging essays with a joke. Located just downhill from the Ben & Jerry's factory, Colbyville was absorbed into Waterbury years ago. Miller uses the symbol to begin a fascinating examination of how the state has transformed itself from rural subsistence into a tourist mecca—a change he doesn't always consider to be for the better.

Morse, Burr. *Sweet Days and Beyond: The Morse Family, Eight Generations of Maple Sugaring.* Poultney, VT: Historical Pages Company, 2005. In this recent history, written by one of Vermont's most established—and colorful—maple syrup makers, Morse writes humorously and endearingly about his family farm, which has tapped maples in Montpelier for eight generations.

Mosher, Howard Frank. A former high school teacher-turned-writer, Mosher captures the quirky spirit of the Northeast Kingdom—and arguably Vermont as a whole—better than any other writer living. His breakthrough novel, *A Stranger in the Kingdom,* about the controversy in a small town when a black minister is charged with impregnating a white girl, is just as powerful now as when it was published in 1989. His latest work, *God's Kingdom,* follows the Kinneson family, whom Mosher introduced in *Stranger in the Kingdom,* and displays a writer still on top of his game.

Perrin, Noel. *First Person Rural: Essays of a Sometime Farmer.* David R Godine, 1978. Perrin—a self-described "peasant"—uses the foibles of country life as a lens on the world. Even if you never use his practical tips on chain saws and maple syrup, this book offers insight and wit.

Stegner, Wallace. *Crossing to Safety.* Modern Library Classics, 1987. Stegner is one of the West's definitive writers, which gives him a fascinating perspective on Vermont. *Crossing to Safety* contains beautiful passages on the Green Mountain's gentle landscapes, contrasted with the dramatic peaks of Stegner's West. Not entirely an outsider, Stegner was nevertheless known to ruffle some local feathers during the years he spent summers in Greensboro. Stegner's fictional take on the town is his *Second Growth* (1947); some townsfolk didn't care for the way they appeared in the book, and after it was published, the Stegners summered elsewhere for several years.

FOOD

Crouch, Andy. *The Good Beer Guide to New England.* Hanover, NH: University Press of New England, 2006. Don't know your Rock Art from your Long Trail? This detailed pub crawl to breweries in New England includes several Vermont favorites.

Hooper, Alison. *In a Cheesemaker's Kitchen: Celebrating 25 Years of Artisanal Cheesemaking from Vermont Butter & Cheese Company.* Woodstock: Countryman Press, 2009. Quite possibly the "cheesiest" book you will ever read, this memoir-cookbook tracks the birth of the artisanal cheese movement in Vermont from one of the pioneers in the field. It also includes plenty of tasty recipes using Vermont Butter & Cheese products.

Lager, Fred. *Ben & Jerry's: The Inside Scoop: How Two Real Guys Built a Business with a Social Conscience and a Sense of Humor.* New York: Three Rivers Press, 1999. If you just can't get enough Chunky Monkey or Cherry Garcia, pick up this book detailing the history of the Vermont local legends.

Lockhart, Betty Ann. *Maple Sugarin' in Vermont: A Sweet History.* Charleston: The History Press, 2008. An encyclopedic recounting of Vermont's famous foodstuff takes in the history of maple syrup, from its earliest discovery by the Abenaki, to its role in the abolitionist movement, to its harvesting by the von Trapp family of *The Sound of Music* fame. The book includes lots of historic photos and excerpts from original sources.

Ogden, Ellen Ecker. *The Vermont Cheese Book.* Woodstock, VT: Countryman Press, 2007. More than just a guide to the varieties of cheese produced in the state, this book takes readers into the farms and kitchens of artisanal cheese makers to explain the process of how each cheese acquires its unique character.

Proulx, Annie, and Lew Nichols. *Cider: Making, Using, and Enjoying Sweet and Hard Cider.* Storey Publishing, 2003. Even hard-core fans of Annie Proulx—the celebrated author of *The Shipping News* and *Brokeback Mountain,* among many other books—might be surprised that her earliest published books covered food and farming. In addition to this book on making cider, Proulx's Vermont writing includes a handbook on grape growing and one on garden structures, penned from the home she built in tiny Vershire.

GUIDEBOOKS

Barna, Ed. *Covered Bridges of Vermont.* Woodstock: Countryman Press, 1996. For the bridge fanatic, this guide gives detailed descriptions and historical information on every bridge in the state, organized into convenient driving tours.

Coffin, Howard, and Jane and Will Curtis. *Guns over the Champlain Valley: A Guide to Historic Sites and Battlefields.* Woodstock: Countryman Press, 2005. This guide takes travelers into the heat of battle, detailing tactics and maneuvers at sites relating to the French and Indian War, the Revolutionary War, the War of 1812, and even the Civil War.

Corbett, William. *Literary New England: A History and Guide.* New York: Faber and Faber, 1993. An excellent guide to sites associated with poets and writers who called New England home, it includes detailed directions to hard-to-find graves and historic locations and houses.

Green Mountain Club. This organization publishes several guides considered gospel by outdoors enthusiasts in the region, jam-packed with no-nonsense directions for hiking and canoeing every inch of the Vermont wilderness. Titles include *Vermont Day Hikes, The Long Trail Guide,* and *360 Degrees: A Guide to Vermont's Fire and Observation Towers.*

Kershner, Bruce, and Robert Leverett. *The Sierra Club Guide to the Ancient Forests of the Northeast.* San Francisco: Sierra Club Books, 2004. Despite centuries of human habitation and exploitation, a surprising number of old-growth stands still exist in Vermont. This guide takes you inside their mossy interiors and explains what makes old-growth forests so unique.

Richards, Andy. *Photographing Vermont's Fall Foliage: Where to Find the Iconic Shots.* Portland: BookBaby, 2012. A godsend for leaf peepers who want to take a bit of fall home with them, Richards's detailed guide for the Kindle includes everything you need to find the best majestic vistas, hidden ponds, and backcountry farmhouses. Specific driving instructions, including routes, landmarks, and even GPS coordinates are included.

HISTORY

Bellesiles, Michael A. *Revolutionary Outlaws: Ethan Allen and the Struggle for*

Independence on the Early American Frontier. Charlottesville and London: University of Virginia Press, 2001. One of the better books to explore the enduring popularity and controversy surrounding Vermont's larger-than-life national hero, this book is less a biography than it is a social history of the founding of Vermont.

Cornwill, Joseph D. *Vermont Covered Bridges.* Charleston, SC: Arcadia Publishing, 2004. While more than 100 covered bridges still survive on Vermont back roads, literally hundreds more have been washed away over the years. This up-to-date book tells their stories—for both the bridges that survived and those that didn't.

Cronon, William. *Changes in the Land: Indians, Colonists, and the Ecology of New England.* New York: Hill and Wang, 1983. The classic study of early New England history debunks myths and shatters preconceptions about Pilgrims and Native Americans and how each interacted with the landscape.

Duffy, Peter. *Vermont: An Illustrated History.* Northridge, CA: Windsor Publications, 1985. This coffee-table book is full of etchings, drawings, and old photographs, along with a narrative hitting all the high points of state history. It's currently out of print, but if you get your hands on it, you'll find a nice overview of the state without much heavy lifting.

Jennison, Peter S. *Roadside History of Vermont.* Missoula, MT: Mountain Press, 1989. Divided into individual towns along five routes across the state, this combination guidebook and history book provides in-depth depictions of some of the local characters and events that have shaped its history. It's just as useful to read as you travel as in an armchair while you plan your trip.

Naylor, Thomas H. *Secession: How Vermont and All Other States Can Save Themselves from the Empire.* Port Townsend, WA: Feral House, 2008. Not as kooky as it might sound, this book makes a compelling case for why Vermont would be better off alone. The founder of the Second Vermont Republic and professor emeritus at Duke University, Naylor makes his arguments in such reasoned prose that, even if you don't agree with them, at least you'll understand them.

Prince, Cathryn J., *Burn the Town, Sack the Banks: Confederates Attack Vermont.* New York: Basic Books, 2006. A very readable account of the little-known "St. Alban's Raid," the only Civil War action in Vermont. The story brings alive the backdrop of spies, soldiers, and politicians behind the desperate last gasp of the South. The courtroom drama of one of the nation's first "celebrity" trials is almost as exciting as the raid itself.

Sherman, Joe. *Fast Lane on a Dirt Road: A Contemporary History of Vermont.* White River Junction, VT: Chelsea Green Publishing, 2009. Probably the best-written history of the last 60 years of the state, this newly updated book contains everything from the beginnings of the ski industry in Vermont to the fight to approve civil unions.

Sherman, Michael, Gene Sessions, and P. Jeffrey Potash. *Freedom and Unity: A History of Vermont.* Barre, VT: Vermont Historical Society, 2004. Written as a companion to the excellent permanent exhibit of the same name at the Vermont Historical Society Museum, this three-inch-tall tome is an exhaustive resource on everything from the Abenaki people to Bernie Sanders, told in an engaging and analytical style that explores the contradictions of Vermont's oxymoronic state motto.

Todish, Timothy J. *America's First World War: The French and Indian War, 1754-1763.* Fleischmanns, NY: Purple Mountain Press,

2002. This book is an illustrated history of the conflict that predated the Revolutionary War and enveloped Vermont in several violent clashes.

Wiseman, Frederick Matthew. *The Voice of the Dawn: An Autohistory of the Abenaki Nation*. Hanover, NH: University Press of New England, 2001. A story of the Abenaki, from their origins to their conquest by Europeans, draws upon archaeological information and firsthand contemporary accounts from an author who grew up as an Abenaki in Vermont.

NATURAL HISTORY AND ECOLOGY

Albers, Jan. *Hands on the Land: A Natural History of the Vermont Landscape*. Boston: MIT Press, 2002. In a gorgeous oversize book, Albers details the various factors—geological, ecological, and economic—that have transformed the Green Mountain State.

Degraff, Richard, and Mariko Yamasaki. *New England Wildlife: Habitat, Natural History, and Distribution*. Hanover, NH: University Press of New England, 2001. This is a no-nonsense guide to every last species of mammal, reptile, amphibian, and bird in the region, along with seasonal information and distribution maps. Note, however, that the book is limited to land species.

Klyza, Christopher McGrory, and Stephen C. Trombulak. *The Story of Vermont: A Natural and Cultural History*. Middlebury, VT: Middlebury College Press, 1999. Well-written and informative, this landscape history book explores how humans have impacted the landscape and its flora and fauna. The book is split into three sections—one on the early history of the state, one on the transformation of the landscape in the last 200 years, and, finally, one on the current ecology of the state.

National Audubon Society. *National Audubon Society Regional Guide to New England*. New York: Knopf, 1998. The amateur naturalist would do well to pick up this guide, which details many local species of trees, wildflowers, reptiles, and mammals, along with 1,500 full-color illustrations.

Thompson, Elizabeth. *Wetland, Woodland, Wildland: A Guide to the Natural Communities of Vermont*. Middlebury, VT: 2000. This comprehensive book goes deep into Vermont's ecosystems, using line drawings and color photographs to depict the flora and fauna you might encounter in each one.

Wessels, Tom. *Reading the Forested Landscape: A Natural History of New England*. Woodstock, VT: Countryman Press, 2005. A good read before heading off into the hills, this book helps put features of the landscape in their proper context.

Zielinski, Gregory A., and Barry D. Keim. *New England Weather, New England Climate*. Hanover, NH: University Press of New England, 2005. From nor'easters to Indian summer, this book patiently explains the meteorological underpinnings to New England's famously wacky weather.

REFERENCE

Duffy, John J., Samuel B. Hand, and Ralph H. Orth, eds. *The Vermont Encyclopedia*. Burlington: University of Vermont Press, 2003. Graze like a Jersey cow over this exhaustive compendium of all things Vermont, with 1,000 entries written by nearly 150 authors about the places, people, companies, and attractions that make the state what it is.

Internet Resources

TRAVEL

Vermont

www.vermontvacation.com

The official state travel website includes useful maps for some of Vermont's scenic byways, as well as links to major destination websites.

Travel Like a Local: Vermont

www.travellikealocalvt.com

Local real estate agent and blogger Erin McCormick has created a well-organized and engaging compendium of her favorite places in Vermont. McCormick is a craft beer and food lover, and her listings for breweries and cideries keep up with recent openings and beer releases.

Happy Vermont

www.happyvermont.com

Stories about exploring Vermont are posted alongside some useful travel resources on this locally run travel blog by Burlington resident Erica Houskeeper, a former communications director for Vermont's state tourism department.

FOOD AND DRINK

The Vermont Cheesemakers Trail

www.vtcheese.com

The Cheese Makers council curates a map of the best places to sample a slice—or buy a wheel—of Vermont's favorite dairy product.

The Vermont Brewery Challenge

www.vermontbrewers.com

This site offers information on visiting the state's breweries; download a passport that you can stamp at every one you visit.

Vermont Distillers' Council

www.distilledvermont.org

The distillers have a trail, too! Not every listed distillery is open to the public, so call ahead.

Vermont Grape and Wine Council

www.vermontwine.com

Twenty-one wineries speckle the landscape; download a passport on the council's website.

SKIING AND RIDING

Ski Vermont

www.skivermont.com

A streamlined but informative guide to the state's best ski resorts, this site allows you to choose your destination by the type of activity (alpine skiing and cross-country to snowboarding), area, or type of terrain you prefer. One of the website's most useful resources is a listing of Vermont cross-country ski areas that offer reciprocity: many offer one free day of skiing to those with a season's pass at another participating spot.

VERMONT HISTORY

Vermont Historical Society

www.vermonthistory.org

Much more than just a portal for the Vermont Historical Museum, the official site of VHS includes an online catalog of its extensive collections of books and manuscripts, lesson plans for teachers, links to local historical societies, and an online store full of books, maps, and other history-related goodies.

Vermont State Historic Sites

http://historicsites.vermont.gov

This basic state-run website has a Vermont Timeline, a map that organizes sites into regions, and detailed write-ups on certain aspects of the past, including Revolutionary War sites and historic homes.

FALL FOLIAGE

Vermont Fall Foliage Report

www.vermont.com/foliage.cfm

Get in-depth and up-to-date foliage reports on each area of the state, starting in early September and continuing throughout autumn. Updated twice per week by the self-dubbed "Leaf Squad," the site tracks and updates Vermont's changing foliage with a color-coded map showing where the leaves are peaking.

Yankee Foliage
www.yankeefoliage.com
Another solid resource for leaf peepers is this frequently updated website produced by the editors of *Yankee* magazine, which includes an up-to-the-minute foliage map based on reports submitted by readers, suggestions for fall activities, and a leaf-peeping app.

Podcasts

Brave Little State
www.vpr.net/apps/podcasts/brave-little-state
Named for a speech when Calvin Coolidge referred to the "brave little state of Vermont," this well-produced podcast covers everything from Vermont's history to culture and politics and makes for great listening as you explore the Green Mountains.

Rumble Strip Vermont
www.rumblestripvermont.com
More of a homegrown effort than the Vermont Public Radio-made Brave Little State, Rumble Strip is a series of leisurely conversations about life in the state by Erica Heilman, whose topics include Vermont's private investigators, contra dances, criminals, and taxidermists.

VPR Café
www.npr.org/podcasts/381443503/v-p-r-cafe
Another show from Vermont Public Radio, VPR Café turns a microphone to the state's food system and can be a great way to discover interesting places to eat and explore.

Index

C

D

E

F

G

H

I

J

K

L

M

N

O

P

QR

S

T

UV

WXYZ

List of Maps

Front Map

Discover Vermont

Southern Green Mountains

Along Route 4

Burlington and the Champlain Valley

Northern Green Mountains

Northeast Kingdom

Photo Credits

Title page photo: David Mcmasters for vermontvacation.com;

All photos © Jen Rose Smith except page 2 © Grant Wieler Photography; page 3 © Stephen Goodhue for vermontvacation.com; page 6 © (top right) Jeb Wallace Brodeur; (bottom) Kent Shaw for vermontvacation.com; page 7 © (bottom right) James Kirkikis | dreamstime; page 8 © (top) Stowe Mountain Resort; page 9 © (top) Dennis Currran for vermontvacation.com; (bottom left) James Kirkikis | dreamstime; page 10 © cosbygerald | dreamstime.com; page 12 © (top) Hubert Schriebl; page 13 © (middle) Mount Snow; page 22 © David Russo; page 27 © (top) Jeb Wallace Brodeur; page 28 © Hubert Schriebl; page 41 © (bottom) Chad Abramovich; page 53 © (bottom) Bennington Museum; page 64 © (bottom) irina88w | dreamstime; page 84 © (top left) Richard Amore for vermontvacation.com; (bottom) Stephen Goodhue for vermontvacation.com; page 87 © Tig Tillinghast/courtesy of Vins; page 93 © (top) Billings Farm and Museum; page 94 © Dennis Currran for vermontvacation.com; page 101 © (top) Chandler Burgess/Killington Resort; page 109 © courtesy Vermont Division for Historic Preservation; page 112 © Skye Chalmers for vermontvacation.com; page 121 © Ethan Allen Homestead; page 135 © Vermont Lake Monsters; page 139 © J. David Bohl/Shelburne Museum; page 168 © (top right) Morse Farm; (bottom) Rock of Ages; page 177 © (top right) Stowe Area Association; (bottom) wangkun jia | dreamstime; page 184 © Morse Farm; page 188 © (top) Grant Wieler Photography; (bottom) Stowe Mountain Resort; page 194 © kan1234 | dreamstime; page 210 © (top left) erikamit | dreamstime; (top right) peanutroaster | dreamstime; page 218 © Morse Farm; page 243 © (top) Jay Peak Resort; (bottom) Jay Peak Resort

MAP SYMBOLS

- Expressway
- Primary Road
- Secondary Road
- Unpaved Road
- Feature Trail
- Other Trail
- Ferry
- Pedestrian Walkway
- Stairs
- City/Town
- State Capital
- National Capital
- Point of Interest
- Accommodation
- Restaurant/Bar
- Other Location
- Campground
- Airport
- Airfield
- Mountain
- Unique Natural Feature
- Waterfall
- Park
- Trailhead
- Skiing Area
- Golf Course
- Parking Area
- Archaeological Site
- Church
- Gas Station
- Glacier
- Mangrove
- Reef
- Swamp

CONVERSION TABLES

°C = (°F - 32) / 1.8
°F = (°C x 1.8) + 32
1 inch = 2.54 centimeters (cm)
1 foot = 0.304 meters (m)
1 yard = 0.914 meters
1 mile = 1.6093 kilometers (km)
1 km = 0.6214 miles
1 fathom = 1.8288 m
1 chain = 20.1168 m
1 furlong = 201.168 m
1 acre = 0.4047 hectares
1 sq km = 100 hectares
1 sq mile = 2.59 square km
1 ounce = 28.35 grams
1 pound = 0.4536 kilograms
1 short ton = 0.90718 metric ton
1 short ton = 2,000 pounds
1 long ton = 1.016 metric tons
1 long ton = 2,240 pounds
1 metric ton = 1,000 kilograms
1 quart = 0.94635 liters
1 US gallon = 3.7854 liters
1 Imperial gallon = 4.5459 liters
1 nautical mile = 1.852 km

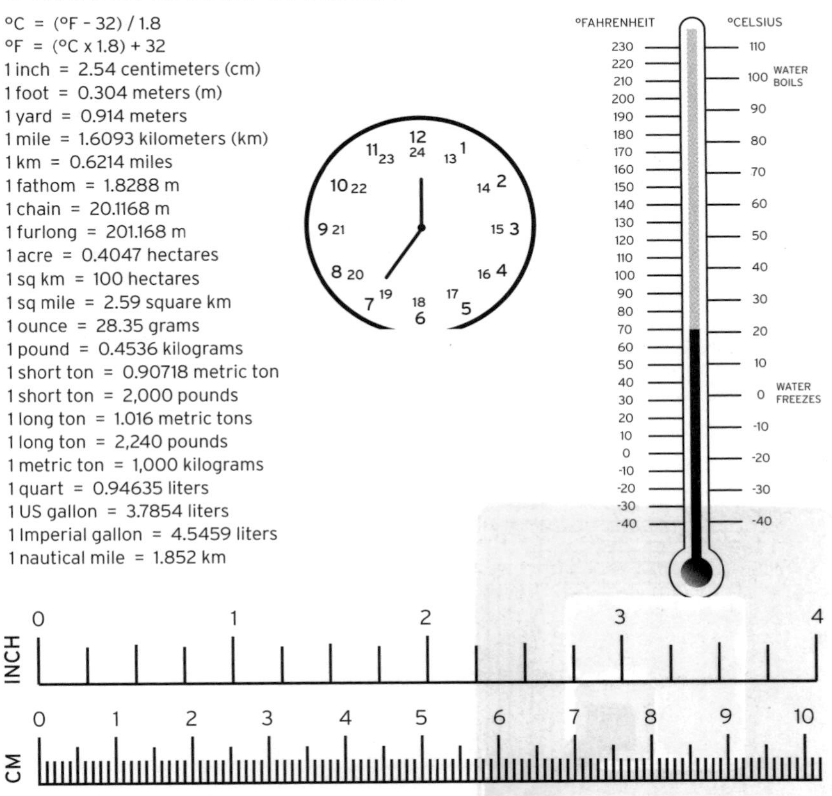

MOON VERMONT
Avalon Travel
Hachette Book Group
1700 Fourth Street
Berkeley, CA 94710, USA
www.moon.com

Editor and Series Manager: Kathryn Ettinger
Acquiring Editor: Grace Fujimoto
Copy Editor: Ashley Benning
Graphics Coordinator: Darren Alessi
Production Coordinator: Darren Alessi
Cover Design: Faceout Studios, Charles Brock
Interior Design: Domini Dragoone
Moon Logo: Tim McGrath
Map Editor: Albert Angulo
Cartographer: Andrew Dolan
Indexer: Greg Jewett

ISBN-13: 978-1-64049-351-3

Printing History
1st Edition — 2008
5th Edition — May 2019
5 4 3 2 1

Front cover photo: Jersey cows feeding in a pasture in the Northeast Kingdom © Reimar / Alamy Stock Photo
Back cover photo: Montepelier © Sepavo | Dreamstime.com

Printed in China by RR Donnelley